W9-DHY-186

BEYOND BLACK AND RED

A SERIES OF COURSE-ADOPTION BOOKS ON LATIN AMERICA:

Beyond Black and Red

African-Native
Relations in
Colonial Latin America

Edited by Matthew Restall

University of New Mexico Press ❧ Albuquerque

© 2005 by the University of New Mexico Press
All rights reserved. Published 2005

09 08 07 06 05   1 2 3 4 5

LIBRARY OF CONGRESS CATALOGING-IN-PUBLICATION DATA

Beyond black and red : African-native relations in colonial Latin America /
edited by Matthew Restall.
     p. cm. — (Diálogos)
     Includes bibliographical references and index.
     ISBN 0-8263-2402-9 (cloth : alk. paper)
     ISBN 0-8263-2403-7 (pbk. : alk. paper)
   1. Latin America—Race relations—History.
   2. Blacks—Relations with Indians.
   I. Restall, Matthew, 1964– II. Diálogos (Albuquerque, N.M.)
     F1419.A1B49 2005
     305.8'00980—dc22

                                        2004028625

Contents

List of Illustrations

List of Tables

Foreword

COLIN A. PALMER

According to the historical record, the first enslaved persons of African descent arrived in the Americas in 1502. Disembarking in Hispaniola, they came at the urgent request of Governor Nicolas de Ovando. With the indigenous population in sharp decline as a consequence of disease, warfare, and mistreatment, the governor pleaded with the royal authorities to send the Spanish colonists African slaves to meet their need for an exploited labor force. Since the enslavement of African peoples had been a feature of Spanish society for centuries, Nicolas de Ovando's request did not represent a departure from Iberian practices. By the time slavery finally ended during the nineteenth century, perhaps as many as 11 to 13 million African-born persons had survived the Atlantic passage to contribute their sweat to the making of the Americas.

Increasingly, historians are devoting their attention to the experiences of these Africans in Latin America and the Caribbean. Building upon pioneering studies by Gonzalo Aguirre Beltrán, Gilberto Freyre, Frederick Bowser, and others, these scholars have refined earlier methodologies and are focusing on the variegated textures of the lives of the enslaved peoples. Consequently, we now know a great deal about how they ordered their lives, the social institutions they created, the nature of their resistance, and their struggles for selfhood.

Unlike their more extensively studied counterparts in North America, the enslaved in Latin America left few first-person accounts of their experiences and their responses to them. Thus, historians have had to reconstruct their lives in essence through the optic of the slave owners and the civil and religious authorities, but interpreting their accounts imaginatively and sensitively. The voices of the enslaved are most frequently encountered in the judicial proceedings of the Holy Office of the Inquisition, but such records, understandably, must be used with great caution.

The chapters in this pioneering collection address an important aspect of the lives of the enslaved blacks, namely their relationships with the indigenous peoples. Taken together, the essays demonstrate the significant advances that have been made in the historiography of the Americas, since a volume with this orientation would not have been possible a decade ago. Each essay is the product of new evidence, and the scholars approach the problems they investigate with much methodological creativity and insight, particularly in their use of the records of the Holy Office of the Inquisition.

Earlier historians, generally speaking, tended to characterize the relationship between the indigenous peoples and those of African descent as one of unrelieved hostility. These oppressed groups competed against one another for their own space at the bottom of the social hierarchy. This shared animus, some scholars maintained, was a function of the efforts of the colonial officials to divide them, thereby facilitating their social control.

This conclusion, to be sure, was overly simplistic and was based primarily on the records of the colonial authorities, who tended to emphasize instances of inter- and intraethnic conflict in their reports. The indigenous peoples—and the Africans too—were often seen as constituting a homogeneous group rather than as peoples with different ethnicities, identities, and loyalties. Issues of cultural misunderstanding were seldom if ever explored, nor did examples of collaboration among the various groups receive much attention.

It is very difficult, even when the sources are abundant, for the historian to capture the animating impulses of particular groups of people, especially those far removed from the experiences of the scholar and very distant in time. Nor is it an easy task to understand the give-and-take of their lives, the nature of their daily social intercourse, and its frequently complex, contradictory, but always dynamic expressions. The essence of the inner lives of those often described as the "Other" sometimes escape the comprehension of the outsider, especially if certain pernicious assumptions interfere with those understandings. Examples of conflict among various groups invite the attention of the authorities and interested observers, but they tend to obscure the instances of compromise, cooperation, cordiality, and even affection that give meanings to people's lives and affirm their humanity.

Not surprisingly, the essays in the volume show that at the interpersonal level, the indigenous peoples and the enslaved blacks behaved like just regular folks with all of their bewildering complexities. They had their conflicts and executed the will of the colonial authorities by fighting on their side against challenges to their control by other blacks or indigenous peoples. In some instances, as on the Florida frontier, they made common cause against the Europeans. Blacks and Native Americans served alongside each other in the military, albeit with different motivations at times. Becoming lovers and spouses, they contested the efforts of the colonial authorities to keep them apart, even at this most basic human level.

These essays complicate our understanding of interethnic relations in the colonial Americas and represent an important stage in the historiography. A major book devoted to the interactions between subaltern groups rather than between the colonizers and the colonized, or the slave owners and their chattel, is an important intellectual moment. The larger implications and consequences of this historiographical watershed are deliciously tantalizing.

Acknowledgments

I am grateful to everyone who made this book project possible: the contributors, for their efficiency and willingness to accommodate my suggestions, however arcane; Colin Palmer, for agreeing to preface the volume; Lyman Johnson and David Holtby, editors of the Diálogos series and of the University of New Mexico Press respectively, for their support, encouragement, and editorial contributions; and to the production professionals at the press, especially Maya Allen-Gallegos, Kathy Sparkes, and Sarah Ritthaler

Matthew Restall
State College, PA
January, 2005

Black Slaves, Red Paint

MATTHEW RESTALL

Biracial people should not be
judged as "half" of anything.
> —*Radmilla Cody,*
> *Miss Navajo Nation 1998*[1]

Black people need witnesses.
> —*James Baldwin*[2]

&G;

In 1796 a militia unit of 115 free black soldiers arrived in their new home in
Yucatan. All had been recruited by and fought for the losing Spanish army
in the war over Haiti and Santo Domingo. They had initially been sent to
Cuba, but the governor there was unconvinced of their loyalties and
ordered them to nearby Yucatan. There the colonial authorities were equally suspicious of the veterans, who were not only black, but most spoke no
Spanish. They were therefore settled near the northeast coast of the peninsula, far from the Spanish centers of Mérida and Campeche but close to the
colony's vulnerable Caribbean shores, where they could be called upon to
aid in the defense of the colony.[3]

Their settlement was named San Fernando de los Negros and was situated in the very center of the ruined ancient Maya city of Ake, dubbed San

FIG. I.1: *San Fernando de los Negros amidst Ake, northeast Yucatan. Photograph by the author.*

Fernando Ake after the Spanish Conquest. Today the site lies within a vast cattle ranch and is inhabited by hundreds of head of cattle and the occasional Maya cowboy; the ruins of the houses built by San Fernando's black residents are still visible in the grassy plazas of Ake, surrounded by overgrown Maya pyramids (see fig. 1.1). The former slaves must have climbed these "hills" to see the Caribbean Sea, from where they were exiled and to which they had once been taken against their will. It is tempting to imagine them pondering the carvings and red-painted images left on the stones by the Mayas who had built and lived in the city until a couple of hundred years earlier.[4]

This image of displaced Africans in an abandoned Maya city is one of symbolic disjuncture. It places native and black residents of the region in completely different historical and cultural spheres. As Patrick Carroll explains in chapter 9, colonial Spaniards tended to view black-native relations as fraught with disjuncture and antagonism, a disharmony that Spaniards saw as inevitable due to perceived black-native differences, as Neil Whitehead observes in chapter 8. Indeed, all the chapters in this volume contain some evidence of hostility between the two groups. Historians of North America have likewise commented on the tendency of native peoples under various circumstances to view involuntary colonists from Africa as "foreigners with black skins . . . more suitable as slaves than as adoptive relatives."[5]

The history of San Fernando after 1796 would seem to reinforce the site's efficacy as a symbol of black-native discord. During its first decade, the community doubled in size, taking in free blacks from elsewhere in Yucatan as well as escaped slaves from the English logging settlements in Belize. Alarmed at this growth, local Spanish officials tried to encourage Mayas, Spaniards, and mestizos to settle in San Fernando, but the town's black leadership refused them. When the legendary traveler John Stephens passed through the region in the early 1840s, he noted the town on his map as "San Fernando chiefly Africans." Shortly afterward, the region was caught up in the internecine violence of the Caste War. According to local legend, Maya forces overran the town and slaughtered its black inhabitants, although historical records suggest that in 1848 the "Africans" of San Fernando fled to Belize.[6]

Such a narrative, however, reveals only part of the picture. Neither the history of San Fernando de los Negros nor that of relations between natives and people of African descent in the rest of colonial Latin America was simply black and white—or black and red. The black leaders of San Fernando to some extent represented racial solidarity in the community in the face of interference by Spanish officials and attempts by nonblacks to settle there. But black leaders in the town were also highly factionalized along language lines, grouped into English, Portuguese, and French speakers. The original soldier-settlers of 1796 brought their military ranks with them, but over the decades this order fragmented as upstarts and new arrivals claimed military ranks too. The original settlers had been born in New York, Jamaica, and Santo Domingo, as well as African locations such as Congo, Guinea, and Senegal.[7] Later settlers coming in from Campeche, Belize, and so on would have likewise been born in a wide variety of places in West Africa, Spanish America, and the British Empire.[8] To assume that Spanish racial designations of *negro* and *pardo* overwhelmed these differences of origin and language would be unfounded; what tied San Fernando's people together was not so much race but location.

Furthermore, despite resistance to attempts by colonial officials to "whiten" the town in its early decades, by 1841 only 57 percent of San Fernando was black; the trickle of Mayas coming in from nearby villages over the decades had become a 40-percent presence.[9] That movement went in both directions. In 1826, for example, a number of black militiamen from San Fernando were listed as having "deserted"; an investigation showed that they had been working *milpas*, or cornfields, some distance from the town for a while and had eventually moved permanently to Maya villages nearer their milpas.[10] These tantalizing hints at long-term interaction between blacks and Mayas undermine the notion that the relationship between the two was one of hostility and disjuncture, even suggesting that the racial integrity of the two groups was illusory. In other words, the Africans of San Fernando were neither massacred by Mayas in the Caste War nor did they all disappear to Belize; for a half century before the town was abandoned, a multiracial population was being forged in northeast Yucatan, one that included—as it does to this day—the descendents of the original 115 black soldier-settlers.

IDENTITY, COMMUNITY, AND CULTURE CHANGE

The dialectical theme of black-native hostility and peaceful black-native interaction (we might call it the hostility-harmony dialectic) is predominant throughout this volume. It is the core characteristic of relations between native Nahuas and Afro-Mexicans in the central Mexican town of Cholula in the seventeenth and eighteenth centuries, as detailed by Norma Angélica Castillo Palma and Susan Kellogg in chapter 4. Gold and silver mines have traditionally been defined as sites of conflict and resistance, pitting native workers, black slaves, and Spanish masters against one another (see the case study upon which Renée Soulodre-La France builds chapter 5, for example). But in chapter 6, Kris Lane shows that mines also served as unique cultural interfaces. After all, for centuries indigenous and African miners lived and worked side by side, mostly without conflict.

In chapter 7, Christopher Lutz and I attempt to unravel the contradictory evidence on relations between Mayas and blacks, beginning with a case from a Mam Maya village in Guatemala, where a mulatto carpenter lived with a local Maya woman and worked for many years until a dispute triggered the expulsion of him and his relatives on racial grounds. The realm of military action found native and black soldiers fighting as comrades as often as adversaries, a phenomenon as true for Spanish America as for Brazil, as shown in the first and third chapters of the volume (by Ben Vinson and myself and by Stuart Schwartz and Hal Langfur, respectively). In fact, this dialectical theme of hostility and harmony crosses more than just the boundary between Spanish and Portuguese colonies; it is also fundamental to the history and historiography of black-native relations in colonies north of the Rio Grande, as Jane Landers shows in chapter 2.[11]

FIG. I.2: A thematic schema of black-native interaction.

The hostility—

harmony

dialectic →→→→ articulated in the arenas of:

        1. identity

        2. community

        3. culture change →→→→ in turn articulated through:

                1. interculturation

                2. informality

                3. diachronic intensification

Within this dialectic a number of closely related topics emerge in this volume, cultural arenas in which the hostility-harmony dialectic is articulated. I will briefly elaborate upon three of these topics here—identity, community, and culture change (see fig. 1.2)—using my discussion of each one to make further references to the chapters that follow.

A substantial and growing body of literature on identity in colonial Latin America exists that I will not attempt to summarize here. Suffice to observe that the issue of how the non-Iberian inhabitants of these colonies identified themselves, and were labeled by others, is a highly complex one. For example, debates continue regarding such topics as the precise nature of ethnic identity among native groups and the relative prevalence of race and class as determinants of rank and identity in colonial cities. What is well established is the highly localized nature of identities throughout the colonies. Larger racial categories, such as "Indian" (or "red," as natives in North America, and to a lesser extent in the Caribbean, came to be colored) and "black" were meaningless at the local community level, where self-identity tended to be rooted. Where such terms were not meaningless, they were ascribed a more local meaning than that intended by Europeans—as in the claiming of pardo (mulatto) identities by Afro-Mexican communities who saw that the Spanish association of the term with militia service could be parlayed into rights and privileges at the local level (that is, for a town or neighborhood, not for all pardos; see chapter 2).

The term "red" is a significant case in point. Long assumed to be a racial, even racist, designation invented by Europeans, "red" was actually a

FIG. I.3:
*"Redskin Cigarettes" packet
from Colombia, c. 1975.*

label invented and adopted by natives in the Southeast of North America in the early eighteenth century, as Nancy Shoemaker has recently shown.[12] Red-white symbolic dualisms were prevalent in southeastern native cultures, suggesting "red" be adopted as an obvious label of reaction—and resistance, as the "red path" meant war—to intrusions by Europeans and their self-identification as "white." Taken as a reference to complexion, the English and French spread "red" as a synonym for "Indian," but the term never caught on among Spaniards and Portuguese, perhaps precisely because it had been invented by natives outside the Iberian colonies (for its use in the Caribbean, see chapter 8). The notion of "red Indians" or "redskins" can be found in modern Latin America, but in reference not to local indigenous groups, but to those of North America—as illustrated in fig. 1.3.

Just as the localized nature of identities among natives and people of African descent in the Americas is becoming better understood, so is it becoming increasingly clear that the multiplicity of identities and identity markers in colonial Latin American societies gave individuals choices. At the same time, the freedom of an individual to select an identity or to emphasize a particular aspect of his or her identity was limited by social circumstances.[13] Thus in terms of social interaction, the conditions of an interactive moment both necessitated and circumscribed identity choices.

For example, in early seventeenth-century Cholula, some Nahua women asserted new, non-native identities through their marriage to free blacks or mestizos (of mixed Spanish-native descent) or *zambaigos* (of mixed African-native descent) and their consequent adoption of non-native dress. As Castillo Palma and Kellogg show (chapter 4), the claim by these Nahua women that such new identities excused them from tribute payments was contested both by Cholula's native governor and by Spanish officials, whose fiscal interests converged to deny the native (or ex-native) women's strategic identity choices. Circumstances could also necessitate the reverse strategy, as in the case (also from chapter 4) of a woman accused of being an *hechicera mulata* (mulata sorceress), who insisted she was an "Indian" to escape Inquisition jurisdiction and as a defense against the Inquisition's stereotypical association of mulatas with witchcraft. Similarly, Whitehead shows in chapter 8 that the self-identities of the so-called Black Caribs of the Antillean island of St. Vincent were bound up in the process of resisting colonial encroachment, while the agendas of colonialist politics underlay contrasting British and French perceptions of how "Indian" or "black" the St. Vincentian Caribs were.

Choices and boundaries also helped define how groups of natives, Africans, and people of various admixtures developed community identities. Despite the Spanish commitment to the myth that their conquests in the Americas were completed by the first generations of conquistadors, in numerous ways the Conquest and colonial rule were part of a single, incomplete, endlessly negotiable and negotiated process.[14] The efficacy and leverage of community integrity in this process reinforced the importance of native municipal communities and fostered new communities of various kinds. I suggested above that efforts by the leaders of San Fernando de los Negros to maintain the settlement's black identity were as much about keeping out outsiders as about promoting racial solidarity; for example, escaped slaves from Belize may have been admitted because there were already English-speaking Africans in the town, not because they fulfilled a simple racial criterion. In the latter decades of its fifty-year history, San Fernando was a multiracial community, comprising blacks, Mayas, and their offspring—but it was still defended as a black militia township by its leaders because that was the community identity that had permitted the town certain privileges and a degree of autonomy. Likewise, Ben Vinson and I argue in chapter 1 that the privileges won by black and free colored militia units in Mexico and elsewhere encouraged a sense of community identity that spread to the larger group of militia families and relatives—yet that sense of identity remained tied to the negotiation of privileges, and it fragmented or shifted as soon as circumstances dictated.

Whatever the ethnic and cultural admixture of the population of a neighborhood, town, or island, the development of community identity involved both internal processes of interculturation and external interaction with other communities and European colonists. Such colonists at times sought to deny identity to communities—trying to wipe out maroon settlements, for example (mentioned in chapters 2, 3, and 5). At times they sought to impose either a native or black identity, threatened and confused by *mestizaje* and cultural hybridity at the community level—as with the Black Caribs discussed by Whitehead.

Attempts by colonists to control native, black, and mixed-race identities were doomed to failure in the face of the slow but steady dissolution of barriers between these groups. Intermarriage and biological miscegenation were the most obvious ways in which boundaries between blacks and natives broke down (see chapter 7, for example), making a mess of Iberian attempts to maintain non-Iberians in discrete subordinate racial categories. But black-native meetings also created "a conversation between cultures" (to steal a phrase from Ulf Hannertz).[15] What kinds of models, if any, have scholars of colonial history developed to illuminate such cultural conversations?

For much of the twentieth century, scholars viewed culture conflict and change in the colonial Americas as a process of acculturation. Their focus was not on multidirectional culture change, but on the ways in which dominant or donor European cultures impacted native cultures. As early as 1960 the anthropologist George Foster noted that "it is well to bear in mind that, although we tend to think only in terms of Indians acculturating to Spanish ways, there were in fact two recipient groups in process of change: Indian and Spanish." Despite this acknowledgment, the overwhelming focus of Foster and his contemporaries is on what Robert Hoover called in 1989 "the enculturation of Native Americans into the European lifeway." In other words, not only has acculturation seldom been viewed as a two-way street, but the emphasis on Europeans and natives has tended to exclude consideration of Africans and African cultures. At the same time, scholars concerned with America's Africans have tended to ignore indigenous cultures. This is the case with groundbreaking studies such as Fernando Ortiz's 1947 study of labor and society in Cuba and Sidney Mintz and Richard Price's 1976 book on Afro-Caribbean societies. Ortiz even suggested that "acculturation" be replaced with "transculturation," a term that grants more agency to non-Europeans in the process of culture change, but he was not

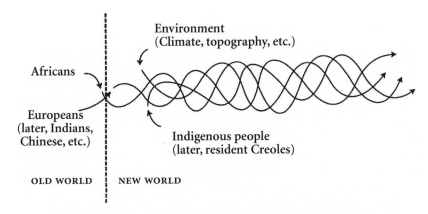

FIG. I.4: *The process of creolization. From David Buisseret, "Introduction," in* Creolization in the Americas, *ed. David Buisseret and Steven G. Reinhardt (College Station: Texas A&M Press, 2000), 6.*

willing to discard the notion that such change was primarily characterized by culture loss on the part of subordinate peoples.[16]

Responding to the need for a model that can accommodate all three groups of the great colonial encounter—Europeans, Africans, and Native Americans—and do so without privileging one group's culture over another, David Buisseret recently proposed the adoption of the term *creolization*. The noun *creole* (*criollo* in Spanish) has historically referred to a European or African born in the Americas. Buisseret suggests that *creolization* adequately describes the syncretic process whereby "new cultural forms came to life in the New World";[17] his diagrammatic representation of that process is reproduced as fig. I.4.

The diagram's image of the swirling, continually intersecting lines of African and native cultures is appropriate to the nature of black-native interaction in colonial Latin America—or at least to our current understanding of that interaction. It may be that in time we will have sufficient data and knowledge to be able to generate a diachronic model that articulates stages of interaction and culture change—as James Lockhart has done for the Nahuas of central Mexico by analyzing written sources in colonial Nahuatl and as has been shown to be partially true of Mixtecs and Mayas.[18] Perhaps, too, a typology will emerge, in which certain circumstances of interaction between natives and people of African descent can be seen to produce predictable hybrid cultural elements.

But for now, Buisseret's diagram serves to loosely illustrate the three forms of black-native cultural interaction that run through the chapters of this volume—three forms that articulate the process of culture change within the hostility-harmony dialectic (see fig. 1.2). The first of these forms is *interculturation*, a term that I recently proposed to describe the impact of Spanish colonial culture on Yucatec Mayas but that is equally applicable to black-native cultural interaction throughout Latin America.[19] Interculturation conveys the reciprocal nature of the process, with cultural influences and accommodations running a two-way street between natives and blacks. One culture may dominate another in certain cases, but as a general principle and by definition, the interculturative process rejects cultural dominance as a structural part of the model.

The second element is *informality*, meaning that there was no systematic or institutional attempt by natives or Africans to impose cultural elements in a way that compares with Spanish efforts at, for example, religious conversion. Instead, archival records reveal people of native and African descent interacting at the quotidian level: playing cards outside a Cholula textile mill, drinking the native Mexican liquor, *pulque*, together, or exchanging potion recipes at the "cultural crossroads of sexual witchcraft" (chapter 4).

The volume's third theme of cultural interaction and change is *diachronic intensification*. Over the colonial centuries, interaction between natives and blacks intensified, leading to the blurring of divisions between the two groups and their cultures. This does not mean that interaction was a syncretic process leading simply and inevitably toward the creation of hybrid cultures. The combination of interculturation, informality, and diachronic intensification meant that it was just as likely for parallel elements to survive within the larger cultural framework as it was for such elements to fuse. Or, more likely still, both processes took place at the same time. But it did mean that the purity of the racial categories created and cherished by Europeans was increasingly undermined, difficult to impose, and divorced from reality— much to the concern of the Spanish colonial authorities and fear of the white minority in the colonies, as Carroll argues in chapter 9.

In the end, our efforts to pinpoint cultural elements within the dynamic of black-native interaction are often in vain—just as colonial Spanish and Portuguese efforts to identify, categorize, and separate black and native Americans were usually fruitless. The complex relationships between Africans and natives were seldom simply black and red.

꧁꧂

NOTES

1. Quoted by James F. Brooks in *Confounding the Color Line: The Indian-Black Experience in North America*, ed. Brooks (Lincoln: University of Nebraska Press, 2002), 16.

2. Quoted by Dwight A. McBride in *Impossible Witnesses: Truth, Abolitionism, and Slave Testimony* (New York: New York University Press, 2001), vii.

3. Archivo General del Estado de Yucatán (hereafter AGEY), Colonial, *Militar*, 1, 13 and 1, 22; Jorge Victoria Ojeda and Jorge Canto Alcocer, "San Fernando Ake: La Comunidad Negra del Nororiente Yucateco (1796–1848)" (unpublished manuscript, 1997), 27–30; Ben Vinson III, *Bearing Arms for His Majesty: The Free-Colored Militia in Colonial Mexico* (Stanford: Stanford University Press, 2001), 216. Other black soldiers from the Haitian war went elsewhere. General Georges Biassou and twenty-five of his men ended up in Florida, for example; Jane Landers, *Black Society in Spanish Florida* (Urbana: University of Illinois Press, 1999), 81.

4. The Maya site of San Fernando Ake covers roughly thirty-two square kilometers, within which 3,500 structures have been mapped by archaeologist Susan Kepecs. The distance from the pyramidal structure in fig. I.1 above to the coast is eleven kilometers, making the sea visible on most days. Note that I have imagined red-painted carvings based on their survival at other sites, although no evidence remains of such carvings at Ake. See Kepecs, "The Political Economy of Chikinchel, Yucatan, Mexico: A Diachronic Analysis from the Prehispanic Era Through the Age of Spanish Administration" (Ph.D. diss., University of Wisconsin—Madison, 1999), 331–42, 367–77. I am grateful to Kepecs for taking me to the site in 1999. Victoria Ojeda and Canto Alcocer (to whom I am grateful for sharing their unpublished manuscript) argue persuasively that Ake was the site of a major battle between local Mayas and a Montejo-led Spanish invasion force in 1528 ("San Fernando Ake," 16). Evidence uncovered by Kepecs suggests that Ake was not finally abandoned by a reduced Maya population until the mid-seventeenth century, if not later ("Chikinchel," 95, 557; "Mayas, Spaniards, and Salt: World Systems Shifts in 16th-Century Yucatan," in *The Postclassic to Spanish-Era Transition in Mesoamerica: Archaeological Perspectives*, ed. Susan Kepecs and Rani Alexander [Albuquerque: University of New Mexico Press, forthcoming]).

5. Theda Perdue, *"Mixed Blood" Indians: Racial Construction in the Early South* (Athens: University of Georgia Press, 2003), 5. For example, Perdue discusses slave-owning among—and the returning of escaped slaves by—Cherokees, Choctaws, Chickasaws, and Creeks in the late eighteenth and early nineteenth centuries (4–7, 9, 64–65).

6. AGEY, Poder Ejecutivo, *Gobernación*, 104; Kepecs, "Chikinchel," 574–75; Victoria and Canto, "San Fernando Ake," 74; Vinson, *Bearing Arms*, 217–18.

7. Vinson, *Bearing Arms*, 216.

8. Based on baptism details in eighteenth-century parish records in Campeche (Archivo Histórico de la Diócesis de Campeche) and Merida (Archivo General del Arzobispado de Yucatán, Jesús María parish).

9. AGEY, Poder Ejecutivo, *Censos y Padrones*, 3, 27; Victoria and Canto, "San Fernando Ake," 40; Kepecs, "Chikinchel," 574.

10. AGEY, Poder Ejecutivo, *Militias*, 2, 25.

11. And as exemplified by a recent publication of essays that in many ways complements this volume: Brooks, *Confounding the Color Line*.

12. See Nancy Shoemaker, "How Indians Got to Be Red," *American Historical Review* 102, no. 3 (June 1997): 625–44. Shoemaker also suggests a variation on this scenario, one in which certain native groups conceived of themselves as "red" before European contact, a conception rooted in origin mythology.

13. I was inspired to look at identity in this way by Jacqueline Toribio's analysis of language use by Dominicans ("Race, Language, and Ethnic Identity among Dominicans," presentation made at Pennsylvania State University, November 2002) and her critique of R. B. Le Page and A. Tabouret-Keller's emphasis in *Acts of Identity: Creole-Based Approaches to Ethnicity and Language* (Cambridge: Cambridge University Press, 1985), 181. Similar approaches can be easily found in the vast anthropological and sociological literature on identity, although there are also hints of it in scholarship closer to the present volume; see Brooks's reference to "situational multiethnicity," for example, in his introduction to *Confounding the Color Line*, 6.

14. See Matthew Restall, *Seven Myths of the Spanish Conquest* (New York: Oxford University Press, 2003), 64–76.

15. Ulf Hannertz, "The World in Creolization," in *Africa* 57 (1987): 546; also quoted by David Buisseret, "Introduction," in *Creolization in the Americas*, ed. David Buisseret and Steven G. Reinhardt (College Station: Texas A&M Press, 2000), 15.

16. George Foster, *Culture and Conquest: America's Spanish Heritage* (Chicago: Quadrangle Books, 1960), 227; Robert Hoover, "Spanish-Native Interaction and Acculturation in the Alta California Missions," in *Columbian Consequences*, ed. David Hurst Thomas (Washington, D.C.: Smithsonian Institution Press, 1989), vol. 1, 395–406; Sidney Mintz and Richard Price, *An Anthropological Approach to the Afro-American Past: A Caribbean Perspective* (Philadelphia: Institute for the Study of Human Issues, 1976), 1; all three quoted by Buisseret, "Introduction," 3–5. Fernando Ortiz, *Cuban Counterpoint: Tobacco and Sugar* (New York: Knopf, 1947), 97–103. See also Richard Price, "The Miracle of Creolization: A Retrospective," in *New West India Guide* 75, nos. 1, 2 (2001): 35–64.

17. Buisseret, "Introduction," 6. For a discussion of how the term has been applied to processes of cultural development in the British West Indies, see O. Nigel Bolland, *Struggles for Freedom: Essays on Slavery, Colonialism and Culture in the Caribbean and Central America* (Belize City: Angelus Press, 1997), 3–33.

18. James Lockhart, *The Nahuas after the Conquest: A Social and Cultural History of the Indians of Central Mexico, Sixteenth through Eighteenth Centuries* (Stanford: Stanford University Press, 1992), 428–36. For a brief discussion of Lockhart's model in the Mesoamerican context, see Matthew Restall, "Heirs to the Hieroglyphs: Indigenous Writing in Colonial Mesoamerica," in *The Americas* 54, no. 2 (October 1997): 249–50.

19. Matthew Restall, "Interculturation and the Indigenous Testament in Colonial Yucatan," in *Dead Giveaways: Indigenous Testaments of Colonial Mesoamerica and the Andes*, ed. Susan Kellogg and Matthew Restall (Salt Lake City: University of Utah Press, 1998), 141–62.

CHAPTER ONE

Black Soldiers, Native Soldiers

Meanings of Military Service in the Spanish American Colonies

BEN VINSON III AND
MATTHEW RESTALL

ဆုင်္ဂ

In 1650, a strong-willed man with vast military experience in the wars of Europe was appointed to the post of governor of Costa Rica. Don Juan Fernández de Salinas y de la Cerda faced a challenging situation. For decades, this sparsely populated colonial holding, which was one of the last regions of Central America to be settled by the Spanish, was plagued with menacing internal disturbances by rebellious indigenous groups. Operating out of the eastern regions along the province's Atlantic coastline were two native groups of particular concern, the Talamanca and the Votos. The new governor's solution was a simple and effective one, original to Costa Rica but tried and true elsewhere in the Spanish colonies. The rebellious natives would be subdued not by Spaniards, but by soldiers of African descent.

The effort to subdue the Atlantic coast was certainly not new. Attempts had been made as early as the sixteenth century, but they were limited by the scarce availability of supplies and the lack of a centrally located base of operations. Only after 1605, with the foundation of the city of Santiago de Talamanca, were more sustained and costly expeditions launched. In 1608, Vázquez de Coronado was contracted to subdue the region, sparking widespread warfare and rebellion that cost the lives of hundreds of Spaniards and natives. War and rebellion continued throughout the 1620s and 1630s as successive governors sought to bring the area under their control. Despite their rebellious nature, the Talamanca and the Votos were seen as potential sources of labor for a slowly maturing economy based upon animal husbandry and the cultivation of corn, cacao, and sarsaparilla. Moreover, the territory they occupied was believed to possess rich mineral resources and was further seen as a potential site for the construction of a lucrative port.

Governor Fernández de Salinas approached the problem differently when he took office in 1650. Rather than relying primarily upon Spanish and *criollo* soldiers, he created the first militia force of free blacks and mulattos to supplement the troop base that was tackling the problem. Between 1651 and 1655, two companies were raised in the capital city of Cartago under the command of Captain Diego de Zúñiga. Their numbers expanded as they experienced military success. By 1672, units were operating out of both Esparza and Cartago, arguably the two most important and populated cities in the province. In Costa Rica, the initial militarization of blacks apparently had a clear purpose: "to defeat the *Indios Votos*." In exchange for their services, the government offered these soldiers three advance paychecks and temporary exclusion from the payment of tribute, to which free people of color were ordinarily subjected. When the government attempted to withhold these rights, as it did in 1662, the soldiers protested vehemently and withheld their services. As long as the colonial authorities extended these privileges, Costa Rica's black soldiers marched willingly onto the field of combat.[1]

The Costa Rican example is but one of many throughout the Spanish colonies that demonstrate the complex and often antagonistic interactions that existed between blacks and natives through the medium of military service. Blacks did not necessarily fight natives because they wanted to or needed to, but because they were recruited for this duty. The rebellious population of Votos in the northeastern sections of the province probably meant little to the black population of Cartago, nearly one hundred kilometers away in the center of Costa Rica.

At the core of armed interactions between blacks and natives was the fact that military service was a duty created by, and ultimately benefiting, Spanish colonial government. Because of this, participating in the military institution represented an act of supreme fealty and colonial citizenship. Blacks understood this aspect of duty, as did natives, who were also eventually recruited into colonial militias. However, black and native soldiers were not simply servants of the Spanish colonial agenda. They sought and manipulated military service for their own ends, to transform individual lives and to better secure the future of their communities. Black and native soldiers involved themselves deeply in the state's project of surveillance and control in that they collaborated in maintaining the structures of colonial dominance that were first erected during the Conquest. But they accomplished this in ways that were also subversive in their ability to alter the crown's perception of their own racial and ethnic categorizations.

In other words, there were a host of interest groups involved in black-native encounters that included the colonial state, whites, blacks, natives, mestizos, the colonial elite, the church, and local bureaucratic authorities. Black-native encounters within the realm of military service involved negotiation and conversations with a variety of these interest sectors. Rarely were their encounters based on black or native concerns alone. This chapter examines aspects of the development of the colonial military and its meaning for blacks and natives. What was the effect of military service upon black and native communities? How did service affect black-native relations? What impact did black and native soldiers have on colonial society?

CONQUEST PRECEDENTS AND THE POSTPONEMENT OF MILITIA FORMATION IN THE EARLY SIXTEENTH CENTURY

The first military encounters between blacks and natives took place during Spanish expeditions of conquest in the Americas. Blacks and natives fought both with and against each other as allies and enemies. Early in the Conquest period, Spaniards realized that their efforts to subdue Native Americans would not succeed if they fought on their own, motivating them to incorporate both blacks and natives into their forces. The best-known example of this phenomenon is the pivotal role played by the Tlaxcalans and their neighbors in the defeat of the Mexica (or Aztec) empire. The Cortés-led Spanish expedition would surely have succumbed to the overwhelming numerical advantage of the Mexica had they not been able to muster the support of indigenous warriors numbering some 200,000 by the end of the Spanish-Mexica war (1519–1521). As Ross Hassig has written, "the Aztecs fought a Mesoamerican war and lost."[2]

Other examples are less well known but just as significant to regional Conquest outcomes. In highland Guatemala in the 1520s Pedro de Alvarado encouraged and manipulated a war between the two dominant Maya groups in the region, the Cakchiquels and the Quichés, using both against smaller native groups in order to establish a Spanish colony. In the Yucatan, the Montejo-led Spaniards sought alliances with ruling Maya dynasties such as the Pech and the Xiu, but the relatively small regions controlled by these dynasties helped make conquest there a protracted affair that left most of the peninsula uncolonized.[3] Meanwhile, the Spanish invasion of the Andes benefited greatly from a civil war between the two Incas (rulers of the Inca empire) rooted in the arrival of smallpox in the region a few years earlier. Both rulers were killed shortly after Francisco Pizarro and his associates reached northern Peru, but disunity among the surviving Inca royalty and nobility allowed the Spaniards to become a permanent presence.[4]

Besieged by Inca rebels in the former Inca capital of Cuzco in 1536, Pizarro was saved not only by native Andean disunity and a relief force of Spaniards; his survival and that of the fledgling Spanish colony in Peru was made possible by a force of five hundred veteran African slaves dispatched from the Caribbean.[5] During the preceding forty years of Spanish activity in the Americas, Africans had seldom fought in such high numbers and they tended to be a minority presence compared to native allies, but they were equally ubiquitous in Spanish Conquest companies. Both willingly and unwillingly, as slaves and as free coloreds, black conquistadors were present on every Spanish expedition of exploration and conquest.

Armed Africans tended to be the personal auxiliaries of individual Spaniards, whether as slaves or servants, though they could also function as free agents later in their conquest careers. For example, the African-born Juan Garrido initially fought in the Caribbean as a slave, beginning in 1503, but participated in the wars of conquest in Mexico as a free man, eventually settling and raising a family in the newly founded Mexico City. A later example is that of Juan Valiente, who arrived in Mexico as a slave after the Spanish invasion and convinced his owner in 1533 to let him go south to seek his fortune in the wars of conquest—provided he share his profits with his owner. Valiente traveled through Guatemala to Peru and then to Chile, where his Conquest career won him a captaincy and an *encomienda* (a grant of native labor and tribute). Valiente's acquisition of rewards usually reserved for Spaniards was exceptional. But he and Garrido were typical in having wide-ranging military experience in the Americas, beginning in their late twenties. They were also typical of black conquistadors in that they were born in Africa, crossed the Atlantic as slaves, and acquired their freedom (either formally, like Garrido, or effectively, like Valiente) through the medium of military service in Conquest companies.[6]

The extensive and often crucial role played by black and native warriors in the Conquest might suggest that non-Spaniards were incorporated into the Spanish military from the onset of the colonial period. In fact, this was not so, largely because the conquistadors themselves were not part of a formal, national army sent to the Americas by the king of Spain. Conquest expeditions, called "companies" by the Spaniards, were formed as private enterprises with the crown's only role being the granting of licenses to explore or conquer—and even these were sometimes given retroactively. In most Conquest companies there were only a handful of professional soldiers; the rest were investors from a variety of professions and occupations, albeit armed entrepreneurs who typically already had battle experience in the Americas. Conquistadors were not ranked like soldiers either. Instead they were typically divided into three groups: the leaders, the principal organizers and prominent investors of the company, who were titled "captain"; those who were not captains but who had brought horses; and the remainder, who traveled on foot. Those on foot did not fight for salaries, but for shares of the spoils and for positions of prominence and profit in the new colonies—such as house plots in the provincial capital, seats on the town council (the *cabildo*), and a grant of native labor (an encomienda).[7]

Natives were never incorporated into these companies, but fought in separate units under their own leaders. Black conquistadors were part of Spanish companies, but mostly as dependents or armed auxiliaries attached to individual Spanish owners (if the dependent was an African slave) or masters (if he was a black or free colored servant). Even the exceptional few, such as Juan Valiente, who rose to become captains, did not command companies composed exclusively of other Africans.

Yet even after the Conquest, when colonial administrations finally began to station and recruit a regular army of some sort in the Americas, blacks and natives were the first to be excluded from consideration for duty. There were three reasons for this. First, deeply rooted ideas about race and social station conditioned how military duty itself was conceptualized. For centuries, the military had served as a key symbol of European power and status. From medieval times, the very title of "nobility" was derived from military origins. In fact, in sixteenth-century Spain, a noble was still defined as a person who was a master of the martial arts and who possessed equestrian skills.[8] Thus while blacks and natives were still used as auxiliaries and

allies in the widespread and protracted military activities of the later conquests, their entry as full-fledged members of the military establishment
became a more difficult proposition.

The scope of the problem can be partly appreciated by examining
how long it took for white criollos or creoles to be finally accepted into the
regular army's officer corps. Although born in the Americas, creoles were
largely barred from widespread entry into elite army ranks in the New
World until the second half of the eighteenth century. Even then it was only
between the years of 1790 and 1799 that the number of creole officers transcended 50 percent.[9] Taking this into account, one can easily see how even
the lowest ranks of the regular infantry, long associated with the European
commoner class and shunned by many New World residents, were difficult
posts for blacks and natives to access. Only in the most extreme circumstances of military necessity do we consistently find blacks or natives serving in regular army forces. The strategic ports situated along the
insalubrious coastal regions of the New World offered one setting. Spanish
soldiers simply could not be stationed here without sustaining tremendous
losses. In the Mexican port of Veracruz, yellow fever brought military death
tolls to a staggering 32 percent in the 1790s. Tucked under the sheets of a
single hospital, 891 soldiers lost their lives in 1799 without firing a shot in
battle. Hundreds more perished in recovery centers and medical facilities
throughout the city.[10] Given that the creole population of whites and mestizos was relatively small, free coloreds were suited up for duty, resulting in
the erection of a permanent fixed battalion of blacks known as the Fijo de
Veracruz. Similar situations could be found in Colombia and Panama.[11]
Still, these cases remained exceptional.

The second factor that inhibited the formal employment of blacks
and natives as soldiers came about as the newly forming colonial governments ruminated over the loyalties of these subordinate groups. It was clear
to certain administrators that the indigenous groups who assisted in the
Conquest effort did so for their own ends. Through helping the Spaniards,
many had hoped to eliminate their enemies, elevate their profile within
their regions, and remove onerous burdens (such as tribute) that had been
placed upon them by their previous overlords. The Tlaxcalans again are an
excellent example. After assisting in defeating the Mexica, they began to
help the Spanish conquer other areas of Mesoamerica, partly in hope of
expanding their power base. Prior to the Conquest, the Tlaxcalans had
entered into an agreement with Cortés, which stated that upon the successful defeat of the Mexica, they would be granted control over various cities,

such as Huejotzingo and Cholula.[12] Of course, the Spaniards reneged on the agreement. They saw in their most powerful allies their most powerful potential enemy. While the Tlaxcalans remained instrumental allies, the Spaniards were keen to play one indigenous group off another to ensure the eventual weakening of the Tlaxcalan state.

Spaniards were as suspicious of blacks as they were of natives. In the sixteenth century blacks were far fewer in number than the indigenous population, but given that so many were slaves who lived in Spanish households, they posed a potential and particularly unnerving threat. The arming of blacks had to be seen in light of the context of slavery. Would blacks with weapons, be they free or slave, engage in wholesale rebellions? Slave restlessness had certainly manifested itself early in the New World. In 1522, slaves had rebelled on the island of Hispaniola, followed by rebellions in Cuba (1533), Colombia (1529), Panama (1552), and Venezuela (1555). Early colonial officials had supported the use of armed Africans in part because of their reputation as good fighting men, but after the Conquest that reputation easily turned into a basis for fearing blacks with weapons.[13] A further concern involved military collaboration with natives: would blacks unite with rogue indigenous groups and pose an even deeper threat to colonists? Although some contemporaries believed that blacks and natives bore an inherent dislike for each other, there was also plenty of evidence of anti-colonial rebels from the two groups successfully joining forces; examples from New Spain included collaborations between the Zapotecs of Oaxaca and runaway slaves and between the Chichimecs of New Galicia and free coloreds.[14] Anxieties over arming the black population also stemmed from the impact of military service upon the stability of the slave regime itself. Since many slaves who participated in the Conquest were subsequently freed in exchange for their duties, military service came to be seen as a possible route to manumission. Indeed, some enslaved blacks came to expect their freedom once they performed military tasks. Consequently, the large scale arming of blacks, especially slaves, offered a potential avenue for mass manumissions, leading to serious decay in the Spanish ability to maintain captive labor forces.

The third factor that delayed the creation of native and black militias was the role played by racial stereotypes. In an effort to ensure that white Spaniards remained atop the social ladder in an environment where racial mixture was becoming commonplace, great energy was devoted toward creating inferior conceptual categories for blacks and natives.[15] The label of *gente sin razón*, or "people lacking the capabilities of reason," was applied to indigenous populations and served as a rationale for their subordination in political, economic, and social affairs. It justified Spanish colonial dominance while at the same time giving leeway toward a type of elite behavior that was routinely condescending toward the indigenous masses.

Blacks and the growing population of free coloreds (variously termed mulattos, *pardos*, and *zambos*) were not categorized as gente sin razón, but may have borne deeper scorn. Given that they were considered "rational people" (gente de razón), they were deemed more accountable for their actions. For example, while natives who committed crimes might have escaped blame on the score of being "unduly influenced by the example of others," blacks bore the full brunt of any criminal charges. Additionally, they found themselves in a situation of double jeopardy since they also had to endure the added weight of prejudices based upon their African ancestry. Blacks were considered inherently immoral, sexually lascivious, "naturally turbulent and defiant," and "cruel and malevolent."[16] There was only a small distance between these thoughts and the notion that blacks were generally unfit to carry weapons, because of their inherent desire to use these weapons for ill as much as for their lack of having the mental faculties to use these weapons appropriately. A blitz of legislation, beginning in the sixteenth century, clearly forbade blacks and mulattos from carrying arms of any kind throughout Spanish America. Similar prohibitions were instituted for natives. In short, even if blacks and natives proved themselves able to live freely and peacefully amidst Spaniards in the colonies, there was still a basic concern in the mind-set of the elite over whether these groups were capable of bearing arms.

The Birth of Black and Native Militias after 1550

Despite the numerous concerns over arming blacks and natives, a precedent of sorts had been set during the Conquest; eventually and gradually, beginning in the late sixteenth and early seventeenth centuries, their involvement in colonial military activities was to become formalized and extended. However, three basic conditions had to be met before blacks and natives could be introduced into the newly evolving military establishment. First, a sense of military emergency had to exist, whether inspired by potential threats from foreign invaders or pirates or by internal threats in the form of rebellions and uprisings. Second, there had to be sufficient development of colonial bureaucratic institutions, including a limited military presence, so that the introduction of black and native troops would not be construed as a direct threat to effective government, but rather a complement to it. Third, the Spanish crown and local colonial governments had to be made to understand that their personnel resources in the New World were insufficient, especially if they planned to build the military establishment solely upon white recruits.

As these various elements gradually came into place throughout the Spanish colonies in the sixteenth century, the hiatus in utilization of black and native soldiers ended.[17] Regardless of how quickly or slowly the three main preconditions for black and native colonial military service materialized in specific regions, the year 1540 marked an important turning point for all of the Spanish colonies. A royal decree (*real cédula*) was passed that required colonists to provide for their own defense by raising militia companies.[18] The legal principles upon which this decree was based rested in medieval Castilian law, where it was written that all subjects and residents of towns were obliged to bear arms when the king called for them to do so or when military operations were conducted in their areas. In the New World, access to weapons, training, and leadership was needed for these militias to become effective defensive forces. Some limited provisions were made by local governments to supply these necessities; however, the most basic and crucial factor for military success was manpower, a scarce commodity in the early Spanish colonies. Between 1535 and 1585, the entire island of Santo Domingo could only post an average of 500 white militiamen, while San Juan, Puerto Rico, could count on just 80 white civilian troops. The entire coast of Honduras barely posted between 50 and 100 men. Havana fared slightly better with 100 militiamen, and Cartagena (Colombia) averaged 200, but lesser ports such as Campeche (Yucatan) had difficulty raising between 20 and 50 militia soldiers. Again, these numbers represented the amount of militia forces that could be mustered among the white creole and Spanish populations. In many cases, even these numbers were hard to come by without a full mustering of the white population from areas distant from the main centers of service. It soon became clear to administrators that most locations could nearly double their militia manpower reserves if blacks and natives were allowed to participate.[19] In 1555, Havana opened its forces, allowing blacks to serve as auxiliaries, as did Puerto Rico (1557), Cartagena (1560, 1572), Santo Domingo (1583), and Mexico (1556–1562). In Santa Marta, natives were used as militiamen as early as 1548 and in Curaçao in 1570.[20]

Militia service could be wholly transformative for blacks and natives in ways that their service in the forces of the conquistadors was not.

Importantly, the state's perception of these individuals could change radically when they were employed as militiamen. Whereas prior to embarking upon military service, blacks and natives might be processed as being oppositional, subordinate, and conflictive to the state's ambitions, after being integrated into the militia, they could be seen as essential components toward maintaining the power structure of the colonial regime.

One of the most vivid examples of this process comes from seventeenth-century Guatemala. For years, the colonial government had been involved in a long and difficult struggle against groups of runaway slaves in the mountains near the Golfo Dulce. However, before the fugitive slaves had been completely recaptured, an even more serious situation developed. Increasingly daring pirate raids began to menace much of the coastline of Honduras and Guatemala, particularly in the zone around Trujillo and the Golfo Dulce.[21] In response, in 1642, the audiencia of Guatemala attempted a bold move. Through the art of persuasion, the runaway slaves were successfully coaxed into relocating and settling in nearby towns, where they proceeded to serve as scouts and soldiers for the crown. The radical change in their status could not have been more marked. Just four years earlier, these same blacks had been the object of scorn and were depicted as a serious threat to the safety of the colony. Now, they were suddenly being trusted enough to bravely defend the kingdom. Not only did these runaway slaves themselves receive a new, elevated status in the eyes of the colonial government, but apparently, so too did the general population of Guatemala's free coloreds. Their overall involvement in the colonial militias seems to have increased significantly during this time, thereby improving their relationship with the colonial bureaucracy.[22]

Slaves, although the least common of black soldiers in the Spanish domain, could also benefit immensely by participating in the militias. As mentioned above, in most instances, serving in the military was a route to freedom, but for a few, it paved the way for acquiring every other conceivable liberty except for manumission itself. In Cuba, despite the duties rendered by thousands of blacks by the middle of the seventeenth century, the crown utilized a small slave contingent to provide added protection for the highly strategic island.[23] Among them were the slaves of the town of El Cobre, who had a long and involved history in Cuba, passing from being privately held slaves in 1600 to being crown property by 1700. Over the course of the colonial period they rendered admirable services to the government, even when in the hands of private masters. For example, in 1662, a contingent of seventy-three slaves from the town dutifully guarded the port of Guaycabón from the English after they had invaded the city of Santiago. After being transferred to crown control, the slaves assumed a more defined function as defenders, serving as a pivotal military buffer between the coast and the capital city of Santiago de Cuba. Partly in exchange for their services, the slaves were able to gain certain amenities, such as a more flexible work schedule and the right to own property and to create their own self-governed community. Additionally, the royal slaves were allowed to run industries and even own other slaves. Although their participation in the military was but one aspect of their multidimensional lives and patronage networks, it offered them some leverage in being able to secure these valuable benefits.[24]

CONQUEST PRECEDENT AND CONCEPTS OF COMMUNITY: THE CASE OF THE ZACATULA FREE COLORED MILITIA IN 1772

In the eighteenth century, some black militiamen were able to conceptually link their military services with the duties that their ancestors had performed during the Conquest era. Black soldiers were able to use their historical memory of the Conquest struggle, their battles against natives over two centuries, and the consequent gains won by whites as a basis for negotiating improvements to their social status and economic conditions. Thus even for militiamen not directly involved in combat against natives in the post-Conquest era, the Conquest persisted as a useful symbol.

An intriguing letter addressed to the viceroy of Mexico, received on the morning of January 23, 1772, spoke to this phenomenon. Three weeks earlier, a small group of free colored militiamen headed by Phelipe Mendoza, Pedro Godoy, and Juan Joseph Manzo had hired a legal representative to conduct transactions on their behalf and to help craft a letter. They were concerned over their future lives as colonial citizens residing in the province of Zacatula. Just north of the port of Acapulco, along Mexico's western coast, Zacatula was a sparsely populated agricultural region whose important cash crops, especially in the seventeenth century, included the cultivation of cacao. A large number of free coloreds lived there, especially in the towns of Ixtapa, Zihuatanejo, Papanoa, Petacalco, and Salinas. By the census of 1803, there were at least 572 free black and mulatto tributaries in the province, meaning that probably well over 1,400 blacks were in residence.[25] Demographically, blacks appear to have outnumbered whites and

FIG. 1.1: *Designs of the uniforms of the regiments of militia infantry of Mexico, Puebla, Veracruz, Toluca, and Códova, the* pardos *of Mexico, and the provincial cavalry of Querétaro. From Archivo General de Indias, Seville, Mapas y Planos:* Uniformes, *roll 18/156/95. Courtesy of the Archivo General de Indias, Seville.*

perhaps even surpassed the number of mestizos and *chinos* (Filipinos) in Zacatula.[26] More importantly, these free coloreds boasted a long tradition of military service, which they provided voluntarily, free of charge, and with enthusiasm for the crown. The soldiers furnished their own weapons and uniforms, which were equal in quality to those of white militiamen (as fig. 1.1 suggests). They also proudly remarked that they did not let their military duties interrupt any of their communal or public labor obligations (*fagina*). As a further testament to their loyalty, the men served under harsh conditions. Tigers, alligators, and other wild animals were endemic to the region, yet none of these dangers thwarted the troops from diligently posting coastal watches (*vigías*) that defended against the landing of enemy ships.

However, the soldiers' letter noted that they were currently facing difficult times. For years, the only form of remuneration they received for their services was exclusion from paying tribute, a head tax to which almost all blacks and indigenous peoples in Mexico were subjected. The removal of tribute obligations, while relieving an important financial burden on many families, did not greatly improve the lifestyle of the nearly one thousand free colored soldiers who inhabited the area. Simply stated, they needed greater access to land, both for their family plots and for raising horses, cattle, and sheep. As a result, slowly, soldiers who had dedicated their lives to crown service were beginning to contemplate evacuating Zacatula in search of better economic opportunities. If they departed, the province would be left defenseless and exposed to attack and insurrection. Mendoza, Godoy, and Manzo's letter expressed concern over preventing the already trickling emigration from transforming into a gushing mass exodus.

There was a simple answer to the problem. Within the province was a large amount of unoccupied crown land (*tierras realengas*). Specifically, surrounding each of the major ports where the militiamen operated (Ixtapa, Zihuatanejo, Papanoa, Salinas, and Petalco) there was fertile farmland that stood "on firm ground" and was ready for cultivation and settlement. In their letter, the militiamen requested access to the land that lay to the north and south of each port, stretching two leagues inward from the shore.[27] The militiamen were fully prepared to pay for this property. A figure of 6,000 to 8,000 pesos was proposed.[28] Certainly, the soldiers argued, if the crown had been willing to offer tribute exemption, which was not a necessity for their basic survival, then surely the crown would be willing to grant them this territory, which was indeed vital to their basic subsistence. Moreover, granting the land to the militiamen was an insurance policy for the defense of the region itself, since Zacatula's ports would remain permanently protected by a robust force of black soldiers and their descendants.

In certain respects, the request appears relatively uneventful, perhaps even routine. Its significance lies in how the militiamen chose to package their proposal. First, the militiamen noted that the most successful petitions for access to crown lands went to communities or "*repúblicas*," rather than individuals. From the soldiers' perspective, their militia represented a form of community that had existed conceptually, if not in physical space. Although the soldiers who constituted the militia were spread out over disparate territories throughout the province of Zacatula, they still shared a common affiliation to crown service. Their military mission and profession bonded them. The same militia institution also provided a chain of command, which gave their units a hierarchical structure under the direction of regional officers. However, the militiamen were not simply appealing to the crown as a community of soldiers alone; rather, they tacitly emphasized that they were a community of pardo and *moreno* militiamen. Consequently, the soldiers' race was an important part of the equation—they were bound together both by profession and skin color. While other types of communities had managed to occupy distinct physical spaces in colonial Spanish America, such as numerous indigenous communities residing in *pueblos de indios* (indigenous townships) complete with their own town councils, this free colored military community had not yet had the chance to do so. Therefore, this moment provided an opportunity for clusters of free colored families to inhabit shared physical spaces while further solidifying their racial and vocational identities. Importantly, the soldiers were requesting that the militiamen have access to the tierras realengas for their private use. Unwanted squatters could be forcibly removed by the pardo and moreno troops, thereby preserving the coherence of the free colored military settlements.

A second important theme of the 1772 letter is the clear opinion of the soldiers that they were entitled to the land because, as militiamen, they were in essence performing the same functions as the early conquistadors who had defeated the Mexica in 1521. The militiamen were careful to compare their services with the Spanish conquistadors rather than with the black conquistador auxiliaries, with whom they may or may not have been familiar. Quite simply, association with the Spanish conquerors invoked more honor and prestige in the eyes of the colonial bureaucrats who would have been reading the militiamen's letter. But interestingly, the comparison conveniently overlooked the fact that it had been centuries since the last major battles had been waged in subduing the province's indigenous population. Indeed, by the eighteenth century, indios represented a demographic minority in Zacatula, much less a threat to the region's security. Nevertheless, the lingering idea of the Conquest, its esteemed place in the colonial heritage, and the valiant struggle against the province's natives were images that were being recalled for manipulation by the black soldiers in their petition. Like themselves, the militiamen argued that the Spanish conquistadors were nothing more than soldiers who had been granted land in exchange for military merit and services. The conquistadors' land was extracted from the indigenous communities that they had conquered. Once in the hands of these Spaniards, the land was passed down from generation to generation. The free coloreds wanted nothing more in exchange for their services. As direct inheritors of the conquistador tradition they felt duly entitled to the land that had been acquired by the conquerors in the first place. Moreover, they remarked that as loyal vassals they would not be asking for the land if they did not truly need it. In order to dampen the effects of any racial stereotypes that the bureaucrats may have possessed, the militiamen explicitly noted that they were not vagabonds and "delinquents," which were two of the typical descriptions used for blacks in administrative circles. Rather they were individuals with honor, but their current lack of provisions was starting to cause them to sacrifice their honor. To avoid any further damage to the integrity of their "communities," they requested the land.

Just over a year had passed before the petition and legal inquiry ended. Unfortunately, the militiamen's efforts did not result in their acquiring the tierras realengas; however, their petition was not rebuffed either. While many of the details surrounding the case are unclear, it seems that the militiamen may have been pressured into terminating their request earlier than expected. Apparently, local government officials in Zacatula had already laid illegal claim to the lands for their own purposes and intervened to frustrate the militiamen's attempts at securing the cherished tierras. Probably as a result, several months into the legal inquiry the soldiers dispatched a representative to end the proceedings. Regardless of the final outcome, this case serves to illustrate a common but little-studied trend regarding the meaning of military service for people of color. At a most basic level, militia duty gave blacks—and even natives—permission to invoke the most sacred images of colonialization for their own purposes. Despite their status as subordinate and marginal populations, both groups, when dressed as soldiers, could appropriate the cannon of the Conquest and its heroes as if they were their own. Keep in mind that Zacatula's black soldiers not only felt comfortable in associating themselves and their duties with the likes of Hernando Cortés, but they fully expected to be taken seriously by the highest levels of government in the process. They expected nothing less than a well-deliberated crown reaction to their strategy at improving their privileges.

THE ROLE OF NATIVE MILITIAS

The indigenous population of the New World also benefited in similar ways by inclusion in the militias. Native men served in units called *indios flecheros*, or "Indian archers" (central Mexico, Yucatan); *indios amigos*, or "Indian allies" (Argentina, Chile, northern Mexico); *indios fronterizos*, or "frontiersmen" (Mexico); companies of *naturales*, or "natives" (Venezuela); and companies named after their captains, called *indios caciques*, or "Indian chieftains" (Mexico and elsewhere). As was the case with black militia captains, service as a native militia officer offered a route to significant social elevation within the colonial bureaucratic apparatus. This was the case in Peru, for example, where by the middle of the eighteenth century there were a total of twenty-one indigenous militia companies in operation, including nine hundred infantrymen and forty-five mounted cavalry. Natives appointed their own officers, one of whom, Mateo Pumaccahua, was the first native to be appointed to the regional court, or audiencia.[29]

Whereas skin color served as a potentially divisive factor among black militiamen, natives could be divided by their ethnicity. However, unlike blacks, the government did not consciously or deliberately segregate natives. Rather, the nature of the recruitment process was largely responsible for creating indigenous companies that represented specific ethnic groups. Most native militia companies were drawn from single, specific townships; namely, semiautonomous, rural indigenous communities (pueblos de indios) that tended to serve as the home of a predominant cultural group. Consequently, achieving ethnic homogeneity was almost a natural occurrence. The Spaniards admittedly benefited from this arrangement, since they were able to manipulate ethnic differences by placing enemy native groups in conflict with each other. This was a particularly valuable and effective strategy in areas where the Spanish population was small and where their presence was hotly contested. In such settings, deeply rooted ethnic feuds and local grievances could be exploited to facilitate Spanish efforts at exerting regional control.

The number of native soldiers who fought against other natives was strikingly large. Indeed, this marks a second feature that typified native military service: it closely paralleled the military undertakings rendered by those natives who served as allies during the conquests of Mexico, Guatemala, Yucatan, Peru, and elsewhere, both in terms of the type of duties rendered and the locations where their services took place. Although a broad-scale survey for native military duty in the New World has yet to be conducted, it appears that native units were mostly set up in frontier regions where conquest conditions persisted for decades. In such areas native groups remained partially or wholly outside colonial control and the Spanish presence was small. Warfare was a constant reality, given the presence of scores of hostile indigenous groups. However, combat typically took the form of small skirmishes and guerrilla warfare instead of large and decisive, pitched battles. While colonial institutions, such as the government and church, operated within conquest environments, these institutions tended to be weak in their overall regional influence, particularly when compared to larger metropolitan centers, such as Lima, Mexico City, and Cartagena. Unlike the fully sedentary societies and imperial polities encountered in Mexico and Peru, indigenous groups in conquest environments tended to be semi-nomadic, non-sedentary peoples—with occasional sedentary groups relatively small in size, as in Venezuela. Prime examples of frontiers featuring long-term conquest environments are northern Mexico, parts of Spanish Florida, and the Mapuche and Araucanian frontiers in Chile.

NATIVE MILITIAMEN ON THE FRONTIER: THE CASE OF SONORA IN THE 1790S

An analysis of the case of northern Mexico offers a deeper understanding of some of the trends and patterns found with indigenous military service as well as a few of the interpolations that existed with blacks and black soldiers. On January 3, 1792, the Mexican viceroy issued a circular to all of his subordinates (*intendentes*) in the colony of New Spain, asking them to describe the state of the kingdom's native militias. He had grown concerned about their number, armament, and geographical distribution. He believed that his early predecessors had been wise to disarm the majority of the colony's natives, "having them to forget entirely the use of their bows, arrows, lances, clubs and axes." By the time he took office, he assumed that almost all natives had been "persuaded" to lay down their arms, except in the northern provinces along the frontier. Recently, however, he had experienced otherwise. Groups of well-armed natives boldly entered Mexico City, claiming that their rights as citizens and soldiers had been violated. Many of them were from regions in central Mexico, and most were upset that crown officials were routinely usurping their *fuero militar*, among other complaints. The fuero was a legal immunity typically extended to militiamen and soldiers based on rank, allowing them to be released from appearing in civilian courts for committing crimes.[30] The commotion the militiamen caused over the violation of their rights was even more disturbing to the viceroy in light of recent episodes of native restlessness. In Peru, Tupac Amaru's indigenous insurgency had posed a serious threat to the control of the central government in the early 1780s.[31] Closer to home, in 1787, Mexico had just experienced serious uprisings in the towns of Papantla and Acayucan, where indigenous groups violently protested changes in tax policies.[32]

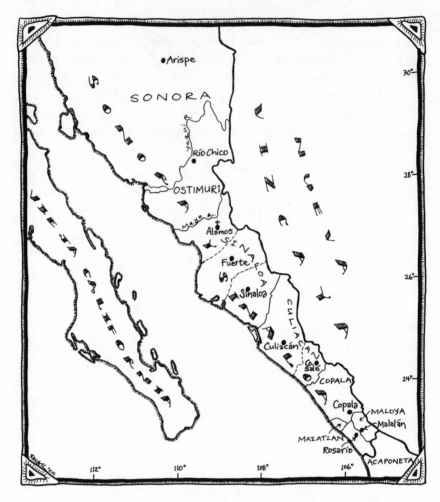

FIG. 1.2: *Sonora y Sinaloa. Map drawn by Matthew Restall,*
    based on a map by Ben Vinson.

Over the next several months, scores of reports streamed into the
viceregal office from throughout the colony, describing native militia duty
in detail. As the viceroy expected, the largest concentration of indigenous
troops was stationed in the northernmost reaches of his colony. One of the
more extensive reports came from Henrique de Grimarest, the Intendant of
Sonora (see fig. 1.2).

Sonora had been a frontier region for centuries. The province had a small white population and multiple hostile indigenous groups, of which the Apache proved most menacing to the settlers. The Apaches were not residents of the province itself, but inhabited its outer fringes, particularly along the northern border. Within the province resided several ethnic groups who sometimes fluctuated between being loyal friends of the government and being its deadly enemies. Of special concern were the Seris, Pimas, and Mayos, who led bloody rebellions throughout the eighteenth century. With hostile indigenous groups housed both within and outside the province, the arming of Sonora's natives followed a certain logic that seems typical of conquest and frontier zones in the Spanish colonies.

Perhaps the most militarized zones of Sonora lay along the extreme northern borderlands, stretching from Ostimuri to the frontier itself. The depth of militarization here was remarkable. The intendant reported that "everyone of an age competent enough to use a bow and arrow" was mobilized so as to defend himself against the Apaches. But despite the high level of militarization there was a startling lack of formal military order. The intendant could not report exactly how many native troops existed, since native soldiers had not been grouped into militia companies of any kind. On occasion, natives joined forces with other colonial residents of the region in league against the Apaches. Only at these times did they operate under the direction of a formal military chain of command, including a captain, adjutant, and lieutenants. At other times, their militarization was effectively independent from the supervision of settlers or the crown. Their duties were no less cherished because of their autonomy. Natives constituted an indispensable human resource, serving to buffer the kingdom and its precious mining communities from the aggression of hostile outsiders. The human buffer created a safe zone just south of the northern borderlands, wherein Spanish settlement could gradually mature and thrive.

Not all native militarization tended to be as informal as in Sonora's northern borderlands. In contrast, military organization was better deeper into the province near some of its middling and southern areas. In the vicinity of Río Yaqui from 1769 to 1792, two to four native companies operated with troop musters varying between one hundred and eight hundred men.[33] These militiamen provided essential duties during Apache attacks as well as auxiliary support for other forces in the jurisdiction of Ostimuri. When needed, they bolstered the defenses of the Buenavista Presidio and helped prevent uprisings from the hostile Seris, Pimas, and Mayos. Of course, the indigenous militias of Río Yaqui had not always been so formally organized. Prior to 1769, these units operated very much in an ad hoc, almost vigilante-like fashion. They responded to emergencies on their own accord and under commanders who had loose, if any, affiliation with the crown.

Both the southern jurisdictions of Maloya and Rosario had formal native militia companies. Rosario's forces were raised in 1734, numbered fifty soldiers, and were placed under the authority of a war captain. In addition to providing military assistance, these militiamen also posted a coastal watchtower duty that helped identify enemy ships off the Pacific coast. Meanwhile, Maloya reported three hundred armed indios flecheros in 1792. They were directed by a full command staff that included a native officer corps, sergeant, and corporals. Maloya's flecheros represented a substantial mobilization of the jurisdiction's native population, which probably numbered fewer than one thousand individuals in the 1790s.[34] While the forces performed few actual duties for the crown and were not further subdivided into tactical units, the militiamen did maintain annual inspections, which may have involved some training exercises.

The examples of Maloya, Rosario, and Río Yaqui reveal that formal indigenous militia companies tended to be created in areas where there was a larger presence of non-native colonial residents. No doubt these colonists played some role in articulating the militia arrangement. The creation of formal units also symbolically represented the crown's ability to order, manage, and control the indigenous population by harnessing it to militia companies. When a region or territory lacked formal companies, this represented the shortcomings of the Spanish bureaucracy and its weakness in supervising its native subjects. On the other hand, military alliances of the type found along Sonora's northern borderlands, as well as other fluid forms of military arrangements, could still be evidence of successful but not deeply rooted Spanish influences and colonial control.

In light of these observations, it is not surprising that formal native militia units were sprinkled lightly and haphazardly across the province, coming gradually into being. The companies of Río Yaqui are an instructive case. These forces were not compiled into recognizable, colonial militia companies until the 1760s. Prior to that period, Río Yaqui's indigenous forces resembled those farther to the north. Their command structure and military functions were more locally grounded and responded more to the needs of native authorities than to the Spanish colonial government. Furthermore, military excursions and defensive activities tended to reflect indigenous concerns. After the 1760s, stronger efforts were made to centralize and augment Spanish bureaucratic authority, resulting in the creation of the formal units that remained in place until 1792. But the militia formation process was contested and negotiated, with frequent competition between indigenous demands and state objectives. The scenario of Río Yaqui took place throughout Sonora. When there was a solid bureaucratic presence, increases in non-native immigration, and a regional commitment toward implementing Spanish colonial aims, the conditions became ripe for transforming loose native military arrangements into more formal ones.

Still, other processes were involved. Some portions of Sonora situated below Ostimuri, such as Copala, Cosalá, Sinaloa, and Culiacán, possessed informal native military arrangements for most of the eighteenth century, despite meeting many of the conditions described above. We do not know exactly how many soldiers operated out of these regions, but during times of need, their military musters were seemingly much smaller than elsewhere, particularly in the lands north of Ostimuri. On the one hand, these zones were not subject to a perennial state of military emergency as in the north. Therefore, an argument can be made that there was a reduced need for military preparedness. But on the other hand, a conscious effort seems to have been made to keep weapons out of the hands of natives in these territories. Specific policies were decreed to prohibit them from carrying arms of any kind, even if they possessed a license from the *justicia*.

Episodes of internal indigenous unrest partly produced the policies that restricted the use of weapons for natives. In 1740, indigenous rebellions rocked the jurisdictions of Ostimuri and Sinaloa, particularly around Alamos, Río Mayo, and Río Fuerte. Although the main incidents of discord lasted for just over a year, resulting in numerous hostilities and deaths, the uprising was not completely quelled until much later in the eighteenth century.[35] In the intervening time, a fragile peace was negotiated in which some indigenous groups agreed not to use their bows and arrows. Anyone seen carrying these instruments could be subjected to the death penalty, even if they were committing no other crime. Unsurprisingly, in the wake of the demilitarization efforts, native men served in formal military roles much more intermittently than before. It was not until 1769, within the context of a wholesale government effort to subdue the region, that two units of indios flecheros were raised. They proved successful in quelling the uprising of seven villages near Río Fuerte, so the decision was made to maintain them under arms. However, in order to prevent widespread weapons use among natives in the region, the flecheros troop rosters were limited to just one hundred individuals. Only enrolled militiamen could bear weapons; any other native was subject to the death penalty, as before.[36]

The Río Fuerte case illustrates another reason why the distribution of native militiamen was uneven within a frontier region like Sonora. Real concerns about native uprisings and efforts to contain them could result in the creation, constraint, or even the reduction of militia forces. As the Spanish bureaucratic apparatus increased its presence and clarified its purpose in the province, unexpected shocks could be produced, resulting in insurgent activity. Therefore, caution had to be exercised about precisely who was armed, how, and when.

BLACK-NATIVE RELATIONS: COMPARING THE MEXICAN FAR NORTH AND THE NEAR NORTH

The province of Sonora, while lightly populated by non-natives, did have a relatively large proportion of blacks in the eighteenth century. A census taken in 1793 revealed that mulattos alone comprised roughly eighteen thousand individuals, representing approximately 54 percent of the non-native population. Even with natives included, blacks may have at best represented a quarter of the entire provincial population.[37] Blacks were generally very active and very well represented among frontier populations in Mexico. They were found working in a variety of occupations, mostly related to mining and ranching. Large numbers were attracted to the borderlands because they found governing institutions to be weaker, producing reduced surveillance and generating fewer encounters with the prejudicial Spanish caste system. Simply put, as people who were already marginal to mainstream colonial society, blacks on frontiers could live freer lives than in many other colonial settings.[38]

On the whole, the interaction between blacks and natives was considerable, and not all of it was positive. A score of blacks were able to acquire positions of authority, serving as constables and justice officials in mission villages. In these settings, it was not uncommon for them to abuse their power, exploiting the natives both physically and financially. Blacks were also taken by natives as war captives and used as spies and warriors for insurgent indigenous groups. Furthermore, Spaniards greatly feared the threat that combined native and black alliances could produce. This generated an air of suspiciousness about black frontiersmen in general. Blacks seen fraternizing with natives were immediately held suspect and could be jailed for merely having a conversation.[39]

There were some good reasons to harbor these fears. In the aftermath of the Tarahumara rebellion in Nueva Vizcaya in the 1690s, Spanish interrogators allegedly discovered that the motive for insurrection was linked to the stirrings of a mulatto named Posilegui. Reportedly, he had inspired the natives to abandon their lives in the missions because he had proof that "the father's teachings are wrong."[40] His efforts to show the natives a new religious path, and his promise to unite them with an armed column of mulattos, produced a war that some natives professed was designed to completely eliminate whites from the region. Blacks and Tarahumara natives also populated *palenques* together along the frontier. These settlements, typically described as runaway slave settlements in the historical literature, took on a different dimension in Nueva Vizcaya. Being more "social" in nature than they were "racial" settlements, these communities did indeed contain fugitive slaves, but they also contained a wide variety of other marginals, including native rebels, thieves, and transient *castas*, such as *lobos, coyotes,* and the like. Wreaking havoc on local estates, the population of these racially mixed communities, sometimes under native leadership, could number in the hundreds.[41]

The high level of interaction between blacks and natives on the Mexican frontier did not translate into the military arena in Sonora. The lack of collaboration seems puzzling, especially since we know that blacks did configure into borderland military forces from very early in the colonial period. Take the case of Francisco López Cueta, who lived in the silver-mining region of San Luis Potosí in the sixteenth century. At the time, this territory lay in the northernmost reaches of New Spain. Francisco's story is interesting in that he had been born in the African city of Cueta during the 1530s or 1540s. The Moors seized him in an assault when he was only fourteen, and after a year in captivity, he traveled to Guinea in a caravel. From there he was taken to Seville, where he resided for nearly five years. He spent some of this time on a country estate, living with a black notable who maintained the registry of the local black population. Finally, at the age of thirty, Francisco boarded a ship called *El Revollo* and journeyed to New Spain, where he became a miner, cowboy, and part-time soldier. It was here that he fought as a militiaman against semiconquered indigenous groups along the Chichimec frontier.[42]

Although Francisco's case comes to us from the sixteenth century and the extent of his global travels make him somewhat unique, many blacks could be found serving along the northern frontier in the eighteenth century as well, both as presidio troops and militiamen. Especially in the role of presidio soldiers, blacks would have been stationed in some of the northernmost reaches of Sonora. However, in the late eighteenth century, it appears that the principal contact that existed between black and native soldiers took place in Sonora's southern regions. In the jurisdiction of Rosario, a pardo militia company was founded in 1734 to assist with efforts at preventing the landing of foreign ships. Watchtower duty (the vigía) was created along the coast, with the responsibilities being shared jointly by black and native soldiers.[43]

The military circumstances of black-native interaction on the Sonora frontier and in the Mexican far north compare interestingly with the situation to the south, in the north-central provinces sometimes referred to as the Mexican near north. To begin with, there were fewer indigenous units operating here and far fewer native soldiers. New Galicia, although still considered part of the northern frontier, was one of the most active areas, counting nearly 807 native militiamen in 1792. In the same year neighboring Michoacan possessed just 301 armed native troops, while Veracruz had merely a single company of armed indios flecheros based in the province of Acayucan. No other region in Mexico reported any appreciable concentration of native militiamen. However, prior to the 1790s, evidence reveals that more native servicemen had populated the colony's central zones. In the early 1770s, for instance, Tuxtla possessed two companies of indios caciques, numbering 154 troops. But that decade witnessed waves of military reforms that seriously streamlined indigenous military participation throughout the colony. In Tuxtla, these reforms took effect in 1775, completely eliminating indigenous military duty throughout the province.[44]

The reduced number of indigenous militiamen in the near north provinces was accompanied by fewer military responsibilities compared to the northern colonial frontier. To begin with, these units were seldom involved in operations against other natives. When their duties placed them in such roles, as in Acaponeta, their militia companies were sometimes referred to indios fronterizos instead of the more common indios flecheros. The name change appeared to carry a certain cachet. The militiamen's duty as frontier fighters was highlighted, thereby elevating their overall value and service to the crown. Indeed, the forces in Acaponeta had actually been instrumental in completing the conquest of neighboring Nayarit in the sixteenth century (see fig. 1.3).

But by the seventeenth century, the near north provinces were no longer a frontier zone; bureaucratic structures tended to be stronger, hostile native populations tended to be smaller, and the presence of non-indigenous colonists tended to be greater. Consequently, native militiamen had

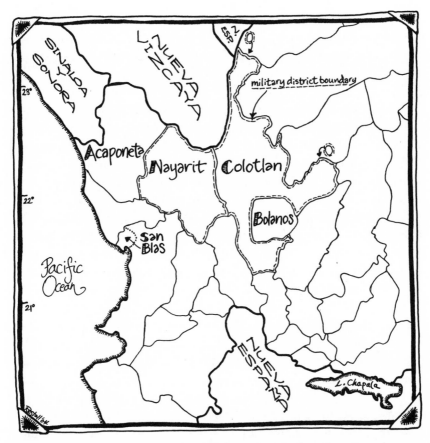

FIG. 1.3: *The Mexican near North. Map drawn by Matthew Restall, based on a map by Ben Vinson.*

lighter duties. Natives were more likely to be required to serve as coastal defenders, and even these duties were by no means extensive. This was the function of the mobilized natives in Michoacan and New Galicia. They performed the critical vigía, as did their peers in the southern portions of Sonora, and were responsible for thwarting numerous coastal incursions. The archival record shows that they were particularly successful in repelling British and Dutch interlopers. A handful of natives even joined the Spanish navy. In New Galicia's naval department of San Blas, groups of indigenous sailors regularly joined expeditions to the Philippines and California. Naval duty was one of the few arenas where racial standards of entry were relaxed throughout the Old and New World. Sailors of all races could be found aboard the ships of the British, Spanish, Portuguese, and even the French navies.[45] Between 1584 and 1641 the Spanish navy itself had nearly one thousand sailors of color, with at least one black ship captain.[46]

While in general, native militiamen in the near northern provinces were limited to coastal responsibilities, there were always exceptions to the rule. The 1722 Spanish assault on the Cora of Mesa del Nayar in Nayarit, a tiny enclave surrounded by other native communities conquered a century earlier, was made possible by the participation of an extraordinary variety of indios amigos—Huichols, Tepehuanes, Guaymatecos, Totorames, and other Coras.[47] In neighboring Bolaños (in New Galicia) (see fig. 1.3), native soldiers held multiple ancillary duties—they worked as guards for the treasury, assisted with police patrol duties, and even performed errands for local justice officials. The native soldiers here were remarkably well organized, and the martial tradition ran strong. Young native boys were groomed into military duty from the age of seven. As their careers matured, a few could aspire to the ranks of corporal, sergeant, adjutant, and even captain. Weekly duties helped mold the companies into an important instrument of local government.

Despite the example of Bolaños, the reduced level of indigenous mobilization and their curtailed military responsibilities meant that blacks and natives did not interact very often as soldiers in Mexico's central regions. Especially in the latter half of the eighteenth century, there were few operations that involved joint participation between units of indios flecheros and companies of pardos and morenos, for instance. One reason was that raising native soldiers tended to be a last recourse of militarization in most of the central territories. If there were ample numbers of whites, mestizos, and free coloreds inhabiting an area, they would be tapped first as the preferred forces for duty. In other words, there existed a race-based hierarchy of militarization that clearly disfavored natives. The hierarchy became increasingly felt as one moved away from the frontier. New Galicia, representing a liminal space between the northern frontier and the colony's interior, serves as a fine example of the process. Between 1753 and 1772, there were thirty-seven companies of whites in the region, compared to twenty-three companies of free coloreds, eight companies of "racially integrated" and mestizo units, and just seven native companies. Wherever native units served in New Galicia, they heavily outnumbered the militarized free colored population and occasionally outnumbered whites. Hence, whenever native companies appeared, it was because few service alternatives existed among the other races. Consequently, when natives were mobilized, there were often few blacks to fight with them.

Another type of indigenous military service dynamic transpired in the provinces of the Mexican near north. Given the higher degree of cultural assimilation that many natives experienced here, their military mobilization carried less ethnic significance, sometimes even to the point that native military duties could barely be distinguished as "indigenous service." For example, whereas the intendant of Sonora could speak rather concretely of the duties rendered by the Pimas, Seris, and other indigenous groups in his region, the intendant of San Luis Potosí was far more pressed to describe the ethnic differences among the indigenous population in his jurisdiction. When mentioned, indigenous peoples were simply spoken of as "indios." The lack of ethnic references partially resulted from generations of interethnic indigenous miscegenation. Shortly after the initial period of Conquest, waves of indigenous groups began to populate and interact with the resident population in San Luis Potosí, including Nahuas from Tlaxcala, Otomis, Tarascans, and Chichimecs. Atop this, Spaniards, mestizos, and mulattos arrived in the area, being attracted by the wealth of developing mining enterprises. Periods of epidemic disease worked to further amalgamate the diverse mix of peoples in the towns of Río Verde and San Geronimo Hedionda; local officials observed that

> the indios do not dress in the clothing they have been
> accustomed to in the past . . . [and] over the course of time
> they have mixed with Spaniards, mulattos and other castes
> such that currently, there are very few legitimate indios.[48]

The ramification of these demographic processes meant that for San Luis Potosí's eighteenth-century military, few companies would be created that were exclusively drawn from the indigenous population. The great distance of nearly two hundred leagues to the frontier further made units of indios flecheros and fronterizos an anomaly in the province. Despite these factors, it is important to stress that natives were not removed from service altogether. Simply, the level and character of their participation had shifted over time. From the sixteenth century, when San Luis Potosí was truly considered a frontier region, until the late eighteenth century, indigenous military involvement increasingly came to reflect both the perspective and services rendered by the broader colonial population. Over the centuries, the external military threats to the safety of indigenous villages (pueblos de indios) had faded, as did the very number and constituency of these communities. When mobilizations occurred, the indigenous population found themselves more involved in dealing with matters that were perceived to be "colonial" threats, rather than ones that could be interpreted as involving their own particular territories and worldviews.

For example, one of the more important mobilizations in the latter half of the eighteenth century came in 1767, when natives from Santa María assisted in quelling the plebeian uprisings that had occurred in the capital city of San Luis Potosí. This was a complex series of stirrings that involved a diverse range of parties with multiple objectives. The vested parties included the church, colonial officials, disaffected miners, and even various indigenous constituencies themselves.

On May 10, 1767, a prohibition on arms use was issued, followed by a series of arrests that took place both in mining districts and indigenous townships. Particularly irksome was the arrest of three natives who were allegedly carrying illegal weapons but were supported in their acts by the native *alcalde*. Mobs of natives protested these actions, bringing violence that inflicted damage on key colonial properties, such as the town hall and tobacco warehouse. Several colonial officials barely escaped their death. In the aftermath, militia dragoon regiments were sent to quell the uprisings. As they handled the crisis they also began removing Jesuit priests from their pulpits, part of a broader, colonywide initiative to expel the Jesuits from New Spain. All of these acts triggered angry reprisals. Rumors began to spread throughout the province that the natives were planning a general massacre of Spaniards on St. James' Day, July 26.

While this event never materialized, other revolts certainly did. In San Francisco, a Jesuit priest goaded the native population to rebel in protest of onerous taxes and militia reforms. In Hedionda and El Venado natives took advantage of the regional mayhem to destroy the estates of wealthy landowners and chase away the local authorities. In San Luis Potosí itself, angry multiracial mobs set out to protect Jesuit priests from expulsion, while others scuffled with the militias or took advantage of the crisis to engage in widespread looting.[49] While it is clear that some natives were integral parts of the discord, others were disaffected by it. The indigenous militias of Santa María, situated ten leagues away from the provincial capital, performed memorable duties in San Luis Potosí. Organized by their caciques "at their own expense," the relief forces supplemented the standing militia of one thousand troops. They were involved in an event that, in essence, had more to do with colonial politics than with anything else. Indeed, their military activities against fellow natives were not part of an extended conquest effort or in quelling semi-conquered indigenous groups. Their mobilization was completely unrelated to the possibility of a foreign military threat. As far as we know from the documentation, the march of Santa María's forces had nothing to do with the safety of the village itself. Rather, the natives here were making a statement of their allegiance to the colonial government in the form of concrete, voluntary military actions in support of the crown's policies regarding armament, taxation, and religious jurisdiction. These activities are the type that we would expect to see of any other locally recruited mestizo or white militia body.

SERVING TOGETHER: MULTIRACIAL MILITIAS IN EIGHTEENTH-CENTURY MEXICO

Native militiamen played an additional military role in Mexico. They participated as soldiers in multiethnic and free colored units. Blacks and natives had fought together since the sixteenth century in various regions of Spanish America but under the circumstances of a particular crisis or threat and not integrated into single, multiracial militia units; an example is the role played by black and native soldiers in the defense of Panama against English pirates in 1596.[50] During the seventeenth century it became more common for native units to be placed with larger free colored militia units. For example, as part of the multiracial force assembled by the governor of Yucatan for the invasion of the Petén in the 1690s, a pardo or mestizo captain named Mateo Hidalgo headed a company of forty-nine men that consisted of thirty-one pardos and eighteen Mayas under their own junior officer.[51]

The presence of black and native soldiers within the same units is not always clearly documented, but it may have been far more common in the core regions of colonies such as Mexico and Peru than has been recognized—especially by the eighteenth century. This was because ethnic and racial identities were becoming increasingly unstable in the late colonial period. In 1792, for instance, shortly after free colored militia service was banned in the city of Puebla, a census was conducted in which the enumerators reported that 8 of the soldiers who were enrolled in the unit of 451 troops were actually indios caciques.[52] There were many difficulties in proving that these militiamen were actually natives. Upon the abolition of free colored duty, a number of blacks attempted to change their racial status so as to continue avoiding tribute payments as they had while in the corps. Some boasted that they were mestizos, while others, plausibly, may have opted to list themselves as caciques, a status that also qualified them for tribute exemption. The fact that each of the married men amongst the indio soldiers took a mestizo, native, or white bride gave their racial claims some credence, but their true racial identity remains in doubt.

In other instances, however, the proof of native heritage was clearer. Juan Josef Martínez, an indio, was apprehended for vagrancy and subsequently incarcerated by colonial authorities in May 1790. He had been missing for over a decade from his native town of San Salvador el Verde, where he had abandoned his wife. During these years, he had completely reconstructed his life, moving to Mexico City and enrolling as a member of the free colored militia battalion, where he actively served for several years. His enrollment accomplished two goals—he was able to avoid paying tribute, and he was able to conceal his true identity by living his life as a pardo.[53]

There were other Juan Josefs in the colony, albeit not many. The free colored forces offered clusters of natives the ability to escape some of the pressures associated with their racial and ethnic designations. For criminals, bigamists, the distraught, and the poor, service offered a chance to hide or start anew. The beauty of the free colored units was that they encompassed an array of hues, ranging from extremely fair skin shades to bronzed browns and midnight black. Natives seeking to alter their identity found the phenotypic diversity of the free colored corps a convenient facilitator for their escape. By contrast, they may have experienced greater difficulties in trying to "pass" in white units, where there was more homogeneity and a stronger premium placed on lighter skin. Of course, passing for white was not altogether impossible, and some whites actually hired both indios and blacks to temporarily fill their militia posts, especially in times of crisis, so that they would not have to be called to active duty themselves. Native success rates at passing in mestizo units were probably highest, and service in these units carried with it a more prized social value than service in the free colored corps, but companies of mestizos were simply not available in all parts of the colony. In such regions, the units of pardos and morenos offered the only military alternative to service in the white militia corps. Unfortunately, we will never know exactly how many natives served in the free colored forces because the archival record preserves only the stories of the few individuals who were caught in the act of passing, rather than those who indeed managed to pass. But the phenomenon existed as an undercurrent to military service and black-native encounters.

A significant proportion of natives living in Mexico's central provinces were categorized as *indios laboríos* or *indios vagos*, which meant that they did not formally belong to indigenous communities (pueblos de indios) and were often itinerant laborers, sharecroppers, or permanent estate workers. Their lifestyle was highly assimilated into Spanish cultural norms. In overall social behavior they tended to resemble New Spain's free coloreds and mestizos, with whom they were often associated by colonial officials, especially in Tuxtla and Tabasco. The bulk of native soldiers found in the units of mixed race were drawn from the population of indios laboríos. These units were particularly prominent along the Gulf coast of Mexico but were also found in the interior. In 1758, just over half of the 1,600 militiamen in the jurisdiction of Veracruz participated in racially mixed companies.[54] While the majority of the rank and file were free colored, a sprinkling of natives manned posts in the corps. However, officerships were generally retained by whites, mestizos, mulattos, and pardos. Even in the case of the Yucatec unit mentioned above, the native officer that headed the Maya troops was subject to the non-native company captain.

CONCLUSION: IDENTITY AND MILITARY SERVICE

The story of black and native soldiers in Spanish America is one both of conflict and collegiality between the two races; men of African and indigenous descent fought together both for and against the Spanish empire, and they also fought against each other under a similar variety of circumstances. Yet a number of significant patterns can be seen within this varied tapestry.

First, while black and native motives for playing colonial military roles also varied, and militiamen were sometimes coerced into serving by colonial authorities, by and large these soldiers appeared to perceive service in terms of self-interest. For native and pardo officers, militia service was a rare avenue of social mobility in colonial society. For native municipal communities, participation in military expeditions brought immediate material rewards and provided the community with a negotiating tool for the alleviation of colonial burdens. For companies of black soldiers, service became the basis for a variety of tribute and taxation exemptions.[55]

Second, patterns and practices of service differed not just according to region, but according to *type* of region. As we suggested above with the contrasting case studies of Sonora and Mexico's near northern provinces, the frontier perpetuated a more intense use of native and black militias, with each serving in distinct units and regularly seeing action, and with Spaniards perceiving such militiamen paradoxically both as potential threats and as invaluable barriers to provincial collapse. This is not altogether surprising, as the first half century of the Spanish invasion (1490s–1540s) set numerous precedents for the Spanish military's use of African and native warriors, without whom the Conquest would simply not have been possible. Despite the reluctance of Spanish settlers to use this history to establish non-Spanish militias in the sixteenth century, the precedent had irreversibly asserted itself by 1600. Where conquest conditions persisted, so did earlier patterns of militia use; closer to the colonial core, militia companies evolved into multiracial units that saw relatively little military action.

Finally, our continual reference in this chapter to "black" and "native" militiamen does not mean that those who served saw themselves in those terms. Spaniards tended to lump native peoples of all ethnicities together as "Indians," and men of African descent were also usually perceived in a single racial category (sometimes separated into negros and pardos, or mulattos). But native militiamen served in groups according to community affiliation, representing their town and following the leadership of the local nobleman who was their unit captain. For native soldiers, a localized group identity preexisted and preempted their militia identity.

In contrast, militia service for blacks played a central role in the formation of group identities. Yet this was probably not a collective identity that encompassed all militiamen of African descent in a given Spanish colony. Certainly black soldiers in Puebla were aware of the privileges negotiated by other black militias in New Spain, but this awareness was based primarily on a desire to find precedents and other legal tools for negotiating improvement to their own conditions. Black militia identities manifested themselves regionally, if not locally. At times—such as in Veracruz from the late seventeenth century into the 1740s—negro and pardo units in the same town even feuded with each other over rights and status.[56] Significantly, the Veracruz soldiers—like most of the warriors and soldiers of African and native descent in Spanish America—conceived of military service neither as a burden of race nor as a colonial privilege but as a medium through which privileges could be won and individual and group identities consolidated.

☙❧

NOTES

1. Rina Cáceres, *Negros, mulatos, esclavos y libertos en la Costa Rica del siglo XVII* (Mexico City: Instituto Panamericano de Geografía e Historia, 2000), 27–29, 100–101.

2. Francisco López de Gómara, *Cortés: The Life of the Conqueror by His Secretary,* translated and edited by Lesley Byrd Simpson ([1552]; Berkeley: University of California Press, 1964), 138; Ross Hassig, *Mexico and the Spanish Conquest* (London and New York: Longman Group, 1994), 101–102, 146.

3. Pedro de Alvarado, *An Account of the Conquest of Guatemala in 1524* ([1525]; New York: The Cortés Society, 1924); Wendy Kramer, *Encomienda Politics in Early Colonial Guatemala, 1524–1544: Dividing the Spoils* (Boulder, Colo.: Westview Press, 1994), 25–99; Matthew Restall, *Maya Conquistador* (Boston: Beacon Press, 1998); Matthew Restall, *Seven Myths of the Spanish Conquest* (New York: Oxford University Press, 2003), chap. 3.

4. James Lockhart, *The Men of Cajamarca* (Austin: University of Texas Press, 1972).

5. Robert Himmerich y Valencia, "The 1536 Siege of Cuzco: An Analysis of Inca and Spanish Warfare," *Colonial Latin American Historical Review* 7, no. 4 (fall 1998): 387–418.

6. Archivo General de las Indias, Seville (hereafter AGI), *México* 204, fs. 1–2; *México* 2999, 2, f. 180; Matthew Restall, "Black Conquistadors: Armed Africans in Early Spanish America," *The Americas* 57, no. 2 (October 2000): 171–205; Restall, *Seven Myths of the Spanish Conquest,* chap. 3.

7. Restall, *Seven Myths of the Spanish Conquest,* chap. 2.

8. James Lockhart and Stuart B. Schwartz, *Early Latin America: A History of Colonial Spanish America and Brazil* (Cambridge: Cambridge University Press, 1983), 4.

9. Juan Marchena Fernández, "The Social World of the Military in Peru and New Granada," in *Reform and Insurrection in Bourbon New Granada and Peru,* ed. John R. Fisher, Allan J. Kuethe, and Anthony McFarlane (Baton Rouge: Louisiana State University Press, 1990), 57.

10. Christon Archer, *The Army in Bourbon Mexico, 1760–1810* (Albuquerque: University of New Mexico Press, 1977), 267.

11. Allan J. Kuethe, "The Status of the Free-Pardo in the Disciplined Militia of New Granada," *The Journal of Negro History* 56, no. 2 (1971): 105–17; Allan J. Kuethe, *Military Reform and Society in New Granada, 1773–1808* (Gainesville: University of Florida Press, 1978).

12. Hassig, *Mexico and the Spanish Conquest,* 149.

13. Sylviane A. Diouf, *Servants of Allah: African Muslims Enslaved in the Americas* (New York: New York University Press, 1998), 145–49; Restall, "Black Conquistadors," 193. The fighting reputation of blacks in Spanish America extended deep into the colonial period and even beyond the Spanish colonies; see, for example, comments about "Spanish negroes" (black sailors from Havana) in New York in 1740, in Peter Linebaugh and Marcus Rediker, *The Many-Headed Hydra: Sailors, Slaves, Commoners, and the Hidden History of the Revolutionary Atlantic* (Boston: Beacon Press, 2000), 188–90.

14. Colin Palmer, *Slaves of the White God: Blacks in Mexico 1570–1650* (Cambridge: Cambridge University Press, 1976), 119–44. Derived from a Nahuatl term that effectively meant "barbarian," *Chichimec* was a generic Spanish label applied to several "untamed" indigenous groups in the northern parts of Mexico.

15. A work that remains relevant in explaining colonial Latin American racial stratification and the caste system is Magnus Mörner, *Race Mixture in the History of Latin America* (Boston: Little, Brown, 1967).

16. J. I. Israel, *Race, Class and Politics in Colonial Mexico, 1610–1670* (London: Oxford University Press, 1975), 73.

17. In some areas, there was no hiatus, as the conquistadors held on to their partisan forces, and in this way, some blacks and native remained under arms even into the early post-Conquest period. However, such services were rendered to a private encomendero rather than to the colonial state itself, and their missions tended to reflect partisan loyalties. Marchena Fernández, *Oficiales y soldados en el ejército de América* (Seville: Escuela de Estudios Hispanoamericanos, 1983), 45–50; Fernández, *Ejercito y milicias en el mundo colonial Americano* (Madrid: Editorial Mapfre, 1992), 13–46.

18. Note that there was a 1536 *cédula* expressing similar obligations for encomenderos to provide for colonial defense. See Santiago Gerardo-Suarez, *Marina, Milicias, y Ejército en la Colonia* (Caracas: Casa de Reeducación y Trabajo Artesanal de El Paraíso, 1971), 26.

19. Paul Hoffman, *The Spanish Crown and the Defense of the Caribbean, 1535–1585* (Baton Rouge: Louisiana State University Press, 1980), 39–42; Jackie Booker, "Needed but Unwanted: Black Militiamen in Veracruz, Mexico, 1760–1810,"

The Historian 55 (winter 1993): 260; Archivo General de la Nación, Mexico City (hereafter AGN), *Indiferentes de Guerra*, vol. 197-B, Narcisso Sagarra, Ildefonso Silva, and Juan Pastor to Marques de Branciforte, June 25, 1795, Mexico City.

20. Hoffman, *The Spanish Crown*, 41.

21. For more on pirates see Manuel Lucena Salmoral, *Piratas, Bucaneros, Filibusteros y Corsarios en América* (Madrid: Editorial Mapfre, 1992), and Kris Lane, *Pillaging the Empire: Piracy in the Americas, 1500–1750* (Armonk, New York: M. E. Sharpe, 1998).

22. Paul Lokken, "Undoing Racial Hierarchy: Mulatos and Militia Service in Colonial Guatemala," *SECOLAS Annals* 31 (November 1999): 28.

23. Herbert Klein offers an overview of the free colored militia forces in Cuba in "The Colored Militia of Cuba: 1568–1868," *Caribbean Studies* 6, no. 2 (1966): 17–27. For additional eighteenth-century discussion see Allan J. Kuethe, *Cuba, 1753–1815: Crown, Military, and Society* (Knoxville: University of Tennessee Press, 1986).

24. María Elena Díaz, *The Virgin, the King, and the Royal Slaves of El Cobre: Negotiating Freedom in Colonial Cuba, 1670–1780* (Stanford: Stanford University Press, 2000), 89–94.

25. Peter Gerhard, *A Guide to the Historical Geography of New Spain* (Norman: University of Oklahoma Press, 1993), 396.

26. This information is extrapolated from evidence taken from neighboring provinces; see Gerhard, *New Spain*, 41, 194. In both of the neighboring coastal provinces of Motines and Acapulco, the black population outnumbered whites and was significantly large when compared to the other non-indigenous population sectors. We do not have a firm notion of how many indios lived in Zacatula.

27. This land may have stretched eastward as well.

28. It is unclear as to whether this was to be an annual payment or a onetime purchase fee.

29. Karen Spaulding, *Huarochirí: An Andean Society under Inca and Spanish Rule* (Stanford: Stanford University Press, 1984), 231. Another example is that of a Huichol named Pablo Felipe, who enjoyed an important career as interpreter and native militiaman in the Sierra del Nayarit region, northwest of central Mexico, especially during the Conquest of the Cora in the 1720s; Rick Warner, "Indios Amigos in the 'Conquest' of Nayarit" (paper presented at the American Society for Ethnohistory, Quebec City, October 2002).

30. AGN, *Indiferentes de Guerra*, vol. 100-A, Viceroy Revillagigedo to the Intendants of Sonora, Guadalajara, Valladolid, Zacatecas, San Luis Potosí, Veracruz, Mexico, and Oaxaca, Mexico City, January 3, 1792; Christon Archer, "Pardos, Natives, and the Army of New Spain: Inter-Relationships and Conflicts, 1780–1810," *Journal of Latin American Studies* 6, no. 2 (November 1974): 244–45; and Lyle N. McAlister, *The "Fuero Militar" in New Spain, 1764–1800* (Gainesville: University of Florida Press, 1957).

31. For good social and racial analysis of the army, see Leon G. Campbell, "Social Structure of the Túpac Amaru Army in Cuzco, 1780–81," *Hispanic American Historical Review (HAHR)* 61, no. 4 (1981): 675–93.

32. Archer, "Pardos," 244.

33. Each company was supposed to have fifty men apiece and in 1792, there were only two functioning companies in the Río Yaqui region. The figure of eight hundred troops came from earlier periods when, although there were only supposed to be four companies of two hundred men, a number of volunteers added themselves to the units.

34. Peter Gerhard, *The North Frontier of New Spain* (Norman: University of Oklahoma Press, 1993), 263.

35. Herbert Priestly, *José de Gálvez, Visitor-General of New Spain (1765–1771)* (Berkeley: University of California Press, 1916), 269. The years 1751 and 1752 brought a new round of intense hostilities as eleven restless villages of Pimas, Altos, and Seris began a general revolt.

36. Ibid., 272–74.

37. These numbers are taken from Gonzalo Aguirre Beltrán, *La Población Negra en Mexico: Estudio Etnohistórico* (Mexico City: Fondo de Cultura Económica, 1989), 228. They represent partial figures. We have chosen to combine the figures for both Sonora and Sinaloa, since the province appears to have functioned under that label in the late eighteenth century.

38. Peter Stern, "Marginals and Acculturation in Frontier Society," in *New Views of Borderlands History*, ed. Robert Jackson (Albuquerque: University of New Mexico Press, 1998), 167.

39. Ibid., 170–71.

40. Susan M. Deeds, "First Generation Rebellions in Seventeenth-Century Nueva Vizcaya," in *Native Resistance and the Pax Colonial in New Spain*, ed. Susan Schroeder (Lincoln and London: University of Nebraska Press, 1998), 22.

41. Stern, "Marginals," 171–73.

42. AGN, *Inquisición*, vol. 146, exp. 1, fol. 21v.

43. AGN, *Indiferentes de Guerra* 100-A, Intendant of Sonora Henrique de Grimarest to Revillagigedo, Real de los Alamos, April 5, 1792. For the role played by the vigía system in the coastal defense of another province of New Spain, see Jorge Victoria Ojeda, *Mérida de Yucatán de la Indias: Piratería y estrategia defensiva* (Mérida, Yuc.: Ayuntamiento de Mérida, 1995).

44. AGN, *Indiferentes de Guerra* 33-B, Antonio de Saavedra to Dn. Juan Fernando de Palacio, Tuxtla, November 12, 1775.

45. Stewart R. King, *Blue Coat or Powdered Wig: Free People of Color in Pre-Revolutionary Saint Domingue* (Athens and London: University of Georgia Press, 2001), 74.

46. Peter M. Voelz, *Slave and Soldier: The Military Impact of Blacks in the Colonial Americas* (New York and London: Garland Publishing, 1993), 46.

47. Warner, "Indios Amigos."

48. AGN, *Indiferentes de Guerra* 100-A, Manuel de Fernandez to Dn. Bruno Diaz de Salzedo, Intendant of San Luis Potosí, Rio Verde, January 20, 1792; and AGN, *Indiferentes de Guerra* 100-A, Gaspar Lechor to Dn. Bruno Diaz de Salzedo, Intendant of San Luis Potosí, San Geronimo de la Hedionda, January 21, 1792. There existed a few "illegitimate" natives in these towns, officials recounted, who claimed indigenous status merely to enjoy certain benefits, privileges, and immunities that the government had afforded the colony's indios. A few had even claimed being "frontiersmen," despite the fact that many towns in the province were nearly two hundred leagues distance from the colonial borderlands. These claims were made based on the previous sixteenth-century status of Potosí as a frontier zone and allowed natives living in these towns to be exempted from paying tribute.

49. Priestly, *José de Gálvez*, 216–21.

50. AGI, *Contaduría* 1468; documents of 1595–1597 excerpted in Carol F. Jopling, ed., *Indios y Negros en Panamá en los Siglos XVI y XVII: Selecciones de los documentos del Archivo General de Indias* (Antigua, Guat., and South Woodstock, Vt.: CIRMA and Plumsock Mesoamerican Studies, 1994), 457–75.

51. For this and a few other examples of black participation in the Conquest of the Petén, see Grant D. Jones, *The Conquest of the Last Maya Kingdom* (Stanford: Stanford University Press, 1999), 144, 229, 259, 260, 267, 467. Spanish campaigns using Yucatec Maya and black and pardo militias against the Lacandon and Itzá Mayas thus featured Mayas and people of African descent fighting both alongside and against each other. An illustrative and vivid anecdote is the fate of an African servant of Juan de Guzmán, who led a Spanish-Maya-African campaign into Lacandon territory in the

1680s; the servant was captured by a Lacandon patrol, who removed his heart on the spot while Guzmán watched, hidden with a few men in a nearby cornfield (Juan de Villagutierre Soto-Mayor, *Historia de la Conquista de la Provincia de el Itza* [etc.] [Madrid, 1701], p. 72).

52. Sudirección de Documentación de la Biblioteca Nacional de Historia, Archivo Judicial de Puebla (AJP), Rollo 2, fols. 1–45v.

53. AGN, *Indiferentes de Guerra* 307-B, Milicias Provinciales Batallon de Pardos de Mexico, Puebla y Veracruz, 1783–1790, unnumbered folios.

54. Ben Vinson III, *Bearing Arms for His Majesty: The Free-Colored Militia in Colonial Mexico* (Stanford: Stanford University Press, 2001), 25.

55. For example (in addition to the cases mentioned above), in the 1620s black soldiers in Peru were given exemption from paying tribute for having helped defend Lima against the Dutch; in the 1650s, tribute exemptions were also being extended in Nicaragua and Costa Rica, and from the 1670s through the early eighteenth century, blacks were making successful appeals for poll-tax relief in Mexico and Guatemala. Additionally, free coloreds used militia affiliations to garner fishing privileges, to liberate friends and family members from jail, and to protect their communities from the abusive practices of local officials. See Frederick P. Bowser, *The African Slave in Colonial Peru, 1524–1650* (Stanford: Stanford University Press, 1974), 306; Cáceres, *Negros, Mulatos, Esclavos*, 100; Paul Lokken, "Transforming Mulatto Identity in Colonial Guatemala, 1670–1720" (unpublished paper presented at the American Historical Association Annual Meeting, San Francisco, January 2002), 11–12.

56. AGN, *Criminal*, vol. 450, exp. 17, fs. 238–68v.

CHAPTER TWO

Africans and Native Americans on the Spanish Florida Frontier

JANE LANDERS

ᏮᏮᎾ

Native Americans, Spaniards, and Africans interacted in Latin America for over three centuries. This contact meant the rapid decimation of the native populations and the enslavement and exploitation of both natives and Africans. Chronic warfare engendered by European territorial and commercial rivalry and, later, colonial wars of independence engulfed both nonwhite groups. Although Spaniards (and later other Europeans of one nationality or another) eventually dominated, nonwhites pursued their own advantage when possible. Some natives and Africans remained within the Spanish orbit, although often on its outer fringes. On the terrestrial and maritime frontiers of Spanish America, *indios y negros ladinos* (acculturated, Spanish-speaking Christians) played important support roles for the Spaniards, including military roles as linguists, scouts, soldiers, and sailors. Many other natives and Africans, however, fled to form *palenques*, or maroon communities, apart from Spanish settlements, in the mountains, swamps, and forests of Spain's vast empire.[1]

The line between maroon and ally was often nebulous and permeable. Native Americans and African-descended maroons became adept at reading the geopolitics in which they were embroiled and astutely gauged their best options. Some who had once been the bane of Spanish colonists later defended their settlements against foreign and internal enemies alike. Those indigenous and African maroons who stuck to the path of resistance were usually undone, although often not before long and costly guerrilla wars. Because of the uneven pace and directions of Spanish settlement, remote frontiers were available to shelter indigenous and African maroons well into the nineteenth century in some regions of the empire. Among these refuges were the Spanish areas of what is today the southeastern United States.

The earliest alliances between Native Americans and African rebels in the Americas began at the turn of the sixteenth century in Hispaniola but shortly thereafter, Africans, free and enslaved, began abandoning Spanish expeditions trekking through what the conquerors called La Florida. The story of black-indigenous alliance in what became the southeastern United States is as old as Spanish history in the region. And even after the Spaniards finally ceded control of Florida to the United States in 1821, Seminoles and their black allies fought two more costly wars against U.S. forces in Florida while their compatriots who survived the "Trail of Tears" fought to retain their independence in the Southwest.[2]

EARLY NATIVE-AFRICAN CONTACTS IN THE SOUTHEAST

European intrusions in the Southeast, and the intertwining of European, indigenous, and African histories in North America, began in 1513, when Juan Ponce de León "discovered" La Florida. Free African veterans of the Taino wars in Hispaniola accompanied Ponce and other conquerors on all expeditions throughout that vast territory, which Spaniards claimed stretched from Newfoundland to the Keys and west to the mines of Mexico.[3] Enslaved Africans first entered the region in significant numbers in 1526. Only five years after the first known American slave rebellion was crushed on Hispaniola, the prominent planter, jurist, and slaver, Lucas Vásquez de Ayllón, transported African slaves from that island to the region near present-day Sapelo Sound, Georgia, to attempt the first major colonization of what is today the United States. How Ayllón selected which Africans might be safely taken to a new and distant frontier is unknown. Disease, starvation, and mutiny undid Ayllón's new settlement, and as winter bore down, some slaves set fires and joined a native Guale rebellion, finally destroying San Miguel del Gualdape.[4] These African rebels disappeared from history and presumably blended into the indigenous population as many of their counterparts were already doing in Hispaniola, Puerto Rico, Jamaica, Cuba, and Mexico.

Despite the slave arson at Gualdape, all subsequent expeditions to La Florida also incorporated Africans.[5] The explorations could not have succeeded without them. Pánfilo de Narváez landed approximately six hundred Spaniards and unknown numbers of Africans somewhere near Tampa Bay in 1528, but that expedition, too, proved a disastrous failure, undone by hurricanes, supply losses, and separation of the forces. Among the four survivors who "came back from the dead" after eight years wandering along the Gulf coast and westward to the Pacific Ocean was Estévan, an African slave whose linguistic and healing talents greatly contributed to the group's survival.[6] Drawing on lessons learned and fortunes won in Peru (where Africans also fought alongside Spaniards against the Incas), Hernando de Soto hoped to succeed in Florida where his predecessors had failed.[7] He outfitted ships in Spain and stopped in Cuba for additional supplies and personnel, including free and enslaved Africans and large numbers of native porters. In 1539 de Soto marched them all on a brutal and circuitous route through eleven modern states in the Southeast, along which many deserted. One enslaved African, Gómez, helped a captive *caci-ca* escape from Spanish control and return to her headquarters near present-day Camden, South Carolina, where he became her consort.[8] Other sub-Saharan and Moorish slaves and Spaniards, too, from this expedition also "went over" to the natives. For the next three centuries the Native American nations of the vast territory of La Florida provided a potential haven for Africans rejecting enslavement.[9]

The first permanent Spanish settlement of Florida was finally accomplished by Pedro Menéndez de Avilés in 1565. As Spanish colonists and their African slaves began building a new settlement and planting crops at St. Augustine, Menéndez made an exploratory tour of his new province and found a shipwrecked mulatto named Luis living among the Calusa nation to the south. Luis had been part owner of a richly laden vessel out of New Spain that wrecked on the Florida coast a decade earlier. His knowledge of the Ays language and customs saved subsequent Spanish shipwreck victims, including some of African descent. Menéndez ransomed eighteen Christians found in the southern villages, including Luis. The Calusa chief, Carlos, released five Spaniards, five mestiza women from Peru, and an unnamed black woman who returned to St. Augustine with Menéndez. There Luis and at least one other African, Juanillo, became official interpreters of indigenous languages, as Africans often did in other areas of the Spanish Americas.[10] However, some of the prisoners Menéndez tried to free chose to stay among their captors, perhaps to avoid separation from families established with native spouses. These included a black woman and a mulatto who had lived among the Calusa since they were children and who could hardly speak Spanish.[11] Knowledge of these mixed families may have inspired the slaves, who according to Menéndez later ran to and intermarried with the Ays.[12]

A year after establishing St. Augustine, Menéndez established a second settlement, Santa Elena, in modern-day South Carolina. Skilled African craftsmen from St. Augustine helped build fortifications at Spain's new and northernmost settlement and thus were reintroduced among the Guale, who had forty years earlier risen against Ayllón.[13] Although Spanish sources do not comment on it, it seems likely the story of the earlier revolt at Gualdape and of the interracial alliances against the Spaniards would have still been known among the Guale and may well have been transmitted to the African laborers from St. Augustine. The new Spanish settlement among the Guale was no more successful than the first, however. Jesuit efforts to prohibit polygamy and to interfere in tribal successions angered the Guale, as did what they considered to be excessive demands for food and services. Finally, in 1576, the Guale revolted again. This major rebellion lasted more than four years and was only defeated after the Spaniards killed many natives and put nineteen towns, granaries, and fields to the torch. Whether black slaves seized this opportunity to again ally with the Guale is unknown, but the black laborers who arrived from St. Augustine in 1583 to rebuild Santa Elena witnessed the aftermath of that tragedy. After another serious revolt was brutally suppressed in 1597, the Guale settlements along coastal South Carolina and Georgia went into a long period of decline, and survivors were gradually relocated to barrier islands. In an all-too-common scenario, the remnants of many different villages were "reduced" to mission sites so that they could more readily supply the Spaniards with food and labor.[14]

Labor was always at a premium in Florida, and soon Spanish authorities initiated a draft, or *repartimiento* system, which rotated hundreds of "Christianized" Guales, Timucuans, and Apalachees into St. Augustine to work. The result was catastrophic. Between 1613 and 1617 a series of "pests and contagions" devastated the native peoples of Florida. The same diseases that felled these groups must have also affected the black population, for by 1618 only eleven aged and infirm slaves were left in St. Augustine; in that year Florida's officials petitioned the crown for replacements from Havana to cut and saw timber for fort and ship repairs. The crown answered, "considering the need existing in Florida for such negroes and the necessity of preserving (sovereignty in) that land," Havana should send as many slaves as it could, "so that for lack of them, royal service does not cease."[15] Another series of epidemics—typhus or yellow fever in 1649, smallpox in 1654, and measles in 1659—took a harsh toll on St. Augustine's limited population, killing many government officials and all the royal slaves.[16]

The combined effect of these plague years was a dramatic decline in the native population, similar to what had happened earlier in New Spain and Peru. The interior of the peninsula was left almost vacant and records describe this as "the starving time."[17] The colony's distress finally led the crown to accede to major land grants and to the introduction of cattle, and in 1645 Florida's governor established a wheat ranch in the lands of the Apalachee, near present-day Tallahassee. In violation of a royal prohibition, he employed black slaves from Angola and a mulatto overseer named Francisco Galindo to supervise the free Indians working on the ranch.[18] Blacks and mestizos, some imported from New Spain, also served as ranch hands on vast new cattle estates in north-central Florida, such as the La Chua ranch, established around 1646 by the Menéndez Márquez family near present-day Gainesville.[19] Such establishments diversified Florida's population as well as its economy and made the colony somewhat more self-sufficient, but much of the surplus production found its way to Havana rather than St. Augustine. Moreover, the ranches' locations in the midst of Indian lands only increased native complaints against the Spaniards: the Apalachee rose in 1647 and the Timucuans in 1656.[20] These rebellions may have also encouraged slave participation or desertion because subsequent documents refer to the need to hold slaves in "the royal fort [at St. Augustine] and with good security so that they may not flee, joined by some slaves that have been brought from Havana to be sold at this presidio as a form of exile because of their being delinquents and incorrigible."[21] The already volatile colony thus periodically received blacks and mestizos from New Spain and Cuba whom Spanish authorities considered troublesome.[22]

Then, in 1670, English planters from Barbados established a colony at Charles Town in South Carolina, "but ten days journey" and within striking distance of St. Augustine. This event dramatically altered the geopolitics of the Southeast as well as the interethnic relations of the frontier. Aided by native and black "volunteers," an undermanned Spanish garrison made a feeble attempt to eject the usurpers but failed. The Carolinians, in turn, instigated more raids against natives allied to the Spaniards and encouraged intertribal warfare among interior tribes to supply their growing trade in slaves. Unable to defend even their island missions, the Spaniards tried to relocate their inhabitants ever southward. In 1711 Spanish officials even evacuated 270 natives of the Florida Keys to Cuba. When those converts proposed transferring as many as 6,000 more of their kinsmen to Cuba, the crown balked at the expense and the plan came to nought.[23] Because the Spanish crown was unable to protect them, many of Spain's former allies switched their allegiance to the English. Almost a century of Anglo-Spanish conflict in the Southeast ensued.[24]

Throughout these hostilities, desperately shorthanded Florida governors, like their counterparts in Cuba and throughout the Spanish Caribbean, relied on native peoples and Africans to supplement their military forces. Florida natives allied to the Spaniards were formed into a provincial militia by the 1650s and a black militia was formed in St. Augustine by at least 1681. These cavalry units, commanded by their own elected leaders, performed reconnaissance and guerrilla operations of critical significance to the Spaniards of La Florida.[25] In 1686 Florida's governor led a combined force of over 153 Spaniards, Timucuan and Apalachee Indians, and members of the new black militia on raids against the new English plantations on Edisto Island, including that of Governor Joseph Morton. The Spanish raiding party killed some of the English settlers and stole thirteen of the governor's slaves before turning southward to burn down the Scottish settlement at Port Royal on their way home to St. Augustine.[26]

The repeated crosscurrents of raids and migrations across the Southeast acquainted many blacks and native peoples with the routes to St. Augustine, and in 1687 the Spanish governor reported the arrival of the first fugitive slaves from Carolina—eight men, two women, and a nursing child who had escaped to St. Augustine in a boat.[27] Perhaps they were the Spanish-speaking slaves captured by English corsairs at Vera Cruz and Campeche, who had the year before asked a Guale man about escaping in canoes to St. Augustine.[28] Despite early uncertainty about their legal status, the Spaniards welcomed the labor and the military services the runaways offered, and so they refused to return them to an English envoy who came seeking them. Instead Spanish officials sheltered them, instructed them in Catholic doctrine, and put them to work. The men became iron smiths and laborers on the new Castillo de San Marcos and were paid one peso a day, the wage paid to the indigenous laborers who worked beside them. The governor placed the women as domestics and paid them half as much. These newcomers claimed to be seeking religious conversion, and after lengthy deliberations, the

Spanish king decided in 1693 to free them, "granting liberty to all ... the men as well as the women ... so that by their example and by my liberality ... others will do the same."[29]

In the next decades more slaves sought asylum in Florida, and they were frequently aided in their escapes by Native Americans. Although the Carolinians set up a patrol system and placed scout boats along water routes to St. Augustine, they were unable to staunch completely the flow of runaways. The English planters complained bitterly of the provocation inherent in this sanctuary policy, for not only did each runaway represent an economic loss and a threat to the plantation economy, but by the beginning of the eighteenth century blacks outnumbered whites in the English colony. Chronic fears of slave uprisings were not baseless. Carolina experienced slave revolts in 1711 and 1714, and in the following year many slaves joined the Yamassee War against the English.[30]

The same year four Yamassee chiefs representing 161 villages pledged their allegiance to the Spaniards, whom they had once terrorized. Spanish censuses indicate that the new villages, which they thereafter subsidized and tried to evangelize, were actually composed of many nations, including the Yamassee, Guale, Timucuan, Apalachee, Casapuya, Ibaja, Mocama, Ocute, and Jororo, but the related Yamassee, Guale, and Ibaja groups predominated. Apparently the governor blended the inhabitants of existing refugee camps with the new influx of Yamassee, making at least an attempt to keep related language groups together. The villages were placed at a considerable distance from St. Augustine, and two of them had forts to which were posted Spanish garrisons. These villages of new converts were expected to help the Spanish hold the frontier.[31]

Although the worst battles of the Yamassee War were over by 1716, hostilities continued through the 1720s, and in this unsettled period the native and black combatants gained military experience, increased geographic awareness, and new contacts among other natives and blacks already living in Florida. The turmoil of the war also gave slaves in Carolina added opportunities for escape. Some probably fled to remote woods and swamps to form fugitive slave communities. Others joined the Yamassee, and some followed them to Florida.

In 1724 a group of ten former slaves accompanied the Yamassee chief Jorge to St. Augustine to seek religious sanctuary. The men of the group had fought for three years alongside Jorge and his warriors against their mutual enemy, the English. After their war went badly, the black and native allies headed for the Spanish settlement, but there they were betrayed and sold into slavery by another Yamassee war captain, Yfallaquisca, also known as Perro Bravo, or Mad Dog.[32] The acknowledged leader of the re-enslaved Africans was a Mandinga who took the name of his new Spanish owner, Francisco Menéndez, when he was baptized in the Catholic Church. The black captain was from a region of West Africa long acquainted with Islam, which may account for his literacy. For the next fourteen years Menéndez led a determined struggle to gain for himself and his followers the freedom promised by the Spanish king. Supported by his Yamassee allies, he filed repeated petitions with the governors and with the auxiliary bishop of Cuba, who toured Florida, but they claimed that since the fugitive slaves arrived during a time of truce with the English, they were not eligible for sanctuary.[33] Finally in 1738, a new governor, Manuel de Montiano, reviewed the case and decided to free all the enslaved people who had fled from Carolina, over the heated protests of their new Spanish owners. Shortly thereafter the governor granted the freed men and women land to homestead and established a town for them two miles north of St. Augustine. In gratitude they swore to be "the most cruel enemies of the English" and to shed their "last drop of blood in defense of the Great Crown of Spain and the Holy Faith."[34] Spanish officials considered the Africans "new converts" and modeled their town, Gracia Real de Santa Teresa de Mose, after the nominally Yamassee villages near St. Augustine. Like those villages, it lay on the periphery of Spanish settlement and was to serve as a defensive outpost and produce food for the Spaniards.

Native American and black mission villages seem to have followed the same design. They consisted of enclosed forts containing the guard- and storehouses and a church and sacristy. Even the houses at Mose, although built by Africans, were said to resemble those of the natives. Franciscan priests were posted at the villages of both blacks and native groups to instruct the inhabitants in "good customs" and catechism, but the villagers were governed by their own leading men, who also led the associated militias. Florida's governors provided the black village with the same items it furnished to the natives, such as corn and arms, and the cost of these supplies was deducted from an annual allotment of 6,000 pesos budgeted in the St. Augustine treasury for "Indian gifts."[35]

These close connections between Native Americans and Africans led to interesting cultural adaptations, of which we can occasionally catch glimpses. The Ibaja Juan Ygnacio de los Reyes, from the satellite village of Pocotalaca, was among the trusted militia guerrillas on whom Florida's governor depended during the siege led by Georgia's General James Oglethorpe in 1740. Described as "perspicacious," he accompanied a Spanish expedition into the Lower Creek country in 1737 to seek alliances and trade. After a group of Uchise attacked the Spanish fort at Pupo the next year, the governor sent Juan Ygnacio and twenty-two of his native militia to reconnoiter and bring back intelligence. In August the governor wrote his superiors, "Juan Ygnacio has not returned and I am very anxious about him, as I fear he may have fallen into the hands of those who came to Pupo: if he has escaped them, I trust he will bring me very sure news." Juan Ygnacio did escape and the same month the governor sent him north to St. Simons "to try, using his native wit, to slip in . . . and discover as much as he could of the plans of the English, and of their condition." Juan Ygnacio pretended to be an escaping murderer chased by the Spaniards and was interviewed at St. Simons by English military officials. Upon his return to St. Augustine, Juan Ygnacio reported the English claimed to have enlisted between five thousand and six thousand indigenous allies to their cause and bragged that all of Florida would soon be English. Florida's governor asked Juan Ygnacio to report the alarming news to the captain general in Havana, but "[Juan Ygnacio] having declared to me that he had made a certain promise or vow, in case of happy issue, to our Lady of Cobre, I was unwilling to put him aboard with violence, and I let him go at his own free will to present himself to Your Excellency."[36]

Nuestra Señora de la Caridad del Cobre was, and still is, the black patron saint of Cuba, whose miraculous discovery was attributed to two indigenous Cubans and an African who were fishing together. La Caridad de Cobre is also the syncretic symbol for Ochun, the Yoruba goddess of pleasure and fertility.[37] Juan Ygnacio clearly understood the saint's function (to ensure happy issue) as well as the Spanish respect for religious vows. It is interesting to speculate how much Juan Ygnacio's contact with Africans in Florida and Cuba may have influenced his choice of a patron—and how many other Florida natives may have also been influenced by this and other Cuban traditions.

Although obviously unable to go among the English as spies, African scouts and cavalry troops performed many of the same important functions as the indigenous militias during the Oglethorpe invasion. Governor Montiano maintained patrol boats on the waterways that were manned by blacks, and he sent black cavalry groups out on joint patrols with native militias.[38] During the invasion, the village of Mose had to be evacuated and was occupied by the English, but its militia fought bravely in the only real Spanish victory of the war—the surprise attack and recapture of their own fort. This event appears in English records as "Bloody Mose" or "Fatal Mose," and it is generally acknowledged to have demoralized the English forces and to have been a significant factor in the English withdrawal.[39]

By 1752 Florida's indigenous Christians were living clustered near the not-very-effective protection of St. Augustine in five refugee villages: Nuestra Señora de Guadalupe de Tolomato, with a population of twenty-six people; Pocotalaca, with thirty-three; a village of eleven Costas Indians; Palica, with twenty-nine inhabitants; and Punta, with fifty-nine.[40] These natives were the pitiful remnants of once powerful nations such as the Ibaja, Yamassee, Timucuan, Chiluque, Casipuya, Chicasaw, Apalachee, and Costas.

By 1759 there were so few *naturales* left that Florida officials congregated the five indigenous towns into two. By then, few families were intact, and many households were composed of widows, orphans, and survivors from multiple families. The Yamassee *cacique* of Pocotalaca, Juan Sánchez, became the leader of Nuestra Señora de la Leche, which incorporated fifty-nine individuals. Thirty-three of these belonged to the Yamassee nation and the rest were Timucuans, Chickasaws, Creeks, and Costas. Nuestra Señora de Guadalupe de Tolomato was still led as it had been in 1752 by the Yamassee cacique, Bernardo Espiolea, and its population incorporated twelve Yamassee and eighteen other individuals of the Chickasaw, Creek, and Uchise nations.[41]

The Mandinga "cacique," Francisco Menéndez, still ruled the nearby free black village of Gracia Real de Santa Teresa de Mose, as he had since its foundation in 1738. Mose's residents had formed intricate ties within their original runaway group, intermarrying and serving as witnesses at each other's weddings and as godparents for each other's children, sometimes many times over. They also entered into relationships with natives, free blacks, and slaves from St. Augustine. Francisco Garzía, a black, and Ana, a native of unstated nation, fled together from Carolina in the 1720s and were among the first homesteaders at the black village of Mose.[42] Other interracial couples resided in indigenous villages. María Luisa Balthazar, from the village of Palica, married Juan Chrisostomo, a slave of the Carabalí nation, living in St. Augustine. Juan later gained his freedom and joined the Mose militia. One of the couple's daughters, María Magdalena, married a free mulatto from Venezuela. The other, Josepha Candelaria, married a native from the village of Punta and made her home there.[43] The polyglot population of Mose was also augmented by freed slaves from St. Augustine, of various origins. In 1759 Mose had a population of sixty-seven individuals and was larger than either of the consolidated native villages.[44]

EXILE IN CUBA

In 1763, the fortunes of European war created additional problems for Florida's multiracial populations. By the Treaty of Paris, which concluded the Seven Years War, Spain ceded Florida to Great Britain, and in an evacuation staggered over the course of ten months, more than three thousand individuals packed their personal belongings and emptied the Spanish colony. "In blind obedience" to their king, Europeans, blacks, and natives from Spanish Florida sailed off to uncertain futures in Cuba and, for a few, Campeche. While the evacuation must have been difficult for all, the already marginalized natives and Africans from Florida had fewer resources and less institutional or social support to call upon in time of need. Although the Spanish crown recognized its responsibility to resettle and temporarily support all citizens dislocated through the fortunes of war, Havana was not prepared to receive such a large influx of immigrants, and the exiled Floridians experienced severe hardships in Cuba. Fifteen "families" of natives from Florida were sent to the Havana suburb of Guanabacoa, an indigenous reserve for over two hundred years. The native Floridians found in Guanabacoa vestiges of familiar institutions, including indigenous municipal and church organizations. Like the Florida natives, those of Guanabacoa also had a tradition of autonomous militias commanded by their own leaders.[45] In Guanabacoa, Florida's indigenous people were at least briefly able to maintain some of their previous institutional and social contacts. Shortly after the exodus to Cuba, María Uriza had her daughter, María Francisca de los Dolores, baptized by Padre Gines Sánchez, the Franciscan friar who had ministered to their village of Nuestra Señora de la Leche outside St. Augustine.[46]

Despite the efforts of Cuban officials or their own parish priests, however, most of the native Floridians came to a sad end in Cuba. Eleven of the fifteen heads of native households died within the next five years. The death of the elderly Timucuan, Manuel Riso, at age ninety-five was probably not unexpected. But for others, like the Yamassee cacique, Juan Sánchez, who was in his mid-thirties when he sailed away from Florida, death came prematurely.[47] Many native women from Florida also succumbed. Ana María, an Ibaja woman formerly of the village of Nuestra Señora de Tolomato, was buried at about age seventy in the church cemetery of Guanabacoa, and the eighty-year-old native woman Juana Rondon followed her to the grave six days later.[48] The poverty of the Florida natives is reflected in the burial records. Most died intestate and were given alms burials, although the elderly cacica of Tolomato, María Francisca, was buried in a two-peso ceremony after receiving full sacraments.[49] Survivors were absorbed into the population of Guanabacoa, leaving few traces of their Florida heritage.

THE BRITISH INTERREGNUM IN FLORIDA

The history of Native American–African alliance in Florida did not end in 1763, however. Although the indigenous nations were virtually extinct or in exile following the colonial transfer to the British, Lower Creek groups who came to be known as Seminoles moved into the vacuum. These newcomers soon established flourishing villages in the interior savannas of northern Florida, where they grew plentiful crops of corn and vegetables and raised large herds of cattle. Runaway slaves who could no longer count on the protection of the Spaniards sought refuge instead with powerful Seminole chiefs such as Payne, Micanopy, and Bowlegs. In return for their freedom, black vassals provided the Seminoles yearly portions of their crops and their military services. They also intermarried with the Seminoles and became their trusted interpreters and advisors in war councils.[50] Some Seminole villages, such as Bowlegs' Town, contained both blacks and Seminoles, but others blacks eventually resided in autonomous villages of their own, such as Pilaklikaha, Payne's Town, Mulatto Girl's Town, King Heijah's Town, Bucker Woman's Town, Boggy Island, and Big Swamp.[51] Archaeologist Brent Weisman argues that the agricultural labor of blacks and their expansion into previously unexploited ecological zones made possible the creation of a surplus and subsequent Seminole entry into a true plantation economy.[52]

After a brief twenty years, European diplomacy once again altered the geopolitics of Florida. At the conclusion of the American Revolution the British retroceded Florida to Spain and Spanish officials and settlers returned from Cuba to resettle their lost colony in 1784. Now it was the turn of British colonists to experience a forced exodus from Florida, and in the chaos of the new transfer another group of slaves escaped from British owners to claim the religious sanctuary promised by the Spanish crown a century earlier. More than 250 former slaves petitioned and received freedom and protection in exchange for their conversion to Catholicism and pledges of loyalty to Spain, and these freedmen and women became the core of an important free black community in St. Augustine.[53]

The new Spanish government of Florida recognized the United States of America as a nation "as ambitious as it is industrious" and worried about

Black Fort Settlements, Black Villages, and Seminole Villages with Black Residents

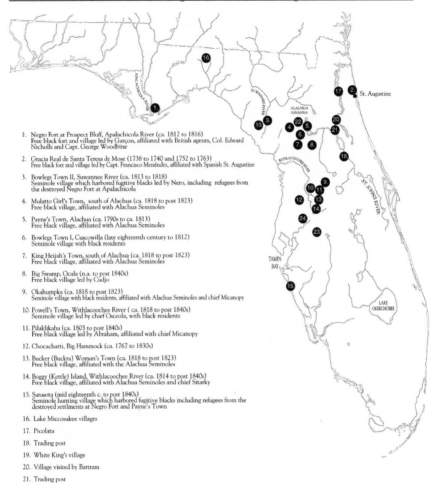

1. Negro Fort at Prospect Bluff, Apalachicola River (ca. 1812 to 1816)
   Free black fort and village led by Garçon, affiliated with British agents, Col. Edward Nicholls and Capt. George Woodbine

2. Gracia Real de Santa Teresa de Mose (1738 to 1740 and 1752 to 1763)
   Free black fort and village led by Capt. Francisco Menéndez, affiliated with Spanish St. Augustine

3. Bowlegs Town II, Suwannee River (ca. 1813 to 1818)
   Seminole village which harbored fugitive blacks led by Nero, including refugees from the destroyed Negro Fort at Apalachicola

4. Mulatto Girl's Town, south of Alachua (ca. 1818 to post 1823)
   Free black village, affiliated with Alachua Seminoles

5. Payne's Town, Alachua (ca. 1790s to ca. 1813)
   Free black village, affiliated with Alachua Seminoles

6. Bowlegs Town I, Cuscowilla (late eighteenth century to 1812)
   Seminole village with black residents

7. King Heijah's Town, south of Alachua (ca. 1818 to post 1823)
   Free black village, affiliated with Alachua Seminoles

8. Big Swamp, Ocala (n.a. to post 1840s)
   Free black village led by Cudjo

9. Okahumpka (ca. 1818 to post 1823)
   Seminole village with black residents, affiliated with Alachua Seminoles and chief Micanopy

10. Powell's Town, Withlacoochee River (ca. 1818 to post 1840s)
    Seminole village led by chief Osceola, with black residents

11. Pilaklikaha (ca. 1803 to post 1840s)
    Free black village led by Abraham, affiliated with chief Micanopy

12. Chocachatti, Big Hammock (ca. 1767 to 1830s)

13. Bucker (Buckra) Woman's Town (ca. 1818 to post 1823)
    Free black village, affiliated with the Alachua Seminoles

14. Boggy (Kettle) Island, Withlacoochee River (ca. 1814 to post 1840s)
    Free black village, affiliated with Alachua Seminoles and chief Sitarky

15. Sarasota (mid eighteenth c. to post 1840s)
    Seminole hunting village which harbored fugitive blacks including refugees from the destroyed settlments at Negro Fort and Payne's Town

16. Lake Miccosukee villages

17. Picolata

18. Trading post

19. White King's village

20. Village visited by Bartram

21. Trading post

22. Cowkeeper's Town

23. Opauney's Plantation

24. Dade City sites

Sources: Klein, Florida Indians. Klein's work is based on lists created by the Mikasuki chief, Neamathla and Captain John Bell at an Indian conference convened by General Andrew Jackson, Sept. 18, 1821; Brown, Jr. Florida's Peace River Frontier; Notices of East Florida; Weisman, Like Beads on a String; Mahon, History of the Second Seminole War; Mulroy, Freedom on the Border. Maps adapted by James R. Landers.

FIG. 2.1: *Map of black fort settlements, black villages, and Seminole villages with black residents. Adapted by James R. Landers from Howard F. Cline,* Florida Indians, *vol. 2:* Provisional Historical Gazetteer with Locational Notes on Florida Colonial Communities *(New York, 1974).*

the land hunger of its southern citizens.[54] Viewing the Seminoles as a buffer against Anglo encroachment, the Spanish government attempted to ensure their friendship by regularly hosting and gifting them in St. Augustine. On at least four occasions groups identified specifically as *cimarrones*, or slave runaways, came to St. Augustine, always in the company of Seminoles, to be presented with gifts.[55] Traveling into St. Augustine, the Seminoles and their black allies would have seen enslaved blacks working on outlying plantations and ranches, but they would also have passed by free black homesteads. In St. Augustine they would have encountered enslaved blacks working in a wide variety of artisanal and service occupations, but they would also have seen freed blacks living next to Spanish planters and running their own stores and small businesses.[56]

Free black militiamen like Juan Bautista Collins traveled regularly from St. Augustine to the Seminole nation to buy cattle for the Spanish government. In 1808 Collins made several trips to the Seminole village of La Chua, where almost two centuries earlier, black and native cowboys had herded Spanish cattle on the Menéndez-Márquez grant. Collins distributed gifts of cloth, handkerchiefs, belts, beads, sugar, tobacco, *aguardiente*, knives, and powder and shot among his Seminole hosts before conducting a series of successful deals. At the Seminole village of Chiscochate, Collins purchased a herd of 125 cattle, 18 of which were sold to him by a black woman named Molly. After a difficult journey of five to eight months, during which he traded independently and tactfully at various Seminole villages, Collins and the black translator and fellow militiaman Benjamin Wiggins brought back herds of several hundred head of cattle for the sustenance of St. Augustine. Through these visits and business negotiations, strong connections developed between blacks and Seminoles, and when Collins was once forced to sue the Spanish government for overdue payment, Chief Bowlegs's sister, Simency, traveled to St. Augustine to testify on Collins's behalf.[57]

Such links proved critical when land-hungry Georgians, styling themselves Patriots, attempted to seize Florida in 1812 and hand it to the United States. On that occasion, as before, the Seminoles and their black "vassals" came to the assistance of Spain. The Spaniards stood to lose their colony, fugitive slaves their freedom, and the Seminoles their rich lands and cattle herds.[58] The Spanish governor posted members of his black militia at Seminole villages, and chiefs Payne and Bowlegs reciprocated by sending some of their own black warriors to fight alongside the Spaniards as a gesture of good faith.[59] Like his predecessors, Governor Kindelán also employed black translators, like Benjamín Wiggins and Tony Proctor, "the best translator of the Indian languages in the province," to promote the Spanish-black-Indian alliance.[60] In July 1812 Tony Proctor recruited several hundred warriors from the Seminole village of La Chua.[61] Blacks like Abraham, who governed the village of Pilaklikaha and who was the trusted interpreter and war council adviser to Chief Micanopy, knew that should the Americans ever gain Florida, it would mean a return to slavery for most blacks. He and others counseled the Seminoles to support the Spanish cause.

The turning point of the Patriot siege came in September 1812, when Lieutenant Juan Bautista Witten, an escaped and freed slave from South Carolina, led a band of twenty-five black militiamen, thirty-two of Chief Payne's blacks, and a handful of Seminoles in a well-executed ambush of twenty U.S. Marines and approximately sixty to seventy Patriots escorting a supply convoy through Twelve Mile Swamp at night. The Patriot accounts (and therefore, most historical treatments based on the English-language sources) reported that the ambush at Twelve Mile Swamp was the work of the Indians, but Governor Kindelán wrote that the "Indians" were actually "our parties of blacks, whom they [the rebels] think are Indians because they wear the same clothing and go painted."[62] Witten's forces took down U.S. Marine captain John Williams, his sergeant, and the wagon horses in the first volley. For two hours afterward they battled the more numerous invading forces, killing many but suffering several casualties as well. That night Witten's men destroyed one wagon and the next morning used the second to transport their wounded back to St. Augustine. This decisive action, like Bloody Mose almost a century before, lifted the Patriot siege and allowed badly needed supplies to reach St. Augustine.[63] Bereft of supplies, the demoralized Patriot and U.S. forces began to pull back. When later that month a force led by Georgia volunteer Colonel Daniel Newnan failed to break up the Seminole towns near La Chua and was mauled by Chief Payne's polyglot warriors, the invasion was spent.[64] Disease, the ferocity of the black and indigenous militias, and weakening U.S. enthusiasm for the land grab when war with England threatened eventually ruined the Patriots. In May 1813 all foreign forces were withdrawn from Spanish Florida.[65]

Although Spain's black guerrillas and their Seminole allies undid the halfhearted Patriot Rebellion, the United States remained firmly committed to an expansionist foreign policy in the Southeast. Its interventions were motivated by territorial ambition, by the lingering fear that Britain would displace the weakened Spanish regimes in the Southeast, and by racial politics. The very success of the Spanish-native-black alliance, in effect, ensured further intervention by Americans, who could not tolerate such dangerous collaboration on their frontier. The War of 1812 and the simultaneous Creek War of 1813–1814 evolved into a long-term effort to push the Creeks, Seminoles, and blacks out of their settlements in western and central Florida and eventually to drive out the Spaniards as well.[66]

In April 1818 General Andrew Jackson led more than three thousand troops in a three-week campaign against the Seminole heartland in what came to be called the First Seminole War. Alexander Arbuthnot, an Indian trader sympathetic to the black-Seminole cause, alleged, "The main drift of the Americans is to destroy the black population of Suwany."[67] The American general Gaines confirmed this when he wrote the Seminoles, "You harbor a great many of my black people among you, at Sahwahnee. If you give me leave to go by you against them, I shall not hurt anything belonging to you." King Hachy (Heijah) responded that some blacks may have taken refuge among the Seminoles during the English war with the Americans, but "it is for you, white people, to settle those things among yourselves. . . . I shall use force to stop any armed Americans from passing my towns or my lands."[68]

Jackson would not be deterred by such threats. Moving eastward, he forced the surrender of the Spanish garrison at San Marcos de Apalachee, where he arrested and executed the most famous Creek prophet Josiah Francis (Hillis Hadjo), who led a nativist effort to unite native peoples from the Great Lakes to the Gulf coast and to roll back U.S. expansion.[69] Jackson also arrested and executed the Bahamian Indian traders Alexander Arbuthnot and Robert Ambrister after a hastily convoked court convicted them of inciting and arming natives and blacks. Evidence at Ambrister's trial included a letter he had written English military officials from the Suwannee, stating that the three hundred blacks there "beg me to say, they depend on your promises, and expect you are the way out. They have stuck to the *cause*, and will always believe in the faith of you."[70]

On April 16, 1818, Jackson's troops burned almost four hundred black and Seminole homes at Bowlegs' Town on the Suwannee River, destroyed large quantities of food supplies, and spirited away herds of cattle and horses.[71] Blacks and Seminoles, who had been forewarned by Arbuthnot, put up a desperate fight, with three hundred black warriors holding back a greatly superior force at the Suwannee to give the women and children time to cross over to safety.

From the Suwannee, General Jackson marched westward and seized Spanish Pensacola, concluding the so-called First Seminole War. Although the Seminoles' northern settlements were ruined, resistance continued.

Black and Seminole refugees dispersed to the west and south of Florida, joining others who had already resettled in traditional hunting villages near Tampa Bay.[72] Captain James Gadsden described Tampa Bay as "the last rallying spot of the disaffected negroes and Indians and the only favorable point from whence a communication can be had with Spanish and European emissaries."[73] The desperate Seminoles and their black allies sent repeated diplomatic missions to the British in the Bahamas and the Spaniards in Cuba, seeking military support. The Spaniards in St. Augustine gave them substantial food supplies and muskets, but the British sent only nominal gifts, not wanting to alienate the Americans, who, by the Adams-Onís Treaty, were soon to take possession of Florida.[74]

When General Andrew Jackson became governor of the new U.S. territory of Florida, he recommended removing the remnant Creeks, Seminoles, and free blacks from the peninsula. As he awaited a response, several hundred Coweta warriors sponsored by Georgia speculators raided the Tampa Bay and Sarasota Bay settlements and carried a number of blacks, cattle, and horses northward. Once again, escaping Seminoles and blacks were forced to flee—this time to the tip of the peninsula at Cape Florida. There, Cuban fishermen and Bahamian shipwreck salvors with whom they had long conducted trade carried hundreds of them "in a famishing state" to safety in Cuba and to Andros Island and Bimini.[75]

Influential black Seminole leaders such as Abraham, Harry, John Philip, and John Cesar or Cavallo stayed on in Florida and resisted removal westward as long as they practically could.[76] Abraham, Chief Micanopy's military adviser, had fought at most of the main battles of the first Seminole War and became the ruler of the free-black village of Pilaklikaha near present-day Bushnell, Florida. But in 1823 the Second Seminole War broke out and once again, Abraham and his followers took up arms. After fifteen more years of miserable war, Abraham turned himself in to the U.S. forces and bowed to the inevitable. In 1838 he wrote commanding general Thomas Jessup:

> We will go with the Indians to our new home, and wish to
> know how we are to be protected, and who is to have the care
> of us on the road. We do not live for ourselves only, but for our
> wives and children who are as dear to us as those of any other
> men. When we reach our new home we hope we shall be
> permitted to remain while the woods remain green and the
> water runs. I have charge of all the red people coming out to
> Pease's Creek, and all are satisfied to go to Arkansaw.[77]

When the Seminoles were "removed" to the western territories, many of their black allies went with them, some of whom eventually sought out a new sanctuary in the frontiers of northern Mexico, where they offered their services to General Santa Anna. Today black Seminoles in Nascimiento and other border settlements still speak Gullah and keep alive the history of their exodus from Florida and of the long maroon tradition on the Spanish frontier. A few blacks and Seminoles remained in Florida and fought one final Seminole war against the United States before retreating far into the then impassable Everglades, where their descendants live today.[78]

The rich lands Seminoles and their black allies left in north-central Florida became homesteads for Anglo settlers, who also usurped much of the land of free blacks ostensibly protected by treaty provisions. Florida's new masters enacted restrictive legislation designed to create a two-caste system in Florida and bring it in line with the rest of the South. In quick succession free blacks were barred from entering the territory and forbidden to assemble, carry arms, serve on juries, testify in courts, or vote. New laws also prohibited interracial marriages and sexual relations between whites and blacks and ended the inheritance rights of children of interracial unions. Finally, manumission was made almost impossible and free blacks had to post bonds guaranteeing good behavior and acquire guardians.[79]

The Florida "frontier," which was deemed for centuries inhospitable for Europeans, was the crucible for Native American–black alliance in North America. For more than three centuries, Native Americans and blacks helped shape the geopolitics of the American Southeast. Aided by Spanish Florida's particular geographic, demographic, economic, and political conditions, they persisted and created viable communities in the face of repeated aggressions. The United States' expansionism ultimately ruined both groups. The purchases of Louisiana and West Florida and the final cession of East Florida in 1821 effectively ended the black and native sanctuaries in the southeastern borderlands.

ⓈⓈ

NOTES

1. Richard Price, *Maroon Societies: Rebel Slave Communities in the Americas* (Baltimore: Johns Hopkins University Press, 1973); Jane Landers, "The Central African Presence in Spanish Maroon Societies," in *Central African and Cultural Transformations in the American Diaspora,* ed. Linda M. Heywood (Cambridge: Cambridge University Press, 2002), 227–41; Jane Landers, "*Cimarrón* Ethnicity and Cultural Adaptation in the Spanish Domains of the Circum-Caribbean, 1503–1763," in *Identity in the Shadow of Slavery,* ed. Paul E. Lovejoy (London: Continuum, 2000), 30–54; Jane Landers, "Conspiradores esclavizados en Cartagena en el siglo XVII," in *Afrodescendientes en las américas: trayectorias sociales e identitarias: 150 años de la abolición de la esclavitud en Colombia,* ed. Claudia Mosquera, Mauricio Pardo, and Odile Hoffman (Bogotá: Universidad Nacional de Colombia, 2002), 181–93.

2. Jane Landers, *Black Society in Spanish Florida* (Urbana: University of Illinois Press, 1999), chaps. 9, 10.

3. Ricardo E. Alegría, *Juan Garrido, el Conquistador Negro en las Antilles, Florida, México y California, c. 1503–1540* (San Juan de Puerto Rico, 1990).

4. Paul Hoffman, *A New Andalucía and a Way to the Orient: The American Southeast During the Sixteenth Century* (Baton Rouge: Louisiana State University Press, 1990), 73–79.

5. Landers, *Black Society,* chap. 1; Matthew Restall, "Black Conquistadors: Armed Africans in Early Spanish America," *The Americas* 57 (October 2000): 171–205.

6. Enrique Pupo-Walker, ed., *Castaways: The Narrative of Alvar Núñez Cabeza de Vaca,* translated by Frances M. López-Morillas (Berkeley: University of California Press, 1993), 51, 56, 64–66, 104–5.

7. Charles Hudson, *Knights of Spain, Warriors of the Sun: Hernando de Soto and the South's Ancient Chiefdoms* (Athens: University of Georgia Press, 1997).

8. Edward Gaylord Bourne, ed., *Narratives of the Career of Hernando de Soto* (New York, 1904), 72.

9. Landers, *Black Society*; Paul H. Hoffman, *Florida's Frontiers* (Bloomington: Indiana University Press, 2002).

10. Florida ration list, 1566–1567, Florida Accounts, Contaduría, 941, Archivo General de Indias, Seville (hereafter cited as AGI), reproduced in Eugene Lyon, *The Enterprise of Florida: Pedro Menéndez de Avilés and the Spanish Conquest of Florida, 1565–1568* (Gainesville: University Press of Florida, 1974), 186. Juanillo was a black captive of Chief Saturiba and served as a Florida linguist until taken to Puerto Plata, Hispaniola, in 1567. Lista de la gente de guerra, Contaduría 941, AGI.

11. The Jesuit missionary Father Juan Rogel complained that he could not trust the interpretive skills of the black woman and the mulatto whom Menéndez found among the Calusa, saying they knew little Castilian because they had lived among the Indians since they were children. Betraying his prejudice, he added that they were not very intelligent because of their race. Father Juan Rogel to Father Didacus Avellaneda, November 1566 to January 1577, cited in *Missions to the Calusa*, ed. John H. Hann (Gainesville: University of Florida Press, 1991), 281.

12. The Ays nation provided refuge again in 1603 for seven black slaves from St. Augustine. Five were later recaptured, but two others were said to have married Indians and were never retrieved. Verne E. Chatelain, *The Defenses of Spanish Florida, 1565–1763* (Washington, D.C.: Carnegie Institute, 1941), 128.

13. Ibid., 138.

14. Grant Jones, "The Ethnohistory of the Guale Coast through 1684," in *The Anthropology of St. Catherine's Island: 1. Natural and Cultural History*, David Hurst Thomas, et al., Anthropological Papers of the American Museum of Natural History, vol. 55, pt. 2 (New York: American Museum of Natural History, 1978), 178–79; David Hurst Thomas, ed. *Columbian Consequences, vol. 2: Archaeological and Historical Perspectives on the Spanish Borderlands East* (Washington, D.C.: Smithsonian Institution Press, 1990), 357–526; Bonnie McEwan, ed., *The Spanish Missions of La Florida* (Gainesville: University Press of Florida, 1993), 1–34.

15. The order suggested Havana provide thirty men of working age and six women to cook and care for the men in illness and noted that Florida's entire *situado* would not suffice if wages had to be paid for the unceasing labor of the slaves. King to Sancho de Alquía, Captain General of Cuba, April 9, 1618, Santo Domingo 225 (hereafter cited as SD), AGI. Florida's governor complained in 1624 that this order had still not been carried out and he repeated the request for slaves from Havana. The Council of the Indies reprimanded Cuba's captain general and again ordered him to comply. Don Luis de Rojas y Borja to the king, May 7, 1624, and Order of the Council of the Indies, May 9, 1624, SD 225, AGI. In the first half of the seventeenth century blacks made up 45 percent of the population of Cuba, so

scarcity was not the problem. Isabelo Macías Domínguez, *Cuba en la primera mitad del siglo XVII* (Sevilla: Escuela de Estudios Hispano-Americanos, 1978), 34.

16. Amy Bushnell, "The Menéndez Márquez Cattle Barony at La Chua and the Determinants of Economic Expansion in Seventeenth-Century Florida," *Florida Historical Quarterly* 56 (April 1978): 419.

17. By the 1720s the indigenous Pojoy, Amacapira, and Jororo had virtually disappeared. Fray Joseph de Bullones to the king, October 5, 1728, cited in Hann, *Missions to the Calusa*, 368–80.

18. Another mulatto supervisor at the Asile ranch was Juan de la Cruz, and at least one ranch hand, Ambrosio, is identified as Angolan. "Documentation Pertaining to the Asile Farm," manuscript translated and annotated by John H. Hann, on file at the San Luis Archaeological and Historical Site, Tallahassee, 4–5, 67; Bonnie G. McEwan, "Hispanic Life on the Seventeenth-Century Florida Frontier," in *The Spanish Missions of La Florida*, 295–321.

19. Bushnell, "The Menéndez Márquez Cattle Barony," 407–31; Lolita Gutiérrez Brockington found that 60 to 80 percent of the permanent ranch hands on Hernando Cortés's cattle ranches were black and mulatto slaves. Lolita Gutiérrez Brockington, *The Leverage of Labor: Managing the Cortés Haciendas in Tehuantepec, 1588–1688* (Durham, N.C.: Duke University Press, 1989), 126–58, 171–72.

20. John H. Hann, *Apalachee: The Land between the Rivers* (Gainesville: University Presses of Florida, 1988); John H. Hann, *A History of the Timucua Indians and Missions* (Gainesville: University Press of Florida, 1996); John W. Worth, *The Struggle for the Georgia Coast: An Eighteenth-Century Spanish Retrospective on Guale and Mocama* (Athens: University of Georgia Press, 1995), 13–15, 51, 69–70, 86, 123–24.

21. Petition of Juan Márquez Cabrera, September 28, 1686, cited in Worth, *Struggle for the Georgia Coast*, 159.

22. Luis Arana, "Military Manpower in Florida, 1670–1703," "The Men of the Florida Garrison," and "Military Organization in Florida, 1671–1702," in *The Military and Militia in Colonial Spanish America, St. Augustine, Florida* (St. Augustine: Department of Military Affairs, Florida National Guard, n.d.).

23. Hann, *Mission to the Calusa*, 370, 391–99, 426.

24. Alan Gallay, *The Indian Slave Trade: The Rise of the English Empire in the American South, 1670–1717* (New Haven, Conn.: Yale University Press, 2002); Verner W. Crane, *The Southern Frontier, 1670–1732* (New York: Norton, 1981).

25. Indian militias continued to defend Florida well into the eighteenth century. In 1759 the Indian cacique Bernardo Lachiche commanded a unit of twenty-eight men by election of the other caciques. Captain Francisco Menéndez commanded the African militia of thirty-five men from the village of Gracia Real de Santa Teresa de Mose. Report of Don Lucas de Palacio on the Spanish, Indian, and Free Black Militias, April 30, 1759, SD 2604, AGI.

26. "William Dunlop's Mission to St. Augustine in 1688," *South Carolina Historical and Genealogical Magazine* 34 (1933): 1–30. Two of the thirteen captured slaves escaped the Spaniards and returned to their English masters. Crane, *Southern Frontier*, 31–33; Worth, *The Struggle for the Georgia Coast*, 146–71; Edward Randolph to the Board of Trade, March 16, 1699, *Records of the British Public Record Office Relating to South Carolina, 1663–1782*, ed. A. S. Salley (Atlanta, Ga., and Columbia, S.C.: 1928–1947), 88–95.

27. "William Dunlop's Mission to St. Augustine in 1688"; Diego de Quiroga to the king, February 2, 1688, cited in Irene Wright, "Dispatches of Spanish Officials Bearing on the Free Negro Settlement of Gracia Real de Santa Teresa de Mose," *Journal of Negro History* 9 (1924): 151–52; royal edict, November 7, 1693, SD 58-1-26 in the John B. Stetson Collection (hereafter cited as ST), P. K. Yonge Library of Florida History, University of Florida, Gainesville (hereafter cited as PKY).

28. Deposition of Mateo, September 27, 1686, cited in Worth, *Struggle for the Georgia Coast*, 154–56.

29. Ibid. The enslaved people who had questioned Mateo about directions to St. Augustine also asked whether he was a Christian; Diego de Quiroga to the king, February 2, 1688, cited in Wright, "Dispatches of Spanish Officials," 151–52; royal edict, November 7, 1693, SD 58-1-26, ST, PKY.

30. Peter H. Wood, *Negroes in Colonial Carolina, from 1670 through the Stono Rebellion* (New York: Norton, 1974).

31. John H. Hann, "St. Augustine's Fallout from the Yamassee War," *Florida Historical Quarterly* 68 (1989): 180–200.

32. Landers, *Black Society*, chap. 2.; Jane Landers, "Gracia Real de Santa Teresa de Mose: A Free Black Town in Spanish Colonial Florida," *American Historical Review* 95 (1990): 9–30.

33. Manuel de Montiano to the king, March 3, 1738, SD 844, on microfilm reel 15, PKY.

34. Memorial of the fugitives, 1724, SD 844, fol. 530, on microfilm reel 15, PKY. Memorial of Chief Jorge, ibid., fols. 536–37; Manuel de Montiano to the king, February 16, 1739, SD 845, fol. 700, on microfilm reel 16, PKY; fugitive negroes of the English plantations to the king, June 10, 1738, SD 844, on microfilm reel 15, PKY.

35. Manuel de Montiano to the king, February 16, 1739, SD 845, fol. 701, on microfilm reel 16, PKY, and September 16, 1740, SD 2658, AGI. Descriptions of the black and native villages can be found in Father Juan de Solana to Don Pedro Agustin Morell de Santa Cruz, April 22, 1759, SD 516, on microfilm reel 28K, PKY. Faunal analysis indicates that they had much the same diet, relying heavily on estuarine resources and wild foods. In addition to net-caught fish and shellfish, they consumed deer, raccoon, opossum, and turtle to supplement the occasional government gifts of beef and corn. Elizabeth J. Reitz, "Zooarchaeological Analysis of a Free African American Community: Gracia Real de Santa Teresa de Mose," *Historical Archaeology* 28 (1994): 23–40.

36. Juan Ygnacio was not the only Indian of importance to the Spaniards. Others appearing frequently in the records of these years, and in similar roles, were his companions, Geronimo, Juan Savina, and the cacique Chislala. "Letters of Montiano, Siege of St. Augustine," *Collections of the Georgia Historical Society* (Savannah, 1909), 20–43; *An Impartial Account of the Late Expedition Against St. Augustine Under General Oglethorpe*, facsimile of 1742 edition, introduction and indexes by Aileen Moore Topping (Gainesville: University Press of Florida, 1978), xv–xvi.

37. Irene Wright, "Our Lady Of Charity," *Hispanic American Historical Review* 5 (November 1922): 709–17; Robert Farris Thompson, *Flash of the Spirit: African and Afro-American Art and Philosophy* (New York: Vintage, 1984).

38. "Letters of Montiano."

39. Phinizy Spalding, *Oglethorpe in America* (Athens: University of Georgia Press, 1984), 110–26.

40. Franciscan censuses, 1752, SD 2604, AGI.

41. Only seventy-nine individuals were listed in the censuses of the towns of Nuestra Señora de la Leche and Nuestra Señora de Guadalupe de Tolomato in 1759. Report of the Bishop of Cuba, October 9, 1759, SD 2584, AGI.

42. Memorial of the fugitives, 1724, SD 844, fols. 593–94, on microfilm reel 15, PKY.

43. Black Marriages, Cathedral Parish Records, Diocese of St. Augustine Catholic Center (DSACC), Jacksonville, Fla., on microfilm reel 284C, PKY.

44. Franciscan censuses, February 10–12, 1759, SD 2604, AGI.

45. In 1659 the Guanabacoa militia was commanded by the Indian captain Francisco de Robles. Leandro Romero Estébanez, *Santiago* (1981): 71–105. Report of Joseph Rodríguez, April 22, 1764, Realengos 67, no. 3, National Archives of Cuba (hereafter cited as ANC), Havana, Cuba.

46. Baptism of María Francisca de los Dolores, October 16, 1763, Pardo Baptisms, fol. 14v, no. 91, Parochial Archives of Nuestra Señora de la Asunción, Guanabacoa (GPA), Cuba.

47. Cacique Juan Sánchez lived at Pocotalaca in 1752 but was relocated to Nuestra Señora de la Leche by 1759. Manuel Riso lived at Nuestra Señora de Guadalupe de Tolomato in 1752 but in Nuestra Señora de la Leche in 1759. AGI, SD 2604, censuses of the towns of Nuestra Señora de Guadalupe de Tolomato, Pocotalaca, Costas, Palica, and Punta, 1752, SD 2604, AGI; census of Nuestra Señora de la Leche, 1759; AGI, SD 2595, "Yndios de las Familias que Componian dichos Pueblos"; ANC, Protocolo de Cabildo, 1754–1764, fol. 90–94, Guanabacoa, Cuba, Resumen de los Yndios Procedentes de la Florida.

48. Burial of Ana María, February 11, 1764, Pardo Burials, vol. 2, fol. 16, no. 136, and Burial of Juana Rondon, February 17, 1764, fol. 16, no. 137, Church Archives of Nuestra Señora de la Asunción, Guanabacoa, Cuba.

49. Burial of María Francisca, October 27, 1765, Pardo Burials, no. 180, Church Archives of Nuestra Señora de la Asunción, Guanabacoa, Cuba.

50. Important works on the geopolitics and cultures of Native Americans on the Southeastern frontier include Gregory Evans Dowd, *A Spirited Resistance: The North American Indian Struggle for Unity, 1745–1815* (Baltimore: Johns Hopkins University Press, 1992); Daniel K. Richter, *Facing East from Indian Country: A Native History of Early America* (Cambridge, Mass.: Harvard University Press, 2001); Claudio Saunt, *A New Order of Things: Property, Power, and the Transformation of the Creek Indians, 1733–1816* (Cambridge: Cambridge University Press, 1999); Greg O'Brien, *Choctaws in a Revolutionary Age, 1750–1830* (University of Nebraska Press, 2002); Kathryn E. Holland Braund, *Deerskins and Duffels: The Creek Indian Trade with Anglo-Americans, 1683–1815* (Lincoln: University of Nebraska Press, 1993); and Joel Martin, *Sacred Revolt: The Muskogees' Struggle for a New World* (Boston: Beacon Press, 1991). On blacks among the Seminoles see Kenneth Wiggins Porter, *The Negro on the American Frontier* (New York: Arno Press, 1971), and Porter, *The Black Seminoles*, revised and edited by Alcione M. Amos and Thomas P. Senter (Gainesville: University Press of Florida, 1996); Joshua R. Giddings, *The Exiles of Florida* (Columbus, Ohio, 1858); George Klos, "Blacks and the Seminole Indian

Removal Debate, 1821–1835," in *The African American Heritage of Florida,* ed. David R. Colburn and Jane L. Landers (Gainesville: University Press of Florida, 1995), 128–56; and Landers, *Black Society,* chaps. 9 and 10.

51. Howard F. Cline, *Florida Indians II: Provisional Gazeteer with Locational Notes on Florida Colonial Communities* (New York: Garland Publishing, 1964). Cline worked from lists created by the Mikasuki chief Neamathla and by Captain John Bell at an Indian conference convened by Andrew Jackson on September 18, 1821.

52. Brent R. Weisman, "The Plantation System of the Florida Seminole Indians and Black Seminoles During the Colonial Era," in *Colonial Plantations and Economy in Florida,* ed. Jane Landers (Gainesville: University Press of Florida, 2001), 136–49.

53. Landers, *Black Society,* chap. 3.

54. The St. Mary's River demarcated the international border separating Spanish East Florida from the United States of America, just as the St. John's River separated Spanish settlements from Seminole lands. Susan R. Parker, "Men Without God or King: Rural Settlers of East Florida, 1784–1790," *Florida Historical Quarterly* 64 (October 1990): 135–55; Report of Nicolás Grenier, November 10, 1784, cited in Joseph Byrne Lockey, *East Florida, 1783–1785: A File of Documents Assembled and Many of Them Translated* (Berkeley: University of California Press, 1959), 307.

55. Cimarrones visited St. Augustine on January 4, 1786; on February 28 and July 31, 1787, and on August 31, 1788. Caleb Finnegan, "Notes and Commentary on the East Florida Papers: Lists of Gifts to Indians, 1785–1788," unpublished research notes drawn from EFP, microfilm reel 160, PKY.

56. Landers, *Black Society,* chap. 4.

57. Simency threatened again that the tribe would sell their cattle to the United States. Despite that threat, the case dragged on until 1816, when Collins finally received payment for the Seminole cattle he had herded to St. Augustine. Suit by Juan Bautista Collins against Don José Antonio Yguíniz, Notarized Instruments, January 16, 1810, EFP, microfilm reel 167, PKY.

58. Landers, *Black Society,* chap. 9; Giddings, *Exiles of Florida*; Porter, *Black Seminoles.*

59. Sergeant Felipe Edimboro and fourteen men served among the Seminoles. Review Lists of the Free Black Militia of St. Augustine, Oct. 12, 1812, Cuba 357, AGI. The Spanish-Seminole alliance held despite the fact that Kindelán had not been able to present them gifts in over three years. Sebastián Kindelán to Juan Ruíz de Apodaca, July 29, 1812, Cuba 1789, AGI.

60. On the important role of black linguists in the Seminole Wars see Klos, "Blacks and the Seminole Removal Debate." Even after the Spaniards left Florida, Seminoles and blacks among them maintained trade and contacts with Spanish Cuba.

61. Edward Wanton to Sebastián Kindelán, July 3, 1812, Correspondence Between the Governor and Subordinates on the St. Johns and St. Marys Rivers, EFP, microfilm reel 61, PKY. The grateful Kindelán felt "obligated to reward the service and loyalty of this miserable slave." In the name of the government he paid Proctor's owner 350 pesos and granted the translator his liberty. Sebastián Kindelán to Juan Ruiz de Apodaca, August 13, 1812, Cuba 1789, AGI. Four years later, on March 8, 1816, Governor José Coppinger also awarded Tony Proctor a military service grant of 185 acres. Historical Records Survey, Spanish Land Grants in Florida, 5 vols. (Tallahassee, Fla., 1940–1941) (hereafter cited as SLGF), vol. 4, 226–27.

62. Sebastián Kindelán to Juan Ruiz de Apodaca, August 2, 1812, Cuba 1789, AGI.

63. Although mortally wounded by eight bullets, marine captain John Williams lived long enough to describe the night battle and the death and scalping of his sergeant. Captain John Williams to Lieut. Samuel Miller, Adjutant, Sept. 15, 1812, Letters Received, #44, Marine Corps 1812 Archives, National Archives, Washington, D.C.

64. Alexander, "Ambush of Captain John Williams"; T. Frederick Davis, ed., "United States Troops in Spanish East Florida, 1812–1813, III," Florida Historical Quarterly 9 (January 1931): 135–55.

65. In the name of the captive king Fernando VII, the Spanish Junta offered the insurgents a general amnesty. Looking for a graceful out, the United States asked Kindelán to honor the offer, and he did, granting rebels three months within which to register for pardon. Major General Thomas Pinckney to Sebastián Kindelán, March 20, 1813, and Kindelán to Pinckney, March 31, 1813, cited in Davis, "United States Troops in Spanish East Florida, 1812–13, V," Florida Historical Quarterly 10 (July 1931): 24–34.

66. During the Creek War (1813–1814), Americans under the command of Andrew Jackson waged a series of pitched battles against the nativist Creeks, or Red Sticks. On March 27, 1814, at Horseshoe Bend, the already decimated Red Sticks lost approximately another eight hundred warriors, or half their remaining force. Survivors, including the prophet Francis, fled to Spanish Florida, where some made a final stand at Prospect Bluff. Dowd, A Spirited Resistance, 185–90.

67. Alexander Arbuthnot to John Arbuthnot, April 2, 1818, cited in *Narrative of a Voyage to the Spanish Main in the Ship "Two Friends,"* facsimile of 1819 ed. (Gainesville: University Presses of Florida, 1978), 216–18.

68. Hachy was also known as Heijah, and in fact he did have blacks among his people. General Edmund P. Gaines to the Seminoly chief and King Hachy to General Gaines, August 1818, cited in *Narrative of a Voyage to the Spanish Main in the Ship "Two Friends,"* 221–22.

69. Dowd, *A Spirited Resistance*, chaps. 5 and 8.

70. Robert Ambrister to Edward Nicolls, 1818, cited in *Narrative of a Voyage to the Spanish Main in the Ship "Two Friends,"* 260.

71. J. Leitch Wright, Jr., "A Note on the First Seminole War as Seen by the Indians, Negroes, and Their British Advisors," *Journal of Southern History* 34 (November 1968): 565–75; William S. Coker and Thomas D. Watson, *Indian Traders of the Southeastern Spanish Borderlands: Panton, Leslie & Company and John Forbes & Company, 1783–1847* (Gainesville: University Presses of Florida; Pensacola: University of West Florida Press, 1986), chap. 15. From Bowlegs' Town, Jackson exulted prematurely, "I have reached and destroyed this and the other town in its vicinity, and having captured the principal exciters of the war I think I may safely say, that the Indian war, for the present, is terminated" (Andrew Jackson to Governor Rabun of Georgia, April 20, 1818, cited in *Niles Weekly Register*, May 23, 1818).

72. Canter Brown, Jr., *Florida's Peace River Frontier* (Orlando: University of Central Florida Press, 1991), 9–10; Canter Brown, Jr., "The 'Sarrazota' or Runaway Negro 'Plantations': Tampa Bay's First Black Community, 1812–1821," *Tampa Bay History* 12 (fall/winter 1990). Arbuthnot had warned, "Tell my friend Bowlegs, that it is throwing away his people to attempt to resist such a powerful force as will be down on Sahwahnee" (Alexander Arbuthnot to John Arbuthnot, April 2, 1818, cited in *Narrative of a Voyage to the Spanish Main in the Ship "Two Friends,"* 217).

73. "The Defences of the Floridas: A Report of Captain James Gadsden, Aide-de-Camp to General Andrew Jackson," *Florida Historical Quarterly* 15 (April 1937): 248. Creeks and Seminoles traditionally migrated to hunting grounds in southern Florida from November to March of each year, and because the Seminole hunters traveled with their families, they established permanent villages around Tampa Bay. Brown, *Florida's Peace River Frontier*, 4–5.

74. Brown, "'Sarrazota' or Runaway Negro 'Plantations'"; Department of Archives, *The Bahamas in the Age of Revolution, 1775–1848* (Nassau, 1989), 16.

75. United States Secretary of War John C. Calhoun denounced the raid and blamed it on the Creek nation; Nassau *Royal Gazette and Bahama Advertiser*, March 20, 1822, cited in Brown, "'Sarrazota' or Runaway Negro 'Plantations.'"

76. Klos, "Blacks and the Seminole Removal Debate"; Kevin Mulroy, *Freedom on the Border: The Seminole Maroons in Florida, the Indian Territory, Coahuila, and Texas* (Lubbock: Texas Tech University Press, 1993); Porter, *Black Seminoles*.

77. Abram to General Jessup, April 28, 1838, Manuscript Box 5, PKY. For a detailed discussion of the sad removals westward of both blacks and Seminoles see Daniel F. Littlefield, Jr., *Africans and Seminoles: From Removal to Emancipation* (Westport, Conn.: Greenwood Press, 1977). While useful, this work depends almost wholly upon English-language sources and thus makes some serious errors about early black-Seminole alliances.

78. John K. Mahon, *History of the Second Seminole War* (Gainesville: University of Florida Press, 1967); Mulroy, *Freedom on the Border*; Porter, *Black Seminoles*; and Canter Brown, Jr., "The Florida Crisis of 1826–1827 and the Second Seminole War," *Florida Historical Quarterly* 73 (1995): 419–42.

79. Canter Brown, Jr., "Race Relations in Territorial Florida, 1821–1845," *Florida Historical Quarterly* 73 (January 1995): 287–307; and Daniel L. Schafer, "'A Class of People Neither Freemen nor Slaves': From Spanish to American Race Relations in Florida, 1821–1861," *Journal of Social History* 26 (1993): 587–609.

CHAPTER THREE

Tapanhuns, Negros da Terra, and Curibocas

Common Cause and Confrontation between Blacks and Natives in Colonial Brazil

STUART B. SCHWARTZ AND
HAL LANGFUR

ුගෙ

In 1814, in the midst of a series of Bahian slave insurrections that shook the foundations of society in that major terminus of the slave trade and center of plantation agriculture, a group of Hausa slaves initiated yet another scheme to gain their freedom. Earlier in that year, at Itapoã, on the outskirts of Salvador, a group of some 250 had risen under the direction of a Muslim religious leader, or *malam*, burning the installations at a whaling station and devastating a number of plantations before a force of government cavalry could check their movement. A second revolt among the Hausas sprang up in March 1814 in the sugar-growing areas of the nearby agricultural zone of the Recôncavo. It too was suppressed, but the Hausas continued to conspire to win their freedom.

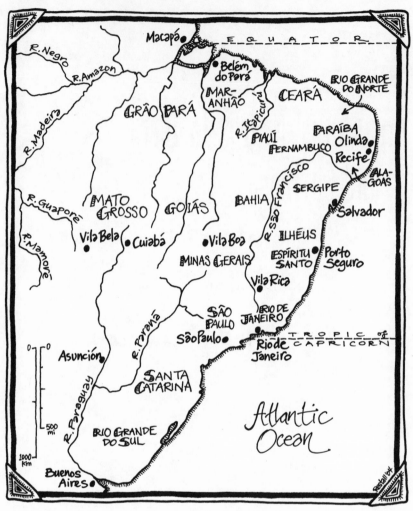

FIG. 3.1: *Colonial Brazil. Map drawn by Matthew Restall.*

A new plot was hatched among urban slave dockworkers and freed artisans in July, but they realized that to have any chance of success, they needed to gain the support of the plantation slaves and of other groups who might potentially be their allies. Local maroon communities, which included some *caboclos*, or natives, were brought into the planned revolt. To this end, they also contacted natives in the region who they supposed would join them in revolt because, as the slaves believed, these natives "wanted their land that the Portuguese had taken from them." Representatives of indigenous groups even arrived in Salvador to speak with the plotters, but they were quickly sent away. Their presence would have raised suspicions among the authorities since natives by the beginning of the nineteenth century were an uncommon sight in the city. Nevertheless, the realization by the slave conspirators of shared grievances with the native peoples of the region, and the willingness of the latter to consider the possibility of collaboration with African slaves against the colonial regime, underlined the political awareness of both and the ironies of their historical relationship.[1]

Interaction and contacts between indigenous peoples and diaspora Africans is one of the least studied and understood aspects of the history of the Americas.[2] What little we do know strongly reflects the interests of the colonial regimes. Thus what blacks and natives thought of each other is particularly difficult to rediscover since the documentation of their relationship is sparse and always filtered through the gaze of colonial observers.

In Brazil, blacks and natives had much in common during the colonial regime. Both groups had been enslaved and both suffered in the creation of the Portuguese colony and from the occupation of the land and the regime of export agriculture. But the parallel sufferings and tribulations of Afro-Brazilians and Native Americans were only part of the story of their interaction because the Portuguese crown and colonists had also deployed the two groups in such a way as to foster hostility and rivalry between them, often to the benefit of the colonial regime or the European settlers and their descendants.

The complex dyadic relationship between Afro-Brazilians and Native Americans cannot be understood by itself, but only within the context of the relationship of both these groups to European society and the colonial regime. Thus, even when contacts took place and relationships, whether friendly or hostile, were formed between Afro-Brazilians and indigenous peoples, white society was constantly a kind of specter, a Banquo's ghost, always present and ever watchful. This was a reality that was implicitly understood but not usually commented upon by contemporaries, and Afro-Brazilians, Native Americans, and the Portuguese all developed strategies within that context to deal with the complexity of forms that these relationships could take.

We must first examine the colonial process of ethnic labeling and the hierarchy that it came to instantiate. The colonial regime demonstrated a proclivity for creating new social categories and spaces in which the language of birth, hereditary status, color, religion, and perceived moral condition contributed to the creation of these ethnic or pseudoracial categories and their ascribed attributes. Thus the term *índios* (Indians) or the other terms that were commonly used in Brazil, such as *gentios* (gentiles), *bárbaros* (barbarians), *tapuyos* (non–Tupi speakers), or *caboclos* (rustics), were chronologically and regionally variable labels of Portuguese origin, created as points of reference to place these peoples within the hierarchical order of colonial society. A similar process also characterized dealing with Africans, but Portuguese attitudes toward them had already been determined to some extent by prior contacts in Africa from the fifteenth century. Whatever the tendencies to deal diplomatically with African states and benignly with those rulers who converted to Christianity, these positive attitudes were undercut in practice by the servile status of most Africans that the Portuguese encountered. That situation led to an attitude of deprecation of blacks, who were associated with slave status. The term *negro* itself implied a servile condition and was often—but not always—used as a synonym for slave. Thus the commonly used label for indigenous people in sixteenth-century Brazil, *negros da terra*, "blacks of the land," revealed a perception of them in a servile status, more or less equivalent to Africans, who were called "*negros de Guiné*." Later, in 1757, when the indigenous mission villages in the Amazon region were secularized in the Directory system, the "unjust and scandalous" practice of calling natives "negros," implying thereby their servitude, was specifically prohibited.[3] In parallel fashion, the first Africans brought to Brazil were sometimes called by the Portuguese *tapanhuns*, a word of Tupi origin that was employed as a quasi-tribal designation. Both the terms *negros da terra* and *tapanhuns* disappeared as native slavery was replaced and large numbers of Africans arrived in the colony. While these categories tended to disappear or to be transformed over time, the process of contact between blacks and natives did produce a progeny of mixed origin called regionally *cafusos*, *curibocas*, or *caborés*. In their own way, these new peoples and new categories further complicated the system of racial hierarchy in the colony.

CONFRONTATION AND HOSTILITY

From the early stages of the Portuguese conquest and settlement of Brazil there were good reasons for hostility between Afro-Brazilians and Native Americans. As black slaves began to arrive in some numbers after the 1560s, natives were increasingly used as a means of controlling them. This function was simply an extension of the use of "tame" or allied natives as protection against "unreduced" indigenous peoples or against foreign interlopers like the French. The Portuguese, like other colonial powers in the New World, promoted a system of "ethnic soldiering," turning some groups into a military force to patrol the territorial and social boundaries of the colony. This policy had begun in the 1520s if not before, and after the arrival of the Jesuits in 1549, the mobilization system was constructed using both independent allied groups and natives in the *aldeias*, or missionary-controlled villages. Portuguese policy had the effect of aggrandizing some "tribes" and creating new identities for those in the mission villages. The ability to mobilize natives for this purpose as well as to deliver them as a labor force to crown and colonists became a standard argument of the missionaries in their justification for control of natives.

The use of indigenous "ethnic soldiers" as a military force on the peripheries of empire was common in the Americas, and the Portuguese were among the first Europeans to employ this practice effectively. The technique was developed early on the Brazilian littoral but then extended across the continent as occupation and settlement expanded. As anthropologist Neil Whitehead has pointed out, such policies had the effect of creating and sharpening "tribal" divisions and hostilities among indigenous peoples and of mobilizing them against European rivals. In colonies where Africans constituted a significant slave population, ethnic soldiering also became a key element in controlling and policing Africans.[4]

In the struggle between the Jesuit missionaries and the Portuguese colonists for control of "domesticated" natives, both sides argued that they were best able to mobilize the potential labor and the military usefulness of those indigenous peoples under Portuguese control. From the 1580s, Jesuit observers made this point consistently, emphasizing "the service performed for God and Your Majesty by converting and domesticating those gentiles." The Jesuit provincial in 1601 in celebrating his Order's service in the pacification of the Potiguars of Rio Grande and Pernambuco claimed that over fifty thousand in 150 villages had been brought under Portuguese control by Jesuit efforts. He argued that

> with the great obedience that the gentio of Brazil have for these
> Religious that it is to be expected not only their conversion to
> our holy faith, but also great service to Your Majesty, helping to
> defend those areas from the French and English who infest
> them and from the Guiné Blacks who rebel, and from Indians
> that resist.[5]

In their struggle against enslavement of natives, the Jesuits emphasized that such a policy would drive indigenous peoples from the coast and create a vacuum that would allow black slaves "to rise with the whole coast as they have attempted in some places with great danger to the Portuguese who in order to defend themselves turn to the *Brazis* [natives] who are the *walls and bulwarks* [emphasis ours] of that state according to the Portuguese that live there."[6] This metaphor of domesticated natives as a protective barrier or wall was repeated throughout the colony's history.

This idea of using natives as both a potential labor force and a defensive cordon appealed to the colonists and sugar planters as well as to the missionaries. In 1603, the absentee donatary of Porto Seguro, the duke of Aveiro, complained that his holdings in Brazil did not prosper because he lacked "gentiles who could populate and defend them." Despite legislation that privileged the Jesuits, he asked for, and received, permission for colonists in his captaincy to bring natives from the interior for this purpose.[7] Similar arguments were made by other sugar planters and by royal officials as well, but in general crown policy supported control by the Jesuits.

As the numbers of African and Afro-Brazilian workers increased on the northeastern plantations after the 1560s, the planters, the Jesuits, and the colonial state all increasingly came to view "domesticated" natives as an essential element of colonial control and essential for the colony's success. Frei Vicente do Salvador, Brazil's first historian, claimed that the depredations of marauding bands of rebellious slaves were only limited by their fear of natives.[8] In the late sixteenth century, as colonists and Jesuits competed for control of the natives under Portuguese control, each side justified its stewardship by arguing that it was best suited to mobilize natives as a defensive force against the threat of foreign interlopers like the French or the Dutch on the coast, the unreduced tribes of the interior, or "domestic enemies," the slaves of the growing number of sugar plantations. In Bahia, for example, the Jesuits argued that their aldeias, or mission towns, of Santo António in Jaguaripe and São Sebastião in Capenema had been established and developed because they stood on the frontier with the hostile Aimorés, an indigenous people who had kept the southern areas of the captaincy in constant danger.[9] The Jesuits had made the service of their charges available to the colonial state. In 1614, natives from the Jesuit aldeia of São João had been mobilized to destroy a runaway slave community in the Bahian interior.[10]

The colonists, anxious to control native labor and no less anxious to have auxiliaries to be used against still hostile groups and against slaves, argued against the Jesuit villages and against Jesuit control of the natives. In

1610, for example, the town council, or *câmara*, of Parahiba contested legislation designed to end enslavement of natives and noted the great value natives provided to the crown as workers and as a counterbalance to the enslaved Africans, the so-called negros de Guiné.[11] The councilors argued that those enslaved were cannibals who had joined with Lutherans (the French) to attack the Portuguese and that the Jesuit aldeias had only made the natives more susceptible to sickness. In this last particular they were probably correct, but their concern was more with the services the natives could provide than with their health.

Both Jesuits and colonists agreed on the utility of the domesticated natives; they only differed on who might best mobilize them. Diogo de Campos Moreno, who prepared a report for the crown in 1612 on the state of Brazil, was greatly in favor of the integration of indigenous people into the fabric of colonial society. As he stated: "The Indians that live together with the Whites are not only better Christians, raising themselves and their children as such, but they also learned the mechanic trades and give benefit to the royal treasury and great assistance in the use of arms on every occasion on the coast and in the interior (*sertão*) of their lands."[12] This defensive function of colonial "Indians," along with their potential as a labor force, was manipulated by both the colonial settlers and the Jesuits. The struggle between the contending sides became a theme throughout much of the history of colonial Brazil.

What was not in contention, however, was the perceived value of the natives as a defensive bulwark and a counterweight to the growing population of enslaved Africans. This was made particularly apparent by a petition of a group of settlers from the Jaguaripe region of Bahia, who in 1613 sought the king's intervention when they complained that the Jesuits had moved their missionary villages away from the frontier where these settlers had their sugar mills and farms and these indigenous bowmen had served to guard the frontier and to control the "black captives" who might rise or flee and join with the French and other enemies.[13] In 1633, Duarte Gomes de Silveira, representing the colonists of Paraíba, penned a long memorial on the use of natives to control the growing number of Africans. He put the matter clearly:

> There is no doubt that without Indians in Brazil there can be
> no Guinea Blacks, or better said, there can be no Brazil, for
> without the Blacks nothing can be done, and they are ten times
> more numerous than the whites; and if now it is costly to

control them with the Indians who they greatly fear... what
will happen without the Indians? The next day they will rebel,
and it is a difficult task to overcome domestic enemies.[14]

This theme of the utility of indigenous troops for the defense of Brazil
against foreign and domestic enemies was continually repeated. In 1697, for
example, Father Pero Rodrigues of the Company of Jesus claimed that the
three principal enemies of the Portuguese were the French, the uncon-
quered Aimoré natives, and the Blacks in *quilombos* (maroon settlements)
and that the best defense against all of them was the use of aldeia natives,
that is, natives under the guidance of the missionaries.[15]

The mobilization of natives by the state, usually under the direction
of the Jesuits, for the purposes of slave control was paralleled by their
employment under other arrangements as well. Natives were often used as
slave catchers by plantation owners on an individual basis. We have some
indication of how the contractual arrangements worked from the entries in
the yearly account registers maintained at Engenho Sergipe do Conde, one
of the largest Bahian sugar estates. Entries in these records speak of payments in small sums as well as shirts, rum, knives, and trinkets paid to
natives for various tasks, including the capture and return of runaway
slaves. Entries such as one for the harvest of 1629–1630, "for money given to
three Indians for tying up a black woman who had run off," or for
1630–1631, "to some Indians who captured three Blacks escaped from the
estate," highlight the nature of the relationship.[16]

Indigenous peoples became a force for the control of the Afro-
Brazilian slave population in two ways. First, the unreduced groups of the
Brazilian interior created a kind of barrier for both whites and blacks, limiting the extension of colonial control but also creating an obstacle for the formation of runaway communities. This situation, along with the predatory
economies of many of these escapee villages, probably contributed to the
fact that most of the runaway communities remained relatively close to the
plantations and urban centers of settlement. The fact that "untamed" natives
provided a barrier to both blacks and whites did not prevent colonial
authorities from contemplating the function of "hostile" groups as a means
of slave control. In particular, these groups were used to combat the numerous runaway slave communities, known as *mocambos* or quilombos. In a letter probably written around 1687, authorities in Pernambuco, anxious to
eliminate the great runaway community of Palmares, called not only for the
localization of domesticated natives and members of the native regiment of

Henrique Camarão in the region of Palmares as a means of control, but also the use of "wild Indians (*gentios bravos*)." The strategy they suggested reveals colonial perceptions of how the problem could be handled:

> There is also much to consider that the wild Indians that surround Palmares and all the mocambos of Blacks are their bitterest enemies, and wish not only to destroy them, but to eat them; and with these gentiles it is possible to enter into communication and to persuade them to go against the Blacks offering them *aguardente*, knives, and other things; and the Blacks, surrounded and in this way squeezed between the gentiles of the interior and our forces from the seashore, will wish to surrender rather than die.[17]

Following the discovery in the 1690s of major mineral deposits in the Brazilian interior, royal authorities extended this practice, countering not only runaway slaves but also renegade settlers and free blacks by enlisting the de facto assistance of uncolonized natives. Relying on hostile hunters and foragers to discourage the smuggling of gold and diamonds eastward to the Atlantic coast from the inland mining district of Minas Gerais, officials sought to create a vast, forested no-man's-land stretching between Salvador and Rio de Janeiro, peopled only by putatively savage and anthropophagous Native Americans. Bands of Pataxó, Kopoxó, Pahame, Maxakali, and Puri natives, among others, served this function while acting in defense of their own territory. Above all, the Aimoré, known more commonly as the Botocudo as the eighteenth century progressed, barred the passage of errant colonists through the coastal forests. These tenacious seminomads thereby furthered official attempts to block unsupervised access to and egress from the mining district.

In the end the scheme could not be sustained as persistent explorers, miners, plantations owners, their slaves, and free black subsistence farmers pushed beyond the periphery of the settled mining zone in greater numbers during the second half of the century. In a striking reversal, the opposing impulse to protect Portuguese vassals on this frontier prompted captaincy officials to recruit blacks to combat the depredations of natives. Governor Antonio de Noronha described such recruits as "*mulatos, mestiços, cabras,* and *negros forros*"—that is, free and freed men of color—"who are sent to people remote places like Cuieté, Abre Campo, and other sites. It is they who compose the squadrons that defend [such frontier outposts] from the invasions of barbarous heathens." When the captaincy's forest squadrons were reorganized and reinforced in the early 1790s as part of a plan to deploy a series of punitive military expeditions against the Puri and Botocudo, one local commander proposed increasing their ranks with "all of the freed *pardos* and *pretos* (mulattos and blacks)" readily available. Mounting clashes between settlers and natives ultimately forced the reversal of crown policy as well, capped by Prince Regent João's declaration of open warfare against the zone's seminomadic bands in 1808. Throughout the ensuing conflict, military authorities continued to enlist blacks to fight the very natives who had once been left at large to prevent runaway slaves and unsupervised freedmen from straying into the coastal forests. The apparent paradox is resolved when we recall that "ethnic soldiering" always depended on pitting one marginalized group against another to serve the immediate interests of the colonial regime.[18]

Minas officials had discovered that unsubdued natives acting as frontier guardians not only impeded runaway slaves and smugglers but also endangered authorized settlers and their captive Africans. Casualties among slaves belonging to such settlers were frequent enough that miners and landowners made it part of their reckoning when deciding whether to reside in the remote sertão or to dispatch some of their black captives to labor there at placer mines and plantations established to provision the major mining towns. Reflecting on the slow pace of settlement in the forests to the east of the mining district, Vicar Manoel Vieyra Nunes wrote in 1769 that until the region's natives were subjugated, the zone's effective exploitation would remain impracticable because the modest resources extracted there did not compensate property owners, who were forced to "consume a great part of their earnings in the payment and purchase of guards" to protect fields and mining operations worked by slaves. The situation had not changed a dozen years later, when Governor Rodrigo José de Meneses traveled through the eastern forests to assess the merits of promoting their settlement. In his account of the trip, he noted a revealing detail: slaves themselves bore arms against the natives. One of his foremost objectives in visiting the area, he wrote, was to determine "if the quantity [of gold] that can be taken out would correspond to the considerable amount goods must cost in that distant place, and the portion of slaves necessary to have under arms to defend themselves from the heathen, while the other portion works." Such considerations, noted the governor, "always enter into the calculations of miners and should equally be considered in the political calculus."[19]

The strategy of using unreduced natives to contain unsupervised migration, in other words, was somewhat unrealistic and difficult to accomplish. Much more feasible was the employment of "domestic Indians," those who had been brought under Portuguese control and settled in Jesuit aldeias or in lay-controlled villages that provided a readily available force for controlling the slave population. Sometimes native groups were moved long distances for this purpose. In the late 1590s, eight hundred bowmen from the powerful Tupian-speaking Potiguars of Pernambuco, who had aided the Portuguese against the French, were sent to southern Bahia to provide protection against the raids of the Aimorés. By the time they arrived, the principal threat had passed and they were eventually distributed not only in Ilhéus, but in the Bahian sugar zone of the Recôncavo as a labor and military force. Some, under their chief Zorobabé, were then deployed against a mocambo of escaped blacks on the Itapicuru River. Zorobabé then sold some of the slaves he captured for a horse, clothing, and military trappings.[20]

While it is difficult to measure the effectiveness of the policy of using natives to control African rebelliousness and insurrection, the lack of large-scale revolts up to the early nineteenth century suggests that the proximity of natives did have some influence, but if such movements were lacking, there was no lack of individual flight and runaways. The military use of "domesticated" natives, especially to suppress slave resistance, found its most common form in the military's employment of them as scouts, bearers, and auxiliary troops in campaigns to stamp out runaway slave communities. Virtually every maroon community in Brazil was attacked or destroyed with the help of natives under Portuguese command.

A major feature in the antimocambo measures was the creation of a force of slave catchers, or "bush captains." These officers, called variously *capitão do campo*, *capitão do mato*, and *capitão dos assalto*, were often themselves black or mulatto freedmen, but they generally operated with the support of native auxiliaries. As early as 1612, the governor of Brazil received a request to create a capitão do campo in all of the eight parishes of Pernambuco. Each of these officials was to have twenty native families under his control to help with his slave-catching activities.[21] Similar arrangements became standard practice throughout many areas of Brazil. In the 1660s, for example, the count of Obidos, as governor of the colony, organized a series of campaigns against mocambos in which natives from the Torre de Garcia d'Avila, from the aldeia of Santo Antonio, and even some veterans of the indigenous regiment of Henrique Camarão were to be employed.[22]

The idea that lay beneath the employment of natives and freed blacks as slave catchers and as a bulwark against unreduced natives and fugitive slaves was that only such forces could be effective in the kind of guerrilla war that such actions implied. In a projected expedition mounted in the 1590s to use Potiguar warriors from Pernambuco against the Aimoré of Ilhéus, it was generally agreed that the campaign was impossible "unless it was [done] with other Indians, forest beings (*bicho do mato*), like them." Similar arguments were made throughout the colony's existence. The Portuguese Overseas Council, discussing the need to subdue the region of Mato Grosso, agreed in 1744, for example, that "the proper people to make war against gentiles are other gentiles along with some whites, and the Bororo because of their bravery and loyalty are the best for this."[23] Similar arguments were made for employing natives or freed blacks against escaped Afro-Brazilian slaves. In a self-congratulatory letter in about 1695, Domingos Jorge Velho, the leader of the expedition that defeated Palmares, claimed that his troops were the most effective against maroons because of the martial skills of the gentio under his command, and that the Paulistas and their natives would be like the Great Wall of China against hostile natives and fugitive blacks, except that they would be more effective and less subject to the forces of nature than the famous Asian fortification.[24]

But such policies were not without difficulties and risks. We can use a Bahian antimocambo campaign of 1636 as an example of ways native forces could be mobilized against runaway communities but also of the dangers inherent in doing so. In 1636, the governor of Brazil and the town council of Salvador mounted an expedition to suppress a large and apparently well-organized maroon community in the Bahian interior. Forces were raised in various locales, and natives from Jesuit villages as well as those under secular leadership were enlisted. Many slaves were recaptured and then sold or redeemed, thus generating a large sum of money to be divided among the members of the expedition. They included Afonso Rodrigues, "captain of his Indians," and Luís de Cerqueira, captain of the aldeia, who received eighty *milréis* to be divided among the natives who participated. Half of that sum went to the Jesuit representative, to be divided among eighty-two natives from the Jesuit aldeias, and smaller amounts went to Cerqueira and Rodrigues for the natives under their command.[25]

This expedition also revealed the difficulties and contingencies of such techniques. As part of the expedition, Rubellio Dias had led his "people," whom he described as "gentio and tapuyos," that is, unconverted non-Tupi-speaking heathens, into the interior. They had encountered a large body of blacks or Tapanhunos and a fierce fight ensued. Many of the maroons were killed or wounded and forty taken prisoner, including their leaders.[26] All were taken back to the mocambo from which they had dispersed, but there was no jail in the encampment where the prisoners could be kept securely. Moreover, Dias feared his own native tapuyos, whom he called "savages." He was forced to deal with the mocambo leader, who promised to bring into camp those fugitives still free in the forest. The leader of the runaway community fulfilled his pledge, but the natives and Dias himself sickened and eventually Dias had to seek further indigenous auxiliaries drawn from villages in Sergipe de-El Rey to the north.

The pattern of using native troops as guides, auxiliaries, and as ethnic soldiers forming the bulk of antimocambo forces became standard practice in Brazil. As noted, Frei Vicente do Salvador, Brazil's first historian, wrote that the only reason the depredations of escaped slaves were not even worse was "the fear that they have of the Indians who with a Portuguese captain seek them out and return them to their masters."[27] In Bahia and Pernambuco such tactics had been employed from the sixteenth century forward, and by the eighteenth century a regular system of mobilizing settled natives for this purpose was firmly in place. The mocambo called "The Armadillo's Hole (Buraco de Tatu)" in Itapoã just north of Salvador was destroyed in 1764 using native auxiliaries from a village of Jaguaripe as well as a militia unit of natives. In 1806, near the Rio das Contas in Ilheús, the quilombo of Oitizeiro was destroyed by the "tropa da Conquista do gentio Bárbaro da Pedra Branca," a contingent of Kiriri natives under the command of António Andrade e Conceição.[28] These two well-documented Bahian cases are simply representative of the general pattern found throughout the other captaincies of the colony. In Rio de Janeiro, for example, where Jesuit aldeias had been created in the sixteenth century, natives continually provided a number of services to the state as laborers and as a force for defense. In 1649, Salvador Correa de Sá, the most powerful figure in southern Brazil, called the natives of the Jesuit villages "a salutary remedy against runaway slaves." During the eighteenth century, natives from the village of São Francisco Xavier de Itinga served as slave catchers for the large estate of Fazenda Santa Cruz nearby.[29]

This policy was not always successful. In the mining zones of Minas Gerais, in south-central Brazil, early governors had sought to emulate the coastal captaincies by creating a network of bush captains in the 1720s and by using natives as slave catchers and auxiliary troops, but these measures proved unsuccessful in the face of the vast extent of territory, the rapidly growing slave population, and the relatively small number of "tame" natives in the region. The count of Assumar, governor of Minas Gerais, commented on the failure of native villages to stop the runaways in 1717, and soon thereafter he began to institute a series of draconian measures and punishments to stop runaways.[30] Such limitations did not preclude revived attempts over the following decades to make use of incorporated natives in Minas Gerais. Among the slave catchers active in the forests to the east of the mining district were "domesticated" members of the Pataxó tribe. Delivering four runaways to a local military commander in 1770, the Pataxó reported that "many more" black fugitives could be found in the area. The captaincy governor responded by redoubling efforts to enlist natives to capture them, with the promise of greater financial rewards. In general, however, the difficult access to the rugged eastern forest tended to frustrate efforts to control the ongoing runaway problem.[31] In other areas as well the changing demography of the colony, which usually included large-scale declines or dislocations of indigenous populations, had the effect of limiting the usefulness of natives as a control on the African and Afro-Brazilian populations.

The patterns of relationships that developed on the Brazilian littoral and in Minas Gerais repeated themselves in the Brazilian north and west. The chronology of indigenous-black relations, however, reflected the realities of the distribution of population. In the Maranhão, for example, the very low levels of the slave trade prior to 1680 meant that there were few Africans or Afro-Brazilians and thus little opportunity for interaction or hostility between blacks and Native Americans simply because there were so few blacks. Economic expansion in the state of Maranhão and a rise in the slave trade in the region changed that situation. As the occupation of the Brazilian interior increased in the eighteenth century and population moved into previously uncolonized areas, the institution of slavery was also diffused and, with it, runaways. In the captaincy of Goiás in the Brazilian far west, the mining economy near Vila Boa and other mining sites attracted migrants, both slave and free, after the 1720s. By 1780, no settled region of the captaincy had a black population that was less than 45 percent of the total inhabitants. But Portuguese settlers and prospectors as well as escaped slaves all had to contend with hostile indigenous groups. Gê-speaking Carijós, fleeing Paulista slaving raids, had re-formed in Goiás as a new ethnicity called Avá-Canoeiros and opposed any encroachment on their territory. Other groups, like the Gê-speaking Krahó, Xavante, and Caiapó, also constituted a barrier to both black and white penetration of parts of the captaincy. These groups were especially active in destroying quilombos.[32] Whereas colonial society had the power to pursue indigenous raiders or negotiate for the return of captives, those alternatives were essentially closed to Afro-Brazilian fugitives. A much closer parity of power existed between them and native groups.

Similar conditions of conflict existed farther north in Amazonia and to the west in Mato Grosso, a region that began to attract settlement in the 1720s after gold strikes in the region of Cuiabá. Fluvial expeditions, the famous *monções*, carrying people and supplies from São Paulo up the Paraguay River, had to battle constantly against the attacks of the Paiaguá, who resisted encroachment on their territory. By midcentury, settlement was regularized in the new captaincy of Mato Grosso (after 1748) around the two major towns of Cuiabá and Vila Bela.[33] Settlers had brought black slaves to work in mining and prospecting, in truck farming, and in the construction of forts and military outposts on the frontier with Spanish America. By 1734, Cuiabá had a population of three thousand: two hundred whites, eight hundred blacks, and the rest natives.[34] The natural outcome of this process was flight and resistance in the form of quilombos. Indigenous peoples resisted both the incursions of the colonists and the presence of escaped slaves, but that resistance was also balanced by the presence of natives in many of the maroon communities.[35] One explanation for this joint flight to forest refuges was that despite royal prohibitions on indigenous slavery, natives captured in settler expeditions to the sertão were, like Africans, often bought and sold in Mato Grosso during the mining boom. As Governor Antonio Rolim de Moura described the problem in 1754, "the major portion of the inhabitants of this Captaincy" were guilty of "selling Indians" or benefiting indirectly from the illegal practice.[36]

Like the militarized international frontier between Florida and the Carolinas, the frontier regions of Brazil became places of considerable interaction and contestation, complicated somewhat by the presence of garrison troops and military deserters. On the north bank of the Amazon, in the Cabo Norte, today's Amapá, or what we could call the Brazilian Guiana, was an international frontier zone with a sparse colonial population and a relatively large number of natives. Indigenous peoples resisted colonial settlement but also the invasion of their territories by white military deserters and escaped Afro-Brazilian slaves. At the same time, colonial authorities and settlers employed both indigenous and African workers together. In 1765, for example, at the fort of Macapá, about 2,600 natives and 2,400 slaves were employed. Of these about an equal percentage (1 percent) of both groups were listed as fugitives from service.[37] In a frontier zone like the Cabo Norte, where the ability to cross over to Caienne (French Guiana) or to sell products there offered fugitives various possibilities, control of runaways became a particularly important issue for colonial government. The basic fear on these frontiers in the eighteenth century was much like that on the coast of northeastern Brazil in the sixteenth century: that escaped slaves might unite with natives to resist the colonial regime. Henrique João Wilckens, after a visit to the Rio Negro region in 1800, wrote that there could be no greater danger than the "clandestine communication of the [settled] Indians with [unsubdued] gentiles and with mocambos" of escaped slaves.[38] A similar situation existed in the northwestern Amazon, where the Dutch at Essequibo continually employed Carib speakers to attack maroon communities and where the problems of deserters and contraband in arms across the frontier complicated antiquilombo measures.[39]

Along the Guaporé River in Brazil's far-western frontier zone, the very existence of the Príncipe da Beira Fortress testified to the multivalent position natives and blacks occupied in Portugal's attempt to secure the colony's border with Spanish America. Soldiers recruited for the fortress's construction and defense during the second half of the eighteenth century included those of both native and African origin, many of whom arrived by canoe, ascending the Amazon, Madeira, and Mamoré rivers from Pará to reach the tropical fortification. The crown hoped this vanguard would provide the impetus for future colonists to populate and thus strengthen the border region. Installed at the fortress, the troops suffered together from malaria and a perpetual lack of food, supplies, munitions, and funds to pay their modest wages, shortages that intensified as the site became a pole of attraction for Native Americans fleeing the Spanish missions of the Mojos region in present-day Bolivia. Inadequately provided for at the garrison, many of these mission natives fled yet again into the surrounding forests, accompanied by deserters from the garrison. To punish the Portuguese for welcoming cross-border indigenous migrants, Spanish authorities offered refuge to African slaves who escaped Brazil to the Guaporé's western bank, some establishing quilombos in Spanish territory, others entering the missions. The pitfalls of relying on those excluded from colonial society to fortify the western border contributed to the short-lived strategic importance of the Príncipe da Beira Fortress in Portuguese geopolitics.[40]

AMIABLE INTERACTIONS

Despite colonial policies and intentions, the similarity in the occupations and status of Africans and natives created opportunities for interaction and cooperation, both within the context of the colonial regime and outside or in opposition to it as well. The period from roughly 1550 to 1600 witnessed the transition from a plantation labor force that was composed primarily of natives to one in which Africans came to predominate. Their coexistence on the sugar estates led inevitably to a variety of contacts. When the sugar estate Engenho São Pantaleão do Monteiro near Olinda was sold in 1577, for example, it had fifteen Guinea slaves and twenty-five negros da terra, or natives.[41] At Engenho Santana in Ilhéus in 1572 there were nine Guinea slaves, one of whom was married to a Tapuya woman. Such unions, however, appear to have been relatively rare. The baptismal register from Engenho Sergipe in the Bahian Recôncavo from 1598 to 1609 listed 176 baptisms of children, but of these only 3 or 4 were the children of mixed African and native couples. But opportunities for such unions did exist. At Engenho Sergipe, Domingos Valente, a skilled black sugar master, married Luiza, who was described as "*negra do gentio da terra*," and by 1591 the couple had two children. Marcos, a Guinea slave who served as a cowherd, married a native woman named Marta. But these cases were relatively rare. Natives at Engenho Sergipe kept to themselves and lived together in a Tupi-style long-house rather than in the *senzala*, or typical slave quarters. It appears that the vast majority of natives married or had sexual relationships with other natives, remaining, for the most part, separated from the others in their immediate world. Still, there were pressures for these contacts to develop. The shortage of African women in the slave trade was a contributing influence forcing African men to seek out and sometimes to marry native or mixed-race women. Although evidence is sparse, in the interior back-lands or sertão, where slaveholdings were smaller and where there was often the use of both native and African workers, unions between them seem to have been more common.[42]

Along with the relationships born out of their similar function as laborers, Native Americans and Afro-Brazilians also developed relations born out of their common military employment. On various occasions both blacks and natives were mobilized to meet the attacks of foreign interlopers and unsubdued indigenous peoples. During the Dutch occupation of northeastern Brazil (1630–1654), both the Portuguese and the Dutch employed indigenous and black soldiers, both slave and free, in the fighting. On the Dutch side, a captain named Antonio Mendes led a combined troop of Tupi natives, mulattos, and blacks.[43] At one point, the famous Luso-Brazilian black regiment of Henrique Dias was composed of 200 blacks and 1,200 natives.[44] Such service might have an international dimension as well. Plans for the reconquest of Angola from the Dutch included the use of Paulistas and their native "*servos de armas*" (armed dependents), and eventually Brazilian natives were used in the reconquest of Angola fighting alongside Luso-African forces.[45]

During the final decades of colonial rule, with the demise of the royal ban on colonizing the forests separating the inland mining camps from the Atlantic coast, natives and blacks served side by side in frontier garrisons and infantry squadrons deployed to subdue the Botocudo, Puri, and other hostile groups. Directing military operations in coastal Espírito Santo, Governor Antonio Pires da Silva Pontes created a corps "composed of men of mixed race, or mestiços of black, white, or Indian origin" in accordance with royal orders. The soldiers were charged with manning garrisons and safeguarding the transport of trade goods and provisions along the Doce River, whose route into the interior through unsettled native territory the crown now envisioned as a commercial corridor. Although two natives were made sergeants, initial experience prompted the governor to complain that indigenous troops "had demonstrated themselves to be unfit for service due to their desertions and weakness in comparison to the mestiço soldiers." A more likely explanation for such conduct is the ease with which natives moved through this familiar forest environment, evading official schemes to control their labor. On one expedition upriver led by the governor himself, forty natives had deserted with their arms and tools, abandoning him in the forest to return to the coast.[46]

Between 1815 and 1817, the German naturalist Maximilian, Prince of Wied-Neuwied, traversed this zone of conflict, venturing up a number of major river basins in both Espírito Santo and Porto Seguro to observe the conquest firsthand. Accompanying a military expedition dispatched to construct a road linking southern Bahia to the mining district, he was struck by "the various races of men" laboring together as foot soldiers. "There were in our company negroes, creoles, mulattos, *mamelukes* [i.e., *mamelucos* or mestizos], natives of the coast, a Botocudo, a Malali, some Maconis, and Capuchos, all soldiers from Minas Gerais"[47] (see fig. 3.2). Up the Jequitinhonha River from the coastal town of Belmonte, encamped at the Arcos garrison among soldiers who were "chiefly people of colour, Indians, or mulattos," the naturalist commented on the harsh daily lives of these multiracial frontier squadrons:

> The soldiers fare very badly; their pay is small, and they are
> obliged to obtain by their own labour all their food, which
> consists of *mandioca*-flour, beans, and salt-meat. The whole
> stock of powder and ball seldom exceeds a couple of pounds;

and very few of the old muskets are serviceable; so that in case
of an attack, they would be under great embarrassment. It is
moreover the duty of these soldiers to convey travellers and
their goods or baggage up and down the river; hence they are
mostly very expert at this employment, and may be considered
excellent boatmen.[48]

Particularly adept at tracking and other military operations in the
tropical forests, the native soldiers suffered the additional burden of men
considered collaborators. "The civilized Indians behave well as soldiers
against their savage brethren," wrote Maximilian. "The latter therefore bear
a violent hatred against them, and are said to aim at them first, because they
consider them as traitors to their country." Not surprising, given such circumstances, was the elevated desertion rate among black and native soldiers
alike, as high as 50 percent in some squadrons.[49]

It was not within the colonial regime, however, but in opposition to it
that the evidence of Afro-native contact and cooperation is most apparent.
Slave runaways were sometimes integrated into Native American ethnic and
kinship networks. At first, the runaways were enslaved natives. The Jesuit
Father Nóbrega reported in 1559 from Bahia that the nations on the
Paraguaçu River and on Itaparica Island were taking in fugitives from the
Bahian sugar estates and refusing to return them.[50] As black slavery
expanded, however, Afro-Brazilian escapees also arrived in indigenous villages. Sugar planter João Fernandes Vieira, as governor of Paraíba, forced
the return of sixty blacks who had been incorporated into the Tapuyas of
the powerful chieftain Janduí by holding his son hostage until their
return.[51] The specter of collaboration between natives and enslaved
Africans against the colonial regime always generated profound feelings of
anxiety and fear. The government occasionally took measures against the
possibility. After the savage Guerra dos Bárbaros, a series of campaigns
against the Cariri in Rio Grande do Norte, a formal treaty was concluded in
1695 that included provisions obligating the Cariri to give military assistance against natives who opposed Portuguese rule and to capture runaway
slaves and return them to their masters.[52] In 1703, Governor General
Cristóvão da Costa Freire received a royal order that blacks, mamelucos,
and slaves be prohibited from going into the sertão, where they might join
with natives who were in revolt.[53]

In areas of the unsettled sertão targeted for incorporation, authorities
employed the power differentials inherent in racial and social hierarchies to

legitimize the suppression of conduct that challenged the colonial project. In particular, the association of nomadism and mobility with resistance, both by natives and persons of African ancestry, linked these outcasts in the minds and policies of those who would command their labor and control the lands they inhabited. Thus, in 1774, when a bureaucrat working in Minas Gerais indexed the "laws, royal charters, notices, and orders" extant in the captaincy archives, he grouped together in one section all legislation pertaining to "vagabonds, Indians, slaves, mulattos, [and] Blacks."[54] Under a single heading, he articulated the nexus of status, race, and—pertinent especially in the unsupervised sertão—mobility that marked both Africans and natives as dangerous. This conflation of suspect social and racial categories had firm royal precedent in Minas Gerais, which the elite would put to their advantage. A royal order issued in 1731, for instance, had authorized the governor to take judicial action against unruly "bastards, Carijós, mulattos, and Blacks."[55]

Evidence of anticolonial collaboration among these groups, given its nature, is scarce, but on occasion the colonial regime and its institutions recorded these links. One such case was in the millenarian Santidade movement that erupted in the region of southern Bahia in the 1560s and lasted well into the seventeenth century.[56] This was a syncretic cult combining Tupi concepts of an earthly paradise or "land without evil" with aspects of Roman Catholicism. A number of the natives involved in the religion had apparently been under Jesuit tutelage while others had been enslaved on the sugar plantations. Followers of the cult worshiped certain idols in ceremonies involving alcoholic drinks and tobacco, and much of the ideology of the participants was directed against the Portuguese and the colonial regime. The region of Jaguaripe, south of the Paraguaçu River in Bahia, became a center of the Santidade and of continuing resistance to the Portuguese. By the 1580s, African and *crioulo*, or Brazilian-born blacks, were also involved in the movement, and the threat they presented together was real enough for it to be mentioned in the royal instructions prepared for a new governor in 1588. By 1610, Governor Diogo de Meneses reported with concern that there were over twenty thousand natives and escaped slaves in the Santidade villages in Jaguaripe, and while as an advocate of the enslavement of natives he may have inflated the figures, there is no doubt that the movement continued. The threat was not only that of a heretical religion, but the harm that these raiders had caused to the sugar economy by their attacks on plantations and the disruption of the supplies of firewood from the Jaguaripe region. There was even a fear that some of the escaped slaves living with the Santidade groups were acculturated and savvy and might seek cooperation with European interlopers as maroons had done in the Caribbean. The raids and colonial responses to them continued well into the 1620s.

We know something of the internal aspects of the movement because in the 1590s a visit of the Inquisition took place in Brazil and over one hundred people were denounced to the Inquisitors because of their attachment to or contact with the Santidade cult.

While the practice of referring to native slaves as *negros* complicates the problem of identifying the origins of the participants, a number of the Inquisition trial records enable us to derive some idea of its composition. Alvaro Rodrigues, a mameluco sugar planter who led an expedition into the interior against Santidade groups, reported that among their followers were many Christianized natives, mamelucos, and baptized Africans. The Santidade cult of Jaguaripe did present the threat of anticolonial collaboration on the part of natives and blacks, but the extent of the collaboration remains unknown. Only 4 of the 104 people accused of Santidade participation by the Inquisition were Afro-Brazilians, although testimony and government reports seem to indicate a much greater degree of collaboration. Nevertheless, the pattern of cooperation and the danger it implied to the colonial regime was a matter of real concern.[57]

Another well-known locale of Afro-native cooperation was in the great maroon state of Palmares. Situated in southern Pernambuco, this group of politically integrated fugitive communities flourished throughout the seventeenth century. The size of Palmares was estimated by some contemporaries to be over thirty thousand inhabitants, which may be an exaggeration, but there is no exaggeration in its ability to defeat punitive expeditions sent out by both the Dutch, who sought to suppress the maroons during their occupation of northeast Brazil (1630–1654) and the Portuguese, who finally did defeat the rebels in 1695 after a long series of expeditions.

Accounts of the expeditions against Palmares reveal both the use of natives as military auxiliaries and the presence of natives within the fugitive communities. Roelof Baro in 1644 led an expedition against the largest Palmares quilombo but had to desist when the Tapuyas under his command revolted. Nevertheless, he returned to Recife, announcing that he had taken some thirty-seven prisoners, among which were seven natives and a number of "mulatto children." The latter may have been the offspring of native-African unions.[58] In 1645, Jan Baer led a larger force, which battered the main quilombo and took a number of native prisoners among the recaptured slaves. While the African cultural elements of Palmares have usually been emphasized, it is important that contemporary observers always noted the presence of natives within the rebel settlements. Moreover, recent archaeological excavations in Palmares sites have revealed indigenous pottery remains indicating either the residence of Tupian women or at least trade networks between the maroons and local indigenous groups.[59]

Fears of blacks and natives collaborating in remote forests and rising together in revolt persisted into the nineteenth century, despite the pervasive myth that by then natives no longer posed a serious threat to colonial society. After Prince Regent João declared war on the Botocudo in 1808, members of the town council of Vila do Príncipe in northeastern Minas Gerais warned the monarch that the region they governed was "surrounded by Botocudo and other wild heathen" who continued to commit "barbarous" crimes. The bulk of the region's free population—described as mulattos, mixed bloods, and creoles, many of them former slaves—were capable of joining the natives in rebellion, the council members cautioned. At the same time, some of these impoverished, often rootless free blacks served a crucial defensive function. These "*vadios* [vagabonds] and useless ones, despite being among the excluded class because of the quality of their color, are in one form or another necessary in this land," the local legislators explained. Itinerant blacks were invariably "the first to send news of insurrections and skirmishes" in outlying frontier zones involving hostile groups, by which the town officials did not specify whether they meant rebellious natives, runaway slaves, or both. Accustomed to "wandering the forests and enduring the rigors of the seasons and of hunger," these free persons of color managed to survive and escape such violence most readily, carrying the news of its destructive consequences with them back to towns and villages on the edge of the frontier.[60] Considering this view of peoples living on the margin of colonial society, we are again reminded of the expediency of a regime that could fear blacks profoundly and simultaneously employ them as a kind of buffer population against native raids, just as it could wage war against some natives while using others as its foot soldiers.

MISCEGENATION AND CULTURAL EXCHANGE

As the prisoners taken by Baro at Palmares in 1644 revealed, the contact between Africans and natives, as runaways were integrated into indigenous villages or as natives were captured by or joining maroon communities, eventually produced a population of mixed parentage. This process of Afro-native miscegenation had, of course, also taken place within the colonial regime and was especially a characteristic of regions like the sertão of northeastern Brazil in the captaincies of Pernambuco, Rio Grande, and Ceará, where a workforce composed of both groups was common. In opposition to or beyond the colonial frontiers, however, we can speculate that these unions had a different valence, and the place in society of the offspring of these contacts probably varied considerably from their usually depreciated position in colonial society.

In colonial Brazil miscegenation was always a matter of concern.[61] At first, that concern was directed to the children of European-native sexual unions. Attitudes toward the offspring of such mixed unions had developed negatively within a generation or so of European arrival. While the first mamelucos or mestizos were considered "the children of Christians," those who lived according to indigenous ways were considered lost souls, and over time their social position fell as the European population grew and the indigenous populations declined, making their role as mediators less important. Even more importantly, with the arrival of large numbers of Africans and the growth of a mulatto population, the status of all persons of mixed origin declined because of the stigma attached to Africans due either to their association with slave status or to racialist ideas. All the intermediate categories tended to become lumped together as pardos. In the southern captaincy of São Paulo, for example, the large population of natives and mamelucos or *bastardos* was simply defined out of existence by eighteenth-century censuses, which increasingly labeled such people as pardos.[62]

Persons of mixed origin were always considered troublesome by colonial authorities. In 1590, the royal inspector Domingos de Abreu e Brito on suggestions from informants in Pernambuco suggested that if five hundred Brazilian mamelucos were sent to fight in Angola, it would produce the double benefit of freeing Brazil of an evil influence and helping in the conquest of Africa, because these men knew how to "suffer the labors of war, having been raised in them."[63] Father Nicholas del Techo, a Spanish Jesuit who complained of the depredations of slave raiders from São Paulo, many of whom were mamelucos against the Jesuit missionary towns (*reducciones*), saw the half-breeds as the devil's helpers: "Satan, angry at seeing the progress of his enemies, united his forces, and then by himself or by the mamelucos, his allies in evil, he sought to destroy the nascent mission towns."[64]

As miscegenation continued in Brazil, producing ever more gradations of racial background, social categories multiplied while the attitudes of the colonial elites tended to lump all the mixed population together. The negative attitudes expressed toward European-native children were even more intense toward Afro-native offspring in colonial society. It is difficult to find any positive comments about them at all. Regions where such people were numerous became known as particularly dangerous. The captain major of Sergipe de el-Rey wrote in 1751 complaining of the "innumerable" slave fugitives that made life unsafe, and he called for companies of blacks or mulattos to be used for this purpose and to control the natives and "caboclos." The sertão in general became linked in the administrative mind with violence and as a place of crime because it was the home of marginal or suspect groups. In 1797, the *ouvidor* (justice) of Jacobina reported that in the last decade there had been 178 murders in his district, mostly carried out by the "four infamous nations of blacks, *cabras*, mestiços, and Tapuyos."[65] *Cabra* was, in this case, the local designation for Afro-native mestizos.

Over time, the permutations of sexual contact began to produce a complexity of racial terms and of regional variations in these designations. An eighteenth-century description from Minas Gerais reported that *carijós*, a term used originally as a designation for Guaraní speakers from southern Brazil, had become a label for mestizos or for the child of a native and a black woman. It also made a linguistic distinction between caboclos, "those who live on the coast and speak Lingua geral (Tupi)," and Tapuyos, who did not speak that tongue. *Curibocas* were described as the offspring of a mulatto and a black or of a mameluco and black, which in the sertão were called "*salta atraz*," or step backward. This terminology seems to be chronologically and regionally specific. In the northeast *caboclo* often meant *mestizo*, while in Grão Pará the term referred to domesticated natives. In Mato Grosso *curibocas* or *caborés* denoted the children of black-native unions.[66]

Whatever the pejorative characterization of Afro-native mixture, colonial society could do little to prevent the continued contacts that such people implied. We have an excellent example of how this reality imposed itself on colonial policy and how the dynamic of native-black relations worked in the diary of an antiquilombo expedition that set out from Vila Bela, Mato Grosso, in 1795. In response to the formation of maroon communities on the Guaporé and São José (formerly the Piolho) rivers, the local government and the governor organized a small expedition, which found the quilombo some thirty-three leagues from Vila Bela. The majority of the residents, however, were natives and caborés who had been born in the quilombo. The commander explained in his diary that a quilombo had been destroyed in the region some twenty-five years before but that the blacks that had escaped that attack had re-formed their community. They had been constantly at war with the Cabixes natives and had raided them for women, which explained the cabon̄és in the quilombo. The community was in a beautiful location, surrounded by fields of manioc, peanuts, corn, beans, tobacco, fruits, and cotton. The river was full of fish, the hunting was good, and they made their own rough cloth for clothing. The commander listed the captured inhabitants of this Quilombo do Piolho: eight native men, nineteen native women, twenty-two caborés, and six blacks, who served as the ruler, doctor, and familial leaders of the community. All were returned to Vila Bela, where they were easily baptized since most had some exposure to Catholic doctrine acquired from the fugitive blacks and all had learned to speak Portuguese from them as well. The fifty-four captives were then transported to a new settlement, to be called Nova Aldeia de Carlota, where it was hoped that they could serve as an example to and help control nearby indigenous peoples and perhaps attract them to commerce with the Portuguese or to bring in alluvial gold deposits.[67]

The glimpse we are offered in this account of the Quilombo do Piolho is a fleeting one. Were its inhabitants really a neoteric native group, or were they the Lusified descendants and remnants of African and Afro-Brazilian fugitives? What was the dynamic of this quilombo's social organization and what were the principles of its political structure and rule? Similar questions could be raised about all of the Afro-native communities on the margins of colonial society. While we have enough fragmentary comments to know how colonial society viewed and manipulated the contacts between blacks and natives, we have little evidence of how blacks and natives saw each other and incorporated each other in their social and cultural practices. Within the colonial regime we have some evidence. Unlike colonial Peru and the U.S. South among the Cherokee, Brazilian natives did not usually own black slaves, at least within the framework of the colonial regime. In 1806, an observer noted the irrationality of natives in their rejection of the logic of Western society. He stated: "The natural character of the natives eludes all philosophy; they have no ambition, they do not value property, and of the most precious property of Brazil, slaves, there is no memory that a native has owned one."[68]

Beyond the frontiers of colonial society in Native American villages and Afro-Brazilian quilombos a number of models operated for the incorporation of outsiders. One was through the structures of kinship, which a number of Native American societies like the Guaraní used to incorporate outsiders. Such kinship ties were used to incorporate whites, other natives, and probably blacks as well. Another was through captive adoption, often of women or children. Dependent or servile statuses existed among a number of indigenous peoples and may have served as a means for bringing out-siders like fugitive black slaves into their communal life. Yet another response to the problem of incorporation was through the structures of myth, seeking to place difficult-to-explain "outsiders" in a network of myth beyond time. Mythopoeic responses often inverted or appropriated "pow-ers" held by outsiders and sometimes, as among western Amazonian peo-ples in the sixteenth century and perhaps among the Santidade followers, produced shaman-led movements that seemed millenarian in content. All of these techniques of integration may have been used as well by Afro-Brazilian communities seeking to incorporate natives as allies, as depend-ents or slaves, and as members.[69]

The contact and cooperation between Africans and Native Americans created sentiments and attitudes that can only be partially recovered in their political manifestations of cooperation in resistance to the colonial regime. Other processes, like syncretism, were at work. One area of Afro-native syncretism was religion.[70] In a number of Afro-Brazilian religions, spread from Amazonas and Maranhão to Pernambuco, Bahia, and Rio de Janeiro, the spirit of the native or Caboclo has joined traditional West African deities. Even within the more conservative Yoruba-centered can-domblés of Bahia, the figure of the Caboclo appears along with the tradi-tional African deities, or orixás.[71] In the more syncretic Afro-Brazilian cults of umbanda, a major cult figure is that of the Caboclo, who is represented as a native and who symbolizes freedom, the hunt, and defense of the terreiro, the site of worship. Possibly, the integration of the figure of a native spirit into Afro-Brazilian religion and the creation of the candomblé de caboclo is really an Afro-Brazilian adaptation of the native as a national Brazilian symbol in the Romantic era of the Independence period of the 1820s and 1830s rather than an outgrowth of their colonial contacts. Be that as it may, present believers have integrated the Yoruba gods with the "spirits that were the original owners of the land we live in."[72]

This integration can also be seen in the self-definition of various popu-lations in Brazil. Interviews conducted in the late 1980s with Afro-Brazilians in the coastal communities north of Salvador, including the suburb of Itapoã, site of an old whaling station and locale of the first Hausa rebellion of 1814, with which this chapter began, revealed popular dances and festival presenta-tions in which natives played a central role. Moreover, oral traditions empha-size the existence of natives in family lineages and celebrate their presence in them.[73] Since the 1950s more generally, a dramatic resurgence in Brazil's indigenous population, by some estimates an increase of 300 percent, can be

FIG. 3.2: *German naturalist Maximilian, prince of Wied-Neuwied, found remarkable the "various races of men"—whites, blacks, natives, and mestizos—whom he observed laboring together on a road-building expedition through Brazil's coastal forest in 1816. From Maximilian, Prinz von Wied,* Travels in Brazil in the Years 1815, 1816, 1817 *(London, 1820), 226. Courtesy of the John Carter Brown Library at Brown University.*

attributed in large measure to peoples once classified as pardos now identifying themselves as natives, claiming or reclaiming a native past.[74] We must be careful with such memories. Being "Indian" is sometimes a way of not being black, and in the nineteenth century, during the struggle for independence and the subsequent formation of the nation, people of African descent, like all Brazilians, came to see the native as a symbol of independent Brazil and of freedom itself. But for both Afro-Brazilians and indigenous peoples in Brazil their relationship was far more complex and contested historically than such symbols have the power to convey.

怃怂

NOTES

1. Details of the plot are provided in Stuart B. Schwartz, "Cantos e quilombos numa conspiração de escravos haussás, Bahia, 1814," in *Liberdade por um fio: história dos quilombos no Brasil*, ed. João José Reis and Flávio dos Santos Gomes (São Paulo: Companhia das Letras, 1996), 373–406.

2. Stuart B. Schwartz and Frank Salomon, "New Peoples and New Kinds of Peoples: Adaptation, Readjustment, and Ethnogenesis in South American Indigenous Societies (Colonial Era)," in *CHNPA*, vol. 3, pt. 2, 467–71. See the classic articles by Nancie González, "The Neoteric Society," *Comparative Studies in Society and History* 12 (1970): 1–13; "New Evidence on the Origin of the Black Carib," *Nieuwe West-Indische Gids* 57, no. 3–4 (1983): 143–72. See also Mary W. Helms, "The Cultural Ecology of a Colonial Tribe," *Ethnology* 8, no. 1 (1969): 76–84. On contacts primarily in the Amazon region, see Flávio dos Santos Gomes, "'Amostras humanas': Índios, negros e relações interétnicas no Brasil colonial," in *Raça como retórica: A construção da diferença*, ed. Yvonne Maggie and Claúdia Barcellos Rezende (Rio de Janeiro, 2002), 27–82.

3. *Directorio que se deve observar nas povoações dos índios do Pará e Maranhão* (Lisbon, 1758), cap. 10. See Rita Heloísa de Almeida, *O Diretório dos índios: um projeto de "civilização" no Brasil do século XVIII* (Brasília: Editora UnB, 1997).

4. Neil Whitehead has emphasized the techniques of "ethnic soldiering" in northern South America. See Whitehead, "The Crises and Transformations of Invaded Societies: The Caribbean (1492–1580)," *CHNPA*, vol. 3, pt. 1, 864–903.

5. Petition of the Provincial and Religious of the Company of Jesus of Brazil (1601?), AGS, Sec. prov. 1461, 104ff.

6. ANTT, Manuscritos da livraria 1116, f. 629. See also "Algumas advertencias para a provincia do Brasil," in Biblioteca Nazionale Centrale Vittorio Emmanuele, Fondo Gesuitico 1255 (38), which makes the same points. This document is discussed in detail in Charlotte de Castelnau-L'Estoile, *Les ouvriers d'une vigne stérile. Les jésuites et la conversion des Indiens au Brésil, 1580–1620* (Paris, 2000), 316–28.

7. AGS, SP 1487 (7 October 1603), fls. 33–33v.

8. Frei Vicente do Salvador, *História do Brasil, 1500-1627*, 5th ed. Notes by Capistrano de Abreu, Rodolfo Garcia, Frei Vinâncio Willeke (São Paulo: Edições Melhoramentos, 1965), 342–43.

9. Serafim Leite, *História da Companhia de Jesús no Brasil*, 10 vols. (Lisbon: Livraria Portugalia, 1938–1950), 5:267.

10. Ibid., 265.

11. Gov. Diogo de Meneses to crown (1 September 1610), ANTT, Fragment caixa 1, n. 6.

12. Engel Sluiter, "Livro que dá razão ao Estado do Brasil," *Hispanic American Historical Review* 29, no. 4 (November 1949): 518–62, quoting 523.

13. BI, King to Gov. Gaspar de Sousa (Lisbon, 24 May 1613), 218-18v.

14. "Información que hizo por mandado de VMg. sobre unos capítulos que Duarte Gomez de Silveira, vezino de Parahiba, embió a la Mesa de Consciencia," AGS, Sec. prov. libro 1583, fls. 382–89.

15. BNRJ, I-31,28,53, cited in Maria Regina Celestino de Almeida, "Os índios aldeados no Rio de Janeiro colonial" (Ph.D. thesis, Universidade de Campinas, 2000), 53.

16. See Instituto do Açúcar e do Álcool, *Documentos para a história do açúcar* (Rio de Janeiro, 1956), 2:157, 174.

17. Ernesto Ennes, *Os Palmares (Subsídios para a sua história)* (Lisbon, 1938), 41–43.

18. See Hal Langfur, "Uncertain Refuge: Frontier Formation and the Origins of the Botocudo War in Late-Colonial Brazil," *Hispanic American Historical Review* 82, no. 2 (2002): 215–56; Governor to Viceroy, Vila Rica, 19 November 1776, BNRJ, Seção de Manuscritos (hereafter SM), cód. 2, 2, 24, fl. 53; and Jozé Bernadinho Alves Gundim, "Plano . . . a respeito da providencia que se deve dar as hostalidades e invazoens dos Indios barbaros no seu respeitivo Destrito," Mariana [1794], APM, Seção Colonial (hereafter SC), cód. 260, fl. 52.

19. Nunes to Governor [Cuieté?, 1769], BNRJ, SM, cód. 18, 2, 6, doc. 203; and Governor to Colonial Secretary, Vila Rica, 31 December 1781, APM, SC, cód. 224, fl. 81v.

20. See Salvador, *História*, 346. The *câmara* of Ilhéus wrote in 1601 to the count of Linhares, owner of the Engenho Santana in Ilhéus, that his sugar estate was one of the best on the Brazilian coast and that to protect it, some gentio who lived near the count's other estate in the Bahian Recôncavo had been moved to guard the property in Ilhéus. See ANTT, Cartório dos Jesuítas, maço 8, n.108 (30 July 1601).

21. BI, King to Gaspar de Sousa (17 August 1612).

22. See Obidos to Capitão do Campo Simão Fernandes Madeira (27 August 1664), *DH* 7 (1929), 185–86; Obidos, portaria (6 June, 1667), *DH* 7 (1929), 301–2; Order given to Capitão do Campo Gaspar da Cunha (20 December 1668), *DH* 11 (1928), 385–86.

23. AHU, Mato Grosso, caixa 1 (22 August 1744).

24. Ennes, *Os Palmares*, 113–38.

25. *ACMS*, 1:327–30.

26. Rubellio Dias's report states that the governor, chief justice (*ouvidor geral*), treasurer (*provedor*), bishop, and two magistrates (*desembargadores*) of the mocambo were captured. He also speaks of battling against three "companies" of rebels. It is difficult to discern if this terminology indicates a highly organized social, political, and military organization in the mocambo or simply a series of equivalencies and references in Dias's mind. See his letter in *ACMS*, 1:329–32.

27. Salvador, *História*, 342.

28. The story of this expedition is reported in João José Reis, "Escravos e coiteiros no quilombo de Oitizeiro, Bahia, 1806," in *Liberdade por um fio*, 332–72. See also APB, "Traslado da Devassa," caixa 287.

29. See Celestino de Almeida, "Os índios aldeados," 209.

30. King to Assumar, AHU, Minas Gerais, pap. avul. (12 January 1719), cited and discussed in Stuart B. Schwartz, *Slaves, Peasants, and Rebels: Reconsidering Brazilian Slavery* (Urbana and Chicago: University of Illinois Press, 1992), 119.

31. Governor to João Teixeira da Costa, Vila Rica, 28 August 1770, and Governor to Jozé Gonçalves Vieyra, Vila Rica, 28 August 1770, APM, SC, cód. 179, fls. 35v–36.

32. On the Avá-Canoeiro see André A. de Toral, "Os índios negros ou os Carijó de Goiás: a história das Avá-Canoeiro," *Revista de Antropologia* (São Paulo) 27/28 (1984–85): 287–325; Mary Karasch, "Os quilombos do ouro na capitania de Goiás," in *Liberdade por um fio*, 240–62.

33. Virgílio Corrêa Filho, *História de Mato Grosso* (Rio de Janeiro: Instituto Nacional do Livro, Ministério da Educação e Cultura, 1969).

34. ANTT, Manuscritos do Brasil, 11, fl. 7.

35. Luiza Rios Ricci Volpato, "Quilombos em Mato Grosso," in *Liberdade por um fio*, 213–39.

36. Governor to King, Vila Bela, 27 January 1754, *Revista do Arquivo Público de Mato Grosso* 1, no. 2 (1982–1983): 69.

37. Rosa Elizabeth Acevedo Marin, "Prosperidade e estagnação de Macapá colonial: As experiências dos colonos," in *Nas terras do Cabo Norte: fronteiras, colonização e escravidão na Guiana brasileira, séculos XVIII–XIX*, ed. Flávio dos Santos Gomes (Belem: Gráfica e Editora Universitária, 1999), 33–62.

38. Flávio dos Santos Gomes, "Fronteiras e mocambos: Protesto negro na Guiana brasileira," in *Nas Terras do Cabo Norte*, 225–318.

39. Nadia Farage, *As muralhas dos sertões: os povos indígenas no rio Branco e a colonização* (Rio de Janeiro, 1991), 97.

40. Denise Maldi Meireles, *Guardiães da fronteira: Rio Guaporé, século XVIII* (Petrópolis: Vozes, 1989), 170–89, and Luiza Rios Ricci Volpato, *A conquista da terra no universo da pobreza: Formação da fronteira oeste do Brasil, 1719–1819* (São Paulo: Editora HUCITEC, 1987), 41–45.

41. F. A. Pereira da Costa, *Anais pernambucanos* (Recife: Arquivo Público Estadual, 1951), 1:455.

42. See Luiz Mott, "Brancos, pardos, pretos e índios em Sergipe, 1825–1830," *Anais da História* 6 (1974): 139–84.

43. José Antônio Gonsalves de Mello, *Tempo dos Flamengos: influência da ocupação holandesa na vida e na cultura do Norte do Brasil*, 2nd ed. (Recife: Governo de Pernambuco, Secretaria de Educação e Cultura, Departamento de Cultura, 1978), 195. When the Dutch surrendered in 1654, Mendes's men were spared but were denied the honor of leaving in possession of their arms.

44. Antonio Vieira to merchants of Brazil (12 September 1646) in John Nieuhof, *Memorável viagem marítima e terrestre ao Brasil* (São Paulo: Editora da Universidade de São Paulo, 1981 [1682]), 299. A number of major engagements in the Luso-Dutch War in Brazil (1645–1654) were fought by large contingents of indigenous troops under European direction. In Rio Grande, for example, a force of five hundred Dutch and eight hundred Tapuya and Pitiguar were routed by the native archers of Felipe Camarão. See Manuel Calado, *O Valeroso Lucideno* (Belo Horizonte, 1987), 2:165–73. See also José Antônio Gonsalves de Mello, *Henrique Dias, Governador dos crioulos, negros e mulatos do Brasil* (Recife: Fundação Joaquim Nabuco, Editora Massangana, 1988).

45. Luiz Felipe de Alencastro, *O trato dos viventes: Formação do Brasil no Atlântico sul* (São Paulo: Companhia das Letras, 2000).

46. Governor to Colonial Secretary, Vitória, 5 November 1800, AHU, Espírito Santo, caixa 6, doc. 445.

47. Maximilian, Prinz von Wied, *Travels in Brazil in the Years 1815, 1816, 1817* (London, 1820), 226.

48. Ibid., 289.

49. Ibid., 181, 290.

50. Serafim Leite, ed., *Cartas do Brasil e mais escritos de P. Manuel da Nóbrega (opera omnia)* (Coimbra, 1955), 343 (letter of 5 July 1559).

51. Pedro Puntoni, *A mísera sorte: a escravidão africana no Brasil holandês e as guerras do tráfico no Atlântico Sul, 1621–1648* (São Paulo: Editora Hucitec, 1992), 123.

52. "Retificação de paz feita com os tapuias janduins da Ribeira do Açu (20 September 1695), AHU, Rio Grande, pap. avul., caixa 1, 40. This treaty and a similar one of 1697 made with the Tapuias Arius *pequenas* that includes the same provisions appears as an appendix in Pedro Puntoni, "A guerra dos bárbaros. Povos indigenas e a colonização do sertão do nordeste do Brasil, 1650–1720" (Ph.D. thesis, Universidade de São Paulo, 1988).

53. Carta régia (Lisbon, 6 June 1706), IHGB, Arq. 1.2.25 from Conselho Ultramarino, VI, 103.

54. "Colecção sumaria das proprias Leis, Cartas Regias, Avisos e ordens que se acham nos livros da Secretaria do Governador desta Capitania de Minas Gerais, deduzidas por ordem a titulos separados" [Vila Rica], [1774], *Revista do Arquivo Público Mineiro* 16:1 (1911): 331–474, quotation 448.

55. Summary of royal order, 24 February 1731, ibid., 449–51.

56. Stuart B. Schwartz, *Sugar Plantations in the Formation of Brazilian Society, Bahia, 1550–1835* (Cambridge: University of Cambridge Press, 1985), 47–50, and the sources cited therein. The most extensive study to date is Ronaldo Vainfas, *A heresia dos índios: Catolicismo e rebeldia no Brasil colonial* (São Paulo: Companhia das Letras, 1995). Interesting details on participation by blacks are provided by Alida C. Metcalf, "Millenarian Slaves? The Santidade de Jaguaripe and Slave Resistance in the Americas," *American Historical Review* 104, no. 5 (1999): 1531–59.

57. Vainfas, *A heresia dos índios*, 139–62.

58. Ivan Alves Filho, *Memorial dos Palmares* (Rio de Janeiro: Xenon, 1988), 33–34. See Roloux Baro, "Relação da viagem ao pais dos tapuyas," in *História das ultimas lutas no Brasil entre holandeses e portugueses*, by Pierre Moreau, trans. Leda Boechat Rodrigues, introduction by José Honório Rodrigues (Belo Horizonte: Livraria Itatiaia Editora, 1979).

59. Pedro Paulo A. Funari, "A arqueologia de Palmares: Sua contribuição para o conhecimento da história da cultura afro-americana," in *Liberdade por um fio*, 26–51; C. E. Orser, Jr., *In Search of Zumbi: The 1993 Season* (Normal:

Illinois State University Press, 1993); for a review of research on Palmares see Robert Nelson Anderson, "The Quilombo of Palmares: A New Overview of a Maroon State in Seventeenth-Century Brazil," *Journal of Latin American Studies* 28, no. 3 (October 1996): 545–66.

60. Câmara [Joaquim Joze Farneze, Antonio Felicianno da Costa, Manoel da Silva Pereira, Simeão Vas Mourão, and Antonio de Brito Teixeira] to Prince Regent, Vila do Príncipe, 9 February 1810, BNRJ, SM, cód. 8,1,8, doc. 1.

61. See Stuart B. Schwartz, "Brazilian Ethnogenesis: Mestiços, Mamelucos, and Pardos," in *Le Nouveau Monde, Mondes Nouveaux: L'Expérience Américaine*, ed. S. Gruzinski and N. Wachtel (Paris: Editions Recherche sur les civilisations: Editions de l'Ecole des hautes études en sciences sociales, 1996), 7–28.

62. See Muriel Nazzari, "Vanishing Natives: The Social Construction of Race in Colonial São Paulo," *The Americas* 57, no. 4 (April 2001): 497–524.

63. Domingos de Abreu e Brito, *Um inquérito à vida administrativa e económica de Angola e do Brasil*, ed. Alfredo de Albuquerque Felner (Coimbra: Imprensa da Universidade, 1931 [1591]), 9.

64. Nicholas del Techo, *Historia de la Provincia del Paraguay de la Compañia de Jesús* (Madrid: A. de Uribe, 1897), 1:4.

65. Captitão-Mór of Sergipe de El-rey to Crown (16 September 1751), APB, Ord. reg. 76, 178–81; Ignácio Accioli de Cerqueira e Silva, *Memorias históricas e políticas da provincia da Bahia* (Salvador, 1925), 3:222–23.

66. ANTT, Manuscritos do Brasil, n. 43, fls. 710–11v.

67. Diario of Francisco Pedro de Mello (Vila Bela, 28 July 1795), in IHGB, Arq. 1.2.5, "Correspondência do governador de Matto Grosso, 1777–1805," fls. 165–77v. It should be noted that the same expedition also raided two other small quilombos, where all the inhabitants were escaped slaves. The eighteen people apprehended were returned to their masters, the quilombos and their crops were destroyed, and "the repeated flights of the slaves of this town and its outliers [arrayaes] suspended."

68. AHU, Rio Grande do Norte, pap. avul., caixa 6 (3 September 1806), cited previously in Stuart B. Schwartz, "The Formation of a Colonial Identity in Brazil," in *Colonial Identity in the Atlantic World, 1500–1800*, ed. N. Canny and A. Pagden (Princeton: Princeton University Press, 1987), 27.

69. The methods of integration are discussed with examples in Schwartz and Salomon, "New Peoples and New Kinds of Peoples," 463–67.

70. In this area the French anthropologist Roger Bastide was a pioneer in his *Les Ameriques noires* (1967), translated as *African Civilisations in the New World*, trans. Peter Green (New York: Harper & Row, 1971), 72–88. The chapter "The Meeting of the Negro and Native" is one of the earliest and still most suggestive essays on the topic of black-native contacts in the Americas.

71. Jocélio Teles dos Santos, *O dono da terra: O caboclo nos candomblés da Bahia* (Salvador: Sarah Letras, 1995).

72. Frances O'Gorman, *Aluanda: A Look at Afro-Brazilian Cults* (Rio de Janeiro: Livraria F. Alves Editora, 1977), 72–74; Tania Almeida Gandon, "O índio e o negro: Uma relação legendária," *Afro-Asia* 19–20 (1997): 135–64. On the symbol of the native, or caboclo, which emerged in the 1820s in the popular commemorations of independence, see Hendrik Kraay, "Entre o Brasil e Bahia: as comemorações do Dois de Julho em Salvador no século XIX," *Afro-Asia* 23 (2000): 49–88.

73. Almeida Gandon, "O índio e o negro," 135–64.

74. See Jonathan W. Warren, *Racial Revolutions: Antiracism and Native Resurgence in Brazil* (Durham, N.C.: Duke University Press, 2001), esp. chap. 1.

CHAPTER FOUR

Conflict and Cohabitation between Afro-Mexicans and Nahuas in Central Mexico

NORMA ANGÉLICA CASTILLO PALMA
AND SUSAN KELLOGG

ⓈⒼ

One of the fundamental characteristics of the Spanish American colonial period was the generation of multiracial societies resulting from the intermixing of the indigenous population with Spaniards and black slaves. Both the Spanish crown and the white elite of Spanish America contributed to the creation of legislation that allowed racial differentiation to be converted into forms of social distinction or segregation. This organizing mechanism of colonial social life was enacted through legislation that imposed distinctive restrictions, rights, and obligations on each racial group as it interacted with the others throughout the colonial period. However, as this chapter will show, not only was a strict segregation impossible to create or enforce, but close relations among all social groups were the norm. These close relationships could be positive or negative, as evidenced by the relationships between

Afro-Mexicans and natives in New Spain. Without fully embracing Patrick Carroll's revisionist argument, made in this volume (chapter 9), that the relations between people of indigenous and African identity were predominantly harmonious rather than conflictive, we argue that there is ample evidence of positive relationships. When conflicts arose, these grew often out of social closeness (in both a spatial and interpersonal sense), not from distance.

We will examine these relationships from the vantage point of Cholula, a city-state (or *altepetl*, in the Nahuatl language native to the region) to the east of the Mexica capital of Tenochtitlán, today's Mexico City (see fig. 4.1). A center of Nahua population and culture throughout the colonial period, Cholula was also the site of the development of important textile *obrajes* (workshops), which had significant labor needs. African slaves accompanied the first Spaniards who resided in the area, and labor requirements for textile production and agriculture ensured that the Afro-descended population would grow. The conditions of life and labor in the obrajes led to both inter-group cohabiting and conflict, the former underlying the dynamic growth of the mixed-race population and the latter responsible for the often tense nature of everyday life for both indigenous and mixed-race groups.

It is worth briefly mentioning some of the legal prohibitions placed upon the indigenous population, who were forbidden to bear arms, dress like Spaniards, or ride horses—although these restrictions were not well enforced and did not usually apply to the indigenous nobility. During the seventeenth century the Spanish crown also decreed restrictive measures that forbade certain women, especially *mulatas* (women of African and Spanish descent), from wearing particular types of dress, principally garments of silk or jewels, but also indigenous clothing. Complementing such sumptuary laws were policies forbidding mulattos, Spaniards, and mestizos (individuals of indigenous and Spanish origin) to live in native communities, or pueblos. In New Spain this policy was known as *separación residencial* (residential separation).

So often repeated in legislation, so little respected in practice, the policy became a source of tension when attempts were made to enforce it.[1] This was the case in 1623 when the hacienda (large, landed estate) owner and merchant don Diego de Coca y Rendón stated that "in the city of Cholula there are many vagabonds of mestizo, black, or mulatto origin who are prejudicial to that Republic [of Indians] and it is convenient that they undertake to begin to serve on Spanish properties."[2] He alluded to a 1593 law of separation of the republics, and he obtained an order stating "that male and female blacks, free mulattos, and mestizos will not be allowed to have housing as

FIG. 4.1: *The Cholula region. Map drawn by Matthew Restall, after a map by Francisco González-Hermosillo Adams and Gabriel Salazar, based on Francisco González-Hermosillo Adams and Luis Reyes,* El códice de Cholula: La exaltación testimonial de un linaje indio *(Mexico City: Gobierno del Estado de Puebla, CIESAS, CONACULTA-INAH, and Porrúa, 2003), 16.*

such" in indigenous pueblos since such residential integration might promote idleness and violence. Nevertheless, his petition again expressed his interest in having mulattos and mestizos already resident in the city and its surrounding area "begin to serve in Spanish houses and those who have trades should present the testing credentials within thirty days."[3]

It was no accident that don Diego de Coca suggested that mestizos, blacks, and mulattos register in order to prove they worked for a Spaniard, since those who did not would be forced to leave Cholula. The reason Coca brandished for undertaking this witch hunt was to root out vagabondage, but behind such legal efforts and supposed social concerns was a larger agenda. This included pressuring free mulattos and Afro-mestizos to enlist as workers on the properties of hacendados like Coca. However, some Spanish obraje owners also succeeded in obtaining licenses to apprehend mestizos and mulattos on charges of vagabondage and having them sentenced to labor in their workshops.[4]

Just as the Spanish subjugation of natives and Afro-Mexicans did not go uncontested, so was the coexistence of these groups not without conflict. Such conflicts led to litigation over alleged debts, robberies, beatings, and insults—and produced the source material for this chapter. The variety of events and the language used to describe them reveal complex patterns of interaction among groups whom the Spanish wished to segregate residentially while at the same time wringing every bit of labor possible out of them. These ambiguous Spanish policies led to forms of interaction and interpenetration and to worldviews (for which we use the term *imaginary* to focus on the stereotypes that different socioracial groups held about each other) that underlay the petty and not-so-petty dramas of daily life. Litigation records show just how deeply intertwined these populations became even as individuals retained what we might term a "flexible consciousness" about their socioracial identity.

It is important to stress, however, that the origin of interethnic conflicts lay in the subjugation of natives and Africans and the abusive behavior of Spaniards rooted in their conviction that they were superior to non-Spaniards. Owing to their marginal and oppressed situation in colonial society and their limited rights in both Spanish and indigenous communities, blacks, mulattos, and *pardos* (darker-skinned persons of African descent) were more often accused of crimes, with some individuals engaging in transgressive behaviors that captured the attention of local authorities. Yet in some cases indigenous communities welcomed black residents, establishing relations of solidarity and aid through friendship, intimate relations, or intermarriage with them. First we will look further at a variety of cases that exemplify the types of conflicts that developed between these populations, then we will move onto examples of alliance, friendship, and cohabitation.

NAHUA IMAGES OF CONFLICT AND COEXISTENCE WITH AFRO-MEXICANS

The image projected in the discourse of indigenous town councilors on relations between slaves and indigenous peoples is one of abusive and exploitative treatment of natives, above all when Afro-Mexicans were employed or enslaved by a powerful Spanish owner who supported them in their actions. For example, in 1593 the native governor and officials of San Pedro Cholula told the viceroy of New Spain "that the owners of livestock and their servants and slaves entered their houses at night and took their provisions and sometimes their women, taking them from their fathers and husbands."[5] In light of these abuses, they asked for reparation and punishment because of the damages they had suffered.

But Cholula was now irreversibly a multiracial society, and the conflicts continued. In 1639 town officials presented new complaints. Cholula's indigenous governor, don Joseph Fránquez, protested to the viceroy, the marqués de Cadereyta, criticizing the refusal of native women to attend to their obligation to pay royal tribute. According to Fránquez the situation was very common since "in this *cabecera* [administrative unit] there are numerous Indian women married to mestizos, *zambaigos* [people of African and indigenous origin], and free blacks."[6] These indigenous women married to community outsiders explained their refusal to pay tribute as well as their abandonment of indigenous-style clothing (since they now wore shoes and jewelry) as based on their marriages to nonindigenous men. Thus the women justified their refusal on the grounds that they had adopted new identities. The official added that the women counted on the support of their husbands and on that of some "powerful people" from the administration in order to avoid paying tribute.[7] This testimony demonstrates two elements of interaction between natives and Afro-Mexicans: first, the union of indigenous women with men who did not share their racial classification; second, the weight that Cholula's natives, both the governor and the women, granted to attire, treating it as if it were a disguise capable of changing identity.

In order to resolve this conflict, the viceroy ordered that the *corregidor* (a Spanish district official) of Cholula permit the indigenous governor to enter the houses of the mixed households, especially those of indigenous women married to outsiders, and, where there should have been an indigenous spouse, to search for the evaders and collect what they owed the crown. Nevertheless, as we will see below, the support of Spanish royal functionaries and the detection of the evading women was not sufficient, for the problem lay with the husbands.

In 1640 Gabriel Pérez, an indigenous noble from the barrio (neighborhood) of Santa María who had filled various offices in the indigenous *cabildo* (city council) of Cholula, spoke of the daily afflictions the indigenous population suffered from the vexations inflicted by the mulattos:

> All the mulattos, mestizos, and blacks from the obrajes of
> the city, who go out on Sundays and holidays to have a good
> time, go to the houses of the natives causing them great
> aggravation and bother, robbing them of chickens and hens,
> and they break the doors of their houses and destroy their
> fruit and *nopal* [prickly pear] orchards and they steal ears of
> corn from the sown fields and they cut the corn stalks before
> they reach maturity. . . . [8]

Pérez's statement illustrates indigenous perceptions of the patterns of criminality developed by black and mulatto workers who cohabited with natives and worked with them in the confined spaces of the obrajes. It also reveals that slaves or free blacks were often defended by their masters, powerful obraje or hacienda owners, thus remaining unpunished for their alleged aggressions against the indigenous population.

Did mulattos and mestizos really view themselves as superior to *indios* (Indians)? The following case suggests an answer to that question. In 1708 an *alcalde* (local judicial and administrative official) of Cholula's native town council appeared before the corregidor to accuse a native woman of failing to pay tribute when he went to collect it. He complained, moreover, that the husband, an Afro-mestizo and weaver of broadcloth, came out to defend her and attacked him verbally and physically. The insults he hurled at the indigenous governor are the most interesting evidence because they reveal the sense of superiority felt by the nonindigenous population. The husband shouted at the Nahua governor and *alguacil* (constable), "Didn't they know he was a gentleman and better than anyone?" followed by insults like, "You are cuckolds, *chichimec* dogs, and drunks." He then threw stones at the faces of the native officials in order to throw them out. All this without the Nahua woman's husband demonstrating the slightest respect for the staff of office carried by the official, which was a sign of authority conferred by the king on indigenous town councils.[9]

MIXED-UP IDENTITIES

In 1701 a group of natives from Cholula denounced an individual by the name of Juan Pinto, identifying him as a *coyote* (person of African and mestizo descent) who cared for the livestock of a Spaniard. The complaint focused on how the ranch hand allowed his mules to graze and endanger the *milpas* (cornfields) of the native community. According to testimony, the natives asked the "coyote, who is in the service of Joseph Barrios, hacienda owner" not to place his mules on their lands. They accused Pinto of having hit them with the mules' reins and described how they responded to these blows by stoning him, hitting Pinto in the head. While the dispute appeared to have quieted, at nightfall Juana Pinto, aunt of the aggressor who had earlier been repelled, herself physically and verbally attacked the Nahuas.[10] To put an end to the ruckus the Spanish hacienda owner, overseer of the coyote and owner of the mules, arrived, accompanied by the alguaciles, in this case Spanish. Those who had wounded Pinto were arrested, and in view of this they demanded justice.

Throughout the proceeding there was no agreement among the indigenous petitioners about the racial classification of the aggressor, indicating their vague and confused sense of his status. One indigenous witness characterized Pinto as "Juan the *gachupín*" (a pejorative term for a peninsular-born Spaniard), another referred to Juan as a mestizo, while the principal witness referred to him as a coyote.[11] When Pinto appeared in subsequent cases of 1702 and 1710 as a witness, he is described as a pardo, a pardo militiaman, or a free mulatto. Pinto's ancestry was likely of mixed African and indigenous heritage, but beyond that his status remained ambiguous.[12]

Seventeenth-century patterns of conflict between indigenous officials and others and Afro-mestizos persisted into the eighteenth century, with the difference being that individual identities became increasingly confused and often contested. For example, in one case from 1712, two Nahuas accused three men of stealing their mules. They recognized among the accused a man whom they described as a "mulatto who carried a dagger" and another who clutched a knife. The men described how the bandits had tied them up and blindfolded them. Hidden, they listened to the crooks yell,

"Mulatto, drive the mules!" According to their declaration the mulattos robbed them of six mules, eight harnesses, clothing, and other things, after which they took refuge in the church.[13]

After being removed from the church and questioned by authorities, the thieves declared who they were. Andrés Xuarez was recorded as being thirty-eight, single, a muleteer, and a *morisco* (a term that in late-colonial Mexico referred to someone of mulatto and Spanish descent). Miguel Matheo was described as a mestizo, twenty-seven years of age, and married to an indigenous woman from nearby Huejotzingo. But the documents emphasize that he was an *hijo de la iglesia* (literally, "child of the church"), a term used to describe those born illegitimately, of unknown parentage, and often of mixed socioracial origins. This label, *hijo de la iglesia*, justified in judicial terms the assignment of the classification *mestizo* with no further knowledge of actual ancestry. But the term was generally used only in entries of baptism or marriage, and its use here may have been a way of either denigrating Matheo Miguel as illegitimate or conversely making a case for treating him less harshly than his allegedly mulatto comrades. This type of maneuver did not help the third delinquent, Antonio Rodríguez, who in spite of being characterized as a mestizo was condemned to the harshest punishment for having been found with a knife. His attempt to claim ecclesiastical immunity failed, and he was condemned to receive two hundred lashes in the pillory. Even worse, his services were auctioned for eight years to the obraje of don Antonio Medina Cataño. The sentence came so swiftly that the *mayordomo* (steward or supervisor) of the obraje, Juan Ponce de León, waited for the prisoner at the court and paid 170 pesos (standard monetary unit) in order to receive him.[14] In the end, it is not clear how racial categories influenced the judicial process because the three "mulattos" claimed to be morisco or mestizo and thereby created ambiguity.

Multiracial Violence: Drinking and Homicide in Obrajes and Bars

The case of the killing of Manuel de Aguilar, a slave in the obraje of Onofre de Arteaga, allows us to re-create the environment of his activities during the little leisure time slaves and other workers were permitted and the violent—sometimes lethal—conflicts that could explode among them.[15] One of the witnesses, Francisco de Montúfar, a slave in the workshop, described how at nightfall he went out to pawn something and upon returning found

Alonso Ximenes, free mulatto, Manuel de Aguilar, a mulatto slave, and Luis Escribano, also a mulatto slave, playing cards in front of the obraje. He noted they were arguing over twenty reales (a real equaled one-eighth of a peso). When Manuel refused to bet at least half a real, a fistfight broke out. Bernardino de la Cruz, a slave described as a *mulato prieto* (dark mulatto), tried to get them to go into the workshop but then entered the fight. Meanwhile the light of the candle went out, and they were left in shadows. In the darkness Manuel continued to resist and hit Bernardino with a club; this blow was answered with one from a spindle, from which Manuel fell to the ground next to a water fountain and died.[16]

Inquisition cases provide another vantage point from which to view interethnic relations and conflict during the colonial period as these relate to socioracial stereotypes. Inquisition records, for example, reveal the close association of Afro-Mexicans with witchcraft (a subject discussed further below). This was partly due to Spanish stereotypes of Africans and partly because the indigenous population was outside the jurisdiction of the Holy Office after 1571. In one such case, a native accused a black man of appearing to him as a devil. In other cases, the opposite occurred as blacks accused their indigenous companions of witchcraft and alleged that native sellers of *pulque* (a common alcoholic beverage made from maguey plants) and owners of cantinas (bars) poisoned them on their drinking sprees. Another example comes from 1728, when the anguished mother of a free mulatto obraje worker, Gertrudis de la Cruz, a free mulata and widow of Juan de Aguilar, who had been a mulatto slave of the obraje of Captain Onofre de Arteaga, appeared before Inquisition officials in Cholula to denounce the indio Juan. According to her, Juan had killed her son, Diego Colex, with a poisonous potion that he gave Diego in a glass of pulque. She stated that the beverage made Diego sleepy and caused his body to stiffen. Gertrudis had don Cristóbal, the city's doctor, examine Diego. The doctor took his pulse, examined the body, and saw that he was poisoned and that there was no hope for him. Don Cristóbal said that they should give Juan some oil to get him to speak and go to confession. When Juan confessed, he said that the conflict "had not had any other beginning and origin than the drink of pulque that Juan had given him [Diego], being so violent the poison or venom that had been injected in the pulque that at two in the afternoon he gave his soul to God, slobbering, with his body all purple and black which goes along with his color."[17] Diego's mother begged that Juan pay for his crime. What these examples, along with the next case, illustrate is the fact that young Afro-Mexicans and Nahuas could enjoy each other's company, with men of all socioracial categories interacting without conflict much of the time. Yet when violence did occur, racial and ethnic stereotypes quickly emerged. Individuals and their families maintained negative images of the "other"—of members of other ethnic groups—and those images could be used to assign blame for misfortunes.

Yet another case featured conflict among mulattos, a Nahua, and a Spaniard. The Spaniard, José García Fajardo, was a farmer and infantry soldier in the Company of Dragoons of the Province of Cholula and married to María Theresa Cardoso. He testified in 1778 that he also ran a small pulque tavern in his house, describing how the night before "at the prayer hour four men arrived at the door of whom he only knew Pedro Tezotpan, an Indian, and the others appeared to be coachmen, and they asked for a glass of pulque."[18] Noticing that they had arrived drunk, he told them that since it was already night he did not have any, upon which one of the three men, who had on leather pants, responded to him "that if here there wasn't any pulque, he would have two problems." The Spaniard responded to the mulatto's demand and implication of violence, "well, neither pulque nor shit, since [if] he had given them a glass of pulque he would be a fool [*pendejo*]." The mulatto or "coyote" of the leather pants answered him: "You are a damned idiot [*pendejo carajo*]!" Upon hearing the insult, the Spaniard took a club and began to thrash Tezotpan from the bridge to the corner until the man screamed, "Enough already!"[19] When the tavern keeper, García, returned to his house, the mulatto with the leather pants threw a stone at him that hit him in the right eye, and he fell unconscious. Upon the tavern owner's recovering consciousness, Tezotpan, even after being attacked by García, offered to cure him. The Spanish tavern owner later admitted having punched Tezotpan even though he had helped him during the flight of the mulattos. And García recognized moreover that among the aggressors was a man named Dionisio, the man wearing leather pants, who worked as a coach driver for a priest.

Multiracial Love in Eighteenth-Century Cholula: Spouses, Lovers, and Sexual Witchcraft

By the eighteenth century marriages between blacks or mulattos and indigenous commoner women were frequent and relatively well tolerated, at times even very well accepted in indigenous pueblos. Some of them were renowned, such as the couple composed of José Crispín, an Afro-Mexican, married to the daughter of Juan Matheo de los Santos, a member of the Nahua community of San Geronimo Caleras (near Cholula). According to testimony, in 1720 the woman's family accepted the union. José Crispín's indigenous father-in-law had been his cosignor for a debt of sixty pesos that Crispín owed to the convent of Santa Clara in Puebla. When the lawyer of the convent had Juan Matheo de los Santos arrested as the guarantor of his son-in-law's loan, the native members of the community asked him to accept them as cosignors until José Crispín, who had fled, returned to pay his debt. Fifty-seven years later we find another record of this couple, and the large and complex household he and his wife had formed, in a commentary made in a census of 1777:

> In San Pablo Xochimehuacán [a locality neighboring San Gerónimo Caleras] there is a family whose head is a free black, José Crispín, who is seventy-eight years old, married to an Indian woman, María Candelaria, who is sixty-one years old. They have seven children who go from [the ages of] thirty-six to the youngest of ten, who must be a child of his older sons. This pair is poor and lives at the expense of the community. They have lived like aristocrats for a long time.[20]

While this description is unique, other documentation exists that reveals black men becoming assimilated into the communities of their native wives. If unions between Afro-Mexicans and natives were not always formal or as long lasting as that of José Crispín and María Candelaria, the parish registers especially offer us many marriages in which both spouses were descendants of African men and Nahua women. On many occasions we can establish that from the baptisms on, the children of these mixed couples were registered as "indios" with the agreement of the priest of the church.

Further examination of the colonial imaginary as manifested in judicial records reveals that one of the stereotypes attributed to mulatas was that of witchcraft and concubinage. They were identified as knowledgeable about the art of love, and we find some denunciations of their weakness for nonmulatto, single or married men, which generated disputes with parents, mothers, or spouses, with sometimes fatal results. In 1718, for example, a Spanish woman, doña Thomasa Zerón, the legitimate wife of Joseph Almazán, asked authorities to punish her husband's lover. The woman had become fed up with the attitude of the mulata lover, who had intentions of moving into her house. Scandalized, doña Thomasa had clearly lost control of the situation, since her husband supported the desires of his lover and abused Thomasa for opposing him. She responded and accused the mulata in the following terms:

> This woman, with little fear of God, tried for a second time to almost come to live in my company, more by means of severity and shame than by courtesy, I did not allow this intention and desire for reasons that would help me not incur the public dishonesty with which the mulata lives. She had the audacity to scream in public to accuse me [of being] a "prostitute" and "that my lover had knocked me about," at present my husband threatens me with death and punishment without any other cause than the said mulata.[21]

Doña Thomasa thus pointed out the mulata's audacious behavior and language by emphasizing how the mulata publicly claimed doña Thomasa's husband as her lover. In order to recover the reins of her home, the woman asked that proceedings be brought against the mulata for having disturbed her and that authorities should order her husband to resume married life with her. It is important to note that doña Thomasa required punishment neither for her husband having hit her nor for his having committed adultery. She only asked that the lover be jailed and that her husband resume married life. As a result, Antonia Jacoba, free and single mulata, was imprisoned in the public jail for three days.

In 1734 the obraje of Antonio Basilio de Arteaga was the setting for another affair and lawsuit. This one concerned a black slave named José, who was jailed for having an affair with a "*china*" of the obraje.[22] The mayordomo became enraged by the law's excessive fines because he wanted to liberate the slave, who had been imprisoned for five days. He exclaimed that "to claim a piece of silver from him was opposed to the Compilation of Royal Laws for the Indies because whichever white man committed a crime of this nature would be compelled to go through with the marriage, without this having to affect the Indians, slaves, and others of similar backgrounds."[23] According to him, the charge established by the royal list of fines was only eight reales and nothing more. Under such pressure, the alcalde mayor responded that the slave would be freed without paying any fine only if he were to get married. It is interesting to note that the mayordomo and the slave did not accept marriage as the route to his liberation. The woman in question never declared her opinion, nor do we know if it was she who demanded the union. All that is clear is that this option was undesirable and that the mayordomo paid a high fine to release the slave.

Another point that emerges is that in the obrajes, mulata slaves sometimes let loose violent passions among the male foremen and weavers. In 1719 don Juan Ponce de León, obraje owner, denounced Nicolás Martín, mestizo, for quarreling and threatening death to another weaver in the obraje, who fled as a consequence. Nicolás Martín injured José de Aguila, also mestizo, and forced him to go out and fight, threatening to kill him. The jealous lover also menaced María de la Cruz, a mulata worker in the obraje, saying that when her master left, he would come in to cut her face.[24] María, the parda slave who had unleashed the conflict, was brought to the tribunal in order to declare the reason for so much violence and confessed "that she had been in an affair that lasted five years with Nicolás Martín, mestizo and weaving supervisor in the workshop. For this cause, they threw him out of the obraje, where she lived."[25] Because he continued seeking María out, Martín's wife complained about this to her mistress. Punished for the reoccurrence of the affair, María decided not to see him again. The scorned lover sent threats to María with another mulata slave, suspecting that she was having relations with the new weaving official.

Imprisoned in the jail, Nicolás Martín confessed that he was married to a mestiza, acknowledged his illicit friendship with the mulata of the obraje of Juan Ponce, and stated that he had had a child with her four years earlier. Nevertheless, Nicolás Martín maintained that when he came across Juan de Aguila, he only asked him why he [Aguila] did not speak to him and if it was because he had entered into a relationship with María, the mulata, insisting he had only warned Juan that "you did bad because the same that was done with me will be done with you."[26] This testimony demonstrates diverse facets of the event. The mestizo weaving official maintained relations with two women—an advantageous union endorsed through marriage with a mestiza and an informal union with a mulata slave inside the obraje where he worked. The child born from this five-year extramarital relationship was considered a slave, as that was the mother's status. The narratives re-create the rituals of seduction, the gallant phrases that the mestizo sent in his messages, visits to a hallway and search for encounters in the balcony, and Nicolás Martín's metaphorical use of the expression "to kiss the hands" to solicit a date.

Another example of the cross-group liaisons or marriages formed by Afro-Mexicans with indigenous or mestizo men and women is the case of the mulatto slave Juan Phelipe. Imprisoned in Cholula in 1735 for having broken into the house of don Manuel Mariano del Castillo, a local priest, Juan Phelipe was accused of beating two servants of the house, a man and a woman, and of being disrespectful to the Spanish justice officials. When a black slave of another local priest arrived at Castillo's house, this slave told one of the witnesses that the witness "should go and seek a mulatto named Juan Phelipe...who has ventured into the [priest's] house and attacked an Indian woman and an Indian man who serve in the house, taking him out to fight" because the indigenous man had come into the house with Spanish judicial officials.[27] Juan Phelipe, the accused, a mulatto who worked as a bricklayer, said "that he gave his word in marriage to the Indian woman Luisa, servant of the priest, and that he saw that an Indian also named Juan was there and that he was jealous, that he [Juan Phelipe] did not disrespect the house but was jealous of the said Indian woman with whom he is to marry."[28] The court sentenced Juan Phelipe to one year in exile.

A long Inquisition case titled "Mónica de la Cruz, the 'famous sorceress' of Cholula" takes us away from these conflicted love affairs and allows us to penetrate further into the female imaginary, particularly the sexual and ethereal role of mulatas in this realm. Through this document we learn of the rites tied to sexual witchcraft, rites based upon the knowledge and handling of herbs, minerals, bodily excretions, and so forth, in order to attract and maintain masculine interest. The complaint against Mónica de la Cruz and her accomplices originated with some of the inhabitants of Cholula, especially in the machinations of some Nahuas who said "they had seen some witches at midnight with their brooms near the plaza" and took them before the Holy Office in 1652.[29]

While the detailed information obtained by the Inquisition judges about this mulata showed she participated in kitchen work and the selling of tamales in addition to her activities as a sorceress, one of the most striking things about this case is the manner in which race was recorded. While the accused was described by others as an "*hechicera mulata*" (mulata sorceress), as likewise were her accomplices Isabel de Montoya and María de Ribera, in her own introductory statement, Mónica de la Cruz brandished her indigenous ancestry. Without presenting further proof than her own words, she asked "to be considered as 'recently converted' and to be punished with greater consideration" than blacks.[30] However, except for Mónica herself, all the witnesses considered her a mulata.

This case demonstrates well the ambiguity and variability in the designation of racial categories among free Afro-mestizos, who could seize upon any indigenous antecedents in order to try to be recognized as predominantly indigenous and not of African descent. We note in this case as in others that the ascending relatives of color are either ignored or designated as Spaniards, as in this case, with neither proof nor witnesses. Mónica de la Cruz affirmed that her father was Spanish and her mother indigenous in the questions of the Holy Office of the Inquisition, arguing "that she was currently working for don Fray Rodrigo de Cárdena, bishop who is leaving for China, [who lived] in the city of Cholula and she said she did not know her age, and by her appearance she is a little over fifty, and her occupation is to make pastries and tamales."[31] She then stated her genealogy in the following way: "that her parents were Phelipe de León, Spaniard, native of the city of Puebla, who is now deceased and she did not know his occupation and her mother, María María, Indian native of a pueblo of New Spain she does not remember."[32]

It is interesting to note that this woman did not have a family of her own, neither husband nor children, nor did she even know by name her paternal grandparents nor any of her collateral relatives, neither uncles, aunts, nor cousins. We also note that data about her maternal genealogy were not taken, apparently because of her claim that her mother was indigenous. In relation to her siblings, she stated "that she only had one sister [actually a stepsister] and she acknowledged that she [the stepsister] was the daughter of a black and died single."[33] It appears important to note that this lack of memory is a more common characteristic of the descendants of slaves than the native population.

In the daily life of Mónica de la Cruz, considered a mulata by the Inquisition and a mestiza by herself, one can observe the interaction of different ethnic groups and the mixed perceptions they sometimes had of each other, as well as her very diverse clientele and suppliers of herbs and powders who were "Indian *pochtecas* [merchants]."[34] Juana de Sossa, a Spanish woman, stated that it was about two years ago,

> that fleeing a certain person from Puebla, she went to Cholula, where she struck up a bad friendship with a certain man (Juan de Sossa), and there she happened to encounter a mestiza or mulata named Mónica de la Cruz, who sold tamales, and on occasion bought some from her, got to know her, and thus learned from her of a certain mulata, María de Ribera, who knew how to make trinkets and spells.[35]

Mónica de la Cruz acknowledged that Juana de Sossa asked her to prepare something so that a black man with whom she had a "bad friendship" would leave her alone.[36] Because of this, the mulata requested her "to speak with some Indian pochtecos" who often came to have a drink of pulque at Sossa's stand, so that they would give her some herbs so that the black man would leave.[37] Mónica, who knew some Nahuatl, spoke with an indigenous woman, "María, old woman, wife of a one-eyed old Indian man, so that she should give her some remedy so that the stated black man would leave."[38] The next day, the native woman arrived by morning and gave Juana an herb "that she did not recognize, so that she would put it in water and from this water pour it on the black man's feet."[39] Juana de Sossa, according to Mónica herself,

> grabbed the said herb and poured it in the water in a gourd. Having seen the black man that night, when his attention strayed, Juana de Sossa poured the water in an area where the black man's feet were, at which he became annoyed and left. . . . And the Indian woman had not told her any words to say while sprinkling the herb in the water, nor pouring the water on the black man's feet.[40]

A mulata told another witness "that she and the said Mónica had two men that had become angry with them, so they made a preparation so that they should return and it was to put salt and *aluzema* (an herb of the Lavandula family) in a new pot and that they should pour it one night on the street in Cholula where they lived."[41] In a few days the men communicated with the women again, saying, "These whores are sorceresses! What have they done to us to make us see them again!"[42] The mulata confronted yet another accusation for recommending the placing of garlic in a house in order to bring good luck. Mónica acknowledged having said it: "It is very true . . . because thus she heard it from the Indian pustecos [pochtecos] that placing (garlic) in the corners of the house or bringing it along was a good thing for frights or against misfortune."[43]

The concoctions that Mónica de la Cruz created obliged her to move around in different ethnic and cultural environments. She had to make use of the knowledge acquired from the Nahuas, often women, known as "the pustecos/as" by the mulatas, in order to obtain their counsel about remedies such as roots or herbs that they used, having equal recourse to notions of sexual witchcraft from her mulata and Spanish colleagues. The documentation provides us with all sorts of details about these interchanges, commercial as well as recipes for potions that would be made, preferably on market days. The contacts with her clients could develop while she sold her tamales.

Mónica's practices, like those of other women knowledgeable about this art, were fed as much from indigenous knowledge about herbs as from European alchemy known by Spanish women. In the cultural crossroads of sexual witchcraft, the mulatas had a central role as experts and as producers of potions, aromatics, powders, and amulets for an ethnically diverse clientele.[44]

INTERETHNIC FESTIVITIES AND CURIOSITY ABOUT THE OTHER

A very different kind of case describes how a celebration that took place one Sunday in August of 1676, in the house of a *cacique* (indigenous political leader), ended in the murder of an indigenous man named Diego de Santiago at the hands of the mulatto Gabriel Sánchez, "the devil" (apparently his nickname).[45] The statements by a slave of the priest of Cholula invited to the fiesta or informal celebration allow us to know in depth the type of relations established between the Nahua elite and the Afro-Mexican population. Some indigenous nobles who had served on the town council appear to have felt a desire to establish relations with local blacks and mulattos. The testimony makes clear that the nobles were curious about and interested in listening to the singing of the blacks. In his narration, Agustín de Peralta, slave of the parish church, said that don Pascual de Mendoza, indigenous noble, called on him to go and "establish friendships" with another native noble, don Juan Nicolás Texeda, and with a mestizo weaver, Juan de León. Just before eleven at night Peralta attended the fiesta with his wife, a mulata. They were eating and drinking wine when Gabriel Sánchez, "the devil," arrived in the company of other mulattos, and Diego de Santiago, an indigenous apprentice of don Pascual, served them a supper.

At the end of the supper and having "established the friendships he had sought," Agustín had sent someone to buy a real of pulque, having been asked to do so by Texeda, when Phelipe de la Cruz arrived, a free mulatto who served as coachman for the alcalde mayor. De la Cruz was searching for Peralta and "with a guitar that he carried with him he began to play and sing some verses that this witness [Peralta] helped him with."[46] Later they said goodbye and Peralta went to sleep in his house in the company of his wife. But a little later, he woke up to blows and screams at the door. Diego de Barrios, mulatto slave of Sebastian de Herrera, hearing banging and yelling, got up and opened the door to the street. The Nahua, Diego de Santiago, came in all bloody, pleading to Barrios for help, saying he did not have any other protection but that of Barrios because "the devil" had slit his throat. Barrios then went to the palace to inform the judicial officials. Note the call for solidarity from Diego de Santiago to the mulatto, telling Barrios "he has no other protection but his," to which the slave responded by carrying Santiago to the palace and to a surgeon. Another element we observe is the detail of the clothing of the wounded man, who used his *tilma*, or cape, to put pressure on his slashed veins.

Called to testify, the Nahua nobles, don Pascual de Mendoza, don Francisco Tejeda, and don Juan Tejeda, all agreed that don Pascual had invited them to dine. After they had finished, the mulattos arrived, drinking and chatting, and some stayed on to sleep in the house of the host, while the others went later with the indigenous apprentice, Diego de Santiago. It was only afterward that the witnesses learned about the killing of Santiago. Another witness alone knew the reason for the outburst from the aggressor, Sánchez. The killer would not stand for the indio Santiago collecting his debts and pointing him out as the thief of some things from the store of the native noble.

CONCLUSION

The cases from Cholula discussed here provide a wide array of information allowing us to reconstruct the economic activities and social lives of the individual protagonists involved in these seventeenth- and eighteenth-century conflicts. Aside from revealing the language (insults, reverential forms, idiomatic expressions, and forms of popular speech) and patterns of interactions among those of different socioracial and economic groups, we see that interaction, while often conflicted in nature, was also frequently rooted in the interpersonal alliances that formed in the streets, workshops, fields, and homes of Cholula's plebeian population.[47] These alliances could be quite close, reflecting the many and multifaceted interactions between those of African descent and those of indigenous descent. While Nahua and other indigenous, African, and mixed-race peoples socialized, formed ties of business and friendship, loved and lived together, and/or disliked and sometimes hated each other, individuals retained a strong consciousness of their socioracial identities well into the eighteenth century. Yet this consciousness does not imply a total fixity for such identities, which could be manipulated to suit both judicial and social circumstances when the need arose.

⟐⟑

NOTES

1. Diego de Encinas, *Cedulario Indiano*, Tomo I (Madrid: Cultural Hispánica, 1945–1946), 341–44. Important works on Afro-Mexicans include Gonzalo Aguirre Beltrán, *La población negra de México, 1580–1810: estudio etno-histórico* (México: Ediciones Fuente Cultural, 1946); Colin A. Palmer, *Slaves of the White God: Blacks in Mexico, 1570–1650* (Cambridge, Mass.: Harvard University Press, 1976); Patrick Carroll, *Blacks in Colonial Veracruz: Race, Ethnicity, and Regional Development* (Austin: University of Texas Press, 1991); Herman L. Bennett, *Lovers, Family and Friends: The Formation of Afro-Mexico, 1580–1810* (Ph.D. diss., Johns Hopkins University, 1993); and Nicolas Ngou-Mve, *La traite et l'esclavage de Noirs au Mexique de 1580–1640* (Ph.D. diss., L'Université de Toulouse-le Mirail, 1987). While the interrelationships between African-descended and indigenous peoples are just beginning to be studied in greater detail, works by Lolita Gutiérrez Brockington, *The Leverage of Labor: Managing the Cortés Haciendas in Tehuantepec, 1588–1688* (Durham, N.C.: Duke University Press, 1993), and Brígida von Mentz, *Trabajo, sujeción y libertad en el centro de la Nueva España: esclavos, aprendices, campesinos y operarios manufactureros, siglos XVI a XVIII* (México: CIESAS and Porrúa, 1999), show the importance of work as the site through which many, though not all, interactions occurred. On the social relations among these groups, see Cheryl English Martin, *Rural Society in Colonial Morelos* (Albuquerque: University of New Mexico Press, 1985), Brígida von Mentz, *Pueblos de indios, mulatos y mestizos, 1770–1870: los campesinos y las transformaciones protoindustriales en el poniente de Morelos* (México: CIESAS, 1988), and Norma Angélica Castillo Palma, *Cholula: sociedad mestiza en ciudad india. Un estudio de las causas demográficas, económicas y sociales del mestizaje en Nueva España, 1649–1813* (México: Plaza y Valdés-UAM, Iztapalapa, 2001). We use a variety of terms in this chapter to designate members of various socioracial groupings. In particular *Afro-Mexican* refers to all individuals of African descent while *Afro-mestizo* refers to individuals of predominantly African and indigenous descent. The terms *indio, indigenous,* and *native* are used in places because we cannot assume that all indios referred to in Cholula's colonial judicial record are Nahuas, though undoubtedly most were. Other terms related to race (by which we refer to the sociocultural classifications of people by color without assuming these have a biological reality) are defined as they appear in the text or endnotes.

2. Archivo General de la Nación (hereafter referred to as AGN), *Ordenanzas*, vol. 4, 1623, exp. 72, fs. 78–79. Note that the concept of the Republic of Indians was a Spanish legal concept referring both to the idea that indigenous communities could govern and adjudicate themselves except in matters that conflicted with Catholic doctrine or important crown policy and to the idea that the indigenous republic was separate from a Spanish republic.

3. Ibid.

4. AGN, *Mercedes*, vol. 11, exp. 110.

5. AGN, *Indios*, 1593, vol. 6, 1a parte, exp. 630, fs. 167–68.

6. AGN, *Indios*, 1639, vol. 11, exp. 165.

7. Ibid.

8. AGN, *Indios*, 1640, vol. 13, exp. 34, fs. 36–36v.

9. Archivo Judicial de Puebla (hereafter AJP), *Fondo Cholula*, 5 de octubre 1708.

10. AJP, *Fondo Cholula*, 1701. "Juan Pinto 'Coiote,' sirbiente de Joseph Barrios (labrador) a quien le reconvinimos no metiera sus mulas." "Pinto nos maltrató de palabra y obra dándonos con unas hixeras de arria, a lo que contestamos a pedradas dándole a Pinto en la cabeza. En la noche Juana Pinto tía de Pinto me aporreó y maltrató de palabra y obra."

11. Ibid.

12. AJP, *Fondo Cholula*, 1702, "Juicio al alguacil José de Soto por disparar a un miliciano pardo."

13. AJP, *Fondo Cholula*, 1712.

14. Ibid.

15. AJP, *Fondo Cholula*, 1720, "Asesinato de Manuel de Aguilar, mulato esclavo del obraje de don Onofre de Arteaga."

16. AJP, *Fondo Cholula*, 1720, julio de 1720 a 20 hr. P.M., "Bernardino de la Cruz mulato esclavo del obraje de Onofre de Arteaga por haber muerto a Manuel de Aguilar mulato, asimismo, esclavo del mismo obraje con un malacate."

17. AJP, *Fondo Cholula*, 1728, "Criminal de Gertrudis de la Cruz mulata contra el indio Juan por hechicería."

18. AJP, *Fondo Cholula*, 1778, *Criminal*, "José García Fajardo español contra Pedro Tezotpan, indio, un coiote y un mulato cochero llamado Dionisio por injurias y golpes." We should remember that the indigenous population did not have the right to use horses. The occupation of coachman in Cholula as well as in other areas of central Mexico was carried out by Afro-Mexicans, so that the word here encompasses a double meaning, stressing that they were dealing with mulattos.

19. Ibid.

20. AJP, *Fondo Cholula*, s. exp. S.F. 1751, Expediente sobre la prisión a Juan Matheo de los Santos, indio de San Jerónimo Caleras, por la deuda de su yerno, Joseph Crispin, negro. Archivo General de Indias, Audiencia de México, Legajo 2577. Puebla de los Angeles. Fieles de la parroquia de San José que pertenence a Cholula, 1777. The reference to "living like aristocrats" ("que viven como patricios") likely is a sarcastic phrase about the higher social place of this family that, nonetheless, had lived at community expense, perhaps for a long time.

21. AJP, *Fondo Cholula*, 1718, "Da. Thomasa Zerón española contra la mulata Antonia Jacoba por inquietarla y hacer vida maridable con su marido."

22. In Puebla, Tlaxcala, and Veracruz, a *chino* or *china* was an individual of both indigenous and African descent, with the term referring to an individual of African heritage mixed with mestizo or indigenous heritage. In Guerrero such individuals were termed *cambujos*.

23. AJP, *Fondo Cholula*, 1718.

24. AJP, *Fondo Cholula*, 1719, "Don Juan Ponce de León español contral Nicolás Martín mestizo."

25. Ibid.

26. Ibid.

27. AJP, *Fondo Cholula*, 1735. "Proceso contra el mulato Juan por entrar con violencia casa del presbitero y golpear a dos indios de servicio."

28. Ibid.

29. AGN, *Inquisición*, 1652, vol. 562, exp. 19, fs. 463–72.

30. Ibid. Note that following the creation of a separate inquisitorial body for native cases in 1571, the claim to be an "Indian" was a common strategy for an accused non-native to attempt to escape Inquisition jurisdiction.

31. AGN, *Inquisición*, vol. 562, exp. 19, f. 499.

32. Ibid.

33. Ibid.

34. The witnesses against them were women who had been clients or accomplices of Mónica de la Cruz: Isabel de Montoya, a thirty-nine-year-old mestiza, accomplice; Isabel de los Angeles, twenty-five years old, Spaniard, accomplice; Juana de Sossa, fifty years of age, Spaniard, accomplice; María de Ribera, free mulata, fifty years old, accomplice and convicted by the Holy Office. Note also the use of the term *pochteca* (and variants), from the Nahuatl term *pochtecatl*, or "merchant," used at this time to refer to indigenous merchants.

35. Ibid.

36. Ibid., f. 526.

37. Ibid., f. 528.

38. Ibid.

39. Ibid., f. 516.

40. Ibid., f. 512.

41. Ibid., f. 517.

42. Ibid., f. 526.

43. Ibid.

44. Luz Alejandra Cárdenas Santana, "El juego del intercambio en el siglos XVII. Inquisición, sexualidad y transgresión en Acapulco," in *Historia urbana Segundo Congres de Investigación urbana y regional*, ed. Elsa Patiño y Jaime Castillo (México: Editorial de la Red de Investigación Urbana, 1999), 31–50; "La transgresión erótica de Cathalina González, Isabel Uruego y Juana María" (paper presented at the VI Encuentro de Afroamericanistas, Xalapa, Veracruz, 1996); Julio Caro Baroja, *Las brujas y su mundo* (Madrid: Alianza Editorial, 1996) (or see Julio Caro Barojas, *The World of the Witches*, trans. by O. N. V. Glendinning [Chicago: University of Chicago Press, 1964]); Ruth Behar, "Brujería sexual, colonialismo y poderes femeninos: opiniones del Santo Oficio de la Inquisición en México," in *Sexualidad y matrimonial en la América Hispánica*, ed. Asunción Lavrin (México: Alianza-CONACULTA [Col. Los Noventa], 1991), 197–229 (or see Ruth Behar, "Sexual Witchraft, Colonialism, and Women's Powers: Views from the Mexican Inquisition," in *Sexuality and Marriage in Colonial Latin America*, ed. Asunción Lavrin [Lincoln: University of Nebraska Press, 1989]), 178–209.

45. AJP, *Fondo Cholula*, 1676, "Gabriel Sánchez, mulato, el diablo, por haber muerto a Diego de Santiago, indio."

46. Ibid., without date or exp.

47. That is, the local equivalent of the urban "plebe" discussed by R. Douglas Cope in *The Limits of Racial Domination: Plebeian Society in Colonial Mexico City, 1660–1720* (Madison: University of Wisconsin Press, 1994), 22–26.

CHAPTER FIVE

"Whites and Mulattos, Our Enemies"

Race Relations and Popular Political
Culture in Nueva Granada

RENÉE SOULODRE-LA FRANCE

ଚଡ଼

"Our *corregidor* is allied to whites and mulattos, our enemies, who want to steal our land."[1] This bold statement describing volatile racial tensions was the complaint presented in a court case brought by the indigenous people of the town of Coyaima, in the interior of Colombia, during the late colonial period. In our study of colonial societies we sometimes operate with implicit assumptions about racial dynamics and the antagonisms that resulted from the imposition of imperialism and the dominant cultural hegemony that came with it. Our unspoken understandings about the sharp divisions between and among dominant and subaltern groups need to be constantly

I would like to thank Sandra Bamford and Thorald Burnham for their helpful discussions of the issues raised in this paper. This research was made possible by the generous support of the SSHRCC/UNESCO/York Nigerian Hinterland Project.

reexamined so that the nuances and complexities of social relationships are not lost. For example, were racial and ethnic relations in fact so starkly delineated in Spanish territories between the sixteenth and nineteenth centuries? If social relations are an ongoing process of negotiation, then ethnicity, as a significant factor, can shift in importance depending on the context.[2] Did questions of race and ethnicity inform all or even most levels of interaction among various groups in this social context?

This chapter will examine the relationships between blacks, or enslaved Africans, and indigenous groups in Colombia, including the element of chance or opportunity that helped shape that interaction. As we examine specific instances when individuals of different races were thrown together the complexities of colonial society are highlighted, as well as the variations of choices that could be made. The questions raised by the contradictory impulses evident in the documentation invite an exploration of the ways that the colonial legal system was used by various ethnic groups and how this helped, in some ways, to secure the hegemony of the dominant colonial culture.[3] Though the voices of subjected peoples are muted and filtered by imperial officials, they can still be heard in the court cases through which they sought to protect themselves. Moments when indigenous groups and enslaved Africans or their descendants applied to the Spanish legal system to uphold their claims provide an important counterpoint to the generalizations made about slave systems and subaltern groups. They show us that we can uncover the complexities and shifting dynamics of social relations in colonial Spanish America, including some of the gender issues that were relevant to these dynamics. They also tantalize with their hints of a popular political culture that belies the notion that an insurmountable divide rent the patchwork of ethnic and racial groups in the colonial context.

BLACK-NATIVE RELATIONS

Relationships between indigenous peoples and enslaved Africans in Nueva Granada by the end of the eighteenth century were completely ambiguous and often simply contradictory. The ways these two subaltern groups behaved was a source of interest to the Spaniards since they often framed their analysis according to racial categories and sought to foster dissension among dominated groups. Certainly, there is evidence of antagonism, as we will see in some of the cases discussed below, such as the events that led to Joseph Ignacio Piedrahita's encounter with the Native Americans working in his master's mines. However, there is rarely any evidence in the documents of an inherent animosity that existed between particular ethnic groups. While tensions between different ethnic contenders could explode into violence, in many cases this appears to have been based on a spontaneous recognition of an opportunity and the willingness to use those occasions to advance specific aims.

An example of such precipitous actions occurred in 1743 near Santa Marta on the banks of the Magdalena River. In the eighteenth century this region continued to suffer hostile incursions by indigenous groups that caused the Spaniards great concern.[4] According to Joseph Fernando de Mier y Guerra, who sent a report from the town of Mompox explaining these events to the viceroy, the Native Americans of the area usually preferred to attack during the summer. He recounted that in August, two blacks, one enslaved and one free, had been fishing in a small boat in the Boca del Cano de Menchiquejo. Suddenly three indigenous warriors swooped down upon them, shooting them with their arrows. Both victims threw themselves into the water, desperate to escape, but they heard one of their attackers saying to another that the blacks should not be killed. The aggressors appear to have been intent on robbery, not necessarily on murder. Another accomplice in the crime swam to the boat and took out a dagger, a crowbar, and a paddle, flinging these items to the shore and then swimming back to the bank. Notwithstanding the attackers' lack of murderous intent, both of the blacks died from their wounds within forty-eight hours, after they had described what had happened to them.

The official reporting the case stated that the arrowheads used by the attackers were made out of metal, clear evidence, in his opinion, that these were warriors from an indigenous group that had already been *reduced*, or brought into missions to be Christianized. He further added that while several members of this group of Amerindians had been imprisoned during a court case earlier that year, the region had enjoyed tranquility and peace. Though the documents regarding these events are scant, they indicate that there was an element of chance at play in this encounter. The indigenous attackers were not particularly hostile toward the blacks since they did not hunt them down and kill them immediately. They did take the opportunity that the fishermen presented, though, in order to rob them of some weapons and tools.

Contrarily, in yet an earlier period, a black slave was accused of hiding some indigenous workers from an *encomienda* labor draft; they were supposed to be working in the mines of Las Lajas. According to the testimony in this case from 1627, the enslaved Sebastian de Medina was harboring indigenous workers who had previously gone into the mines and become very ill. They had taken refuge with him and were working for him on his master's *estancia*. He denied the charges, saying that there was only one Muisca native, named Miguel, who worked for him.[5] The accusations came from the native *teniente*, who was in charge of fulfilling the labor draft, and they demonstrate how race could be transcended as a cohesive collective concept in particular situations. Such occasions could be played out at the expense of ethnic solidarity, of course. This was the case in the example from the area of Guatequi, when a community of Panche insisted on defending its white teniente and refused to accept an indigenous one because he was in league with the priest and other non-Panches. In these cases, questions of ethnicity and racial solidarity became secondary before other interests.[7]

This is not to say that race and ethnicity were not issues of importance in colonial society. In the case of the enslaved Sebastian de Medina, for example, his defender needed to state that he "is a Christian, fearful of God our Lord and of his conscience, and that he is stating the truth, and just because he is black we cannot presume that he is not."[7] Indigenous and African spoke of each other and of whites in the court documents, and degrees of race were highly recognized and strongly attacked or defended. The issue of race or "quality" often came up in cases of contested marriages, such as when the mestiza doña Tomasa de Salazar opposed her daughter's marriage to a mulatto in 1783. She claimed that both his parents were mulattos, that they were "old, without teeth, half dumb, or incapable of speaking properly, they were the colour of dark brown sugar, they had wide noses, and curly hair like legitimate or very close descendents of Ethiopia."[8] To be called a mulatto or a zambo was unquestionably pejorative and offensive, and many legal contests were fought over this issue.[9]

There is no doubt that the Spaniards sought to foster animosities between Africans and indigenous populations.[10] For example, they offered to pay indigenous groups who turned in runaway slaves, they used indigenous allies in their military campaigns against *palenques* (maroon settlements or runaway slave communities), and they promulgated colonial legislation that sought to limit the contact between the different groups.[11] This was also a favored tactic used by the Portuguese in Brazil, although the demographic context in those colonies was different than in many parts of Nueva Granada.[12] Furthermore, the Spaniards used the ostensibly "natural" antagonisms between blacks and Native Americans as an excuse to impose social controls upon the enslaved. For example, in the city of Santa Fé de Bogotá, the supposed damage that vagrant slaves were wreaking on the indigenous population was used to legitimize antivagrancy laws, prohibitions on freedom of movement and association, and the imposition of curfews upon enslaved Africans in the sixteenth century.[13] According to the law, grave crimes were being committed in the city against property and against the *naturales* (as the indigenous population was called); these acts of robbery, violence, and murder were "presumed to be committed by black slaves," and so those ill-doers needed to be controlled.[14] At times, though, these same animosities, which were generally encouraged, could create problems for the Spaniards, such as in the case of the Chimila raiders who attacked and killed the slaves watching the herds in the province of Santa Marta, disrupting agricultural production in that region during the eighteenth century.[15] Such depredations also occurred in the Chocó during the seventeenth century, when the Citara indiscriminately attacked Spaniards and their African slaves, mulattos, mestizos, and indigenous porters from the interior.[16] All those people associated with the colonizing project in the area were targeted by the indigenous rebels.

The use of Native Americans to control blacks could also be reversed, and so enslaved Africans were sometimes used by the Spaniards to control Amerindians. Indigenous perceptions that Africans were in league with the Spanish developed as the two subordinated groups were forced to labor together in various contexts. Trusted slaves were put into positions of power over indigenous labor on haciendas and in mines and became the targets for native resentment.[17] Of course, in the legal documentation it is the moments of discord that are highlighted, and those occasions when Africans and Native Americans coexisted harmoniously are not necessarily represented. Perhaps the best evidence of such accommodation, then, is the incidence of *zambos*, or the mixing of the two races through biological and cultural intercourse. This reality became a defining feature of the area around Mompox, one of the key points on the transportation route along the Magdalena River (*el Río Grande*). The canoe men of the river were living examples of the ubiquity of miscegenation despite continuous prohibitions of such racial mixtures by the colonial authorities.[18] The same kind of racial mixing occurred in Cartagena province, although according to Adolfo Meisel Roca, this was usually accomplished through force as indigenous women were stolen from their communities by men of African descent. One of the main motivating factors in this development was the relative absence of women of African descent in the rural areas of the region. This is why the coastal region of Cartagena was one of the most racially mixed regions of Nueva Granada in the census of 1777,[19] although to a lesser degree, this historical process was also at work in Tolima Grande, in the center of the viceroyalty. By the end of the eighteenth century such racial mixing led to the definition of many towns in the region as towns of *libres*, free people of color.[20] An outstanding example of this was the town of Guayabal. Because of its location near the gold fields that were worked by enslaved Africans, close to the important transportation routes in the center of the viceroyalty, it experienced a high level of race mixture by the time of the 1778 census.[21]

Still, as we have already seen, moments of contention and violence occurred between the races. For example, in 1658 the natives of the town of Piedras, in the jurisdiction of Mariquita, the center of the silver-producing region of Nueva Granada, complained to the courts about the abuse they were suffering at the hands of a slave, Gonzalo Angola, who belonged to their *encomendero*. The Native Americans claimed that he persecuted them with harsh punishments and through rigorous treatment.[22] The Spaniards considered people of African descent to be their natural allies when the time came to conquer rebellious indigenous populations or to resist their attacks. Thus in 1681 the governor and captain general of Nueva Granada ordered that all of the mulattos in Mariquita should be pressed into service to defend the Spaniards against hostile indigenous attacks.[23]

In the same way, on some occasions during the eighteenth century Native Americans betrayed runaway slaves. When the corregidor went to pick up the tribute payments from the town of San Francisco de Yguira in 1771, the inhabitants told him that there was a mulatto there who belonged to the former Jesuit hacienda of Doyma. The Indians brought in the runaway, Pasqual Viva, one of the slaves who had been missing from the hacienda.[24] There is no indication in the document why the indigenous group betrayed the mulatto, except that they charged the corregidor four pesos for the mulatto's maintenance. Even though runaway slaves at times sought the support of indigenous groups and thought they might be able to make common cause, there was no guarantee this would work, as in the case of the palenque Egoyá, whose location was betrayed to the Spaniards by a native man.[25] Indigenous groups and enslaved Africans related in equally ambiguous ways in the Pacific lowlands of the Chocó. Sometimes they escaped Spanish domination together, and on other occasions they attacked each other mercilessly.[26] In the early nineteenth century a Spanish official in the region stated that the Native Americans were "close to the whites and enemies of the blacks." While we cannot simply accept this assessment at face value, neither can we dismiss it as a complete fabrication.[27] At the very least it indicates that some Spaniards analyzed social relations in the colony very much in terms of race and consciously sought to impede concerted African-indigenous action.

Just as native groups feared that runaway blacks, or *cimarrones*, would attack their settlements and steal their women, at times individuals of African descent feared the same from natives. In 1776 the governor of Panama took the testimony of two free black women who had been stolen from the town of Marea in Darién and sold into slavery.[28] The two women, Maria Luiza Navarro and Gerbacia de Galagaza, both of whom were *criolla*, or born in Nueva Granada, described in detail how a year and a half before, Native Americans had attacked their town. The attack came at about two o'clock in the afternoon, and at least seven people were killed while as many of their neighbors as could fled to the mountains; they and three other women and four boys were captured and taken back to the native town as booty. The captors tried to sell them to some Englishmen who had come ashore, but they reprimanded the indigenous would-be traders for trying to sell the women. Eventually, though, an Englishman whom the natives called Captain Verga bought them and transported them to Jamaica, where they were sold. Luckily their new owners agreed to help them make their way back to Panama and to freedom. One of the governor's main motivations for taking their testimony was to try to glean as much information as possible about the location and strength of the natives, all in the interests of subordinating them to Spanish rule.

Some of the cases of friendly or harsh relations between indigenous and African populations discussed thus far were no doubt the product of long histories between particular groups or individuals. However, in some instances, circumstances led people into specific acts that then had varied consequences, sometimes providing unforeseen opportunities. This appears to be what happened in the case of Joseph Ignacio Piedrahita's experiences with the Native Americans of Antioquia.

In 1772 in the gold-mining region of Antioquia the black, enslaved Joseph Ignacio Piedrahita did something we might consider relatively unexpected.[29] The events were outlined in a letter that Joseph's owner, don Carlos Piedrahita, wrote on October 22, 1772.[30] In that letter don Carlos explained to his father that he had gone into the mountains looking for gold mines, which he found and registered. Subsequently he brought in some slaves to work the mines at considerable expense because of the transportation costs.

On October 14 there was a great disturbance, and some Native Americans who worked in one of the mines alongside the slaves attacked him. Don Carlos explained that the natives wanted to kill him, and his only defense was Joseph Ignacio, who "because of his great loyalty defended my life. At great risk to his own life, he was wounded seven times." Don Carlos added, "I had to give him his liberty, a large favor it is true, but one he merited after having risked his life to save mine." The other slaves were also attacked and two of them injured, but they all managed to escape into the hills, as did don Carlos. He stated that it had been fortunate for him that he had not been armed, since the attackers would have cut him to pieces if he had taken a more threatening stance. A copy of this letter survives in the National Archive in Bogotá as part of a larger case dealing with the question of Joseph Ignacio's plea for freedom, based on his heroic actions in saving his owner's life and on don Carlos's promise that he would be freed.

Unfortunately the documents do not provide any indication about the background to the struggle, so we do not know why the indigenous workers rebelled and attacked, nor why the enslaved African defended his white master.[31] These documents present us with an intriguing story, but a story about what? Within it we find elements of power struggles between races and within families; it is thus in part a story about frustration, injustice, and the fight for freedom. It touches upon the delicate subject of relations between genders in the Spanish colonial world since it turned out that Joseph did not really belong to don Carlos at all, but rather to his mother, and thus opens up for us those relationships between male and female within the family. It is the story of an individual, but it exposes for us the workings of the Spanish legal system and the possibilities it provided for subaltern groups to develop a political philosophy that might answer their needs while it simultaneously helped to legitimize Spanish imperialism and colonial social structures. This story also allows us a forum to discuss the legal distinctions that were made between indigenous, African, enslaved, and free, which help to further define the nature of racial and ethnic dynamics in this context.

Joseph Ignacio's claim to freedom appeared to be more or less an open-and-shut case, given that his master had offered him his liberty in writing. It is impossible to know whether or not Joseph Ignacio had calculated the advantages he might gain by defending don Carlos. From the description of these events in the documents it appears that everything happened very quickly and that his reaction may very well have been an automatic defense of his master without any conscious decision making.

Though these events occurred in 1772, in 1775 Joseph Ignacio went before the colonial courts, asking to be granted the freedom that had been promised by don Carlos. The case had been immediately complicated by an objection raised regarding Joseph Ignacio's ownership in a letter written by don Matheo Alvarez del Rino, uncle to don Carlos and brother to his mother.[32] Alvarez stated that the enslaved Joseph Ignacio did not belong to don Carlos at all, but to the young man's mother, doña Gertrudis Alvarez. In this letter and some of the other communications extant in the case are indications about the dynamics within this family. First of all, in the original letter to his father, don Carlos suggested that he was embarrassed to write to his uncle to tell him that he had been attacked and bested by the indigenous workers, indicating that his uncle was a powerful influence in the family. Through the missive from the uncle we learn that doña Gertrudis had made a most unfortunate marriage, in her brother's opinion. Her husband had quickly gone through her entire dowry, leaving her with nothing but a few "*esclavitos*," one of whom was Joseph Ignacio.[33] Her brother, don Matheo Alvarez, had magnanimously provided her with a small house in which to raise her children and a monthly stipend to feed them. Thus the enslaved Joseph Ignacio had never belonged to don Carlos, but had been lent to him, and he therefore had no right to offer him his freedom. Don Matheo also added that even though he had saved his master's life, the enslaved man had probably been only looking out for himself. It had probably been purely coincidental that he had saved don Carlos, and his subsequent acts of defiance toward his superiors surely canceled any former act of ostensible heroism.[34] Legally, if don Carlos had been able to reimburse his mother for the value of the slave, then he could have been granted his freedom; however, it turned out upon examination that don Carlos was insolvent.

In a strange turn of events, don Carlos and Joseph Ignacio appeared before the notary (*escribano*) of Antioquia City at some point between 1772 and January 1774 and signed an agreement on this issue. Since they both recognized that don Carlos really did not have the wherewithal to free Joseph Ignacio, they agreed that don Carlos had to revoke his offer of freedom. Joseph Ignacio voluntarily released him from the agreement with the understanding that the two would pursue this matter again if the time should come that the master, don Carlos, was in a position of wealth; then he would fulfill the promise. The agreement was duly notarized and signed by don Carlos, and Joseph Ignacio made his mark since he could not sign the document.[35] Thereafter Joseph Ignacio continued to serve the Piedrahita family.

By the time that Joseph Ignacio's demand for freedom was brought before the royal court (*real audiencia*), it was 1777. He had pleaded his case before the governor of Antioquia, don Juan Geronimo de Encissa, and then his successor, don Francisco Silvestre. At least Silvestre showed some interest in the case since he ordered don Carlos to appear before the courts to explain his side of the story.[36] However, Joseph Ignacio could not force the provincial judges to move on the case, and when don Carlos failed to make his court appearance, he was able to stall the entire process. In the end Joseph Ignacio had no other recourse but to seek the "sovereign protection" of the royal court, so he made his way to Santa Fé de Bogotá to ask the Procurator of the Poor to take on his case. Within the Spanish legal system, by the latter part of the eighteenth century an enslaved individual could use the institutional mechanisms available to force his or her owner into court, even though it might take much time and persistence.[37] It was only after Joseph Ignacio pursued his case in the viceregal capital with his new owner's permission that don Carlos was finally forced to testify, which he did in 1778. At that time don Carlos stated that yes, he had in fact written the letter, mistakenly offering the slave his freedom. He had done this without reflecting on the fact that Joseph Ignacio did not really belong to him, but rather to his mother, an act of spontaneous generosity. He then added that even if he had owned the slave, he could not have freed him because of all the debts he owed to various individuals and because the slave actually belonged to his mother's dowry and thus was supposed to be inalienable.[38] Later that year, in June 1778, don Carlos's father, don Ignacio Piedrahita, was forced to disclose how many slaves he owned, their names, and their ages as the judges sought to get to the bottom of the case.[39]

One of the major changes that occurred in the legal status of enslaved Africans or their descendants during the eighteenth century was that they gained access to the services of the crown defender (*procurador de pobres* or *procurador defendor de esclavos*). This crown official was charged with presenting the cases of those who could not pay for the services of attorneys. Access to these services by blacks was part of the humanistic trend of the eighteenth century even while the rest of the colonial authorities shored up the traditional system of slavery.[40] Two crown defenders, Josef Antonio Maldonado and Luis Joseph Camacho, presented Joseph Ignacio's case. They provided several interesting interpretations of the series of events that had led to Joseph Ignacio's bid for freedom in the royal courts. First, Maldonado explained how "the donation of liberty in remuneration for an act [such as Joseph Ignacio's saving of don Carlos's life] is not revocable."

He also stated that don Matheo's testimony and letter should not be admissible evidence because don Carlos had told his parents in the very first letter that he wanted to free the enslaved individual and since they did not contradict this, the son could act for the father and a freedom certificate (*carta de libertad*) should be issued for Joseph Ignacio.[41] Later, by 1778, the public defender claimed that in essence Joseph Ignacio had been free since 1772, but because of his good will and his appreciation he had returned to the home of his first owners and worked for them, but not as a slave, simply to show his gratitude.[42]

The relationship between the enslaved Joseph Ignacio and his owners, the Piedrahita family, is never presented in the court records as an antagonistic one. In fact, the events that are described in the documents suggest a surprisingly warm and harmonious relationship between Joseph Ignacio and don Carlos as well as don Carlos's parents. In 1774 the notary (*escribano publico*) of Medellin, Juan Joseph Lotero, wrote that he had known Joseph Ignacio since he was very young. He had always been very humble, obedient, and a loyal slave, to the point that even after he was promised his liberty, he continued to accompany his previous owners, serving them in complete obedience.[43] How, then, did the situation deteriorate to the point where Joseph Ignacio was forced to ask the royal courts (real audiencia) to intercede on his behalf? This is when the dynamics within the Piedrahita family itself played a major role. It seems that at one point, don Joaquin de Piedrahita, don Carlos's brother, ordered Joseph Ignacio to go and get a mule at a distant pasture. Since Joseph Ignacio would have to take the same road as his brother, who was also enslaved by the Piedrahita family and who had been sent on another errand, they decided to go together. Apparently they did not make the trip quickly enough, and upon his return, don Joaquin angrily tried to strike Joseph Ignacio with a stick to punish him. Joseph Ignacio grabbed the stick from him in order to protect himself and told him, "You are not my master; my master is señor don Carlos." As he was walking away, the enraged don Joaquin took out a knife and tried to stab him in the back but was prevented from doing so by another of his brothers. The fact that Joseph Ignacio's brother was also enslaved by the Piedrahita family may have influenced his decision to stay on with them even after he had been theoretically freed. However, it is evident from this altercation that he felt a particular affinity to don Carlos, an affinity that did not extend to don Joaquin.

Naturally don Joaquin could not allow this affront to his dignity to go unchallenged, and so, according to his father, they agreed to punish Joseph

Ignacio, tying him to a cartwheel and whipping him. In spite of this, don Joaquin was not satisfied, and he ran to inform his uncle, don Matheo, about what had happened. According to the father's testimony, at that point don Matheo behaved with despotic authority. He came and took the enslaved Joseph Ignacio away and sold him to doña Catherina Velasquez as a further punishment.[44] Don Ignacio's testimony helps us to situate the antagonistic feelings between the brothers-in-law. He indicated that don Matheo had sold the slave against don Ignacio's will and then, to add insult to injury, had kept the money from the sale.[45] All of this had occurred before 1774. It was in November of that year that doña Velasquez signed a statement that she was granting Joseph Ignacio permission to appear before the courts in order to pursue his interests.[46] Joseph Ignacio thereafter began the long process of trying to get the manumission document out of the Piedrahita family, once it became evident that he had been betrayed in his expectations that the family would freely grant him his liberty. This case helps to highlight the precarious nature of the bonds that enslaved individuals could develop with their owners as well as how they could get caught up and used as pawns in family disputes.

The relations between male and female in colonial society are also touched upon in this case. This issue was broached in don Matheo's letter, when he informed the courts that Joseph Ignacio belonged to his sister's dowry. Despite this, the only litigants who appear in the case are the male family members. Doña Gertrudis's interests were discussed by her husband, brother, and sons in this patriarchic society. Her brother portrayed her as a helpless, easily duped, weak creature. In a very ironic twist, Joseph Ignacio equated a slave's legal rights to a married woman's situation. One of his dispositions stated that "when the slave litigates for his freedom he can appear on his own behalf before the law in the same way that a married woman who has no one to appear in law for her to deal with matters of her dowry can."[47] Again the use of such a concept was a double-edged sword. While Joseph Ignacio made the point that his use of the courts was a legitimate act, to justify his case he had to undermine his own masculinity and approach the courts as a married woman would. This example demonstrates the way gender constructions were, to a degree, a metaphor of the relations between ethnicity and race in colonial society and the relative power that particular individuals could be expected to exercise. These issues were mirrored in the ways Spaniards depicted indigenous groups and enslaved Africans, with Africans generally occupying an intermediary position between the masculine Europeans and the feminized indigenous males.[49]

Finally, after many years of persistence and having fled to Santa Fé de Bogotá, Joseph Ignacio's case was closed. On August 26, 1778, don Carlos was ordered to give him his freedom letter, and if doña Gertrudis Alvares's dowry was to suffer, she should recoup the amount from her son don Carlos. In the end, the racial divisions that had flared up in the Antioqueño Mountains when Native Americans attacked the white mine owner had provided the opportunity for Joseph Ignacio to make the first steps down the long and tortuous road to his freedom. He seized the possibility with his defense of the Spaniard and was able to transform that action into his liberty.

POPULAR POLITICAL CULTURE

Though by the end of the eighteenth century enslaved Africans could lay claim to some legal protection as we have seen above, historically indigenous groups had enjoyed many more legal rights in colonial Nueva Granada than legally enslaved Africans.[49] The long history of Spanish legislation, of course, did not always provide even minimal protection for Native Americans, but it helped to shape the worldviews of the colonized. Thus in New Spain a native could state that he was a "vassal and tributary of His Majesty" and conclude that he was owed protection.[50] The institutional protection offered indigenous groups could sometimes appear rather attractive to other marginalized individuals in colonial society. For example, in 1780 Francisco Mora tried to pass himself off as a Native American, although the corregidor testified that he knew him and his parents and they were reputed to be whites, without any native mixture. In the end, the protector stated that Francisco Mora had claimed to be a native so as to gain access to the court's protector for naturales, though why he sought to do this remains unclear.[51]

In many cases, any benefits that indigenous groups might gain in their struggle to maintain themselves under the weight of colonial oppression were at the expense of the imported African population. By the end of the eighteenth century Africans and their descendants were at least nominally protected by law, although the application of those laws varied hugely in time and place.[52] This codification of general customs and accepted practices finally promulgated in the Instruction from Aranjuez in 1789 led to the creation of offices such as the procurador defendor de esclavos discussed above. The general underlying assumption behind this codification was that there were accepted practices within colonial society. The notion that local custom and justice (*equidad*) should be upheld by the colonial courts was pervasive throughout Spanish colonial society.[53] Historians have noted an escalating number of acts of insubordination by the enslaved by the end of the eighteenth century, possibly because slave owners were failing to uphold the requisite norms within the slave system.[54] Certainly the enslaved on former Jesuit haciendas used the argument that traditional customs and rights were being undermined by their new owners in order to litigate against them and in some cases to justify their rebellion against those owners.[55]

Both indigenous groups and enslaved Africans were quick to learn the various options opened to them by the Spanish legal system. While indigenous communities and Africans in Nueva Granada may have had a common cause in their exploitation by whites, the concerns that they brought before the courts differed because of the varying ways they were exploited by the Spanish or by each other. By the end of the eighteenth century many indigenous communal lands were under attack, and the Native Americans tenaciously used the courts to try to protect their property, as in the case of the indigenous town of Coyaima, cited at the outset of this chapter. They also complained of abuses by royal officials who theoretically existed to protect them and, very often, of abuse by their priests. Enslaved Africans, on the other hand, resorted to the courts to gain their freedom, as in the case of Joseph Ignacio, or to beg the courts to force their owners to treat them better, or to sell them to other masters. Thus the types of exploitation to which they were subjected had a racial component because of the legal, cultural, and productive context of the exploitation.

In spite of the obvious potential areas of conflict between indigenous and African in the Spanish colonial context, as well as the different interests with which they were concerned, these two subordinated groups were willing to use the Spanish legal system. The language with which they presented their cases hints at an underlying popular political culture that transcended race, ethnicity, status, and class within the Spanish imperial system.[56] Acts of insubordination like the creation of maroon communities by runaway Africans, court challenges demanding freedom like in Joseph Ignacio's case, and the Coyaimas' continued legal challenges against the officials in charge of managing their communities indicate an underlying understanding about the possibilities for redress that existed in the Spanish legal system and within the Imperial compact—as well as the limits to those possibilities.

The Spanish colonial legal system was predicated upon the notion of the judicial figure of the king. Within this paradigm the monarch was the impartial and benevolent arbiter who would see that justice was done.[57]

This type of philosophy also existed in Brazil and in the British Caribbean, where enslaved Africans looked to the king as a protector against abuses by their owners.[58] Indigenous groups were known to be highly litigious in the eighteenth century, and in using the courts they employed a language designed to reflect their acceptance of their place within colonial society and the role of the king as their protector. At times they implied very strongly that when they were treated unjustly, it was at the expense of the king's authority, since he was their benevolent father and they his obedient vassals. It was in this vein that several individuals from Coyaima complained about the persecution they were suffering at the hands of their corregidor and his friends. "They have no respect for you and for the protection that has been given us by our king and natural lord."[59] They finished their plea by emphasizing that "in this sad state of anxiety we have no other refuge and consolation after God and we attach ourselves to your powerful protection, asking and begging, prostrated at your feet."[60]

Indigenous and African had to accept on some level that they somehow belonged to the colonial world that was imposed upon them, but they also molded that world through their acts of resistance and accommodation. To gain greater access to the assumptions and understandings that subordinated groups held in this colonial context, we can examine the language that they used in presenting their pleas to the courts. Naturally we must consider that this language may have been imposed upon the supplicants by the scribes and officials who wrote up their cases and presented them to the courts. But there may very well have been cases where these were the words offered by the enslaved and the oppressed themselves. At the very least we can suggest that they recognized an underlying logic to the paternal language that was used and sought to push the rhetoric of the king as the head of a family that included all his subjects. And if the king was not accessible, then his representatives, even at the lowest levels, were viewed and addressed in familial terms. As late as 1805, the *teniente de naturales* (the town representative) of the indigenous town of Coyaima wrote to the corregidor stating that the Amerindians were being abused by a colonial official, and in signing the letter, he finished with the plea, "We have no other father to which we can turn."[61] Joseph Ignacio Piedrahita also referred to the protector as a "father in which miserable persons like me encounter our refuge and protection."[62] Besides this, when the enslaved Joseph Ignacio made his statement about how the enslaved were like married women before the law, he indicated very straightforwardly that he knew that the law was supposed to serve and protect his rights. He also had a strong opinion about how his saving of his master's life should be interpreted legally. He suggested that when a slave risked his own life to save his master's, he deserved to be compensated with his freedom.[63]

Sometimes enslaved Africans used the justice system in surprising ways. For example, in 1790 the owner of the hacienda Melgar, don Josef Ygnacio de San Miguel, complained to the judges of the real audiencia that five of his slaves had run away to Santa Fé de Bogotá and surrendered themselves to the public prison of that city. They complained that their owner did not feed them, that they had too much work, that he punished them excessively, and that when they were sick, he did not have them treated.[64] As noted above, one of the trends in this period was that there were accepted norms of behavior for slave owners, and while they were able to extract the surplus of their enslaved property, they could not go beyond certain limits. At this point the five slaves chose to seek justice within the colonial legal system, trusting in that system to correct their owner's behavior or to protect them. Their defender suggested that it would be appropriate to protect these unhappy beings, especially since the owner was acting in contravention to the royal order regarding the treatment of the enslaved.[65] Again Joseph Ignacio provides us with more of the imagery with which popular groups may have envisioned the legal system and the crown when he stated that he was "prostrated before your feet with the most profound respect applying to your innate piety as a source of justice and where there is the certain shelter that the poor and disvalued solicit."[66] Again the protector to whom he was applying reinforced the notion that a particular code of behavior was expected from slave owners. He wrote that "to deny the black and oppose his liberty would never be well viewed."[67]

CONCLUSION

The fact that indigenous communities and blacks were willing to use the colonial legal system may have been a reflection of their desperation and their exhaustion of other alternatives. However, it is also a testimony to the complexities of racial relations in colonial Nueva Granada and to the underlying assumptions that fashioned that colonial world. Those assumptions helped shape a political culture that could transcend race and ethnicity as defining categories and functioned to help theorize the practical relations that were worked out, fought over, and negotiated over time within these communities. Since members of indigenous communities and enslaved Africans and their descendants persisted in their use of the colonial legal system, they helped to legitimize that system, but at times they also were able to benefit from it. Their use of paternal language and their claims for justice helped to concretize the rhetoric of colonialism. Meanwhile, the language used by their defenders indicates that there were accepted norms that applied to the ways individuals, notwithstanding their race, should be treated, and when these were transgressed, the entire social body was threatened.

Relationships between indigenous groups and Africans were based on far more than irreconcilable racial and ethnic antagonisms. On some occasions individuals from the subordinate levels of society acted together to evade the Spanish colonizers and at other times they acted against each other. Those moments when Africans and Native Americans attacked each other are rife with tinges of spontaneity and opportunism that belie the interpretation that the two groups were inherently antagonistic. This relatively intangible element that pervades many of the examples of relations between these groups should give us pause when we analyze racial tensions. As individuals fell into or were pushed into potentially confrontational situations by the Spaniards, they saw the opportunities that suddenly appeared and sought to maximize the benefits they could obtain. This element of chance helps explain the often contradictory reactions that characterized the relationships between indigenous groups and those of African origin in colonial New Granada.

ᘒᘒ

NOTES

1. Archivo General de la Nación, Bogotá, Colombia (hereafter AGN-C), *Colonia, Caciques y Indios*, Tomo 59, fl. 554 (translations are by the author): "Que nuestro corregidor... colgarse con los Blancos y mulattos nuestros enemigos que nos quieren quitar nuestras tierras...."

2. Roy Wagner, *The Invention of Culture* (Chicago: University of Chicago Press, 1975).

3. In discussing the notion of a popular political culture shaped and influenced by the hegemonic dominant culture, we must take into account that dominance can never fully penetrate every level of daily life and all of the interstices of a society. For a poignant discussion of this issue, see Bejamín Arditi, *El Deseo de la Libertad y la Cuestión del Otro: Ensayos acerca de la Posmodernidad, el Poder y la Sociedad* (Asunción: Criterio Ediciones, 1989), 75.

4. This case is in AGN-C, *Negros y Esclavos de Panama*, Tomo IV, fls. 5r–6v.

5. AGN-C, *Colonia, Caciques y Indios*, Tomo 29, fls. 732–42.

6. This case is cited in Margarita Garrido, *Reclamos y representaciones: Variaciones sobre la política en el Nuevo Reino de Granada. 1770–1815* (Bogotá: Banco de la Republica, 1995), 242–43.

7. AGN-C, *Colonia, Caciques y Indios*, Tomo 29, fl. 737: "El dicho mi parte es christiano temeroso de dios nuestro senor y de su conciencia y de quien no se puede presumir lo contro respeta de lo dicho como por ser Negro que trata verdad. . . ."

8. Cited in Pablo Rodríguez, *Sentimientos y vida familiar en el Nuevo Reino de Granada* (Santa Fé de Bogotá: Editorial Ariel, 1997), 177.

9. See Nina S. de Friedmann, *La Saga del Negro: Presencia Africana en Colombia* (Bogotá: Instituto de Genetica Humana, Facultad de Medecina, Pontificia Universidad Javeriana, 1993), 66.

10. Mateo Mina, *Esclavitud y Libertad en el Valle del Río Cauca* (Bogotá: Fundición Rosca de Investigación y Acción Social, 1975), 33.

11. See Rebecca B. Bateman, "Africans and Indians: A Comparative Study of the Black Carib and Black Seminole," in *Slavery and Beyond: The African Impact on Latin America and the Caribbean*, ed. Darién J. Davis (Wilmington, Del.: Jaguar Books on Latin America, Scholarly Resources, Inc., 1995), 30, and Adolfo Meisel Roca, "Esclavitud, mestizaje y haciendas en la Provincia de Cartagena 1533–1851," in *El Caribe Colombiano: Selección de textos históricos*, comp. by Gustavo Bell Lemus (Barranquilla: Ediciones Uninorte, 1988), 119. See also Virginia Gutiérrez Pineda and Roberto Pineda Giraldo, *Miscegenación y cultura: La Colombia Colonial, 1750–1810* (Santa Fé de Bogotá: Ediciones Uniandes, 1999), 48.

12. See Stuart B. Schwartz, *Slaves, Peasants, and Rebels: Reconsidering Brazilian Slavery* (Urbana and Chicago: University of Illinois Press, 1992), 110.

13. Gutiérrez Pineda and Pineda Giraldo, *Miscegenación y cultura*, 35.

14. Ordinance from 1558, cited in ibid.

15. See Lance Grahn, *The Political Economy of Smuggling: Regional Informal Economies in Early Bourbon New Granada* (Boulder, Colo.: Westview Press, Dellplain Latin American Studies, no. 34, 1997), 70.

16. See the discussion of a Citara rebellion in 1684 in Caroline A. Williams, "Resistance and Rebellion on the Spanish Frontier: Native Responses to Colonization in the Colombian Choco, 1670–1690," *Hispanic American Historical Review* vol. 79, no. 3 (1999): 417.

17. Adolfo Triana Antorveza, "Estado-Nación y Minorias Etnicas," in *Grupos Etnicos, Derecho y Cultura* (Bogotá: Funcol-Quadernos del Jaguar, 1987), 116.

18. David Ernesto Peñas Galindo, *Los Bogas de Mompox: Historia del Zambaje* (Bogotá: Tercer Mundo Editores, 1988), 8, 50. See also the discussion of this issue in Jorge Conde Calderón, *Espacio, Sociedad y Conflictos en la Provincia de Cartagena, 1740–1815* (Barranquilla: Artes Gráficas Industriales, 1999), 107.

19. Adolfo Meisel Roca, "Esclavitud," 101, 119.

20. Angela Inés Guzmán, *Poblamiento e Historias Urbanas del Alto Magdalena, Tolima: Siglos XVI, XVII, XVIII* (Santa Fé de Bogotá: Eco Ediciones, 1996), 109.

21. Ibid., 99.

22. AGN-C, *Colonia, Caciques y Indios*, Tomo 62, fls. 91–94.

23. AGN-C, *Colonia, Negros y Esclavos del Tolima*, Tomo II, fl. 8.

24. Ibid., fl. 523.

25. Gutiérrez Pineda and Pineda Giraldo, *Miscegenación y cultura*, 211. In another case, the hideout of runaway slaves was betrayed by an indigenous person in 1785 after a punitive expedition was organized by the alcalde of Cerritos in the area of the Cocama. See Hermes Tovar Pinzon, "De una chispa se forma una hoguera: Esclavitud, insubordinación y liberación (1780–1821)," *Nuevas Lecturas de Historia*, no. 17 (1992): 29.

26. For an interesting discussion of the cultural developments occurring during the eighteenth century in this part of Nueva Granada, see Erik Werner Cantor, *Ni Aniquilados, Ni Vencidos: Los Emberá y la gente negra del Atrato bajo el dominio español, siglo XVIII* (Bogotá: Instituto Colombiano de Antropología e Historia, 2000), 135, 185. Interestingly, in the latter case, where two enslaved men murdered an indigenous family, one of them had established ties of fictive kinship with the family.

27. Ibid., 186.

28. AGN-C, *Colonia, Negros y Esclavos del Magdalena*, Tomo IV, fls. 303v–305.

29. AGN-C, *Colonia, Negros y Esclavos de Antioquia*, Tomo II, fls. 674–762. For a comprehensive study of this region during the eighteenth century, see Ann Twinam, *Miners, Merchants and Farmers in Colonial Colombia* (Austin: University of Texas Press, 1982).

30. AGN-C, *Colonia, Negros y Esclavos de Antioquia*, Tomo II., fls. 674v–675.

31. As noted above, though, in certain circumstances the concept of ethnicity was not a fundamental element in determining the relations people established. "Significantly, illicit trade in northern New Granada cut across both class and ethnic lines" (Grahn, *Political Economy of Smuggling*, 189).

32. AGN-C, *Colonia, Negros y Esclavos de Antioquia*, Tomo II, fls. 686–87.

33. Ibid., fl. 677v. The use of this diminutive indicates the way enslaved individuals were viewed as children who needed the guidance and paternalistic care of their owners.

34. Ibid., fl. 677.

35. Ibid., fls. 686–87.

36. Ibid., fl. 691.

37. See Jane Landers, "African-American Women and Their Pursuit of Rights through Eighteenth-Century Spanish Texts," in *Haunted Bodies: Gender and Southern Texts*, ed. Anne Goodwyn Jones and Susan V. Donaldson (Charlottesville and London: University Press of Virginia, 1997), 68.

38. AGN-C, *Colonia, Negros y Esclavos de Antioquia*, Tomo II, fl. 756.

39. Ibid., fl. 733.

40. Gutiérrez Pineda and Pineda Giraldo, *Miscegenación y cultura*, 2, 43. The institution of the procurador defensor de esclavos is considered by these authors as having been the vanguard of the legal advances made by blacks in this period (46).

41. AGN-C, *Colonia, Negros y Esclavos de Antioquia*, Tomo II, ffs. 691–691v.

42. Ibid., f. 758.

43. Ibid., f. 741.

44. Ibid., fls. 680–680v.

45. Ibid., fl. 703.

46. Ibid., fl. 674.

47. Ibid., fl. 679.

48. Laura A. Lewis, "Colonialism and Its Contradictions: Indians, Blacks and Social Power in Sixteenth and Seventeenth Century Mexico," *Journal of Historical Sociology* 9, no. 4 (December 1996): 419.

49. de Friedmann, *La Saga del Negro*, 59, and Peter Wade, *Gente negra, nación mestiza: Dinámicas de las identidades raciales en Colombia*, trans. Ana Cristina Mejia (Bogotá: Ediciones Uniandes, 1997), first published as *Blackness and Race Mixture: The Dynamics of Racial Identity in Colombia* (Baltimore: Johns Hopkins University Press, 1993), 63.

50. Cited in Lewis, "Colonialism and Its Contradictions," 415.

51. This case is in AGN-C, *Colonia, Caciques y Indios*, Tomo 43, fs. 487–505v.

52. For a discussion of the different types of cases brought before the courts by enslaved Africans, see Renée Soulodre-La France, "Socially Not So Dead! Slave Identities in Bourbon Nueva Granada," *Colonial Latin American Review* 10, no. 1 (2001): 87–103. For further examples of how people of African descent used the Spanish legal system, see Margaret M. Olsen, "Negros horros and Cimarrones on the Legal Frontiers of the Caribbean: Accessing the African Voice in Colonial Spanish American Texts," *Research in African Literatures: The African Diaspora and Its Origins* 29, no. 4 (winter 1998): 52–71.

53. Charles Cutter, *The Legal Culture of Northern New Spain, 1700–1810* (Albuquerque: University of New Mexico Press, 1995), 43. This notion is very similar to that presented by E. P. Thompson in "Moral Economy of the English Crowd in the Eighteenth Century," *Past and Present* 50 (February 1971): 76–136.

54. Tovar Pinzon, "De una chispa," 18. See also Gutiérrez Pineda and Pineda Giraldo, *Miscegenación y cultura*, 43.

55. See, for example, the cases discussed in Renée Soulodre-La France, "'Los Esclavos de su Magestad!' Slave Protest and Politics on Jesuit Haciendas in Late Colonial New Granada," in *Slaves, Subjects, and Subversives: Blacks in Colonial Latin America*, ed. Jane Landers (Albuquerque: University of New Mexico Press, forthcoming).

56. Lewis, "Colonialism and Its Contradictions," 416. This author suggests that a "legal consciousness" had developed in colonial society.

57. Cutter, *Legal Culture*, 48.

58. A. J. R. Russell-Wood, "'Acts of Grace': Portuguese Monarchs and Their Subjects of African Descent in Eighteenth-Century Brazil," *Journal of Latin American Studies* 32 (May 2000): 332. Russell-Wood suggests that the use of the legal system by the enslaved in Brazil "may have reflected an almost paternalistic notion of monarchy in which an individual monarch was responsible for the well-being of his individual subjects."

59. AGN-C, *Colonia, Caciques y Indios*, Tomo 59, fls. 554–55. "Sin tener respeto a la autoridad de usted y amparo que nos franquea Nuestro Rey y Senor Natural."

60. Ibid., "En tan lastimosa constitucion y angusta no no queda despues de Dios otro refugio y consuelo que acogernos al podoroso amparo de usted como lo egecutamos pidiendo y clamando postrados a los Pies de usted."

61. AGN-C, *Colonia, Caciques y Indios*, Tomo 43, fls. 355–56, "No tenemos otro padre a quien apelar."

62. AGN-C, *Colonia, Negros y Esclavos de Antioquia*, Tomo II, fs. 682.

63. Ibid., fls. 682–682v.

64. AGN-C, *Colonia, Negros y Esclavos del Tolima*, Tomo IV, fl. 529–31.

65. Ibid., fl. 530.

66. AGN-C, *Colonia, Negros y Esclavos de Antioquia*, Tomo II, fl. 684v.

67. Ibid., fl. 759v, "Mas negarle al Negro y oponerse a su libertad nunca seria bien visto."

CHAPTER SIX

Africans and Natives in the Mines of Spanish America

KRIS LANE

ᘉᘉ

In 1643 word reached Quito, modern capital of Ecuador, of a knife fight
between two women in the main church of Santa María del Puerto, a
small gold-mining camp now called Barbacoas, Colombia. Apparently
Juana de la Cruz, a gold mine owner's wife, had attacked an indigenous or
mestiza woman named Bárbara Pérez, slashing her across the face with a
knife and calling her a variety of names, all beginning with *puta* ("whore").

The scuffle, which took place in full view of many witnesses, including a
horrified priest and several slaves, was apparently over charges of bona fide
prostitution. Doña Juana exclaimed to an *alcalde*, or town official, who tried
to break up the fight: "Allow me, Your Mercy, Señor, to settle up with this
Indian bitch who let my husband take her skirt off, the little slave trader!"[1]

Various witnesses claimed that they had heard doña Juana's denunciations of Bárbara Pérez at other times. She had said: "That innkeeper's
whore goes out to the mines, looking after the six or seven lovers that she
has," and, "She should have been cut when Francisco Serrano caught her

with the mulatto Pedro Sánchez, who was found on top of her."² Juana de la Cruz's insulting terms, which everyone agreed were "very injurious" and even "too ugly to repeat," included the words *tambera* (*tambo-*, or innkeeper), *mulatera* (mule driver/keeper), *negrera* (slave trader), *buzamona*, and _pechera. Though clearly tinged with racism, all these terms were essentially status- or class-based insults, the most blatant being *pechera*, literally: "tribute-paying commoner."

To be called a tribute payer, an innkeeper, a mule skinner, and a slave trader (the meaning of *buzamona* is unclear) was apparently every bit as damaging in this seventeenth-century Colombian gold camp as being called a prostitute.³ Bárbara Pérez, more than a "hypocrite, deflowerer of hypocrites," was denounced as a commoner, a member of the vile plebe, and furthermore an Indian.

Meanwhile, in the faraway silver mines of Zacatecas, Mexico, a slave named Juan de Morga was struggling to survive. Morga, the illegitimate son of a Spanish-born priest and an African woman, had been sold to a Mexico City accountant while still in his teens.⁴ Literate, of mixed heritage, said to be handsome, he might have lived in relative comfort in the bustling viceregal capital. After all, Mexico City, like many other urban centers in colonial Spanish America, had a substantial population of mulatto footmen and artisans. Their *cofradías*, or religious confraternities, were active and highly visible in urban ritual and everyday social life.

But Juan de Morga, like most teenagers, cherished freedom more than security, and whenever he could, he ran away, sometimes for months on end. Exasperated, his bookkeeper-master sold him to the mines (roughly Spanish America's equivalent of being sold downriver) in 1646. In Zacatecas, Morga would experience the darkest horrors of the slave system. His new owner, a petty mining and milling contractor named Diego de Arratia, was apparently a sadist. Arratia would punish his young slave's willful temperament almost daily.

By his early twenties Juan de Morga had been successively slashed across the face, branded, publicly flogged, dragged behind a horse, confined in shackles for extended periods, and beaten about the mouth with a hammer (to break his teeth). The ordinary horrors of mine and mill work, discussed in detail below, were almost irrelevant in this case. In fact, according to Morga's later testimony, it was during work stints at sites like the Little Creek Mine and adjacent mills that he pondered suicide. Once he imagined placing his head beneath the powerful hammers of a water-driven stamp mill, on another occasion of leaping into a mine shaft deep within the mountain.

Finding himself incapable of suicide, Morga ran away to Mexico City to petition for a new master (Spanish law required investigation of *sevicia*, or excessive punishment claims). Rejected, even by initially helpful Mercedarian priests, and ultimately recaptured by bounty hunters sent by Arratia, Morga returned to Zacatecas to face new torments. An attempt at suicide by self-poisoning failed along the way.

Having exhausted all avenues of escape, Juan de Morga did the unthinkable: he sold his soul to the devil. Apparently a sympathetic indigenous shaman and fellow mine worker in Zacatecas, having witnessed Morga's ongoing predicament, had advised total renunciation of God and the saints. About his neck Morga was to wear a small protective pouch filled with herbs. Incredulous, he found that the shaman's magic worked; Arratia's sadism seemed positively checked.

By early 1650, however, Morga began to doubt his choice. A baptized Catholic and son of a priest, he feared for his soul. Yet as soon as he destroyed the talisman and began making plans to confess, he sensed the return of his master's wrath. In response, Morga stole a horse and escaped, first to the northern desert, then to the south. At Jilotepec, north of Mexico City, he was captured and detained. Only Morga's literacy and—ironically now—the strange story of his temporarily successful Faustian bargain could save him. He was given paper and quill by a local magistrate, and he quickly penned a detailed confession. As a measure of his desperation, Morga asked to be investigated by the Holy Office of the Inquisition.

For some reason, the confession letter was not delivered. Again desperate, Morga shifted to drama: he threw himself wildly into faked bouts of demon possession. Frightened by this horribly scarred, possessed, and apparently dangerous man, the town officials of Jilotepec at last delivered Juan de Morga to Mexico City's inquisitors. His case was heard and a number of testimonies taken. Several witnesses supported Morga's chronic abuse claims against Arratia. Ultimately persuaded that this wretched youth was more victim than backslider or heretic, the Inquisition used its enormous influence to force his sale. Persistence and suffering at last compensated, albeit in a small way, Morga was moved to Mexico City to join the retinue of a wealthy householder.

Though perhaps atypically dramatic, the cases of Juan de Morga and Juana de la Cruz highlight features of midcolonial life in Spanish America's many and scattered precious-metals mining camps. Beneath the violent surface are hints of day-to-day work regimes; of local demography, economy, and religion; and of various forms of social and sexual interaction. Both cases suggest frequent—sometimes amiable, sometimes antagonistic—contact between men and women of African and indigenous heritage.

This chapter examines first African-indigenous interaction in Spanish American gold camps, beginning with the Caribbean and moving south through the Andes. Discussion of gold camp life centers on what is known to date about demography, work conditions, technical exchange, and social interaction. Part two of the chapter continues with these same themes, but treats Spanish American silver towns, focusing first on the well-researched cities of Zacatecas (Mexico) and Potosí (Bolivia), then on life in the more marginal camps of the Andes and Central America.

A few generalizations are worth making beforehand. First, over the course of the colonial period most silver mining was carried out by coerced (but not enslaved) indigenous workers and most gold mining by African slaves and their descendants. That said, there was considerable overlap of these populations in both the goldfields and silver mines, with notable change over time. Second, since much more silver than gold was ultimately produced, silver mining has been most intensively studied. Less is known about gold-industry labor patterns, productivity, and so forth. Finally, silver mines tended to be located in the remote, dry, and often cold high-country interior of Spanish America, whereas gold mines were mostly distributed in lower, hotter, and wetter zones. African-indigenous interaction would be greatly inflected, if not determined, by these geographical and demographic tendencies.

GOLD

Although not as central to the huge Spanish imperial enterprise as the more famous silver mines in the long run, it was in the goldfields of the Caribbean basin and north Andes that indigenous and African miners came into the most frequent and often sustained contact. Similar, isolated cases of gold mine camaraderie could be found in sixteenth-century Peru and western Mexico, but this sort of mixing was the rule rather than exception in the vast and scattered goldfields of what is now Colombia. Before this area was developed, however, the Spanish established numerous gold mines on the islands of Hispaniola, Cuba, Puerto Rico, and in various river basins dotting the circum-Caribbean mainland. With few exceptions these mines were exhausted within a few decades of discovery. Still, they lasted long enough to serve as mine-labor testing grounds and important cultural interfaces.

The Caribbean Crucible

Having visited Portuguese slaving and gold posts in West Africa, Christopher Columbus set the tone for Spanish American colonization by obsessing constantly over Caribbean gold.[5] Unfortunately for the native peoples of the region, and soon after for a steady stream of West Africans, he found it. The location of gold deposits in northern Hispaniola, in particular, touched off a mad rush to the island's rugged interior, mostly centered on the hill districts of Cibao and San Cristóbal.

As Dominican historian Frank Moya Pons has noted, a genuine gold economy took shape on Hispaniola as early as 1499, relying principally on enslaved indigenous labor. The theoretically ameliorative *encomienda* was being tried by the time of the Ovando administration (1502–1509), but already Africans were being transshipped to join native miners as well.

Within a dozen years of Columbus's landfall, West Africans and Caribbean natives were working side by side, digging and panning for gold. These work gangs included not only male miners, although men predominated, but also females, skilled women (and probably also girls) who were entrusted with the *batea*, or wooden gold-pan cleanup. This, the final separation of gold dust from black sand, was the most critical stage of gold placering.[6]

In outline, placering for gold was simple: one located, excavated, and washed gold-bearing stream deposits, then melted the resulting gold particles—sifted with the aid of gravity—into bars. Even in dust form, gold circulated freely as money. Word of such "easy money" got out quickly, and many Spaniards headed for the Indies to dig for treasure (or rather, to try to find someone else to dig it for them). Close on their heels came crown officials acting as magistrates, assayers, and tax collectors.

When compared with silver mining, universally an underground affair yielding fairly impure ores, gold placering entailed much less investment in equipment, chemicals, and fixed capital like tunnels and vents. Consequently, gold mining of this sort was extraordinarily attractive, especially to those lacking technical skills and money.

To their chagrin, European fortune seekers quickly discovered that viable gold placering was by no means as simple or cheap as it appeared. There was the problem of finding reliable deposits, of course, and also of defending oneself against claim jumpers and other enemies, but an even more fundamental truth emerged: in order to be profitable over any stretch of time, gold washing required massive inputs of labor. Whether one preferred Native American or African workers or some combination (white

Come les esclaues naigres trauaillent ẽ cherchẽ l'or aux mynũ en la terre nommuẽ Beauguel

Ceste terre est fort dangereuze les naigres y viuent peu de temps ꝯ ni se passent Jour ꝯ nuit qui ne pleuuẽt auẽ grands esclairs ꝯ tonnuerre Couse ꝯ Jaelle terre est proche de la ligne ẽquinoctialle estant peu fertille en blena Mais yal grand nombre de bon or Le Roy des paigne permect aux espaignols qui som aux yndes de si habituit pẽfaire minũ ꝯ auoir l'or estant en Jaelle ꝯ luy paians la cin q ẽ payhe de tribus de Xonis ꝯ ẽ ꝯ deuenent fans d'or argẽt que piorurie

FIG. 6.1: *Illustration of gold panning from* Histoire Naturelle des Indes, *a French edition of Gonzalo Fernández de Oviedo's* Historia General y Natural de las Indias *of 1535. Reproduced courtesy of The Pierpont Morgan Library, New York (MA3900 f. 100).*

slaves and indentures being unavailable in the Spanish colonies), in gold-mining scale was key. Yet the more miners one employed, the more mouths to feed, bodies to house and clothe, and so on.

Gonzalo Fernández de Oviedo, among the first chroniclers of Spanish American colonialism, devoted considerable attention to the early Caribbean gold cycle. Oviedo, who served for a time as crown smeltery officer on Hispaniola, observed that at least four support workers were needed for every miner; thus "ten bateas" translated into fifty "*indios*." Under this formula only prominent encomenderos and large-scale enslavers of Africans and alleged Carib cannibals (i.e., the only legally enslaveable native peoples of the Caribbean and surrounding mainland) could expect to profit from gold mining.

But could these larger operators strike the right balance and keep the gold flowing? Excepting all other limiting factors, the rudimentary farming and food preservation technologies of the day alone meant that long-term mining enterprises would be difficult or at least very expensive to sustain. It was thus proposed, by Queen Isabella herself, that indigenous labor be reserved for agriculture, with surplus manioc and other produce used to feed gangs of enslaved African miners.

Arrangements would never play out this neatly on the ground, but Portuguese slavers with ties to Seville responded immediately to crown and colonist demands for bonded African labor. Oviedo remarked that within a generation of Spanish arrival on Hispaniola, West Africans outnumbered native islanders in several districts. That "Guinea blacks" should be made to mine gold in the so-called torrid zone of the Spanish Indies struck many contemporary European observers as a natural development. What of the miners' point of view?

As noted above, the early goldfields were not strictly a man's world. Men almost universally excavated riverbanks with iron tools, but panners, as Oviedo noted, were "for the most part Indian or black women." It is possible—even likely—that some enslaved West African women had prior experience in the great Bambuk, Bouré, and Akan fields of the upper Senegal, upper Niger, and middle Volta rivers, respectively.[7] On a darker note, since mercury was already being employed in the cleanup, these women were probably among the first American miners to suffer the crippling effects of this insidious toxin. It is not unreasonable to assume, furthermore, that a number of mining-camp children, indigenous, African, and mixed, were born with mercury-related neurological problems.

Always the keen observer, Oviedo also noted that many African men brought to work in the mines of Hispaniola quickly adopted the native practice of tobacco smoking, citing its powers to suppress appetite and fatigue. Oviedo was for some reason outraged by this bit of native-African cultural exchange, comparing tobacco smoking to the supposedly repugnant ancient Scythian practice of inhaling cannabis fumes.[8] The colonial record is silent on lung ailments and mouth cancers, but probably few miners lived long enough to die from the effects of tobacco.

Before one assumes that all Caribbean mining was gold panning of the crudest sort, the Puerto Real mines of Hispaniola deserve mention. Archaeologists have recently described early underground gold-copper works east of modern Cap Haitien, Haiti. Here at the fringe of one of the earliest municipalities to be established in the Americas, the Spanish combined African and indigenous slave labor to extract copper ore as early as 1505. King Ferdinand himself was said to have sent seventeen African slaves to help start the project.[9] In following initially mineral-rich veins into bedrock, the Puerto Real mines went deep underground. Gold was at first a significant by-product, but the deposits seem to have played out entirely by the 1520s. It was undoubtedly here that Africans and Native Americans toiled underground together for the first time.

Ferdinand apparently ignored the advice of Juan de Ayala, an early Hispaniola settler who recommended in a 1503 letter that no more Africans be sent to the island. Ayala complained that these unwilling transatlantic sojourners were already fleeing "to the Indians among the forests" in groups.[10] There is also suggestion of African slaves engaging in theft, a principal means of subsistence for so-called maroon groups from here forward. Ayala advocated forced indigenous mine labor via two institutions: *repartimiento*, or government-mandated corvées, and slavery—the latter reserved for, as he put it, "the Indians who refuse to obey."

Columbus and his heirs and followers—men like Ayala—were in large part responsible for the speedy depopulation of the Caribbean islands, and their lust for gold, as Las Casas and others later claimed, was also a key factor.[11] In the rush to riches indigenous peoples of various ethnicities were hastily enslaved or otherwise forced to labor in muddy pits from Cuba to Puerto Rico. Their six- to eight-month work stints in the mines entailed concentrated resettlement near contaminated streams, poor nutrition, and frequent physical abuse. The several diseases that ultimately killed the majority of native Caribbean islanders may have been inadvertently introduced by Europeans, but the conditions of mine work no doubt did much to accelerate their spread and deadliness.[12]

The decline in native Caribbean numbers spurred Spanish colonists to import African slaves for mine labor. Population decline was quick and disastrous, such that even Las Casas, for all his championing of Native American rights, initially agreed that African slavery was a legitimate stopgap.

The die was cast. As if following an unalterable script, the Caribbean transition from indigenous slavery to encomienda—then to African slavery—would be repeated elsewhere in Spanish America, in some cases into the early eighteenth century. (For purposes of comparison, similar processes took place in other sectors besides mining, as happened in the Colombian river transport system and Venezuelan cacao industry.[13])

ANDEAN CONTINUUM

Indigenous and African workers shared much the same fate in the goldfields of early Venezuela, Panama, Nicaragua, Honduras, and Mexico, but the region that would emerge from independence as the Republic of Colombia, for a time split between the audiencias, or high courts, of Quito and Bogotá, stood out in this regard.

Geographer Robert West, in his 1952 classic *Colonial Placer Mining in Colombia*, noted that "Western Colombia was the largest mining area in the Spanish colonies in which [African] slaves eventually replaced Indian labor."[14] This seems a straightforward enough observation, but its significance has been routinely overlooked by historians. For our purposes, the long transition from indigenous to African labor in all of colonial Colombia's goldfields made for an unusually large and varied set of opportunities for close interaction, friendly and otherwise.

Conquest-era plunder of indigenous ornaments and funerary offerings in the land of El Dorado quickly led to mining gold at the source. The relatively accessible placers of the vast Cauca and Magdalena drainages were exploited first, but forays and raids soon extended deep into the more forbidding terrain of upper Amazonia, the Central Cordillera, and the wet Pacific coast. Gold was practically everywhere in the north Andes, but nowhere in great concentrations. Major underground, or vein type, gold mines were rare.

As West and others have noted, indigenous demographic decline in Colombia followed the tragic Caribbean script with few variations. Disease, coupled with nearly incessant warfare, alien labor demands, rapid relocation to unfamiliar climates, malnutrition, and a host of other shocks led to near-total annihilation of some indigenous groups. Some, like the Paezes and Pijaos of the Central Cordillera and the Sindaguas and Noanamáes of the Pacific coast, fought tenaciously to keep gold seekers out. Rather like certain Caribs of the Lesser Antilles, they were successful for over a century. Emerald prospectors were similarly harassed by the Muzos and other bellicose groups in the hot country north of Bogotá.[15]

In the southeastern Putumayo and neighboring districts of upper Amazonia, indigenous resistance to colonial prospecting and military expeditions was generally more successful. In many places, such as the Mocoa district east of Pasto, this resistance outlasted the colonial period. A similar mix of outcomes was to be found in the gold-bearing lowlands of eastern Ecuador.

Perhaps the most spectacular resistance to Spanish gold lust and accompanying labor demands outside of Chile emerged in the vast "Jívaro" heartland east of Cuenca and Loja (southern Ecuador). It appears that by about 1620, if not before, the Shuar, Achuar, and other Jivaroan speakers had overwhelmed a half dozen or so isolated mining camps, some of them capable of producing tens of thousands of ounces of twenty-three-karat gold annually. We know that African slaves were present here as early as 1549, but only a few fragmentary account books from these lost, early colonial mines remain.[16]

On balance, more indigenous peoples lost than won in the long struggle for control of the north Andes. By the second half of the sixteenth century, colonial officials throughout the region petitioned King Philip II for subsidized shipments of African slaves to repopulate the gold mines. No such subsidies were forthcoming, but—in sharp contrast to contemporary Mexico and central Peru—in early Colombia, African slaves were not simply viewed as potentially skilled auxiliaries: they were deemed an absolute necessity if the colony was to survive at all.

As in the cane fields of Brazil and tobacco plantations of the early Chesapeake, Colombia's early gold camps blended indigenous and African-descended workforces until the former all but disappeared. Where the encomienda predominated, indigenous tributes in kind fed and clothed incoming slaves, and tributes in gold dust served as a base for Spanish capital accumulation. Once encomendero mine owners had cash income, merchants extended them credit. With credit they purchased more slaves. Meanwhile, indigenous and African mine workers shared not only prospecting techniques, but also survival and fighting skills and various habits and forms of material culture.

By the early eighteenth century, African and African-descended slave crews, or *cuadrillas de negros de mina*, routinely numbered in the hundreds and were found throughout colonial Colombia. As one result, the Chocó region of the north Pacific coast, the great gold frontier of the eighteenth century, is still a virtual neo-Africa today. Here colonial indigenous and African resistance, sometimes in combination, was fierce.[17] By independence, Colombia counted an African-descended mining population—everywhere a mix of free and enslaved individuals—in the tens of thousands. As the most obvious reminder of long-term cultural interaction, the racially blended population was substantially larger.[18]

A Gold Mining Frontier

An illustrative example of an Afro-indigenous Colombian mining frontier is Barbacoas, the southwest Pacific coast district where Bárbara Pérez and Juana de la Cruz came to blows in 1643. Barbacoas had been reconnoitered over a hundred years earlier in the days of Francisco Pizarro, but the interior remained in essence unknown to Europeans until the first decades of the seventeenth century.

The first African slaves to mine gold in Barbacoas arrived in the 1620s from Panama. Many were immediately captured and killed by a marauding indigenous group called the Sindaguas, but after their conquest in 1635 the slave population increased dramatically. With help from native Barbacoans held in encomienda (the Sindaguas being only one of several subdued groups), slaves learned to build pile dwellings and dugout canoes in the local style, to trap fish, and to grow critical subsistence crops in various rain forest microclimates.[19] Indigenous persons interacted frequently with slaves, sometimes sexually, sometimes by trade, and several remote groups, including the Awá, Chachi, and Tsáchela of northwest Ecuador and southwest Colombia, adopted the marimba and other African musical instruments.

Vastly outnumbered, slave owners and encomenderos established mine ordinances in 1668 forbidding mixed African-indigenous settlements and also mixed mining work gangs.[20] Due to Barbacoas's peculiar geology and topography, the standard process of indigenous *congregación*, or forced clustering, was generally rejected. Instead mine workers, overseen not by masters or majordomos but rather African-born *capitanes de cuadrilla*, or "work gang captains," lived in widely scattered riparian camps, virtually independent of their owners. Fearful of disease, many slave owners preferred to live with their families in the cool highlands. Production quotas were periodically set or negotiated with these absentee masters, with surplus gold dust (i.e., that exceeding quotas often collected independently in unclaimed areas on Sundays and feast days) used by the slaves to purchase market goods and even freedom.[21]

102

FIG. 6.2: *Illustration of a gold forge from* Histoire Naturelle des Indes, *a French edition of Gonzalo Fernández de Oviedo's* Historia General y Natural de las Indias *of 1535. Reproduced courtesy of The Pierpont Morgan Library, New York (MA3900 f. 102).*

The relative independence of slave gangs and their leaders caused some masters to express fear of concerted, indigenous slave uprisings.[22] In 1668 slaves and native Barbacoans were said to be establishing kinship and godparentage ties and thus seriously threatening the apartheidlike encomienda ideal. A ban was also placed on African-descended *caciques,* or native headmen, strong suggestion that powerful cross-cultural marriage alliances were being formed.

Other ordinances aimed at curbing behaviors like that ascribed to Bárbara Pérez. Following the 1668 rules, indigenous men and women "of ill repute" were to be forcibly placed in upstanding elite households in Santa María del Puerto, the regional capital, where they would serve as domestics. Africans and Native Americans caught engaging in gaming activities or prostitution were to be flogged in public. Finally, the sale of alcoholic beverages to indigenous persons was strictly forbidden.

It appears from surviving documents that the violent encounter between Bárbara Pérez and Juana de la Cruz was not anomalous. The Barbacoas district was in fact the site of several high-profile murders in the later seventeenth century, including those of two visiting tax officials. There were also slave uprisings in the eighteenth century and much talk of indigenous people finding refuge within growing communities of free people of color. A maroon community called "El Castigo" was built in the rugged foothills to the east and successfully resisted repeated militia attacks in the 1710s and 1720s before succumbing to a major expeditionary force in 1746.

Everyday resistance in Barbacoas could include assault sorcery, or "black magic," as well, as evidenced by a strange case from 1700. Here a predatory master's sexual attack on an indigenous encomienda subject spawned a deadly vengeance cycle ultimately involving a number of families and several African slaves. In taking testimony, investigators pitted slaves against Native Americans and against one another, but in the end it was agreed by all parties that subject Barbacoans of varying colors and ethnicities had effective means to, as they put it, "tame the master." As in the case of Juan de Morga of Zacatecas, indigenous shamanic practices were universally regarded as potent tools of resistance.

Forgotten Fringes

Mixed workforces could be found in the central and southern Andes as well. Soon after conquest African slaves were taken to the gold mines of Carabaya, east of Cuzco, and to lowland Chachapoyas, northeast of Cajamarca.[23] Relatively large numbers of Africans and indigenous encomienda charges appear to have worked together in these temporarily rich gold washings, but little is known of social consequences beyond later Spanish mention of small resident "mulatto" (primarily Afro-indigenous) populations. Presumably these new peoples, mixed and mostly non-European mining communities like those found throughout interior Brazil and Venezuela even today, survived by combining subsistence activities like hunting and fishing with seasonal gold panning.

Better documented is a series of "black-and-red" uprisings in early seventeenth-century Vilcabamba, like Carabaya a remote district in the lowland hinterland of Cuzco, Peru. In this case a large group of African and creole slaves, along with a number of native Andeans, local and displaced, forged an alliance of sorts from their shared experience of placer mining.[24]

Led by an indigenous man named Francisco Chichima, a large portion of Vilcabamba's mining workforce of over two thousand slaves and an unknown number of Andeans rebelled against their Spanish oppressors in 1602. Chichima and his followers were not only interested in flight, but also hoped to touch off a regionwide anticolonial rebellion. Several slave-staffed *estancias*, or wheat farms, were consequently destroyed and their owners threatened. For a time panic gripped Cuzco, but ultimately luck fell on the side of the Spanish. Chichima and his retinue were hunted down and captured. It is uncertain whether unusually harsh treatment in the goldfields, relative personal mobility among some workers, geographical isolation, or some combination of these and other factors spurred this outburst.

Much farther south, in the gold mines of early colonial Chile, it is clear that African slaves worked alongside indigenous encomienda subjects and war captives. Reliable numbers and distribution patterns have yet to be described, but Eugene Korth has cited conflicting statements regarding the use of African slaves in early Chilean mines. Whatever the case, some five thousand Africans, mulattos, and *zambos* (Afro-indigenous persons) were said to be living in the colony in about 1600, roughly twice the Spanish population.

As in backcountry Peru, within a century of Spanish arrival in central Chile there was serious talk of a combined African-indigenous uprising. A rumored 1630 rebellion failed to materialize, as did another in 1647, but the panic generated was palpable.[25] The first rumor was linked to a massive mobilization of Mapuche warriors in the south, the second to an earthquake. As in Colombia and the early Caribbean, slaves and free people of color were perceived as highly dangerous—even in relatively small numbers—precisely because they had so much in common with Native Americans. The isolation that typified gold camps rendered them all the more explosive, politically and socially.

Silver

Although silver mines were more often staffed by indigenous workers, Juan de Morga was no rarity. In fact, people of African descent were present in virtually every silver camp from northern Mexico to southern Peru, and sometimes in large numbers. People of color were routinely conspicuous and active members—sometimes full-fledged citizens—of mining communities. Furthermore, as in the gold camps, there is abundant evidence of sustained interaction between African-descended and indigenous peoples.

Silver Cities

Two of the most famous and productive silver towns in colonial Spanish America were Potosí, in modern Bolivia, and Juan de Morga's adopted home of Zacatecas, in central Mexico. Peter Bakewell, who has written extensively on both Potosí and Zacatecas in their colonial heyday (c.1550–1650), suggests that most laborers in these silver camps were indigenous, perhaps 80 percent or more.[26] In Potosí, the *mita* draft, established in the mid-1570s by Peru's Viceroy Toledo, was the principal means of supplying workers to Spanish mine owners. Despite demographic and other shocks, the mita was revived a number of times and was still in effect just before independence.

In Zacatecas, on the other hand, mitalike repartimiento drafts rather quickly declined in favor of wage labor. As early as the mid-seventeenth century, mine owners throughout north and central Mexico were forced to compete for a limited number of free indigenous, mestizo, mulatto, and even immigrant Spanish hands. This was not workers' paradise, by any means, as many laborers—even if not enslaved and abused like Juan de Morga—were tricked or coerced into permanent residence through debt encumbrance. As happened in many other colonial cities and industries, mine and mill owners advanced food, clothing, and other goods, along with basic shelter and promises of protection, to free, but highly vulnerable (usually illiterate) laborers. Debt peonage could entail paternalist reciprocity, but it was notarized service contracts and a rural quasi-police force (called the Santa Hermandad, or Holy Brotherhood) that ultimately kept workers tied to one master.

Why was slavery less prevalent in the silver districts? In Potosí, where indigenous labor drafts were fairly effective, mine owners had little incentive to purchase Africans. Also, by contrast with Brazil or the Caribbean, slaves were consistently quite expensive in the Andean highlands and were thus no mean investment. In Zacatecas, slaves appear to have been only slightly less expensive than in the high Andes, but the ineffectiveness of crown recruiting of indigenous labor and competition for free workers seems to have encouraged more Mexican mine owners to purchase slaves. In either case, presumably, the lure of metallic income had to be carefully weighed against the risks of losing a slave to a cave-in, fall, or other mine-related disaster.

Such safety considerations apparently did not deter mine owners from employing approximately eight hundred African slaves at Taxco, another of New Spain's rich silver districts, by 1569.[27] These workers almost certainly toiled alongside indigenous counterparts, most of them technically free (i.e., not enslaved or even held in encomienda) by this time. Concern over respiratory diseases like silicosis would probably not have been a disincentive to slave labor either, since these ailments tended to manifest themselves only gradually, after the afflicted worker's purchase price had been recouped. Underground mining was known to be unhealthy, but the specific effects of chronic quartz dust exposure on human lungs were only clinically described in the late nineteenth century, well after the end of the colonial period.

NUMBERS

By about 1600, or a little before, Potosí—by then one of the largest cities in the Western Hemisphere—counted a mostly temporary indigenous population in the tens of thousands. Some 6,000 were Andean male draftees. They shared the city and environs with an African and African-descended population—male and female—of about 5,000.[28] Zacatecas in the early seventeenth century was much more modest in size, with an indigenous male worker population of about 1,500 and an African-descended one of only about 800.[29] Counting women and children, Zacatecas's indigenous and Afro-Mexican communities probably totaled three or four times these numbers.

Most enslaved and free persons of African descent were not engaged in mine work in Potosí, but nearly all were in Zacatecas, where they constituted a substantial portion of the total labor pool. The same was true in Pachuca, Guanajuato, Taxco, and a number of lesser Mexican camps.[30] A census of slaves (i.e., not counting free persons of color) working in all the silver mines of New Spain in about 1597 suggests they accounted for nearly 14 percent of the total workforce. Free indigenous workers made up the majority, nearly 70 percent, and native draftees only about 18 percent.[31]

There is no reason to suspect that these early Mexican miners were forcibly segregated by race, although presumably more "blacks" worked in refining, as was true of Potosí. In both New Spain and Peru calls for royal subsidies to expand the slave labor force in the silver mines were incessant in the sixteenth and seventeenth centuries, the period of sustained and occasionally catastrophic indigenous demographic decline.[32] Although subsidies never materialized, Spanish-Portuguese unification (1580–1640) and expansion of the Angolan slave trade after 1590 did result in a sizable influx of slaves in all parts of the colonies.

In Potosí a modestly large number of slaves worked in the mint, but most were privately owned domestics, aides, porters, artisans, and so on. According to several contemporary commentators, the mines' altitude (greater than 4,000 meters, or about 14,000 to 15,500 feet) was considered debilitating for African laborers by the 1570s, if not before. Since such altitudes, however high, are still below the level of major genetic physiological adjustment documented in Central Asia (living day to day above about 5,000 meters), it is certain that the descendants of Africans brought to Potosí would have adapted as readily as any other humans to its rigors.[33]

This is not to say that hypoxia, or prolonged oxygen deprivation, was not a serious concern in the Andean highlands. Certainly mine owners who subjected slaves to hard labor at extreme altitudes without allowing for proper acclimatization (at least two weeks of near-constant rest, high caloric intake, and massive consumption of liquids) were likely to watch their workers die gasping from pulmonary ædema and other acute, altitude-related sicknesses. The same fate would have met most Spaniards thrust into the mines of Upper Peru and also most coastal or lowland Amerindians (Spanish law restricted movement between *temples*, or "proper human habitats"). In sum, Potosí's persistently cold, dry, and thin air would certainly have been a shock to natives of West Africa or Amazonia, but altitude was not a problem of race, as the Spanish argued, but of short- to medium-term human physiological adaptation.

The approximately 2,500-meter (about 8,000 feet) altitude of Zacatecas, by contrast—though certainly high by coastal standards—was much less of a concern. Relative isolation from population centers, both Spanish and indigenous, meant that here workers of native and African heritage faced other challenges, most likely a mix of the personal and industrial. As the case of Juan de Morga demonstrates, altitude could be the least of one's concerns.

By the late eighteenth century (approximately 1779), the combined African and mulatto population of Potosí was only about one thousand; this in a city of nearly twenty-three thousand inhabitants, now about two-thirds indigenous. Obviously slavery had not been embraced here, but there were several reasons for this. Most significantly, the mines' output had declined considerably, pushing the cost of slave labor out of reach following the late sixteenth-century boom, and was only now, almost two centuries later, being revived.

In the meanwhile, some "black" adaptation to the rigors of altitude must have occurred, since African-descended men and boys were routinely drafted into mine-labor *mingas*, or task-specific musters.[34] These draftees labored alongside indigenous and mestizo men on a daily basis. The mita was still also employed on a large scale in late colonial Potosí, and it was the constant appropriation of indigenous labor from as far afield as Cuzco and environs, not the unsuitability of Africans for work at altitude, that ultimately shaped the city's population history.

WORK CONDITIONS AND DAILY LIFE

As a general rule, silver mining entailed many more objective hazards than mining gold. Since African slaves were frequently entrusted with the job of smelting, which continued to be practiced in many places, they and their families must have been unusually susceptible to lead poisoning.[35] Of far greater concern, of course, was the toxicity of mercury, used in far greater quantities in silver refining than in that of gold. Indigenous men were made to walk bare-legged through great vats and cakes of amalgamating ore, an unhealthy practice to be sure, but slaves working in the refineries in fact had it much worse. They were routinely subjected to the far more dangerous mercuric vapors emitted by retorts, or condensing ovens. Massive mercury use in all of the silver camps contaminated not only workers' bodies, but also clothing, bedding, water, and air. As in the goldfields, wives and children also suffered.

Potosí's wealthy mine and mill owners had the money for slaves if anyone did, but most African and African-descended men and women were kept indoors as squires, cooks, laundresses, and wet nurses. The famous early eighteenth-century chronicler of Potosí, Bartolomé de Arzans y Orsúa, used the vehicle of moral tales to condemn certain levels of intimacy between elite families and enslaved African and housebound indigenous women.

In describing the short and unhappy life of one seventeenth-century elite creole woman born in Potosí, Arzans claimed that her evil ways had an easily identifiable cause. "Vices," he claimed, "are transmitted and transplanted in children in milk with indescribable ease."[36] One can only speculate as to the mutual psychological effects of wet nursing by women of color followed by abrupt separation and a stream of racist admonitions, but the opinion of Arzans and other elites was clear: indigenous and especially African-descended persons, in this case women, were assumed to be morally suspect. Interracial intimacy was thus regarded as socially disruptive, even polluting.

In carrying on this racist theme, Arzans makes examples of a number of male slaves and freedmen of African descent. They appear in many contexts in midcolonial Potosí. Some, like their Native American and mestizo brethren, served as military auxiliaries in the prolonged feuding between Basques and "Vicuñas" during the seventeenth century. In this case people of color were bit players in a deadly moral and ethnic, but basically European, drama. When focusing specifically on the character of African and African-descended men, however, Arzans consistently casts them in a harshly negative light.

The most extreme example of this is the case of Antonio Bran de Bizuela, a.k.a. "el Duende" (roughly, "the Wizard"), a legendary mid-seventeenth-century rogue slave. As if drawing from an established script, Arzans blames Bran for countless crimes and misdemeanors, among them theft, rape, witchcraft, and general mayhem. Here is the scene Arzans describes following what amounted to El Duende's lynching: "His body appeared hanging from the balcony of the cabildo, to the considerable satisfaction of the whole city."[37]

By contrast, apparently loyal slaves—most often women—are occasionally mentioned, if not exactly championed, by Arzans. These relatively abstract examples might be regarded as simple reminders of Spanish expectations rather than celebrations of individual will. All told, Arzans makes clear, if perhaps somewhat inadvertently, that despite their relatively small numbers, persons of African descent were a significant social presence in what historians tend to think of as the quintessentially "Indian" Imperial City of Potosí.

Meanwhile, in north-central Mexico, gross demography trumped Andean moralizing and storytelling. As David Brading has noted for late colonial Guanajuato (approximately 1792)—by then New Spain's richest and largest mining camp—mulattos accounted for over 40 percent of mine laborers. They were followed by roughly equal numbers of mestizos (29.6 percent) and Spaniards (28.6 percent).[38] Furthermore, nearly all of these workers, almost two thousand in total, were free. Slavery, as a general rule, had not taken root here either, but "black," or "free colored" (*pardo libre*) labor certainly had. Though not labeled as such in census records, a considerable proportion of Guanajuato's "casta" workforce was no doubt Afro-indigenous. As elsewhere in the colonies, "black" and "red" cultural inter-action had proceeded to the next logical level: widespread *mestizaje*.

MORE FORGOTTEN FRINGES

A somewhat different pattern emerges in early colonial Honduras, where the modest (and relatively low-altitude) silver mines of Tegucigalpa and Guaçucaran were developed in the second half of the sixteenth century. Unlike Zacatecas and quite the opposite of Potosí, indigenous workers were here almost totally excluded from underground mine labor, which was car-ried out solely by African slaves.[39] Indigenous and Spanish workers appar-ently engaged in the sort of support and refining tasks performed by Africans in many other silver districts. Lower slave prices may have been a factor encouraging this seemingly inverse development, but as happened throughout the mining districts of Spanish America, Honduran operators and officials soon pleaded with the king for large numbers of "discount" Africans to increase productivity.

Other mineral-dependent towns, like Peru's great mercury supplier, Huancavelica, developed after 1564, depended almost wholly on indigenous labor. Huancavelica's mines were nearly as high as Potosí's (about five thou-sand meters), but it was crown monopolization of mercury sale and distri-bution and crown-managed mita labor, not altitude, that most accounted for this situation. Work conditions here were positively atrocious, and few slave owners would have been so rash as to risk their investments for the modest profits afforded by mercury.[40] Nevertheless, some 240 African slaves were said to be living and working in Huancavelica by 1592, and the slave trade to the nearby (and equally high) silver camp of Castrovirreyna was apparently on the rise.[41]

AN ANDEAN SILVER CAMP

The case of Castrovirreyna may be worth mentioning, in part because so little is known about this second-rank Peruvian silver town. In this regard it may be comparable to the gold camp of Barbacoas. The famous indigenous polemicist Guaman Poma de Ayala wandered through Castrovirreyna sometime around the turn of the seventeenth century and uncharacteristi-cally declared its citizens "calm, noble, and God-fearing," although he noted that they mistreated indigenous subjects from time to time and failed to pay them proper wages.[42]

Silver had been discovered here around 1555, but it was only after 1590 that crown officials redirected substantial mita labor from lesser projects to the Castrovirreyna district in order to stimulate production. *Yanaconaje*, or nonvillage indigenous servile labor, was also growing in importance. African slavery, perhaps spurred by the relatively close proximity of the coastal Pisco and Ica vineyards, where Africans and Native Americans had been working side by side for decades, soon followed. By 1616 a single mining-ranching outfit in the region counted eighteen slaves and fifty-two indigenous mitayos.[43]

Although relatively few details about slavery and black life in Castrovirreyna have thus far come to light, the first decades of the seventeenth century marked a difficult moment in local Spanish-indigenous relations. In 1613, 150 Andean shamans accused of leading their followers into apostasy and idolatry were marched into the center of town. According to Steve Stern, all were publicly humiliated and their alleged objects of worship destroyed in a great bonfire. Thirty of the shamans were said to have committed suicide within five days.[44]

FORGOTTEN FRINGES

Not all mining towns matched the blended cosmopolitanism of Castrovirreyna. Slaves of any heritage were all but absent in the silver mines and even the town of seventeenth-century Oruro, although they worked alongside *yanaconas* (nonvillage indigenous laborers) in the vineyards of Pilaya y Paspaya.[45] For the later colonial period, only a very small number of house slaves and mixed-heritage (pardo) majordomos lived in Oruro and surrounding mines. A number of household slaves of African descent were said to have been murdered in Oruro during the antipeninsular uprisings of 1781. In this case it was not millenarist native Andeans (although they soon appeared on the scene) but rather disgruntled Hispanic creoles who led the attack.[46]

Kendall Brown and Alan Craig note a small number of free mulatto and zambo, or Afro-indigenous, workers in the late-eighteenth-century silver district of Huantajaya, in the Atacama Desert of Chile, and Carlos Contreras mentions modest numbers of African slaves and free people of color in the similarly late-discovered mines of Hualgayoc, just north of Cajamarca.[47] It would probably be safe to say that virtually every Spanish American silver camp, no matter how high, had at least some residents of African ancestry in colonial times. As to how this undoubtedly noticeable African presence affected local or displaced indigenous cultures remains to be examined, but tantalizing evidence abounds.

CONCLUSIONS

African-Native American interaction of the face-to-face and daily sort began in the earliest mines of Hispaniola, and it continued in the great goldfields and silver towns of New Granada, Peru, and New Spain until well after independence. In some places the African population was in time absorbed into the larger indigenous or mestizo one. In others it was Africans and their descendants who did the absorbing. Whatever the outcome, in demographic or genealogical terms, traces of the colonial interface remain.

Mining camps had their own peculiar dynamics. In the case of gold, scattered and transient mine works were often the site of intermarriage (or at least sexual union), concerted rebellion, and quite extensive cultural exchange. In Colombia, African influences were very strong, and, while one still acknowledges the power and complex processes of creolization, persist to this day.[48] In the case of silver, remote mountain districts became the home of a more mixed, and over time less coerced, workforce. In Peru indigenous workers, and hence traditions, predominated, yet Africans, as seen in the case of Potosí, were very much a part of mining life. In Mexico workers of mixed heritage, mestizo, mulatto, and Afro-indigenous, totally transformed the silver camps by the eighteenth century.

As seen in the cases of Juana de la Cruz and Juan de Morga, Spanish American mining towns were also sites of performed womanhood and manhood and often the sites of chronic and often gendered violence. As is still true today, mining camps were odd and isolated fringes, transient human congeries where money had a different meaning and labor was often assumed to be refractory. The social conventions of the center did not always hold, yet at the same time many individuals could be seen desperately grappling their way up the social hierarchy. Mining precious metals was, perhaps more than anything, hard and dangerous work. "Black" or "red," male or female, the miner's ethos appears to have become enmeshed in seemingly opposite instincts: to survive and to keep digging.

ᏚᏋ

Notes

1. ANHQ Fondo Especial, caja 1, vol. 3, #142 (4-x-1643), f. 81v ("quando la apartó el alcalde dixo dexeme Vmd Sr compe con esta perra yndia que mi marido le quitó el anaco negrera").

2. Ibid., ff. 80–81 ("que si no sea cortava quando Francisco Serrano la avia coxido con el mulato Pedro Sánchez que hallandolo ensima de ella").

3. The seventeenth-century dictionary of Sebastián de Covarrubias (*Tesoro de la Lengua Castellana o Española* [Barcelona: S. A. Horta, 1943, 1674 edition, orig. 1611]) notes under the entry for *buz*: "beso de reverencia y reconocimiento que da uno a otro; y entre monerías que la mona hace es el buz, tomando la mano y besandola con mucho tiento, *summis quod aiunt labiis*, y luego ponerla sobre la cabeza." The nature of this child's game suggests that a "buzamona" was akin to a sycophant. The act of slashing the supposed prostitute's face was perhaps also symbolic, though I have found no similar cases.

4. This narrative is drawn from Solange Alberro, "Juan de Morga and Gertrudis Escobar: Rebellious Slaves," in *Struggle and Survival in Colonial America*, ed. David G. Sweet and Gary B. Nash (Berkeley: University of California Press, 1981), 165–88.

5. Carl O. Sauer, *The Early Spanish Main* (Berkeley: University of California Press, 1966), 23.

6. Frank Moya Pons, *Despues de Colón: trabajo, sociedad, y política en la economía del oro* (Madrid: Alianza Editorial, 1987), 43.

7. On the use of slaves in gold mining in West Africa, see Paul Lovejoy, *Transformations in Slavery: A History of Slavery in Africa*, 2nd ed. (Cambridge: Cambridge University Press, 2000), 33. See also Ivor Wilks, "Wangara, Akan, and Portuguese in the Fifteenth and Sixteenth Centuries," in *Mines of Silver and Gold in the Americas*, ed. Peter Bakewell (New York: Variorum, 1997), 1–39.

8. Gonzalo Fernández de Oviedo, *Historia General y Natural de las Indias* (books I–VIII, Biblioteca de Autores Españoles, v. 117) (Madrid: Atlas, 1959), 117, 154–67.

9. William H. Hodges and Eugene Lyon, "A General History of Puerto Real," in *Puerto Real: The Archeology of a Sixteenth-Century Spanish Town in Hispaniola*, ed. Kathleen Deagan (Gainesville: University Press of Florida, 1995), 96.

10. Juan de Ayala, *A Letter to Ferdinand and Isabela, 1503*, ed. and trans. Charles E. Nowell (Minneapolis: University of Minnesota Press, 1965), 45.

11. Bartolomé de las Casas, *A Short Account of the Destruction of the Indies*, trans. Nigel Griffin (New York: Penguin, 1992), 13, 18–19, 24.

12. See Noble David Cook, "Sickness, Starvation, and Death in Early Hispaniola," *Journal of Interdisciplinary History* 32, no. 3 (winter 2002): 349–86, and Massimo Livi Bacci, "Return to Hispaniola: Reassessing a Demographic Catastrophe," *Hispanic American Historical Review* 83, no. 1 (February 2003): 3–51.

13. Robert J. Ferry, "Encomienda, African Slavery, and Agriculture in 17th-Century Caracas," *HAHR* 61, no. 4 (November 1981): 609–35. For the water transport industry along the Magdalena River, see Thomas Gomez, *L'envers de l'Eldorado: Economie coloniale et travail indigene dans la Colombie du XVIème Siecle* (Toulouse: Assosiation des Publications UTM, 1984).

14. Robert West, *Colonial Placer Mining in Colombia* (Baton Rouge: Louisiana State University Press, 1952), 83.

15. See Luis Enrique Rodríguez Baquero, *Encomienda y vida diaria entre los Indios de Muzo, 1550–1620* (Bogotá: ICCH, 1995), 31–59.

16. Jorge Garcés G., ed., *Las minas de Zamora: Cuentas de la Real Hacienda, 1561–1565* (Quito: Archivo Municipal, 1957).

17. See William F. Sharp, *Slavery on the Spanish Frontier: The Colombian Chocó, 1680–1810* (Norman: University of Oklahoma Press, 1976), and Caroline A. Williams, "Resistance and Rebellion on the Spanish Frontier: Native Responses to Colonization in the Colombian Chocó, 1670–1690," *HAHR* 79:3 (August 1999): 397–424.

18. Anthony McFarlane, *Colombia Before Independence: Economy, Society, and Politics under Bourbon Rule* (Cambridge: Cambridge University Press, 1993), 76–79.

19. See Norman Whitten, *Black Frontiersmen: Afro-Hispanic Culture of Ecuador and Colombia* (Prospect Heights, Ill.: Waveland Press, 1986).

20. Kris Lane, "The Transition from Encomienda to Slavery in Seventeenth-Century Barbacoas (Colombia)," *Slavery & Abolition* 21, no. 1 (April 2000): 80.

21. See Mario Diego Romero and Kris Lane, "Miners and Maroons: Freedom on the Pacific Coast of Colombia and Ecuador," *Cultural Survival Quarterly* 25, no. 4 (winter 2002): 32–37.

22. Kris Lane, "Taming the Master: Brujería, Slavery, and the Encomienda in Barbacoas at the turn of the Eighteenth Century," *Ethnohistory* 45, no. 3 (summer 1998): 500.

23. James Lockhart, *Spanish Peru, 1532–1560: A Colonial Society* (Madison: University of Wisconsin Press, 1968), 26, 185–86.

24. Frederick Bowser, *The African Slave in Colonial Peru, 1532–1650* (Stanford, Calif.: Stanford University Press, 1972), 176–77.

25. Eugene V. Korth, *Spanish Policy in Colonial Chile: The Struggle for Justice, 1535–1700* (Stanford, Calif.: Stanford University Press, 1968), 37–38, 222–23.

26. See Bakewell's superb summary treatment, "Mining," in *Colonial Spanish America*, ed. Leslie Bethell (Cambridge: Cambridge University Press, 1987 [1984]), 203–49.

27. Robert C. West, "Early Silver Mining in New Spain, 1531–1555," in *Mines of Silver and Gold*, ed. Peter Bakewell, 128.

28. Peter Bakewell, *Miners of the Red Mountain: Indian Labor in Potosí, 1545–1650* (Albuquerque: University of New Mexico Press, 1984), 98, 192.

29. Peter Bakewell, *Silver Mining and Society in Colonial Mexico: Zacatecas, 1546–1700* (Cambridge: Cambridge University Press, 1971), 122–24.

30. Colin Palmer, *Slaves of the White God: Blacks in Mexico, 1570–1650* (Cambridge, Mass.: Harvard University Press, 1976), 76.

31. Peter Bakewell, "Notes on the Mexican Silver Mining Industry in the 1590s," in *Mines of Silver and Gold*, ed. P. Bakewell, 184–85.

32. Palmer, *Slaves of the White God*, 77–82; Bakewell, *Miners of the Red Mountain*, 192.

33. See, for example, E. R. Buskirk, "Work Capacity of High-Altitude Natives," in *The Biology of High-Altitude Peoples*, ed. P. T. Baker (Cambridge: Cambridge University Press, 1978), 173–87.

34. Enrique Tandeter, *Coercion and Market: Silver Mining in Colonial Potosi, 1692–1826* (Albuquerque: University of New Mexico Press, 1993), 43, 79.

35. Alan Probert, "Bartolomé de Medina: The Patio Process and the Sixteenth-Century Silver Crisis," in *Mines of Silver and Gold*, ed. Peter Bakewell, 102.

36. Bartolomé Arzans de Orsúa y Vela, *Tales of Potosí*, ed. R. C. Padden, trans. Frances López-Morillas (Providence, R.I.: Brown University Press, 1975), 103.

37. Ibid., 57.

38. D. A. Brading, *Miners and Merchants in Bourbon Mexico, 1763–1810* (Cambridge: Cambridge University Press, 1971), 258–60.

39. William L. Sherman, *Forced Native Labor in Sixteenth-Century Central America* (Lincoln: University of Nebraska Press, 1979), 232–35.

40. Kendall Brown, "Workers' Health and Colonial Mercury Mining at Huancavelica, Peru," *The Americas* 57, no. 4 (April 2001): 467–96.

41. Steve J. Stern, *Peru's Indian Peoples and the Challenge of Spanish Conquest: Huamanga to 1640* (Madison: University of Wisconsin Press, 1982), 142. On Huancavelica, Stern cites Bowser, *The African Slave in Colonial Peru*, 93–94 and 410, but these references are equivocal. Bowser's general view was far more conservative: "In sum, outside of the gold mines in such tropical provinces as Vilcabamba, the African's role in Peruvian mining consisted of the rare slave here and there who served in a supervisory capacity" (122).

42. Felipe Guaman Poma de Ayala, *El primer nueva corónica y buen gobierno*, ed. John V. Murra and Rolena Adorno, 3rd ed. (México: Siglo XXI, 1992), 965. Steve Stern mentions two cases of very violent abuse and even execution of mitayos by Castrovirreyna's corregidor in *Peru's Indian Peoples*, 104.

43. Stern, *Peru's Indian Peoples*, 142.

44. Ibid., 176.

45. Ann Zulawski, *They Eat from Their Labor: Work and Social Change in Colonial Bolivia* (Pittsburgh: University of Pittsburgh Press, 1995), 176.

46. Oscar Cornblit, *Power and Violence in the Colonial City: Oruro from the Mining Renaissance to the Rebellion of Túpac Amaru (1740–1782)* (Cambridge: Cambridge University Press, 1995), 66, 150, 169.

47. Kendall W. Brown and Alan K. Craig, "Silver Mining at Huantajaya, Viceroyalty of Peru," in *In Quest of Mineral Wealth: Aboriginal and Colonial Mining and Metallurgy in Spanish America*, ed. A. K. Craig and R. C. West (Baton Rouge: Louisiana State University Press, 1994), 312, and Carlos Contreras, *Los mineros y el Rey, Los Andes del norte: Hualgayoc 1770–1825* (Lima: IEP, 1995), 88.

48. See Richard Price, "The Miracle of Creolization: A Retrospective," *New West India Guide* 75, nos. 1, 2 (2001): 35–64.

CHAPTER SEVEN

Wolves and Sheep?

Black-Maya Relations in Colonial Guatemala and Yucatan

CHRISTOPHER LUTZ AND
MATTHEW RESTALL

Blacks and mulattos "are for the natives worse
than wolves among sheep."
—*Tomás Espinosa, oidor of the*
audiencia *of Guatemala, 1585*[1]

ⱺ⊙⊱

In the 1680s a mulatto carpenter named Joseph Barrientos lived with his family in the small Mam Maya village of Chalchitán (today's Aguacatán). This was an unlikely place to encounter a man like Barrientos: the Maya pueblo lay just to the east of the district capital of Huehuetenango in the Cuchumatán region of northwest Guatemala, a mountainous and chilly area that offered very few agricultural opportunities, modest mineral resources, and a scattering of resident Spaniards. In fact, we would probably never have known about this mulatto carpenter and his family if Barriento's son, Manuel, had not succeeded in attracting the ire of the Maya town council (the *cabildo*) of Chalchitán. According to the accusations of the cabildo, the Barrientos family was victimizing the native population; most seriously, Manuel had been stealing cattle and conspicuously living with a local Maya woman. The cabildo formally complained in a petition to the *audiencia* (the governing court of the colony) in the provincial capital of Santiago. Without any apparent investigation into the allegations by the Maya village authorities, the audiencia ordered the entire Barrientos family to pick up and move at least twenty leagues distant from Chalchitán.[2]

Over a century later, almost due north of Chalchitán, in another Spanish colony, that of Yucatan, another incident occurred in which Spanish officials adjudicated an apparent conflict between a man of African descent and a Maya community. One spring night in 1816 a twenty-four-year-old black slave named José Antonio Marcín escaped from his owner's house in the colonial port town of Campeche and headed up the *camino real* (royal highway) toward the capital of Mérida. At dawn Marcín reached the edge of the Maya village of Kopomá, where he exchanged words with several local inhabitants before falling into a fight with a group of Maya men; believing them to have been sent by his owner, Marcín refused to accompany them into the village and as a result received a head wound that put him in the hospital in Mérida. There he was arrested not only for escaping, but also for theft, assault, and rape. But as Marcín's trial progressed over the months that followed, the Maya witnesses against him evaporated; the frustrated judge concluded that the charges had stemmed from the "dissemination and lies" of the Mayas of Kopomá, and he ordered Marcín to be sent back to his owner.[3]

These two cases have been selected to open this chapter in part because they reflect the geographical and chronological scope of our study; the chapter focuses on the two principal Spanish colonies in the Maya area, those of Yucatan in the north and highland Guatemala in the south (see fig. 7.1), during the 250 years from the late sixteenth to early nineteenth centuries. But they have also been chosen because of the way they seem to illustrate the hostile nature of black-Maya relations in these colonies—as though Spanish colonization had indeed introduced African "wolves" among the native Maya "sheep."

Our contention, however, is that this reflects only one side of black-Maya relations. These cases passed into the written historical record only because conflict broke out; by definition, such records seldom contain evidence of harmonious coexistence between Mayas and Africans. In addition, there are clear signs in these cases of Spanish interference in the development of the conflict and its outcome—such as a willingness to believe

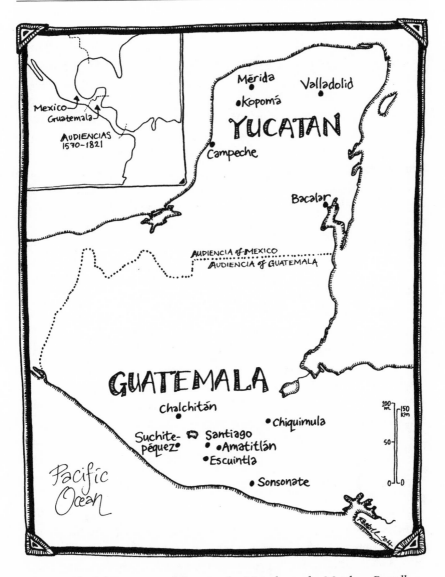

FIG. 7.1: *Colonial Yucatan and Guatemala. Map drawn by Matthew Restall.*

stereotypes about African criminality and licentiousness and a concern to segregate subject groups (see Patrick Carroll's emphasis on this factor in chapter 9 of this volume). Furthermore, our brief summaries above remove the cases from their larger contexts; Chalchitán and Kopomá were small Maya pueblos that never became centers of African settlement, whereas Campeche, the town from which Marcín escaped, had a significant African population and—like the two colonial capitals of Mérida and Santiago—became an increasingly multiracial community during the colonial period. Sometimes Mayas played sheep to African wolves, but at other times the situation was reversed, and more often than not, the Spaniards were the wolves and both Mayas and Africans were their potential prey. And just to further complicate the metaphor, sometimes the wolves lay down with the sheep; the Barrientos case most obviously illustrates hostility toward Africans in Maya communities, but note that Manuel was living with a Maya woman. One of the most significant patterns of African-Maya interaction was that of miscegenation—as we shall see.

In order to sort through the varying circumstances and complexity of black-Maya interaction and discern patterns within its kaleidoscope, we have structured this chapter around discussion of two determinants. Following a brief demographic summary (that is, an outline of where Mayas and Africans lived and in what numbers), we turn first to changes over time and second to regional differences—principally those between urban centers and rural communities.

PATTERNS OF MAYA AND AFRICAN SETTLEMENT

Guatemala's geography is more complex than Yucatan's, being marked by numerous rivers, mountains, and plains and valleys at varying altitudes. In contrast, Yucatan is a flat limestone peninsula with no large rivers or mountains. As a result, the native peoples of Guatemala—whom we call Mayas but who did not themselves recognize a common identity—were divided into numerous subgroups, each with their own language or dialect of a language (all of which we call Mayan). Yucatan was more linguistically homogeneous: all its natives spoke Yucatec Maya. Nevertheless, soil conditions, access to water, and other factors produced concentrations of settlements in certain parts of both the Yucatan peninsula and the Guatemalan highlands. Whereas in Yucatan, Spaniards settled and brought Africans to the main areas of Maya settlement, a different pattern evolved in the more diverse topography of Guatemala. There the Spaniards mainly settled in the mountain valleys (5,000 feet, or approximately 1500 meters above sea level or lower), while the majority of the surviving native population centers were at higher elevations to the north and west and, therefore, less appealing to the Iberian settlers, who wanted to raise wheat and sugarcane.

Around 1520, right before the Spanish invasion, the southern Guatemala population and the Yucatec Maya population were roughly the same size—about 2 million each.[4] Mayas were as hard hit by disease as other Native American groups, and all Maya populations declined dramatically during the sixteenth century, with the indigenous Guatemalan population reaching its nadir of an estimated 128,000 in the 1620s and the Yucatec population bottoming out close to a mere 100,000 in the 1680s. Recovery after this point was slow and uneven. In Guatemala, the increase in native numbers was apparently more steady in the highland area to the north and west of Santiago (the capital from 1541 to 1773, today called Antigua) than elsewhere (some regions never recovered). Yucatan saw a series of stalled recoveries in the seventeenth and early eighteenth centuries, finally climbing to about 400,000 by 1820—roughly the same number as the Guatemalan Maya population at this time. Thus by the end of the colonial period there were still barely a fifth as many Mayas in highland Guatemala and Yucatan as there had been three centuries earlier, although they remained the majority population, constituting some 70 percent of the total population in each province in the final half century of the colonial period (1770–c. 1820).[5]

Meanwhile, there was a growing African population in the Maya area. How did this come about? Throughout the Americas, black slaves arrived with their Spanish masters during the earliest campaigns of explorations and conquest—as detailed in the first chapter of this volume.[6] Francisco de Montejo purchased a license to bring one hundred African slaves into Yucatan, one of whom, Sebastián Toral, fought for decades as a conquistador and became a free settler in Mérida after its founding in 1542.[7] Pedro de Alvarado likewise brought Africans into Guatemala to assist in the Spanish Conquest there and in 1534 wrote to the king of Spain that he had two hundred more in the colony ready to take with him to Peru (some of whom returned with Alvarado when he was bought off in Ecuador).[8] By the early 1540s entire boatloads of African slaves were landing at the Atlantic coast ports of Honduras, much of their human cargo bound for Guatemala, and by the end of the decade black slaves had begun reaching the fledgling Spanish colony of Yucatan through the Gulf port of Campeche. As table 7.1

TABLE 7.1: Estimates for the African
Population of Yucatan, 1570–1805

YEAR	BLACKS	PARDOS/ MULATTOS	BOTH
1570	265	20	
1574			500
1600	500		
1605		350	
1618			2,000
1646	497	15,770	
1742	274	35,712	
1779	1,490	17,605	
1790	2,800	43,426	
1791			45,201
1805			28,100

Sources: Gonzalo Aguirre Beltrán, *La Población Negra de México* (Mexico City: FCE, 1989 [1946]), 197–222 (for 1570, 1646, 1742); Manuela Cristina García Bernal, *Población y Encomienda en Yucatan bajo los Austrias* (Seville: Escuela de Estudio Hispano-Americanos, 1978), 154–58 (for 1574, 1600, 1618); Sherburne F. Cook and Woodrow Borah, *Essays in Population History: Mexico and the Caribbean, Volume II* (Berkeley: University of California Press, 1974), 79, 95 (for 1605, 1805); Robert W. Patch, *Maya and Spaniard in Yucatan, 1648–1812* (Stanford, Calif.: Stanford University Press, 1993), 234 (for 1779); *Documentos para la Historia de Yucatan* (DHY) (Mérida, Yuc.: Compañía Tipográfica Yucateca, 1936–1938, 3 vols.), I, 99 (for 1791); and J. Ignacio Rubio Mañé, *Archivo de la Historia de Yucatan, Campeche, y Tabasco* (Mexico City: Imp. Aldina, Robredo y Rosell, 1942, 2 vols.), I, 250 (for 1791). A version of this table was published in Restall, "Otredad y ambigüedad: las percepciones que los españoles y los mayas tenían de los africanos en el Yucatán colonial," *Signos históricos*, II, no. 4 (2000): 19, and in "La falacia de la libertad: La experiencia Afro-Yucateca en la edad de la esclavitud," *Rutas de la Esclavitud en Africa y América Latina*, ed. Rina Cáceres (San José: Editorial de la Universidad de Costa Rica, 2001), 294.

suggests, patterns of importation persisted, albeit erratically, both under royal license and through illegal trading, throughout the next two-and-a-half centuries.[9]

Where in Guatemala and Yucatan were Africans and their descendents concentrated?[10] Tribute records can be used to give some sense of African settlement patterns. For example, the contrast in amounts of tribute paid from

TABLE 7.2: Tribute Paid by Free Blacks, Free Mulattos, and
Indios Naborías in Guatemala, 1576 and 1592

Year	Jurisdiction	Amount Paid
1576	Villa de la Trinidad de Sonsonate	252 tostones
1592	Santiago	529 tostones
1592	Ysquintepeque (Escuintla)	162 tostones, 2 reales
1592	Guazacapán	70 tostones
1592	Chiquimula de la Sierra	46 tostones

Source: Archivo General de Indias (AGI), *Contaduría*, legs. 966, 968, published in
Christopher H. Lutz, "Evolución Demográfica de la Población No Indígena," *Historia
General de Guatemala*, vol. II, ed. Jorge Luján Muñoz (Guatemala: Asociación de Amigos
del País, Fundación para la Cultura y el Desarrollo, 1994), 249–58. The original tribute payments were recorded in *tostones*: a toston was an amount equivalent to four reales or half a
peso (so the Sonsonate total was equivalent to 126 pesos, and so on).

region to region—as shown in table 7.2—suggests that an Afro-Guatemalan
population had by the end of the sixteenth century become concentrated in
the capital of Santiago, along the Pacific coastal plain from Escuintla, and
eastward into Sonsonate (in present-day El Salvador), with lesser numbers
beginning to appear in eastern Guatemala. As a result, a multiracial society
began to emerge in these areas—as rather fancifully depicted in an illustration for a seventeenth-century travel account (fig. 7.2).

By the late colonial period, the Spanish authorities were compiling
more regular and thorough census records; table 7.3 is an example of how
estimates of the Afro-Yucatec population can be extracted from such a census. As in Guatemala, people of African descent were living throughout the
colony, but were overwhelmingly concentrated in the capital city (Mérida)
and in and near the port town of Campeche (Yucatan's demographic equivalent to Guatemala's Pacific coast). There were two other Spanish towns or villas in Yucatan, Valladolid and Bacalar, but they remained economically and
demographically insignificant relative to Mérida and Campeche and thus
never contained a sizable Afro-Yucatecan population, as table 7.3 illustrates.

Despite these population concentrations, by the late eighteenth century a sizable mixed-race population was scattered throughout the colonies
of Guatemala and Yucatan. As was the case in most Latin American
provinces, mixing of all kinds eventually occurred among Iberians,

FIG. 7.2: *A Maya, two Africans, an Englishman, and a Spanish priest in seventeenth-century Guatemala. From the frontispiece to a 1693 German edition of Thomas Gage's* Description of the West Indies. *Courtesy of the Centro de Investigaciones Regionales de Mesoamérica, Antigua, Guatemala.*

TABLE 7.3: Distribution (by Percentage) of the
African Population in Yucatan, 1779

REGION	DISTRICT	BLACKS	PARDOS/ MULATTOS	BOTH
Southwest	**Campeche**	73.9	22.9	26.9
	Other districts	1.5	10.4	9.6
Northwest	**Mérida**	15.4	10.1	10.5
	Other districts	3.1	40.8	37.9
Northeast	**Valladolid**	0.9	3.9	3.7
	Other districts	1.3	10.7	9.9
Southeast	**Bacalar**	3.7	1.2	1.4
		100%	100%	100%

Note: The one Spanish city and three Spanish villas (towns) are in bold.

Source: Table created from data in Robert W. Patch, *Maya and Spaniard in Yucatan,
1648–1812* (Stanford: Stanford University Press, 1993), 235.

Africans, and Native Americans but with a strong tendency toward miscegenation between enslaved African men and native or mixed-race women
and, to a lesser extent, between female slaves and Spaniards. Some of these
unions were formal, church-sanctioned marriages, but most were informal.
Due to the "law of the womb," whereby children fathered by slaves were
themselves born slaves only if their mothers were enslaved, a large slave and
free population of African descent emerged. These children of mixed
descent were almost always identified as being mulatto (the favored term in
Guatemala) or *pardo* (the favored term in Yucatan), whether their second
parent was Maya or Spaniard.

According to one study of Santiago, in the middle decades of the sixteenth century most people of Afro-Maya descent lived outside the
Guatemalan capital, while most Afro-Spanish mulattos remained in the
city.[11] This was probably true in Yucatan too (with respect to Mérida and
Campeche) and is not surprising in that most Spanish settlers chose urban
life, leaving rural communities in both Maya-area colonies overwhelmingly
native. While people of African descent in Spanish cities and major towns
were more likely to be black, in smaller settlements and rural communities

they were far more likely to be mulatto or pardo (especially in the early colonial decades); also, while the black population grew slowly in early colonial times but more quickly in the eighteenth century (the boom century of the Atlantic slave trade), its growth was dwarfed by the steady increase in mulatto numbers (by the end of the colonial period there was one mulatto for every ten Mayas in both Guatemala and Yucatan).

EARLY PATTERNS: MAYAS AND AFRICANS IN THE SIXTEENTH CENTURY

Having initially been imported for labor purposes related specifically to the conquest of Maya groups—to fight as black conquistadors (see chapter 1) and to provide services as unarmed porters and other camp auxiliaries—African slaves were subsequently purchased in Guatemala and Yucatan for a wide range of economic and social reasons. The Maya area never became the site of sugar or tobacco plantations on a scale comparable to Brazil or the Caribbean or even Mexico, but wherever Spaniards sought to exploit natural resources, they invariably brought Africans in small numbers to carry out the most skilled tasks or to supervise skilled or unskilled Maya workers.

The local indigenous population met most but not all colonial labor demands, leaving African slaves from the onset to constitute a permanent labor force that was more directly and closely tied to the Spanish colonists than Mayas were. In Santiago, Mérida, and Campeche, slaves served as servants in Spanish households or often as highly skilled employees in their masters' businesses, encompassing virtually all areas of Spanish economic activity. In these varied urban activities, black and mulatto slaves lived and worked beside free blacks, mulattos, and other mixed-race peoples as well as Maya workers. Free people of African descent tended to live where Spaniards did—primarily in the Spanish cities and major towns—and where Spaniards found the right conditions to establish agricultural enterprises on which they grew wheat, maize, sugar cane, and cattle (and in Guatemala, indigo and cacao, the latter usually grown on native lands but its trade increasingly in the hands of non-Mayas).

Some important patterns were established during these early decades of colonial rule. One of these was the inability of the Africans to become part of either the *república de indios* (the native community) or the *república de españoles* (the Spanish community), at least as these two social and political entities were conceived by the colonists. In other words, Africans could not participate in either Spanish politics in city and town or Maya politics in the countryside. People of African descent were similarly caught in the middle socially, neither entirely rejected nor entirely accepted by either the colonists or the natives.[12]

The second pattern was one of black-Maya interaction through the medium of Spanish economic practices. As alluded to above, African slaves with specialized artisan skills and the confidence of their masters and mistresses supervised the work of native peoples. These blacks, usually male, supervised mostly female natives in Spanish households and mostly male natives in workshops, bakeries, and other businesses. Such natives tended to fall into one of three categories: Maya men and women performing personal service duties (*servicio personal*), later replaced by the *repartimiento de indios* (a form of poorly paid urban and rural corvée labor); *indios naborías* (hereditary native servants independent of a particular barrio or pueblo) who were mostly Maya but could also be Nahuas brought from central Mexico by Alvarado, Montejo, and their fellow conquistadors; and finally, non-Maya native slaves, who after 1550 became free workers and were gradually absorbed into the larger Maya population.[13]

The third pattern that was established in the mid- and late sixteenth century relates to settlement. The urban neighborhoods (barrios) and pueblos that surrounded the small Spanish cores, or *trazas*, of Santiago, Mérida, and Campeche had initially been entirely native; rather than mix natives with Africans, the early Spanish settlers had housed their black slaves either at the edges of their own urban properties or in special neighborhoods squeezed in between the Spanish traza and native barrios. But free blacks and persons of mixed descent born in the Spanish households, as well as married servant couples freed of their contractual obligations, soon sought house plots (*solares*) and houses in these native barrios. This pattern had begun at least by 1570, probably earlier, and intensified as the traza became crowded and free blacks, mulattos, mestizos, and eventually poorer Spaniards acquired land and homes in native barrios, turning them into multiracial communities where people of native and African descent started informal unions or married, had children, and engaged in a variety of social and economic relations.[14]

Although this process began in the cities and towns, it soon spread to the larger Maya communities in the regions adjacent to those towns. By 1600, Spaniards, accompanied by their black slaves and servants, had moved far into the Maya countryside, acquired land from native pueblos, and begun raising wheat, maize, cattle, and sugar (as illustrated by the family of

Manuel Barrientos).[15] Spaniards preferred to live in the city and, if they could afford to, were more likely to leave black slaves or servants in charge of rural properties; this setup led to black-Maya social interaction of the kind mentioned above but also to antagonism between black and mulatto supervisors and Maya workers—especially where the Mayas were forced to work for little or no pay under the exploitative repartimiento system.

These, then, were the patterns of interaction between Africans and Mayas established in the sixteenth century: a socioracial colonial system that placed people of African descent in an often uncomfortable position between Spaniards and Mayas, colonial economic practices that made blacks and mulattos supervisors to Maya laborers, and settlement patterns that turned native communities adjacent to Spanish centers into multiracial ones. Was this pattern altered or intensified by developments in the seventeenth century?

LATER PATTERNS: MAYAS AND AFRICANS IN THE SEVENTEENTH AND EIGHTEENTH CENTURIES

Records of slave imports into Central America during the first few decades of the seventeenth century show that this was a boom period for the trade in African men and women. The early decades of conquest violence had passed and the small colonies in highland Guatemala and Yucatan were growing and prospering, creating not only a demand for black slaves but the capacity to afford them. The size of shipments ranged from a handful to as many as 150, the number of slaves from "Guinea" on a ship that reached Campeche in the summer of 1599. Eight shipments to the ports that fed Guatemala between 1613 and 1628 each brought an average of 119 enslaved Africans.[16]

Had this level of importation continued throughout the century, the Spanish colonies in the Maya area might have looked very different by 1700. But the trade declined quite dramatically after 1635, with no large shipments into Guatemala at all between that date and 1699.[17] Slave imports to Guatemala picked up again in 1700 but never again reached the levels of the early seventeenth-century boom. In Santiago's most wealthy, Spanish-dominated Sagrario parish, baptismal records show that small numbers of African-born slaves (bozales) were bought and baptized during the mid- to late seventeenth century, with a marked increase in bozal baptisms in the period 1700–1770. But even for the years 1710–1719, a decade that saw a greater influx of African-born slaves into the Spanish households of the

Sagrario parish than any other decade in the eighteenth century, baptismal records suggest that on average, no more than ten slaves were imported annually.[18] The pattern in Yucatan has yet to be established in detail, but it appears to have been a milder variant on the Guatemalan one, with a modest flow of slaves into the colony in the seventeenth century, followed by a steady increase in the eighteenth—although the number of bozales baptized in Mérida's Spanish parish of Jesús María in the mid-eighteenth century was, as in Santiago's Sagrario parish, an average of only ten a year.[19]

This long-term pattern of reduced African slave imports meant that the complexion of Guatemala's and Yucatan's slave populations literally lightened as a result of miscegenation between the mid-seventeenth century and the early nineteenth century. During the period of low levels of slave importation in the seventeenth century, the mulatto population, both enslaved and free, grew dramatically. By the last decades of the seventeenth century Santiago's Spanish elite had become increasingly concerned about the growing numbers of mulattos both in the urban and rural sectors and the perceived crime and social disorder they might cause.[20]

The seventeenth century thus established a pattern of miscegenation that persisted in the eighteenth century, despite—if not because of—the return of a higher level of bozal imports. An estimated 56 percent of slaves sold in eighteenth-century Guatemala were identified as black, the remainder mulatto, but if such data were to be broken down by decades, no doubt the slave population would be identified as more black in the early decades and more mulatto in the latter part of the century.[21] As we shall discuss below, the process of miscegenation was particularly pronounced in Spanish cities and towns; first, however, we turn to rural trends in the second half of the colonial period.

BLACKS IN THE MAYA COUNTRYSIDE: RURAL PATTERNS

A fascinating starting point for our survey of rural trends is the Guatemalan town of San Juan Amatitlán. Around 1680, Amatitlán had over 970 Maya tributaries—that is, a total population of approximately 4,000 men, women, and children, making it a sizable native town for late seventeenth-century Guatemala.[22] San Juan Amatitlán was encircled by sugar estates (*ingenios*), owned by Spanish religious orders and a few individuals, as well as by a large number of wheat farms, or *labores de panllevar*, all owned by Spaniards. Large numbers of black and mulatto slaves lived on all of the sugar estates, some working as supervisors of the less skilled and unskilled Maya workers who were forced to work there under the repartimiento de indios or corvée labor system. As was not uncommon in Guatemala, where the repartimiento was especially onerous, a full quarter of adult men (between eighteen and fifty-five) from San Juan—243 of its tribute-paying males—were assigned to twenty-four different ingenios and labores for the meager daily wage of one real.

Half of these Maya men were sent to the five large sugar estates, where they were supervised by African slave overseers. In a detailed inspection of labor conditions, called a *visita*, in 1679, many Maya officials and workers as well as slaves of African descent and their Spanish cleric masters testified as to the treatment of the native workers by slave overseers. Almost without exception, the Maya officials (who were exempted from repartimiento service), the black and mulatto slave supervisors, and their Spanish masters all asserted that the native workers were well treated and paid the specified amount. In contrast, a number of the Maya laborers complained of verbal abuse and whippings at the hands of their African overseers and of dangerous working conditions that resulted in serious injuries and even death. As a result of these complaints, a number of the black and mulatto slave supervisors were thrown in the royal jail in Santiago but were soon released, and their Spanish masters fined between fifty and two hundred pesos for the labor infractions. Conditions for the workers of San Juan Amatitlán presumably continued unchanged; the fines were not steep (less than the value of a single able-bodied slave), and Spanish officials seemed to understand that if black slaves were abusive, it was because they were under orders to get as much work as possible out of their underpaid Maya laborers.[23]

While black-Maya labor relations were often tense and, at times, violent, other aspects of daily life in and around San Juan Amatitlán resulted in close bonds between the Pokomam Maya community and the large sugar ingenio slave population. Some slave masters, including priests, encouraged enslaved African men to marry their female counterparts, in the hope that they would thus engender more slaves. But significantly, roughly half of black slaves who were formally married in the church in the late seventeenth century married Maya women. Such marriages forged bonds between the slave community and the Pokomam Maya population and created an ever-larger intermediate free population of mixed descent identified as mulattos in San Juan Amatitlán and other areas of highland Guatemala.[24]

The example of San Juan Amatitlán in the late seventeenth century illustrates three of the four points of black-Maya contact in the highland

Guatemalan and Yucatec countrysides about which we have information: labor relations, the growth of a rural mulatto population, and marriage. The fourth point of contact was a cultural one—folk religious and medicinal practices. Unfortunately, our information on these topics is uneven: Africans remain virtually unstudied in colonial Yucatan and Guatemala, especially when compared to Spaniards and Mayas, and the history of their interaction with Mayas is even less broken ground. However, we have been able to compile a patchwork of cases and data that give a good sense of the larger pattern. In this section we shall look first at a pair of cases of African-Maya conflict that attracted the attention of the Inquisition in Yucatan; second, at census data from Guatemala in 1683 and 1804 and from Yucatan in 1779; and third, at marriage patterns in Guatemala in the 1671–1701 period, with some hints as to comparable Yucatec patterns (with the first point of contact listed above, labor relations, touched upon again in the section on urban patterns).

Our pair of Inquisition cases from Yucatan are dated almost a century and a half apart and suggest (as much as a sample of two can) how African-Maya relations in the countryside might have hardened over the decades from suspicion to hostility. The first case is an incident from 1580. A sexagenarian African named Cristóbal, the slave of a Spanish priest, is investigated for his alleged participation in "idolatrous" practices in a Maya community near Campeche. Testimony alleged that Cristóbal consumed food and drink left out as an offering to a Maya deity. Inquisition officials feared this was a kind of diabolist ritual consumption. After questioning Cristóbal and seven Maya witnesses, however, the investigators concluded that the slave's motive was nothing more than hunger.

The investigation recorded a conversation between Cristóbal and one of the local Maya officials, Andrés Cuyoc. According to the accounts of both men, Cuyoc happened upon Cristóbal eyeing an offering that had earlier been placed upon a ceremonial stone outside the village. The slave asked the Maya man if the bread was good to eat; Cuyoc said it was, and the slave ate it. He then asked about the other items, with the same response and outcome. The exchange seems stilted, strained perhaps, as though each side were sizing the other up, each hoping to avoid open hostility, each aware of the cultural barrier between them. The African wanted the food and hoped to get it peacefully; the Maya wanted to safeguard the offering but preferred to avoid an unpleasant incident.[25]

If the 1580 incident suggests mutual ignorance accompanied less by hostility than by bemusement, a 1722 case suggests that by late-colonial times,

Mayas were no longer willing to tolerate what they perceived as mulatto interference in ritual or cultural matters. The Inquisition prosecution of a mulatto *curandero* (healer) named Joseph Zavala in that year was made possible by the Maya town councillors of Xechekan, who denounced Zavala for practicing his arts in the district after he successfully cured a dying Maya woman in the community. In part, Zavala's crime was that he was an outsider—not just a non-Maya, but a non-member of the Xechekan community. But race seems to have played a role as well: Maya witnesses consistently referred to Zavala not just by name, but by the Spanish term *mulato*.[26]

The impression given by these two cases is one of greater African-Maya contact leading to a more overtly hostile relationship. How accurate is this impression? One way to find an answer to such a question is to approach it through a very different type of source: the census. For example, what can census data tell us about changes in the settlement and dispersal of blacks and mulattos in the late colonial period? Figs. 7.3 and 7.4 show the distribution of all nonindigenous families in Guatemala (including Soconusco, today part of Mexico, and Sonsonante, today in El Salvador). In 1683 (fig. 7.3), most non-Maya rural settlers lived in regions south and east of the Valley of Guatemala, while few Spaniards and Africans lived north and west of the capital.

By 1804 (fig. 7.4), the black and mulatto population, slave and free, had in many areas been integrated into a more amorphous middle sector, called *ladinos*. The low levels of black slave importation in the mid- to late seventeenth century and centuries of miscegenation had greatly reduced the separate and distinct nature of Afro-Guatemalan identity. Even though there remained areas where free mulattos had not become part of a larger ladino population and still identified themselves as mulattos or *gente parda*, the 1804 census identified all non-natives (who were 30 percent of the total population) who were not Spaniards as ladinos.[27]

Thus districts of colonial Guatemala that were once completely Maya had during the eighteenth century experienced large increases in their numbers of non-Maya inhabitants. While there were only 20 non-Mayas in Verapaz in 1683, for example, by 1804 there were 615 Spanish and ladino families, and in Tecpán Guatemala there were 60 non-Indians in 1683 but 495 Spanish and ladino families in 1804. The implications of this demographic shift for land control and use are extensive. Not only did Spanish and ladino expansion cause the loss of Maya lands, but the development of wheat and cattle operations near Maya pueblos brought the added burden of repartimiento demands: Spaniards and ladinos needed not only Maya lands but

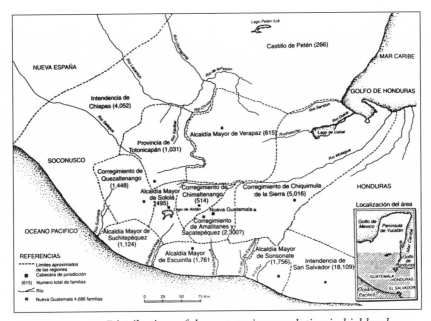

FIGS. 7.3 AND 7.4: *Distributions of the non-native population in highland Guatemala, 1683 and 1804. From Jorge Luján Muñoz, ed.,* Historia General de Guatemala *(Guatemala City: Asociación de Amigos del País, Fundación para la Cultura y el Desarrollo, 1994), vols. II and III. Reproduced courtesy of the Fundación para la Cultura y el Desarrollo, Guatemala.*

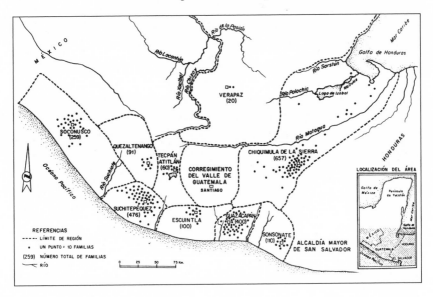

also Maya labor.[28] As occurred elsewhere in colonial Mesoamerica, low native population levels in the seventeenth century permitted informal acquisition of native lands by non-natives, leading to land conflicts in the eighteenth century once indigenous populations began to recover.[29]

In the lowlands the Spanish and ladino population growth was explosive, tripling in Escuintla, for example, and increasing even more than that in Sonsonate and San Salvador (where there was an indigo boom after 1750). Although ladino families were less likely to live in native communities in the Pacific lowlands than up in the highlands, in the lowland districts of Chiquimula and Escuintla there was an in-migration of non-Mayas that raised levels of *mestizaje* (racial mixing, in this case largely outside marriage), led to the loss of indigenous lands, and even caused the gradual decline—if not disappearance—of some lowland Maya pueblos.[30]

The final decades of colonial rule in Yucatan saw a population boom in all ethnic sectors, but again this was most pronounced among pardos (mulattos) and mestizos. All Afro-Yucatecans—pardos and blacks combined—grew from constituting 8.8 percent of the province's population in 1779 to 12.4 percent by 1791, when they therefore outnumbered Spaniards. Even with mestizos and Spaniards grouped together, as they were in the 1791 census, blacks and mulattos were almost as numerous: the former were counted in that year as 14.8 percent of the Yucatec population, with blacks and mulattos as 12.4 percent and Mayas the remaining 72.8 percent.[31]

The population boom was least pronounced among blacks, who by this time constituted less than 1 percent of the total population in the colony.[32] In fact, blacks were disappearing as a separate category toward the end of the century, merging into a single pardo category with mulattos, just as both groups were merging in Guatemala into the ladino category.

Although this process of miscegenation resulted to a considerable extent from informal unions, marriage practices and patterns help to show how the process unfolded over the generations—and underscore the crucial point that while the vast majority of Mayas and people of African descent in Yucatan and Guatemala married others like them, enough families were forged from black-native relationships to have an impact on that process of miscegenation.

Marriage records from throughout the Maya area have yet to be studied in detail, but we do have—by way of a case example—a recent study by Paul Lokken of marriage trends in several regions of Guatemala between 1671 and 1701. We mentioned at the start of this section the tendency in San Juan Amatitlán for black men to marry Maya women, while free mulattos married among themselves; this was also true of the whole Valle de las Vacas region around Amatitlán. To the east lay the larger region of Chiquimula de la Sierra, which stretched to the present-day borders of El Salvador and Honduras. Out of a total adult population of ten thousand, some 12 percent were considered Spaniards, mestizos, and mulattos, and they were concentrated in a few key towns. Without sugar estates, there was no large black population, free or enslaved, but a third of Chiquimula's non-Maya population was free mulatto. Although there were three cases of mestizas marrying Indian husbands, no Maya–free mulatto marriages were recorded. Likewise, to the north, in the more sparsely populated Acasaguastlán region, where a tenth of the total population was of African descent and seven-tenths were Mayas, almost no Maya–free mulatto intermarriage occurred. This does not mean, of course, that there were no informal unions between Mayas and mulattos (as suggested earlier by the case of Manuel Barrientos in Chalchitán).

The final region for which Lokken was able to extract information on marriage patterns was Guatemala's Pacific coast. Here, by 1680, there was a diverse population of various Maya groups, Pipil, and Xinca, numbering some forty thousand. There were also some four thousand Spaniards, mestizos, blacks, and mulattos. The degree to which Mayas married non-Mayas—in particular blacks and mulattos—varied a little through the region. Three districts can serve as examples. In Escuintla (called Escuintepeque at the time), the Pipil-speaking natives tended to live at the higher elevations away from the lowland coastal hot lands where blacks and mulattos were concentrated, yet as black men grew in number during this period (1671–1701), a tendency developed for them to marry native women. In Zapotitlán (also known as Suchitepéquez), Spaniards were proportionately more significant than in Escuintla, while the total non-native population was outnumbered by Mayas twenty-five to one. The smaller African population thus had less opportunity for endogamy and was disappearing by the early eighteenth century as blacks married Mayas and mulattos married mestizos and lower-ranking Spaniards. Finally, in Guazacapán, a Pipil district that was 10 percent non-native, church marriages between Mayas or Pipils and free mulattos were rare, but some black men married Maya women, and it seems certain that black and mulatto informal unions with indigenous partners resulted in significant mestizaje here and throughout the entire coastal region. In Lokken's words, "The non-Indian population of much of Guatemala's Pacific coast was distinctly mulatto in character as the eighteenth century dawned."[33]

Thus despite the dispersal of people of African descent throughout these regions of Guatemala, no general pattern of *significant* black-Maya or mulatto-Maya intermarriage emerged. A *weak* pattern of marriage emerged between the two groups, most pronounced in the Valle de las Vacas, where black slaves sometimes married Maya women, and in some parts of the Pacific coastal plain, where some intermarriage took place between Mayas or other natives and free blacks or mulattos. In particular, Mayas who married people of African descent seem more likely to have been *indios laboríos* (independent native laborers), who were more independent than most Mayas, having weaker ties to the communities of their birth and able to avoid the onerous tribute and labor obligations attached to community membership. Manuel Barrientos, therefore, as a free mulatto living in an informal union with a Maya woman in the late seventeenth century, represents well the pattern of domestic interaction between Mayas and people of African descent.

MAYAS AND AFRICANS IN THE CITY: URBAN PATTERNS

Despite Barrientos and his Maya wife and other examples of black-Maya unions in the countryside, without question the three most important centers of intermarriage and mestizaje were the two Spanish provincial capitals in the Maya area, Santiago and Mérida, and the port town of Campeche.[34]

As we have already seen, most of the blacks in Yucatan lived in the town of Campeche and the district around it, while the same area held more mulattos (or pardos) than any other region in the province. As the peninsula had no reliable road connecting it to the outside world, the colony was effectively an island, making the port of Campeche Yucatan's gateway; this fact helps explain why Campeche developed more of an Afro-Yucatec community than any other place in the peninsula and may also explain why more blacks and mulattos did not move out into the Maya countryside (as they did in Guatemala). As the provincial capital, Mérida was also a logical place for Africans to be concentrated. Indeed, the districts of Mérida and Campeche, combined with the three districts that more or less lay between them (Camino Real, Hunucma, and Sierra), contained 62.8 percent of the colony's pardos in 1779 and 90.7 percent of its *negro* residents.

Fig. 7.5 shows, using the example of Campeche, how mixed the populations of Yucatan's urban centers had become by the late eighteenth century. Furthermore, as this data includes "district" populations (meaning Maya communities in the urban hinterlands), the non-Maya presence within the city walls would have been even more pronounced.

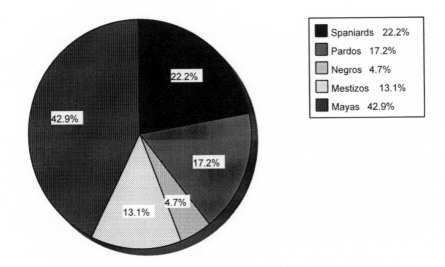

FIG. 7.5: *Racial distribution of the Campeche district population of 23,479 in 1779. Created from data in Robert W. Patch,* Maya and Spaniard in Yucatan, 1648–1812 *(Stanford, Calif.: Stanford University Press, 1993), 234. For a similar pie chart presenting Mérida's population at this time, see Matthew Restall,* The Black Middle: Slavery, Society, and African-Maya Relations in Colonial Yucatan *(Stanford, Calif.: Stanford University Press, forthcoming).*

Campeche, Mérida, and Santiago were all important settings for a variety of interactions between all of the hybrid groups that resulted from social and biological mestizaje. Beginning in the early sixteenth century, Africans, Mayas, and Spaniards came together in what became—over more than two centuries—multiracial urban population centers of some size (Santiago being the largest, with Yucatan's urban population split between Campeche and Mérida). These urban centers generated push-and-pull dynamics. Population growth and inequality of economic opportunity pushed poorer residents out into the valleys, hinterlands, and larger Maya towns. At the same time, labor demands brought newly enslaved Africans from across the Atlantic or from other regions of Spanish America, while Spanish settlers were pulled into the cities by family connections and Maya migrants by illusions of opportunity or coercive colonial practices.[35]

Table 7.4 illustrates the situation in one corner of the colonial Maya world—the environs of Campeche in the 1780s. In these Maya communities, situated within the urban orbit of Campeche but not inside the city, pardos (meaning in this case all Afro-Yucatecans) were settling in similar numbers to Spaniards, with non-Mayas nevertheless remaining very much a minority. Likewise, the Maya neighborhoods that ringed Santiago, having seen a growth in their native population early in the seventeenth century, also became steadily less Maya between 1650 and 1750 (even while rural Maya villages were growing)—a demographic shift probably related to the increase in the free mulatto population of Santiago.[36] Thus the trend in Maya communities around Campeche, illustrated in table 7.4, can be seen in comparable communities around Santiago through the intrusion of mulattos into these neighborhoods—where they bought house lots (*solares*) and houses from the native inhabitants, became engaged in small-scale businesses, legal and illegal, and, at times, found Maya spouses.[37] As mulattos were pushed out of the city and into the urban hinterland, Mayas seem to have been pushed farther out from the city. The pattern is complex, for this pushing was taking place even while other Mayas were moving into the city from the countryside. In 1716, for example, the town councilors of San Juan Amatitlán complained that over 280 of their tributary residents had fled to the Santiago region, a movement that may have partly stemmed from the disruptive influence of the sugar industry in the Amatitlán area, with its large Afro-Guatemalan workforce.[38]

Labor roles were central to this push-and-pull dynamic and to the rapidity with which Spanish cities in the Maya area became multiracial. Within these cities and their surrounding communities, Mayas and Africans were supposed to be segregated. In theory, Mayas were part of the república de indios, residing in self-governed communities that included no non-Maya inhabitants. Africans did not have their own "republic," nor did they fully fit into the república de españoles. The concept of a bifurcated society, therefore, was deeply flawed in its failure to take into account both a significant African presence in the colonies and the rapid growth of mestizo and mulatto populations resulting from widespread miscegenation.[39]

Both the African presence and the process of miscegenation resulted from colonial labor demands. This was broadly true in that labor demands underpinned African slavery in the Americas, but it was also specifically true in the context of the work Africans did in colonial cities. In the early colonial period, when the Maya population was hit hard by epidemic disease, Spaniards placed black and mulatto slaves—and, increasingly, free

TABLE 7.4: Racial Distribution of Recipients of Church Rites in the Parishes Immediately outside the Walls of Campeche, 1781–1787

	BAPTISM	MARRIAGE	BURIAL
Spaniards	5.6	8.2	6.3
Pardos	4.8	7.0	5.7
Mayas	<u>89.6</u>	<u>84.8</u>	<u>88.0</u>
	100%	100%	100%

Source: Created from data presented in Robert W. Patch, *Maya and Spaniard in Yucatan, 1648–1812* (Stanford, Calif.: Stanford University Press, 1993), 235. The parishes were San Francisco Campeche (the Maya head town right outside the Spanish city's walls) and Santa Lucía, Lerma and Sambula, Hampolol, and San Diego and Cholul. By the 1780s the category of *pardo* was often used, as it is here, to denote all Afro-Yucatecans.

blacks and mulattos—in the skilled trades to fill positions once held by Mayas. A 1604 sales tax (*alcabala*) census of the eighty non-Maya artisans in Santiago showed that more than fifty of them were blacks and mulattos.[40] It is not clear if epidemic disease was the main factor or if blacks and especially mulattos somehow gradually pushed Mayas out of construction and other trades after 1600.[41] Either way, Mayas had dominated the building trades in the sixteenth century, but during the seventeenth these trades came to be dominated by and associated with blacks and mulattos.

However, workers and artisans of African descent did not just replace Mayas; as dependents of their Spanish owners or employers, blacks and mulattos were also used as supervisors of Maya laborers. In the urban centers of Yucatan and Guatemala, as in other Spanish American cities, Spaniards delegated their authority first to black slaves and later to mulatto slaves, free blacks, free mulattos, and mestizos—who served as overseers, majordomos, tax collectors, and intermediaries between Spanish colonists and the native majority. Whereas Mayas initially filled most positions as servants in Spanish households, workshops, and stores, African slaves and then free blacks and mulattos gradually came to occupy these roles too. Whether in a domestic environment, on a construction site, or in the central marketplace in Campeche, Mérida, or Santiago, Mayas would have found themselves in almost daily contact with people of African descent.

Indeed, the fact that much of the African population was enslaved and the Maya population was not (with the exception of Guatemala before 1550, when the wars of conquest produced Maya and other native slaves) did not mean that Mayas enjoyed a social or economic status above Africans. The standing of these groups with respect to each other was highly complex, even when one casts aside the fact that an increasing sector of the urban population was descended from both.

One dimension of this social ranking was the fact that Mayas both from the cities and the surrounding villages and towns were obligated to perform rotational labor duties in the city—duties that often involved degrading, unskilled, and punishing work, for little or no monetary compensation. It was Mayas who swept and weeded the city streets and government properties, cleaned out public latrines, and provided fodder for Spanish urban livestock. Maya men from the Santiago region, for example, had to dig accumulated silt from the Pensativo River bed to prevent it from flooding in the rainy season. Inhabitants from the Maya villages on the camino real were forced to carry firewood and logs (to be made into building beams) into Campeche. Mayas from Mérida and a scattering of towns around it complained for years over the hard unpaid labor they put in at the construction site of the Mérida *ciudadela*, or fortress, in the 1660s.[42] In very few of these cases did non-Mayas have to perform similar duties, as they stemmed from membership in native municipal communities (in sum, the república de indios). In this sense, blacks and mulattos shared an exemption and privilege with Spaniards, one that created some social distance between them and Mayas.

Still, the factors that kept Mayas and Africans apart could not ultimately offset the biological implications of coresidency in the Spanish cities. For example, based on estimates of legitimate and illegitimate births, it is calculated that Santiago's *gente ordinaria* (non-Spanish) population numbered approximately 13,720 in the 1590s, 21,717 in the 1650s, 24,620 in the 1680s, and 25,041 by the 1750s.[43] No other region in Guatemala could match this population growth nor this level of mestizaje, and the same was true for Mérida and Campeche with respect to Yucatan. To get some sense of how mestizaje worked at the level of family formation, we again turn briefly to evidence of marriage (and baptism) in Santiago and in Campeche.

Marriage records for Santiago's native (mostly Maya) communities were kept by the religious orders, but unfortunately, all have been lost. There are, however, long runs of parish registers from the city's central parishes administered by the secular clergy, from as early as the late sixteenth century

TABLE 7.5: Racial Classification in Non-Spanish Marriages,
Campeche (Central Parish), 1688–1700 (n = 66)

	NEGRA	PARDA	MULATA OR MORENA	INDIA	MESTIZA	ESPAÑOLA
Negro	5	2	—	2	—	—
Pardo	—	34	—	8	8	1
Moreno	1	—	2	—	1	—
Indio	—	1	—	—	—	—
Mestizo	—	1	—	—	—	—
Español	—	—	—	—	—	—

Source: Archivo Histórico de la Diócesis de Campeche (AHDC), Caja 90, Libro 650 (marriages of non-Spaniards), fs. 2–23.

up through the 1770s. These records reveal much about black and mulatto intermarriage with Mayas.[44] Similar to the pattern in the San Juan Amatitlán and Escuintla regions, in seventeenth-century Santiago a clear trend existed of black slaves marrying Maya women. Similar to black slave–naboría unions, mulatto slave–naboría marital patterns were strongest in the late sixteenth and early seventeenth centuries before declining gradually but remaining significant up to 1720. Why did these ties weaken in the eighteenth century? We think this is due to both a decline in the mulatto slave population and the stronger tendency for even mulatto slaves to marry within their own group, whether their chosen spouses were slave or free. At the same time, indios naborías also showed a strong tendency to intramarry or, in some cases, to marry mestizos and, to a lesser extent, free mulattos. While free mulatto–indio naboría intermarriage was stronger prior to 1690, this trend weakened between that date and 1770. In Santiago indio naboría marital relations with all slaves were generally stronger than they were with either free blacks or free mulattos.[45]

The comparable marriage records from the central parishes of Campeche and Mérida reveal similar trends; table 7.5 offers data from a sample decade—Campeche in the 1690s. Here again we see evidence that most marriages were racially endogamous; that is, two-thirds of the unions are between partners of African descent, most of them classified by the priest as *pardo/parda*. However, while it was rare for a native man to marry a woman of African descent, there was a small but significant tendency among black or mulatto men to marry women of Maya ancestry (29 percent of all cases); once again, a familiar pattern.[46]

The gender balance within some of these groups helps explain marriage patterns between them, in particular high rates of intramarriage. Exact censuslike data are unavailable for Santiago's and Campeche's naboría population, but from numerous other sources it is clear they were as a group heavily tilted toward women, who were most needed in urban households to perform domestic chores. This lack of gender balance among the city's indios naborías complemented the heavy tilt toward males among the early black slave population. Naboría women continued to migrate to the city (often escaping tributary status and thereby becoming naborías once in the city), while most incoming slaves were men, encouraging marriage between the two groups (especially between mulattos and Maya women).

Another archival angle from which black-Maya miscegenation can be approached is that of baptismal records: these can offer access to the existence of informal unions that are obviously not documented in marriage records, in particular by allowing historians to unearth illegitimacy rates. While the registers for Maya neighborhoods in Santiago are lost, we do have two sets of baptismal records, one set for Spaniards and another for everybody else, the so-called gente ordinaria. A comparison between the two main parishes of Santiago (1630–1770) is instructive.

While gente ordinaria illegitimacy in the parish of San Sebastián was never under 36 percent, it was consistently lower than in Sagrario, a parish characterized by large, Spanish-headed households, often with numerous black and mulatto slaves and Maya servants. A few slaves, usually mulatto, resided in the bigger houses in San Sebastián, and there was probably at least one Maya woman servant in almost every non-Indian household. So no part of a city of some thirty thousand persons was immune to gente ordinaria illegitimacy. But multiracial illegitimate births were especially common in the larger, more elite households of the Spanish urban core.[47]

A similar pattern can be seen in records from Campeche's central parish, where the Spanish masters of African slaves and servants brought infants to be baptized. For example, all thirty-two entries in the 1690s name the child's mother, but only twelve name the father. The implications of this go beyond simple illegitimacy. Godparents were also listed, so no doubt in many cases the father was present but named as master and godfather. Many of these children were therefore the illegitimate offspring of extramarital unions between Spanish masters and their African slaves or servants, children conceived and born in the master's household.[48] Thus in Campeche as in Santiago, large, multiracial households were without doubt the engines of mestizaje, especially positioned to produce and raise children of part-Spanish, part-African, and/or part-Maya descent.

CONCLUSION

We have examined black-Maya relations in two categories, urban and rural, but of course under some circumstances the two intersected. One of these was the highway that led in and out of the city, a place where worlds met, often in disjunctive fashion—where the metaphor of wolves and sheep seemed particularly apposite.

The case of José Antonio Marcín, described at the beginning of this chapter, offers one example of how such meetings came about. In the escaped-slave scenario, an urbanized African, accustomed to interacting with Mayas in Campeche, misreads and is misunderstood by the rural Mayas of Kopomá, who are not accustomed to seeing black strangers in their village. Why were rural Mayas so distrustful of Afro-Yucatecans or Afro-Guatemalans?

One explanation is rooted in another circumstance of highway encounter. The camino real that Marcín took out of Campeche also led Mayas from the countryside into Campeche and Mérida, as did the roads that ran from highland Guatemalan villages into Santiago. Some Mayas came to Spanish cities to escape the burdens of tributary status and to seek permanent work, but many others journeyed in for shorter periods in order to perform the labor duties assigned to their towns and villages, to deliver twice-yearly tribute payments to Spanish officials or encomenderos, or to deliver goods (cotton or woolen cloth and thread; in Yucatan, wax; and in Guatemala, charcoal) or foodstuffs (especially maize and wheat) to sell in the city's plaza or to merchants. When traveling alone or in small numbers, these Mayas were vulnerable to assault and theft. Early-colonial evidence comes from Thomas Gage, the English traveler who claimed that in the 1630s in highland Guatemala escaped slaves "often come out to the roadway, and set upon" the mule trains.[49] An example of late-colonial evidence comes from Yucatan in 1821, when the Spanish authorities arrested, convicted, and in a few cases executed the members of a Campeche gang who had allegedly committed a series of violent robberies along the highway and in

212 CHRISTOPHER LUTZ AND MATTHEW RESTALL

nearby Maya communities; the accused were all black or pardo militiamen, and most of the victims were Mayas.[50]

Native travelers were also vulnerable to the abuses of *regatones*, a pejorative term for the middlemen who came out from the city to intercept inbound natives on the road. Regatones pressured travelers to sell their goods on the spot and were often accused of forcing below-market sales that amounted to highway robbery. In the sixteenth century regatones tended to be the Maya servants or African slaves of Spanish colonists, but by the mid-colonial period the business had become dominated by free blacks and free mulattos, who worked for themselves or for merchants, bakers, weavers, and artisans, who might be Spanish or mestizo or in some cases also black or mulatto.[51]

These highway encounters reflected the way the intrinsically exploitative nature of Spanish colonialism could color relations between Africans and Mayas. For native travelers, the journey into Santiago, Mérida, or Campeche was overshadowed by the knowledge that one's cargo might be stolen or sold cheap under duress; for free blacks and mulattos, the regatón scene was an opportunity to bypass the economic restrictions that stemmed from colonial monopolies and discriminatory practices.[52] In other words, to fully understand black-native relations, we must always be aware of the role played by the Spanish colonial crucible into which Africans and Mayas were placed.

To return to the cases that opened the chapter: the Maya cabildo of Chalchitán were able to settle their dispute with Barrientos in their favor with such rapidity because they found a ready ally in the Spanish authorities, an ally willing to accept without question that a mulatto family was troublesome; likewise, a closer reading of the Marcín case reveals how a simple highway encounter could become an imagined criminal rampage through the intervention of Spanish officials and the highly suggestive questions they put to Maya witnesses. In the words of the official report on the 1789–1791 Merino y Cevallos governorship of Yucatan, mulattos living outside city walls were "vagrants [*bagamundos*]" and "the only people from whom the Indians receive frequent abuse [*frecuentes vejaciones*]."[53]

Spaniards made sporadic attempts to keep Mayas and Africans apart while wittingly or unwittingly fostering prejudice between the two groups. The success of these attempts, and the degree to which they amounted to a concerted state policy of segregation (even apartheid, as Carroll argues in chapter 9 below), remains unclear. There is plenty of evidence from Guatemala and Yucatan of Spanish prejudices and fears, but it does not suggest an organized and sustained campaign of segregation. Furthermore, Spaniards provided several urban environments in which Mayas and Africans worked together, lived together, and together produced a new mixed-race population that would grow to outnumber the Spaniards themselves. The Spanish ideal of two subject populations, native and black, segregated from each other except under controlled labor circumstances, only worked for a brief moment at the start of the colonial period. By the late sixteenth century, the key patterns of African-Maya interaction had become well established and would intensify over the centuries that followed: working together leading to living together leading to the creation of a mixed-race population, beginning first in the cities of Santiago, Mérida, and Campeche and then spreading out to towns, Maya communities near cities, and eventually into the countryside. Conflict between those of Maya and African descent paralleled these developments, but it was not a sign of their incompatibility, as Spaniards suggested. On the contrary, ongoing and even increased instances of Maya-black conflict was probably a symptom of the intensification of interaction between the two groups and the gradual breakdown of barriers between them.

၆၀

NOTES

1. Tomás Espinosa to the king, 30 March 1585, Archivo General de Indias (hereafter AGI), *Guatemala* 10, cited in Magnus Mörner, "La política de segregación y el mestizaje en la Audiencia de Guatemala," *Revista de Indias*, Año XXIV (enero–junio 1964): Núms. 95–96: 137–51. Quote on p. 139 (translation by Christopher Lutz).

2. See Paul Thomas Lokken, "From Black to *Ladino*: People of African Descent, *Mestizaje*, and Racial Hierarchy in Rural Colonial Guatemala, 1600–1730" (Ph.D. diss., History, University of Florida, Gainesville, 2000), 169–70. The Spanish colonial history of Chalchitán, a social division or clan forming the eastern side of the town of Aguacatán, is discussed in a regional context in W. George Lovell, *Conquest and Survival in Colonial Guatemala: A Historical Geography of the Cuchumatán Highlands, 1500–1821*, rev. ed. (Montreal and Kingston: McGill-Queen's University Press, 1992), 82ff. For the Chalchitán and Aguacatán population (about 167 tributaries and an estimated total of 670 souls), see AGI, *Guatemala* 29, "Autos hechos . . . Año de 1684," f. 17v., as transcribed by Genoveva Enríquez

Macías, "Nuevos documentos para la demografía histórica de la Audiencia de Guatemala a finales del siglo XVII," *Mesoamérica* 17 (1989): 136.

3. Archivo General del Estado de Yucatan (hereafter AGEY), *Criminal* 1, 11a. This is the same case to which Patrick Carroll refers at the start of his chapter in the present volume. It is also briefly discussed in Matthew Restall, "Otredad y ambigüedad: las percepciones que los españoles y los mayas tenían de los africanos en el Yucatan colonial," in *Signos Históricos* 2, no. 4 (July–December 2000): 15–38.

4. The Guatemalan figure includes an estimated one hundred thousand non-Mayan Pipil speakers in the Southeast, on the border of modern El Salvador, and covers the area of the present-day republic without the Petén.

5. On Guatemala: W. George Lovell and Christopher H. Lutz, "'A Dark Obverse': Maya Survival in Guatemala, 1520–1994," in *Geographical Review* 86, no. 3 (July 1996): 400, table 1; and W. George Lovell and Christopher H. Lutz, *Demography and Empire: A Guide to the Population History of Spanish Central America, 1500–1821* (Boulder, Colo.: Westview Press, Dellplain Latin American Studies No. 33, 1995), 7. For the Guatemalan Northwest see Lovell, *Conquest and Survival*, 145, table 16. On Yucatan: Matthew Restall, *The Maya World: Yucatec Culture and Society, 1550–1850* (Stanford, Calif.: Stanford University Press, 1997), 173–74.

6. See also Matthew Restall, "Black Conquistadors: Armed Africans in Colonial Spanish America," *The Americas* 57, no. 2 (October 2000): 171–205 (which cites, among many other sources, Gonzalo Aguirre Beltrán, *Población negra de México, 1519–1810: Estudio etnohistórico* [México: Ediciones Fuente Cultural, 1946]).

7. AGI, *México* 2999, 2.

8. Restall, "Black Conquistadors"; Adrián Recinos, *Pedro de Alvarado: Conquistador de México y Guatemala* (México: Fondo de Cultura Económica, 1952), 141–55.

9. In Guatemala there was apparently a major hiatus from the 1630s until near the end of the seventeenth century; see J. Joaquín Pardo, *Efemérides para escribir la historia de la muy noble y muy leal ciudad de Santiago de los Caballeros del Reino de Guatemala* (Guatemala: Tipografía Nacional, 1944), 8, and Christopher H. Lutz, *Historia sociodemográfica de Santiago de Guatemala, 1541–1773*, Serie Monográfica: 2 (CIRMA: La Antigua Guatemala, 1982–1984), chap. X, esp. pp. 219–23. For Yucatan, see Matthew Restall, *The Black Middle: Slavery, Society, and African-Maya Relations in Colonial Yucatan* (Stanford, Calif.: Stanford University Press, forthcoming). For an early-colonial example of a royal license granted for the importation of large numbers of slaves, in this case three hundred to be brought in

through Tabasco in 1618, see AGI, *México* 136; in a revealing reflection of how Spaniards saw Africans and Mayas as fulfilling labor needs in complementary ways, the colonists in Tabasco also won the right to bring down from Yucatan three hundred married Mayas (*indios casados*) to meet labor needs, although it is not clear if the relocation ever occurred.

10. If it is a challenge to collect data on the size and distribution of the colonial Maya population, it is nearly impossible to find data of comparable quality for the slave and free population of African descent. This is because while from early on, Mayas were forced to pay an annual head tax or tribute to either their Spanish encomendero or to the Spanish crown, black and mulatto slaves of African descent paid no tax and the records of African slave importation by ship (under the *asiento*, or royal license system) and their individual sales and purchases are time-consuming to find and retrieve from notarial records—even if such records have survived. Our ability to track down the whereabouts and numbers of free blacks (*negros libres*) and free mulattos (*mulatos libres*) is made somewhat easier due to the imposition by the late sixteenth century of a tribute burden (called the *laborío* tribute) on these free groups of African descent and on indios naborías. See Robinson Antonio Herrera, *The People of Santiago: Early Colonial Guatemala, 1538–1587* (Ph.D. diss., History, University of California, Los Angeles, 1997), chap. 5; Lutz, *Historia sociodemográfica*, Apéndice VII, pp. 445–47; and Restall, *The Black Middle*. On the laborío tribute, see Christopher H. Lutz, *Santiago de Guatemala, 1541–1773: City, Caste, and the Colonial Experience* (Norman: University of Oklahoma Press, 1994), app. 7, pp. 253–54. An indio naboría or naborío was a hereditary native servant who was free of normal native tributary status and the obligations that entailed; the term *naboría* was used to describe this group in colonial society or an individual woman of that group (see Lutz, *Santiago*, 315, glossary, and discussion in text).

11. Herrera, *The People of Santiago*, 260.

12. For a full elaboration of this thesis, see Restall, *The Black Middle*.

13. This last category pertains primarily to Santiago and very little to elsewhere in Guatemala or to Yucatan. Unlike any other Spanish settlements in the Maya area, Santiago's native population came from a variety of Mayan ethnolinguistic groups, as well as Pipil (Nahua) speakers from Guatemala's southeastern Pacific coast, Nahuatl speakers from central Mexico, and indigenous immigrants and former (post-1550) native slaves from elsewhere in native America. See Lutz, *Santiago*, and Karen Dakin and Christopher H. Lutz, *Nuestro pesar, Nuestra aflicción/tunetuliniliz, tucucuca: Memorias a Felipe II, enviadas por indígenas del Valle de Guatemala, en lengua náhuatl hacia 1572*, Instituto de Investigaciones Históricas (México: UNAM, 1996).

14. Lutz, *Santiago*, 45–78; Restall, *Maya World*, 29–37.

15. Christopher H. Lutz, *Historia sociodemográfica*, chap. XIV, and Christopher H. Lutz and W. George Lovell, "Core and Periphery in Colonial Guatemala," in *Guatemalan Indians and the State: 1540–1988*, ed. Carol Smith (Austin: University of Texas Press, 1990), 35–51.

16. Aguirre Beltrán, *Población negra*, p. 40; Restall, "Otredad y ambigüedad," 17; Lutz, *Santiago*, 85. African slaves primarily reached Guatemala and Yucatan through Spanish American ports, but there was also a lesser trade by land from Belize to Yucatan (as English settlements developed in Belize in the seventeenth century) (Restall, *The Black Middle*) and by land into Guatemala from Mexico in one direction and Panama in the other.

17. The reasons for this decline are not entirely clear but may be rooted in the seventeenth-century depression in the region and perhaps also the fear often expressed by Santiago's cabildo of the high numbers of blacks in the colony. Murdo J. MacLeod first pointed out the post-1635 seventeenth-century decline in African slave imports but notes a revival in the 1690s in *Spanish Central America: A Socioeconomic History, 1520–1720* (Berkeley and Los Angeles: University of California Press, 1973), 298; the same book also details the seventeenth-century depression. For *bozal* (slaves born in Africa) baptismal data, see Lutz, *Santiago*, 86, and for post-1700 research see Beatriz Palomo de Lewin, "Esclavos negros," in *Historia General de Guatemala*, gen. ed. Jorge Luján Muñoz (Guatemala: Asociación de Amigos del País, Fundación para la Cultura y el Desarrollo, 1994), vol. III: 135–48. Paul Lokken has uncovered information on the illegal disembarkment of over eighty slaves in Trujillo in 1641 and an apparent foiled Dutch effort to smuggle slaves in through the same port in 1660: "From Black to *Ladino*: People of African Descent, *Mestizaje*, and Racial Hierarchy in Rural Colonial Guatemala, 1600–1730" (Ph.D. diss., University of Florida, Gainesville, 2000), 30–31, fn. 29. On the antiblack fears of the Santiago cabildo, see Martha Few, *Women Who Live Evil Lives: Gender, Religion, and the Politics of Power in Colonial Guatemala, 1650–1750* (Austin: University of Texas Press, 2002). Similar fears were expressed in early-eighteenth-century Yucatan: the bishop warned of social unrest because blacks "disdained to be equated with Indians," while around the same time the procurator in Mérida reported the Spanish fear that the increasing number of mulattos in the Sierra region would result in them abusing the local Mayas and provoking a general African-Maya conflict; both cited in Robert W. Patch, *Maya and Spaniard in Yucatan, 1648–1812* (Stanford, Calif.: Stanford University Press, 1993), 95–96, the latter also in Manuela Cristina García Bernal, *La Sociedad de Yucatan, 1700–1750* (Seville: Escuela de Estudio Hispano-Americanos, 1972), 19.

18. Lutz, *Santiago*, 86.

19. Archivo General del Arzobispado de Yucatan (hereafter AGAY), Jesús María IV-B-7, *Bautismos*, vol. 3; Restall, *The Black Middle*; Restall, "Otredad y ambigüedad," 19.

20. Few, *Women Who Live Evil Lives*. The irony of—and in some sense a stimulant to—Spanish fears about mulattos was the fact that colonists became increasingly dependent in the seventeenth century upon militiamen of African descent to defend the kingdom (see chapter 1 of this volume).

21. Palomo de Lewin, "Esclavos negros," 140.

22. For San Juan Amatitlán's population see AGI, *Guatemala* 27, "Visita de ingenios y trapiches en que trabajan indios. Año de 1679," f. 104 v.

23. AGI, *Guatemala* 27, "Visita de ingenios y trapiches en que trabajan indios. Año de 1679." On slave values in Yucatan, see Matthew Restall, "La falacia de la libertad: La experiencia Afro-Yucateca en la edad de la esclavitud," in *Rutas de la Esclavitud en Africa y América Latina*, ed. Rina Cáceres (San José: Editorial de la Universidad de Costa Rica, 2001), 291; for this data in the larger Spanish American context, see Restall, *The Black Middle*.

24. See Lokken, "From Black to *Ladino*," 129–40. Lokken (p. 127) quotes the colonial chronicler and local landowner Francisco Antonio Fuentes y Guzmán as noting that San Juan had a "great number of Spanish, mulatto, mestizo, and black *vecinos*" (vecino is a legally recognized citizen of free status).

25. AGN, *Inquisición* 125, 69, fs. 254–63.

26. AGN, *Inquisición* 1164, fs. 210–319. For a discussion of African influences on Maya folk culture in Santiago, especially "magic" and related beliefs and practices, see Martha Few, *Women Who Live Evil Lives*; the title of this very suggestive work expresses the bias of Inquisition officials, but of course one person's witch (*bruja*) could be another person's midwife (*partera*) or healer (*curandera/o*).

27. See Ann F. Jefferson, "The Rebellion of Mita: Eastern Guatemala in 1837" (Ph.D. diss., University of Massachusetts, Amherst, September 2000). This use of the term *ladino* was particular to Guatemala; it was not used commonly in Yucatan, for example. Originally in the sixteenth century *ladino* was used in Guatemala to describe Indians who had become Hispanized, especially in language and dress. By the late seventeenth and eighteenth centuries it was still used in the earlier sense, but more generally it referred to those of mixed descent, some combination of indigenous, European and/or African. It came to be a catchall term for all those who were neither Spanish (or white) nor culturally indigenous; if, for example, a Maya "passed" as a ladino, he/she was a ladino. In some cases *ladino* was also a synonym for *pardo*, mulatto, and

mestizo. See "Glosario," *Siglo XVIII hasta la Independencia*, vol. ed. Cristina Zilbermann de Luján, in *Historia General de Guatemala*, gen. ed. Jorge Luján Muñoz (Guatemala: Asociación de Amigos del País, Fundación para la Cultura y el Desarrollo, 1994), vol. III, 701.

28. For a Pacific coastal (Michatoya drainage) case of this type of problem, see Lawrence H. Feldman, "Vanishing Transhumant Cacao Planters: The Xinca of the Michatoya Drainage, Guatemala," in *Actes du XLII Congrés International des Americanistes* (Paris: Société des Américanistes, 1976), vol. 8, 95–101.

29. See Lovell, *Conquest and Survival*, 122–26, and Arturo Taracena Arriola, *Invención criolla, sueño ladino, pesadilla indígena: Los Altos de Guatemala: De región a Estado, 1740–1850* (San José, Costa Rica: Editorial Porvenir, 1997), 44–49, 58–63. Each provides a brief but convincing case study of the taking of Maya lands in western highland and Pacific coast Guatemala.

30. José Antonio Fernández Molina, "Colouring the World in Blue: The Indigo Boom and the Central American Market, 1750–1810" (Ph.D. diss., University of Texas, Austin, 1992); Julio César Pinto Soria, *Estructura agraria y asentamiento en la Capitanía General de Guatemala: Algunos apuntes históricos* (Guatemala: Universidad de San Carlos, Centro de Estudios Urbanos y Rurales, 1980), cited in Lovell and Lutz, *Demografía e imperio*, 181–83. These same problems confronted Pipil and Xinca communities as well in eastern, coastal Guatemala and into today's El Salvador; see Feldman, "Vanishing Transhumant Cacao Planters."

31. From a total population of 364,022, including Tabasco; from *Documentos para la Historia de Yucatan* (Mérida, Yuc., 1936–1938, 3 vols.) (DHY), vol. I, 99 (Wolfgang Gabbert, *Becoming Maya: Ethnicity and Social Inequality in Yucatan since 1500* [Tucson: University of Arizona Press, 2004], 147, also uses this census). For discussion of Yucatan's late-colonial population in a contemporaneous source, see the "Discurso sobre la constitución de las provincias de Yucatan y Campeche" of 1766, Biblioteca Nacional de México (BNM)–*Fondo Franciscano*.

32. Aguirre Beltrán, *La Población Negra*, 222; Patch, *Maya and Spaniard*, 233–34; J. Ignacio Rubio Mañé, *Archivo de la Historia de Yucatan, Campeche, y Tabasco* (Mexico City: Imp. Aldina, Robredo y Rosell, 1942), vol. I, 250.

33. These paragraphs are drawn from Lokken, "From Black to *Ladino*," 129–30, 138, 141–48, 174, 184ff., 194–99, 204–11 (quote on p. 211).

34. Santiago was Guatemala's colonial capital of longest duration, lasting from 1541 until 1773; it was preceded by Santiago en Almolonga, 1527–1541, and succeeded by La Nueva Guatemala, or Ciudad de Guatemala, founded

north of the Valle de las Vacas after the civil authorities decided to move the capital after the old capital of Santiago (today's Antigua) was badly damaged by earthquakes in 1773.

35. See Lutz, *Historia sociodemográfica*, for a brief discussion of the late Richard M. Morse's theory of centrifugal movement of people out of colonial Latin American cities and the centripetal movement of persons into national period Latin cities, 278, n. 35, and 328–39, n. 55. On Yucatan, see Marta Espejo-Ponce Hunt, "The Process of the Development of Yucatan, 1600–1700," in *Provinces of Early Mexico*, ed. Ida Altman and James Lockhart (Los Angeles: UCLA Latin American Center, 1976), 33–62; and Restall, *The Maya World*, 24–40, 173–77. Our evidence and that of others suggests that colonial population movement was not so unidirectional, at least, not in Spanish Guatemala and New Spain. See, for example, Gabriel Haslip-Viera, "The Underclass," in *Cities and Society in Colonial Latin America*, ed. Louisa Schell Hoberman and Susan Migden Socolow (Albuquerque: University of New Mexico Press, 1986), especially 286–87 on colonial Mexico City. See Richard M. Morse, "Latin American Cities: Aspects of Function and Structure," *Comparative Studies in Society and History*, vol. IV (1961): 473–93.

36. See Lutz, *Historia sociodemográfica*, Cuadro 3, 11–12; Cuadro 14, 163. While the three barrios of Espíritu Santo, La Merced, and San Francisco saw an increase in tributaries between 1581 and 1638 of 13 percent, this was followed by a sharp reversal, a decline of 35 percent between 1638 and 1684, and an even steeper decline of 64 percent between 1684 and 1754. On the distribution of water in Santiago and its implications for population pressures, see Stephen A. Webre, "Water and Society in a Spanish American City: Santiago de Guatemala, 1555–1773," *Hispanic American Historical Review* 57, no. 1 (February 1990): 57–84.

37. For a discussion of cases of free mulattos marrying Mayan women tributaries, see Lutz, *Historia sociodemográfica*, 170–75.

38. For a discussion on the uncovering of networks of communication and petty trade, see Few, *Women Who Live Evil Lives*, and Lutz, *Historia sociodemográfica*, 348–51. Regarding Mayan migration generally, see Christopher H. Lutz and W. George Lovell, "Survivors on the Move: Maya Migration in Time and Space," in *The Maya Diaspora: Guatemalan Roots, New American Lives*, ed. James Loucky and Marilyn M. Moors (Philadelphia: Temple University Press, 2000), 11–34.

39. For a thoughtful discussion of this subject see Magnus Mörner, "La política de segregación y el mestizaje en la Audiencia de Guatemala," *Revista de Indias*, Año XXIV (Enero–Junio 1964): Núms. 95–96: 137–51. Mörner points

out that this segregationist policy was not meant to thwart mestizaje as "interracial marriages" continued to be possible and legal (137). In this article Mörner focuses on the process of mestizaje in the rural sector, especially the cacao-rich district of Sonsonate in modern El Salvador.

40. Francisco de Paula García Peláez, *Memorias para la historia del antiguo reino de Guatemala*, Notas e índice onomástico y toponímico de Francis Gall, Biblioteca Goathemala, vols. XXI–XXIII, 3rd ed. (Guatemala City: Sociedad de Geografía e Historia de Guatemala, 1968–1973), vol. II, 30–31. Mayans were not counted as they were exempt from paying the alcabala.

41. Paul Lokken leans toward the push or displacement hypothesis: "From Black to *Ladino*," 202, n. 68, based on García Peláez, *Memorias*, vol. II, 31. It is important to point out that the importance of demographic movements and epidemic disease to colonial Spanish American historiography did not become more widely accepted until the mid-twentieth century, so García Peláez, writing in the mid-nineteenth century, considers "*despoblación*," but saw it as caused by the wars of conquest, not epidemic disease. See *Memorias*, vol. I, 95–103.

42. Dakin and Lutz, *Nuestro pesar, Nuestra aflicción*, on Santiago. The Yucatec examples are documented in AGN, *Civil* 2013, 1 (sample petitions from which are published in Matthew Restall, Lisa Sousa, and Kevin Terraciano, *Mesoamerican Voices* [Cambridge: Cambridge University Press, forthcoming]), and AGI, *Escribanía* 315B (which contains complaints from the Mérida communities of Santiago and San Cristóbal as well as the nearby ones of Chubulna and Kanasin among a large quantity of other records on the ciudadela affair).

43. Lutz, *Santiago*, app. 4, 239–42. The gente ordinaria ("ordinary people") included indios naborías, all blacks and mulattos, free and enslaved, and any mestizos who did not get counted as Mayas or Spaniards.

44. See Lutz, *Santiago*, esp. chaps. 4 and 5, for a more detailed analysis of marriage patterns both by parish and citywide. Due to loss of Santiago's Maya barrio registers all of our information is drawn from records relating to indios naborías contained in the parish registers for gente ordinaria.

45. Lutz, *Santiago*, 122–32 (sentence above paraphrased from 131).

46. Similar percentage breakdowns can be gleaned from data based on Mérida's marriage records—as presented by Francisco Fernández Repetto and Genny Negroe Sierra, *Una Población Perdida en la Memoria: Los Negros de Yucatán* (Mérida: Universidad Autónoma de Yucatán, 1995), 28–36—although by the late eighteenth century men of African descent were marrying Mayas or mestizas as much as 44 percent of the time (also see Matthew Restall, "Manuel's Worlds, Richard's Worlds: Black Yucatan and the Colonial Caribbean," in

Slaves, Subjects, and Subversives: Blacks in Colonial Latin America, ed. Jane Landers [Albuquerque: University of New Mexico Press, forthcoming], and the analysis of AGAY baptism records in Restall, *The Black Middle*).

47. See Lutz, *Santiago,* app. 3, 233–37.

48. AHDC, Caja 1, Libro 3 (baptisms of blacks and mulattos), fs. 26–62 (1690–1695).

49. Gage, *The English-American,* 195–96.

50. AGEY, *Criminal* 3, exp. 2.

51. See Lutz, *Historia sociodemográfica,* and Lutz, *Santiago,* for a more complete consideration of this phenomenon with respect to the city of Santiago.

52. Christopher H. Lutz, "Santiago de Guatemala (1700–1773)" in *Siglo XVIII hasta la Independencia,* vol. ed. Cristina Zilbermann de Luján, *Historia General de Guatemala,* gen. ed. Jorge Luján Muñoz (Guatemala: Asociación de Amigos del País, Fundación para la Cultura y el Desarrollo, 1994), vol. III, 185–98; Lutz, *Santiago*; and Lutz, *Historia sociodemográfica* all contain varied and different information on Spanish colonial monopolies, racial discrimination, and free casta and ladino reactions to these restrictive policies and practices.

53. AGI, *México* 3042, f. 53v.

CHAPTER EIGHT

Black Read as Red

Ethnic Transgression and Hybridity in Northeastern South America and the Caribbean

NEIL L. WHITEHEAD

༺ྀ

T he colonial conquest of northeastern South America and the Caribbean stimulated the emergence of unfamiliar and "transgressive" or unacceptable forms of ethnic identity. Such new human kinds were taken as evidence of the existence of various "monstrous races"—such as anthropophages or people eaters and giant Amazons—that were part of the European medieval imagination of the outer limits of the earth. By the eighteenth century such human kinds were no longer thought to be peculiar divergences from the rest of humanity and so were categorized according to universal Enlightenment ideas of "race," "nation," and social evolution.

This chapter examines the way such classifications emerged, particularly where a phenotypical blackness in the indigenous population was "read" as

An earlier version of this chapter was presented as a paper in the symposium "Contact and Power," organized by the Borders Studies Research Circle at the University of Wisconsin–Madison, April 1997.

FIG. 8.1: *The Caribbean of the Caribs. Map drawn by Matthew Restall.*

"red," that is, native.[1] A clear example of this process occurred among the Carib Indians of the Caribbean during the period of colonial conquest. This case example is still of political and social significance today, as the Caribs of Dominica and St. Vincent are prominent among the descendants of the native people who first encountered Columbus.

Despite continuing predictions of their demise over the past five hundred years, they still stubbornly survive as an independent community within the modern island state of Dominica. At the time of first contacts the Caribs were a powerful trading people whose canoes plied the waters of the Caribbean and coastal South America. During the colonial period this pre-eminence in sea and river traffic ensured them a significant place within the colonial "cockpit" of conflict that was the Caribbean. As a result they were a magnet for dispossessed and fleeing Indians as well as the black runaway slaves from the island plantations. This also led to a steady infusion of escaped black slaves into Carib society and the eventual emergence of "Black Caribs" as a distinct population. Nevertheless, issues of blackness and Carib ethnic authenticity were exploited by the colonial regimes of the region in an effort to stimulate internecine conflict among the various Carib communities in both the islands and Guyana and Surinam. These issues and the history of that colonial legacy are still very much alive in community debate today.[2]

By the middle of the nineteenth century, the Caribs still persisted on Dominica, Martinique, and St. Vincent, despite being severely reduced in numbers—thousands of the so-called Black Caribs were forcibly transported to Honduras and Belize at the end of the eighteenth century, following the British war against the Black Caribs in Dominica. For those Caribs still on the islands of the Antilles the stabilization of colonial regimes throughout the region meant that their special niche as interisland traders was severely curtailed. In this context they relied increasingly on agriculture and fishing as a means of participation in the national cash economy. By the advent of the twentieth century their socioeconomic position was indistinguishable from that of the freed black slaves, who were their main economic competitors in the wage labor economy.

Since independence from the former colonial power, Britain, in 1978, the economy of Dominica, like that of the other Windward islands of the Antilles, has been based on agricultural export, principally bananas, and tourism. However, as part of its independence package Dominica, for example, retained a special economic relationship with Britain that allowed the sale of bananas at well above the world market price. It is in this context that the Caribs are now deploying their cultural and historical heritage to ameliorate and improve their situation within the island economy as a whole. This marketing of cultural heritage in turn has fed debate on the nature of that heritage, particularly over who best exemplifies it, since, as already suggested, Carib society on the islands has been exceptionally pluralistic in the past. The idea of Carib "purity," that is, a "purity" that excludes blackness, has begun to be mentioned especially when such claims are also being used to negotiate between competing kin groups on the official reservation of Salybia itself for leadership of the Carib Council.

In colonial times, when native identities escaped the limits of racialized cultural boundaries in this way, as in the case of blacks "read as red" (i.e., Caribs), it doubly threatened the old colonial schema of identity. First, it directly challenged the validity of the existing classification. Second, it was a demonstration of the generally imperfect attempts to make such classifications. Such hybrid identities were thus threatening to established forms of colonial political and social authority, even creating at times a common interest in the suppression of the ethnically ambiguous on the part of persistent colonial rivals, such as the British and French. This was precisely the case with the eighteenth-century emergence in the Lesser Antilles of the so-called Black Caribs, discussed below. I hope to show that by examining examples of ethnic transgression across the colonial boundary of red and black, we can gain a better appreciation of the dangerous nature of such transgression and how that transgression influenced the dynamics, cultural contact, and formation of colonial power relations.

READING RED

In the borderlands of the medieval world the episodes of contact with the Americas, and the forms of power unleashed there, forced numerous transgressions of established and fixed norms of thought and action. The elaboration of such contacts into the drama of colonial conquest and occupation of the South American continent and Caribbean islands thus also engendered many new forms of identity, and then the mixing or "hybridity" of those forms.[3] Such challenges to the medieval sociocultural order were mediated through an initial assimilation of these new kinds of being into the marvelous and the monstrous categories of European thought. As a result the "new" world became a site for the reproduction of the "old" and headless men, cannibals, and giants were continually "discovered" in the novel American context, thereby bringing the natives under epistemological if not yet political control.[4]

Alongside this assimilation of new categories of being to the monstrous marvels of medieval thinking was also a debate on "savagery" and "civilization" whose intellectual roots were in the classical world.[5] Emerging from the battle with "barbarian" Islam, Spain's imperial encounter with America shook up a simple opposition of Christian Spain to Islamic Africa. In this context the Native American population was not simply assimilated to the categories of the *Reconquista*, but stimulated a new debate on the evangelical responsibilities of the Castilian state, the idea of universal humanity, and the historicity of biblical myth. With the persistence of the colonial project and its dispersion across the globe, such categories necessarily became part of the Enlightenment juxtaposition of the ideas of race, nation, and progress.

In this context indigenous peoples enter European philosophical debate as exemplars of political evolution in two ways. On the one hand, they are seen as "Hobbesian brutes," playing out the political philosophy of Thomas Hobbes, who suggested that in the absence of state power there was nothing but a perpetual war of all against all, leading to the idea that in tribal societies life was "nasty, brutish, and short." On the other hand, the peoples of indigenous America were also seen as "Rousseauean nobles," after

the views of Jean-Jacques Rousseau, who argued that tribal peoples lived in
a sort of simple harmony and freedom. Both of these powerful images continue to vie in the European imagination as timeless contexts for the working out of humanist principles of government; just as the philosopher John
Locke used the example of life in the huts of the Tupinambás as evidence of
the existence of universal philosophical principles. However, the continuous nature of such intellectual inquiry also suggests its inherent limitations.
If "America" was truly new and different, then it could not be understood as
new by means of analogy to old European forms of culture, society, or ethnicity. In consequence, the categories of conquest and colonization were
continually reassessed and asserted in the face of indigenous actions and
ideas that refused to neatly fit in with the colonial moral and natural
schema to which they were assigned.

Preeminent among these classificatory schema in northeastern South
America and the Caribbean was the ethnology of Columbus, which still
forms the analytical bedrock of colonial and modern ethnologies alike.[6] I
refer here to the notorious conceptual opposition of *caribe* and *guatiao*
("not hostile") and the later supravening term *aruaca* (Arawak), through
which native cultures were assigned to either the spiritual persuasion of the
missionaries or the martial discipline of the conquistadors. Fixed in their
unquestionable status through origins in the documents of discovery and
an "authentic" presence in native oral testimony, the idea of caribes as invasive cannibals and aruacas as legitimate and tractable savages came to form
complementary oppositions in the field of savagery. This in turn allowed
colonial ethnologies to generate complex schema of ethnic classification,
according to the degree to which groups exemplified these polar characteristics. As a result, an active program of colonial ethnography was prosecut-
ed by the missionaries.[7]

Of course, native practice continually threatened this neat bifurcation
of Native American identity, as did competing ethnological schema emerging
from French and Portuguese colonial activity along the Brazilian coast. In
Brazil, all were cannibals, and thus the forms of savagery reflected not a "savage" culture, but the lack of culture altogether. This supposed primitiveness is
then demonstrated empirically in some indigenous groups, such as the Tupi,
by their cannibalistic customs and the practice of perverted and inhuman
sexualities. However, other groups, such as the Guaraní, who were allies of
the Europeans, were argued to be "good" cannibal Indians, and much interest
was shown in their cosmology and polity in order to provide a rationale for
their cannibal proclivities. Indeed, such anthropophagic rites were overtly

compared to the Christian Eucharist. It is not, therefore, simply the cannibal urge, but also its *meaning*, which is important in these discourses.[8]

As a matter of intellectual history, the interaction between these two forms of discourse on American savagery produced a complex web of differing accounts and investigations of "cannibalism." This meant that when new groups were encountered, their ritual and symbolic practices were often explained by reference to these initial contacts with the Tupi and Guaraní in Brazil. Accordingly, French colonial ethnology, marked deeply by the encounter in Brazil, found Tupi-ism among the Iroquois, just as the Spanish eventually found Caribism in Argentina. It will come as no surprise to learn that the intellectual effort made to bring such schema into line with the experience of colonial practice was substantial indeed. This is reflected directly in the fact that virtually no published work of travel reportage fails to offer some observation that is thought to bear on certain vexing questions thrown up by these classificatory exercises—are the Caribs really cannibals and the Arawaks really friendly? Or are the Tupi savage eaters of men or participants in a Brazilian Eucharist? And underlying all these ethnological concerns, the fundamental colonial interrogation—*who is what?*

The term *transgression* thus indicates the way certain kinds of political alliance and ethnic sentiment, especially those that upset existing understanding and categorization, were threatening, if not actively dangerous. As a result, debate in colonial sources with regard to the emergence of forms of ethnic sentiment and practice that were seen as "hybrid" was wider than just the case of black-red transgression and also emerged with regard to such categories as "white Tupi," or "civilized Indians." All these ethnic ascriptions perforce implied a transgression of established ethnic and cultural boundaries of colonial understanding. As such, the mere possibility of the existence of these hybrids clearly threatened the credibility of colonial schema for native identity. For these reasons, the manner of debate and investigation of these transgressive and hybrid categories, both within colonial writing and in the enactment of colonial policy, becomes a useful window onto the rhetorical forms of colonial mastery, that is, the discursive means by which a threatening and monstrous hybridity is transmuted into an exotic, but reassuring, alterity (or quality of difference).

It is also useful to make a distinction between issues of alterity and those of hybridity, since hybridity suggests a monstrous and unnatural novelty, alterity a difference of known or predictable elements. This distinction then helps to unravel the special vilification and near prurient interest shown toward such transgressive identities as caribes who are blacks, Tupi who are white yet eat human flesh, and wild Indians who display a civilized majesty. Within the constraints of this chapter I will only consider black-red transgressions, but it certainly appears from a review of the colonial literatures that interest in other such hybrid identities was no less intense, if unencumbered by the political implications of potential alliances between black slaves and wild Amerindians.[9]

The reason for this is, of course, that such curiosity was driven not by the value-free research programs of an abstracting ethnological science, but by the dynamic urgencies of colonial conquest. By the end of the sixteenth century the presence of such unnatural and asocial categories of persons invited and induced renewed discursive efforts to tidy up the terms of ethological classification that had been derived from initial contacts. At this moment we therefore witness the invention of *Guaymures*—the tribe of white cannibals—lineal descendants of the "squaw men" who represent a New World marvel of categorical and cultural incontinence, one that burst open European conceptual rectitude and scientific parsimony.[10] But this paradox is also what allows an ethnological closure since, no matter what the monstrosity of human form that is thrown up in the course of cultural contact, the ability of a scientific classification to domesticate such savagery through acts of iteration and description stabilizes the dynamic, incontinent, and threatening qualities of hybridity. How this was done with regard to red-blacks, and the political and economic benefits for colonial mastery in doing so, is the subject of the rest of this chapter.

BLACK CARIBS

In the case of Black Caribs in the Caribbean territories, such colonial mastery, as exercised through existing ethnological ideas of "Carib savagery," was not sufficient for the purposes of colonial stability. This was because Black Caribs represented a challenge to the neat bifurcations of colonial understanding—master/slave, white/black—to which the "Indian" added a third and suddenly unpredictable term. Moreover, black and native alliances also threatened a continuing political rupture in colonial relationships since the presence of Black Caribs manifestly incited similar transgressions among still captive slaves. As a result various attempts were made by colonial regimes to utterly destroy the Black Caribs militarily or otherwise suppress their political influence. However, the categorization of various populations as "Black Carib" was highly reminiscent of the earlier

Spanish classifications in the Caribbean that bifurcated the population into aruacas and caribes. Although this was achieved by reference to cultural habits (cannibalism) and political orientations (to the Spanish) and less by allusion to skin tones, the net effect was strikingly similar. In both cases the complexity of the actual ethnic sentiments and history of a people was resolved by the production of exclusive categories that signaled alternatively tractability and rebellious opposition. In short, the "blackness" of eighteenth-century Caribs was no more natural or evident than their predilection for cannibalism of a hundred years earlier. Moreover, we shall see that the presence of "blacks" among the Caribs was a matter of concern and comment from the very inception of the colonial presence. The colonial nightmare of free association and alliance among its subject peoples was thus very much part of how the complexity of ethnicity in the Caribbean was rendered more emotively controllable and intellectually reassuring.

Today the historical and popular representation of "Caribs" in the Caribbean, including Guyana and Venezuela, still strongly reflects these rhetorics of colonial mastery. As a result, the Caribs are seen as both savage, given their indelible association with "cannibalism," a term cognate with *caribe* in the orthography of Columbus, but also marginal to the politics of postcolonialism in the sense that they did not oppose white colonial rule in the way that black African slaves did. However, the actual prevalence of such interrelationships and the pattern of colonial repression of both Amerindians and rebel blacks created the basis for the emergence of a common sense of exclusion. This was the fertile ground for the formation of the people we know today as Black Caribs in St. Vincent and Surinam or as the Garifuna in Belize. However, it should be emphasized that "blackness" here is no less a construct of the colonial observer and cannot be taken as a given of ethnic sentiment among those designated as "black" by the colonial authorities. Indeed, the formation of such identities was predicated on the colonial process itself, which, through the ethnocide of warfare, slavery, and epidemic disease, forced ethnogenesis right across the continent.[11] The idea of "Black Caribs" has its bases in the categories of colonial understanding; these categories differentiated the rebel black from the intractable savage in their opposition to white dominance, seeking to pit the one against the other.

At the same time, we should not ignore the fact that indigenous ethnic philosophies also evinced their own principles of exclusion and difference and so in turn produced their own categories of hybridity.[12] However, in the case of Black Caribs, although they were apparently sometimes opposed by other Amerindians, this should not be seen as stemming from indigenous ideas that mirrored colonial discourse on the purity and hybridity of race. Rather, such antagonism, where it existed, was strongly stimulated by the colonial authorities themselves, both intellectually and in policy terms. In this way intellectual commentary on red-black antagonism was used to present such differences as inevitable, making it seem as if both colonial and native ideologies of ethnicity shared a negative idea of "blackness." This was the case with the Spanish idea of Caribism in the fifteenth and sixteenth century Caribbean since, even before the extensive transportation of black slaves had begun, attributions of Caribism carried analogous negative connotations to those of "blackness" in the eighteenth century. Nonetheless, this dangerous conjunction of Carib with black was already foreshadowed by judicial inquiries in Puerto Rico in the sixteenth century that sought to establish the role of escaped black slaves in Carib raids on local haciendas. This clearly suggests that issues of Black Carib origins are as much about the stability of colonial classification as about the history of demographic change in the Caribbean. As a result, purported "evidence" of Amerindian racism toward blacks cannot be simply treated as an exemplar of a universal, "natural" racialism that was shared by whites and Amerindians, although colonial commentary certainly sought to naturalize differences in just this way. Rather, for Amerindians, blackness was a sign of exteriority, like whiteness, and a proper understanding of indigenous attitudes must necessarily take account of this.

THE DOCUMENTARY RECORD

In a brief chapter it is impossible to fully explore extended case studies, but even a limited examination of documentary sources from the Lesser Antilles can give us a window onto the general character of the conjunction of "blackness" and "Caribism" in different contexts, separated by some 150 years. Each may then stand as an exemplar of the processes referred to above and will be the subject of concluding commentary.

THE CAPTIVITY OF LUISA DE NAVARRETE (1580)

From the inception of Spanish settlement in the Caribbean, the Amerindians of the Lesser Antilles bore the reputation of being intractably warlike. Although the experiences of the non-Spanish colonizers were often very different, there can be little doubt that both local shipping and the isolated farms and plantations of the Spanish settlers were often attacked by caribes. Although European adult males were killed outright during such attacks, many other individuals were simply taken into captivity as wives, servants, and perhaps future victims of ritual war dances (*areytos*). In 1576 just such a raid on the island of Puerto Rico resulted in the capture of a creole woman, Luisa de Navarrete. Despite the attention that was given to the captivity of Luisa, her plight was not that uncommon. Estimates of there being up to three hundred European and African captives on Dominica, as well as the imprisonment of the son of Juan Ponce de Leon II, indicate that this was by no means an exceptional fate. The following extracts from the petition of Bernaldez de Quiroz, procurator general of Puerto Rico, are a summary of Luisa de Navarrete's testimony on her captivity:[13]

> I, the said Pablo Bernaldez de Quiroz, Procurator General, present...as a witness Luysa de Nabarrete, black-skinned, free and of good name and Spanish-speaking, and a resident of this city.... [The caribes] took away this witness and left her in Dominica as the captive of an Indian *casique* in Dominica, here they held her captive 4 or 5 years, and this witness has seen that...they arm themselves every year and cross to this island of Puerto Rico and rob and destroy whatever they can.... This witness has seen that the three times they have come to this island...they have carried away a great quantity of Blacks and left some in Dominica and distributed the rest amongst the Indians of these islands, which they take to their lands in order to serve them.... This witness saw that one of these times that they carried off a quantity of Blacks that they had stolen, that they took from Luisa a white boy, son of one Domingo Pinero, and another time that their armada came.... They took from this island two other Blacks that this witness knew, and the Indians said that they had carried off others to another island.... The said Indians always used to go boasting and making great fiestas saying that they had burnt and destroyed many farms in this island and killed many people, and this witness saw...that they attacked, overcame, burnt and robbed a ship...and then carried off and killed three or four of the principal Spaniards who were traveling in the ship. They held all these people captive, and many more from before this witness was captured; they held there the ones that serve them and treat them very roughly, making them work and go about naked by day and night, and they paint them like themselves,

making them sleep on the ground, not allowing them to eat
meat except lizards and rats and snakes and some fish, and they
do not let them roast this nor cook this, but they are made to
eat it raw, and they tell them to eat human flesh.... They get
drunk, take the female captives and force them, knowing them
carnally, making them do as they wish, and the wives of the said
Indians, seeing this, shoot arrows at the other captive women
in parts where they do not kill them, and when the said Indians
want to eat others that they have captured they make their
areytos and call to and speak with the Devil.... There in their
areytos they agree to kill one, and so they kill him and eat him,
and when it is agreed that they kill some Christian of another
nation, they kill him and throw him in the sea, and when some
Indian who holds captives dies, they kill some of his captives
and say that they kill them in order that they should go on
serving him, and, if it were not for this there would be many
more captives than there are ... and this witness knows and
saw in the said island of Dominica that there are two [black]
women and a man who were already as much caribes as the
rest of them, and the women say that they no longer remember
God, and the man neither more nor less so, and he eats human
flesh and they do just as the Indians do, neither more nor
less ... and another man comes with these said Indians that has
now become as caribe as them and likewise eats human flesh,
and this witness and other Christians speaking with this man
asked him why he did not remember the mother of God, since
he was a Christian, and the said man replied that since the
mother of God had not remembered to take him from here
in forty years, neither did he wish to remember her, and this
witness saw the same among the other Blacks who eat human
flesh and do as the Indians do.

These extracts make it very evident that integration of black slaves captured
from the Spanish into caribe society began from the very inception of
European settlement. Furthermore, integration involved a range of social
possibilities—from outright captivity, through to a modified domestic service, up to intermarriage with the Caribs and the adoption of their political
and cultural practices. Notable too is the distinct ways black and white captives were treated.

These themes are still evident 150 years later, underlining the point that European colonialism had a constant role in shaping the relation between escaped or captured slaves and Amerindians throughout this region. Moreover, it will also be evident that a simple bifurcation of the population of the Caribbean outside of direct colonial control into blacks and reds cannot do justice to the complexity of this history. This is also very evident in the information supplied from the initial intelligence gathered on the "Black Caribs" of St. Vincent. This report aimed, among other purposes, to delineate historically and culturally the difference between Black Caribs and a supposed "native" red or yellow Carib substrate.

First Reconnaissances of the Black Caribs (1700–1723)

As the early documents indicate, although the presence and social integration of black runaway slaves within the Amerindian societies of the Caribbean certainly had begun as early as the mid-sixteenth century, it was not until the eighteenth century that "Black Caribs" become ever more clearly delineated in the colonial sources as a fully distinct social element with separate, and at times conflicting, interests to the "real" Amerindian population. Most of all on St. Vincent, possibly due to the intense colonial rivalry for a clear possession of the island and because of the way in which all elements of the general population were utilized by the colonial authorities as proxies, the Black Caribs came to form a powerful and enduring element in colonial strategies on the island. The purpose of the following short extracts is to illustrate the growing alertness on the part of the Europeans to the possibilities for exploiting differences among the population of St. Vincent not under their control and their attempts to exploit nascent divisions between Black Caribs and a supposedly aboriginal "red Carib" population. The historical documents certainly suggest in a general sense that such activities by the Europeans were an important element in the formation of Black Carib identity during the eighteenth century, and this was manifestly so in the case of the Garifuna, or Black Caribs, of Central America. It was their ancestors who were deported en masse from St. Vincent in 1797, when the British took complete control of the island at the end of the second Carib War.[14] With the goading of an intense French and English rivalry over the settlement of Dominica, St. Vincent, and Grenada in the eighteenth century, Black Caribs under the leadership of the chieftain Chatoyer emerged as a significant organized anti-British military force. Ethnological curiosity as to the sources and implications of such an ethnic formation thus derived from the fact that Black Caribs represented a potent and novel element in colonial political calculations.

FIG. 8.2: *Chatoyer, chief of the Caribs of St. Vincent, with his five wives. From Bryan Edwards,* The History, Civil and Commercial, of the British Colonies in the West Indies, *vol. III (London: Printed for J. Stockdale, 1801), opp. p. 179.*

The following extract is taken from a report made in 1700 by the Comte d'Amblimont and alludes to a shipwreck off St. Vincent as a possible origin for the considerable number of "negroes" reported there. It is also suggested that the favorable currents from Barbados to St. Vincent were an important factor in augmenting the black population here. However, in light of the preceding considerations, this becomes as much an attempt to "naturalize" the construction of "blackness" in opposition to indigenous identity as it was an objective report of the actual demography of St. Vincent. As we shall see later, this is borne out by the way estimates of the Black Carib population vary wildly according to the colonial positioning of the commentator, although the potential significance of "blackness" was a mutually shared ideology by French and British alike.

> There are a considerable number of Negroes in St. Vincent who established themselves here a long time ago having their families and their *carbets* [longhouses] in parts where they are separated from the *Caraibes*. This island of St. Vincent is the one where the Caraibes maintain themselves in the greatest number since the establishment of the Europeans in the Caribbean, and similarly through the trade between the French, English and Caraibes it has been convenient that they have been left with their property, as also on Dominica, without anyone being allowed to trouble them there. It happened that there was a long time before this a ship full of Blacks wrecked and lost on the windward of St. Vincent, many of the black men and women . . . escaped on shore and were received kindly by the Caraibes; it is this event that began settlement of these Blacks on St. Vincent. . . . There were male and female Blacks, they had children, and some of these Blacks married Caraibe girls, on account of which they have grown in number. . . .
> It is true that many Blacks have deserted from the islands possessed by the Europeans who have put themselves among those on St. Vincent, but few have deserted the French islands [because of the currents]; of all the islands the one from which it is the most easy to reach St. Vincent is Barbados, it is not necessary to do anything other than drift on the currents. . . .
> It is possible to come very easily from Barbados; that is why among the Blacks of St. Vincent there are few who come from the French islands. As far as removing all these Blacks from

St. Vincent is concerned . . . these Blacks are settled on the
windward of St. Vincent and all this windward coast is full
of dangers and obstacles. . . . It will be the most practicable to
disembark on the leeward side in the area occupied by the
Caraibes. . . . This will also be very difficult, unless the Caraibes
here will allow it.

This passage presents the key ideas that were also the basis for British imag-
ining of the Black Carib, which was given its clearest expression as a kind of
post hoc justification for the Carib Wars in the writings of William Young.[15]
It may well be that there was such a shipwreck, as is alluded to in these
accounts, but no less important is the imagery of an invasive and ever bur-
geoning "blackness" among the aboriginal inhabitants, the caraibes. The
caraibes are then seen as vainly holding out against this tide of negritude
until or unless the hand of colonialism can sweep clean the island of its
contaminants. D'Amblimont, in this early report, is clearly aware of some
of these ambiguities over ethnic definitions and how they may relate to
political proclivities. He continues:

The opinion most common is that the Caraibes of the said
island wish that the Blacks that are settled here would flee
elsewhere, some of these Caraibes who come here testify the
same, it seems also that this would be in their interest, because
they are subject to the fear that these Blacks are multiplying
and growing in number, would become stronger and more
powerful than them and afterwards maltreat them. . . . On the
other hand it is not possible to be at all assured that this will
occur because there are a great many of these Blacks allied with
some of the Caraibes and who live together on good terms, and
one ought not at all to absolutely rely on the specific words of
these Caraibes, who speak little, who take a long time to explain
themselves, and who judge most cleverly what one desires them
to say. . . . It is a very steadfast sentiment that they prefer to
see two thousand Negroes settled in their island, than to see
disembarking here only 50 armed Frenchmen. This is why
one is able to certainly plan that one would have no agreement
from these Caraibes for this enterprise, and that in order to
try it is necessary to risk war with them, as well as the Negroes
of the said island of St. Vincent.

Peter Hulme has recently closely examined French materials relating to this crucial question of the categorization of the Black Caribs as an aspect of colonial rivalry.[16] In particular, he cites the commentary of Moreau de Jonnés, who fought with the Black Caribs against the British.[17] As Hulme points out, it is also important to remember that the small-scale individual farming practiced by French planters in the region contrasted strongly with the large-scale plantation projects that were envisaged by British financiers in their investments in St. Vincent sugar. This alone would tend to suggest that the emphatic "blackness" of St. Vincentian Caribs in British eyes was derived as much from the obstacle they presented to an exclusive occupation of the island as from any observation of skin tones. In short, although Moreau lived and fought with so-called red Caribs, his estimates of the "black" element of the Carib population are far smaller than those of his British contemporaries.[18] This pointedly raises the question as to how "black" those Caribs deported from St. Vincent by the British may have been. It also suggests that in British eyes, "blackness," like "caribism" for the Spanish, really originates in a political opposition to colonial designs. This intractability is then progressively conflated with specious racial classifications that overall served to both justify and motivate the Carib Wars of the 1790s.

CONCLUSION

It will be appreciated, then, that resistance to colonial encroachment was an active context in which ethnic identities evolved and that this process of ethnogenesis was not just a matter of self-identification, but also overt manipulation by colonial regimes. In fact, colonial political designs *were* substantively impeded, not just by Black Caribs, but also by the interconnections of maroon (or escaped slave) societies and Amerindian groups, even though these connections might also facilitate the control of maroon groups in other colonies, such as Berbice (Guyana). It is also clear that it was not just the categorical offense that hybrid identities gave to the dominant categories of ethnic classification that accounts for their cultural significance, but also a colonial fear of categorical incontinence and the resulting uncontrollable proliferation of human kinds. This fear itself stemmed from the way such schema were ideologically connected to the overall design and functioning of colonial occupation and control and leads not to a critique of cultural chauvinism, but demonstrates precisely how hybridity can actually *reinforce* such notions.[19]

More generally, such considerations about the existence and development of ethnic plurality and hybridity in native and colonial society strongly suggest that our picture of what constitutes "tribes," "groups," or "ethnicities" is theoretically very limited. As yet we are unable to do justice to the complexity of historical formulations of ethnicity and, more importantly, the meaning of hybridity within such schema. Hybrids mark boundaries; they act as the null case to claims of identity and so are necessarily part of a sociocultural conception in which purity is the other term. Recent work in anthropology argues that while hybrids are indeed marginal figures, isolated in the distance of borderlands, this emphasis on their ideological and cultural isolation as persons obscures the fact that they are indivisibly connected to the discourses of identity and purity.[20] In such discourses hybrids function as the cutoff point, markers of the limits of intelligibility, and so signal transition to other forms or allow recombinant forms to develop—as the cases presented here suggest.

As anthropologist Mary Douglas long ago recognized, ideas of purity and danger are central to the explanation of cultural categories.[21] Where the notion of hybridity is useful is in distinction to scientific forms of social-cultural analysis that claim an empirically unchallengeable status for conceptual or methodological distinctions and categories. By bringing the idea of hybridity to the center of debate about ethnicity, rather than the standard focus on issues of "authenticity," it is possible to challenge the notion that historical analysis must proceed by the progressive exclusion of evidence that does not fit normative categories in a vain search for the core or essence of ethnic sentiment. This procedure results only in an erasure of subtle differences in an attempt to bring all items of "evidence" within existing conceptual schema. Otherwise such schema become hopelessly inflated to allow for and naturalize the new classes of phenomena that hybridity seems to present. However, the transgressive and hybrid is the permanent exception, the remainder, the detritus of these acts of scientific purification. But the relevance of hybrids to these cultural acts of scientific classification is that such categories are dramatically undermined by the hybrid's paradoxical and contradictory qualities. As Mary Douglas states:

> The very reaction to ambiguous behavior expresses the expectation that all things shall normally conform to the principles which govern the world. ... [But] in painting such dark themes, pollution symbols are as necessary as the use of black in any depiction whatsoever. Therefore we find corruption enshrined in sacred places and times.[22]

Both "blackness" and "caribism" emerged at the inception of European settlement of the Caribbean as key tropes of colonial ethnology, involving a range of social possibilities between persons of distinct origins—including slavery, intermarriage, and transculturation into native practices. However, it was not until the eighteenth century, and in the context of intense colonial rivalry, that social and political notions of Black Caribs emerge in colonial sources. These notions were forceful and fatefully enacted toward the population of St. Vincent with a view to removing the obstacle of Carib prior settlement, and to this end Black Caribs were identified as the primary source of seditious opposition to the British. In winning the Carib War of 1796–1797, the British were then able to seek a final solution to their Black Carib problem through the mass deportation of a huge portion of the Carib population.

That these deportees were Caribs, whatever their skin tone and political beliefs, is amply demonstrated in the fact that it is the Garifuna who have continued to use the aboriginal language, Karinagu. Once spoken by all island Caribs, it is now only the descendents of those deported to Central America in the eighteenth century who still speak Karinagu—and recall in oral history and ritual customs the memory of their deportation. Assertion of their indigenous and independent political traditions and their "blackness" must be understood as no less a token of their American origins than it may be of more distant African ones—they are blacks who demand that we read them as red.

ᘓᘛ

NOTES

1. The term *yellow* was also used in the Caribbean to denote indigenous people who were thought to show no phenotypical African admixture.

2. See Peter Hulme and Neil L. Whitehead, eds., *Wild Majesty: Encounters with Caribs from Columbus to the Present Day, an Anthology* (Oxford: Oxford University Press, 1992); Neil Whitehead, "Native Society and the European Occupation of the Caribbean Islands and Coastal Tierra Firme, 1492–1650," in *A General History of the Caribbean*, vol. III, ed. C. Damas and P. Emmer (London: UNESCO Publications, 1999), chap. 7; "The Crises and Transformations of Invaded Societies (1492–1580)—The Caribbean," in *The*

Cambridge History of Native American Peoples, vol. III, ed. F. Salomon and S. Schwartz (Cambridge: Cambridge University Press, 1999), chap. 10.

3. For a discussion of ethnogenesis in this region, see Neil Whitehead, "Ethnogenesis and Ethnocide in the settlement of Surinam," in *History, Power and Identity: Ethnogenesis in the Americas, 1492–1992*, ed. J. Hill (Iowa City: University of Iowa Press, 1996), 20–35.

4. Stephen Greenblatt, *Marvelous Possessions: The Wonder of the New World* (Oxford: Clarendon Press, 1991).

5. R. Bartra, *Wild Men in the Looking Glass: The Mythic Origin of European Otherness* (Ann Arbor: University of Michigan Press, 1994).

6. Neil Whitehead, "Ethnic Plurality and Cultural Continuity in the Native Caribbean: Remarks and Uncertainties as to Data and Theory," in *Wolves from the Sea: Readings in the Archaeology and Anthropology of the Island Carib*, ed. N. L. Whitehead (Leiden: KITLV Press, 1995).

7. Neil Whitehead, "Native Society and the European Occupation"; "The Crises and Transformations of Invaded Societies"; and "Lowland Peoples Confront Colonial Regimes in Northern South America, 1550–1900," all in *The Cambridge History of Native American Peoples*, vol. III, ed. F. Salomon and S. Schwartz (Cambridge: Cambridge University Press, 1999), chap. 14.

8. F. Lestringant, *Cannibals* (Berkeley: University of California Press, 1997); Neil Whitehead, "Hans Staden and the Cultural Politics of Cannibalism," *Hispanic American Historical Review* 80, no. 4 (2000): 721–51.

9. In the case of the white Tupi, or "squaw men," French colonial policy in Brazil created a class of indigent traders. The ability of individual traders to work with native leaders was crucial, and later successes in the settlement of Brazil can be directly linked to the activities of their "white Tupi" offspring. Yet such traders were still a source of anxiety for the formulators of imperial design since they actively married into the "savage tribes" and adopted or mimicked their customs, even to the point of participation in that most sacred of indigenous rites—the anthropophagy of enemies and kin. However, as their moment of political significance passed, these "squaw men" became conflated in the literature with the other hybrid creations of that early colonial moment. These include such as the half-breed Tapuyas, remnant Tupi mercenaries, and denationalized white adventurers such as El Peregrino Vendado (Lope de Aguirre) or Aleixo Garcia, who invaded the Inca empire with a native Guaraní army nearly a decade *before* Pizarro.

10. White-reds also haunted the margins of Caribbean history. Thomas "Indian" Warner was the son of the English governor of St. Kitts and a carib woman. A French source describes him thus (Hulme and Whitehead, *Wild Majesty*, 91):

"Although this Bastard was born of a female Savage & slave, there appeared in him nothing of the Savage but the colour of his skin and hair, and although he had very black hair, he combed and dressed it, contrary to the custom of the other Savages." Warner's father died in his adolescence but he effected a reconciliation between the English and Caribs, and so Lord Willoughby, governor of the Caribbean, took him to England, making him appear at court. There he comported himself as a Christian with the English and dressed as they did, "but being returned he rid himself of these clothes, and comported himself as an infidel with the Savages, and went naked and covered with body-paint just as they do; but he never touched a single woman." The English gave Indian Warner a commission to subject the Caribs of Dominica to the crown and he came to play a pivotal role in a series of confrontations between the French, English, and Caribs. European patrilineal theory held that Warner had an inherited capacity for proper and civilized behavior, as reflected by his facility in enacting the correct codes of appearance at the English court. As such, hybrids of Warner's type might be usefully contrasted with the case of the white Tupi—naturals of Europe but morally *defective* through participation in indigenous culture, whereas Warner appears as a natural of the Caribbean but morally *effective* through overt participation in colonial culture; clearly even this thin borderline was difficult to traverse.

11. Neil Whitehead, "Tribes Makes States and States Make Tribes: Warfare and the Creation of Colonial Tribe and State in Northeastern South America, 1498–1820," in *War in the Tribal Zone*, 2nd ed., ed. R. B. Ferguson and N. L. Whitehead (Santa Fe, N.Mex., and Oxford: School of American Research Press and James Currey, 1999), 127–50.

12. This was particularly so where groups came to act as "ethnic soldiers" for the colonial regime, thus more fully adopting the colonial political viewpoint of ethnic differences; see Neil Whitehead, "Carib Ethnic Soldiering in Venezuela, the Guianas and Antilles: 1492–1820," *Ethnohistory* 37, no. 4 (1990): 357–85.

13. A fuller version, from which this extract is taken, appears in Hulme and Whitehead, *Wild Majesty*, 171–79.

14. See ibid., 216–30.

15. The key extracts are given in ibid., 189–210.

16. See Peter Hulme, *Remnants of Conquest: The Island Caribs and Their Visitors, 1877–1998* (Oxford: Oxford University Press, 2000); and Peter Hulme, "Yellow and Black in the Caribbean: Racial and Ethnic Classification on St. Vincent during the Revolutionary Wars of the 1790's" (paper given to the Department of Anthropology, University of Wisconsin—Madison, March 2000).

17. The memoirs of Moreau de Jonnés (1858) were composed at the age of eighty, but he had served on St. Vincent as a young man and had there been

lodged with the "Caraibes." His questioning of the blackness of those judged to be Black Caribs is therefore very pertinent (see n. 18 below).

18. As Hulme, "Yellow and Black in the Caribbean," points out, the British sources suggest that there were around 3,000 Black Caribs and only very few red Caribs, but Moreau, who was in an excellent position to judge, estimated that there were only some 1,500 Black Caribs and more than 6,000 red Caribs. It would certainly seem that the construction of "blackness" in these circumstances was very much a matter of political positioning.

19. This is also shown, perhaps even more starkly, in the case of Indian Warner (see n. 10 above). Warner's specific tragedy was that he was never able to firmly convince either colonial or savage as to his human capacity for ethnic authenticity and political fidelity and so, as soon as local colonial and indigenous politics had resolved the uncertainties of identity and alliance that were created during this initial occupation of the islands, Warner fell between those worlds. In an act of near-classical tragedy, he was killed by his own white half-brother, Philip, who was commanding a joint military expedition against "enemy" Caribs and who also ordered a wholesale massacre of Thomas's allies: "Afterwards an Indian calling himself Thomas Warner's son came on board Col. Warner's ship, and told him that as he had killed his father and all his friends, he prayed him to cause him also to be killed, holding his head of one side to receive a blow, this, by Col. Philip's order was given him, and his body thrown overboard" (Hulme and Whitehead, *Wild Majesty*, 101–2). Indian Warner had been warned that Colonel Warner was plotting to kill him, but he had replied that he was "better assured of his kindness and fidelity, being his own half-brother." The reaction that this murder induced in the English crown is unprecedented and indicates the powerful way Warner's hybrid status impacted English actions and self-image. Charles II ordered that "a speedy and exemplary justice be done upon the person guilty of this inhuman act, and his Majesty's pleasure is that blood that hath been so barbarously spilt be fully avenged. His Majesty leaves it to the Governor to give the Savages of Dominica a public demonstration of his justice upon the authors by sending them some heads" (Hulme and Whitehead, *Wild Majesty*, 101). Thus the ambiguities of Indian Warner's status provoked this strange colonial mimesis of the Dominican savages—an Englishmen's head as a token of Charles's love for his savage subjects; a wild majesty indeed!

20. M. Strathern, "Cutting the Network," *JRAI* 2, no. 3 (1996): 517–35.

21. Mary Douglas, *Purity and Danger: An Analysis of the Concepts of Pollution and Taboo* (London: Pelican, 1971).

22. Ibid., 210.

CHAPTER NINE

Black-Native Relations and the Historical Record in Colonial Mexico

Patrick J. Carroll

☙☙

In the spring of 1560, Viceroy don Luis de Velasco publicly decried *negro* depredations in Guanajuato. He claimed that lawless blacks roamed the countryside at will, committing all sorts of criminal acts—destruction of property, thefts, assaults, rapes, and murders. Some of the victims were whites, but most were Amerindians. According to the viceroy, blacks preyed heavily upon native females, violating them at will, even in their own homes and in front of their families. Worse yet, blacks sometimes carried off indigenous women, never to be seen again.[1]

Chapter 7 of this volume tells the story of a runaway slave from Yucatan named José Antonio Marcín. Matthew Restall and Christopher Lutz recount that in 1816, Maya villagers dragged a wounded Marcín before Spanish authorities and charged him with a variety of crimes ranging from robbery to rape. After reviewing court records, Lutz and Restall surmised that the indictments more likely derived from natives' predisposed negative perceptions of blacks' behavior than from any crimes the slave actually committed. Armed with a small sword for personal protection, Marcín was seen as a threat. In the Mayas' minds, a black man with a weapon on the royal road was an outlaw, and they interpreted everything he did as criminal activity. For their part, Spanish authorities harbored their own racist attitudes toward blacks and were only too ready to believe the black's Maya accusers without any corroborating evidence. In support of this assumption, Restall and Lutz point out that Marcín's experience did not represent an isolated case. After examining charges against a number of other blacks brought before the office of the Inquisition in colonial Mérida, Lutz and Restall concluded that throughout the colonial period, both whites and Mayas in Yucatan often viewed blacks as dangerous undesirables.

Indeed, Spanish American criminal and church records abound with references to hostile black-native relations. Don Alonso de la Mota y Escobar, the early-seventeenth-century bishop of Puebla, provided one particularly gruesome account of such conflict. In 1609, while traveling through the Veracruz section of his diocese, he came upon two frightened merchant brothers and their Nahua servants. Both Spaniards related a terrifying tale. The previous night their party had set up camp along the royal road between the port of Veracruz and the town of Jalapa. Just after dark a band of *cimarrones*, or runaway slaves, set upon them. First, the fugitives took the Spaniards' strongbox containing over a hundred pesos. They then seized all the pack animals and loaded them with the victims' trade goods. In the process they killed the merchants' teenage brother, who tried to resist the assault. Yet this was not what had frightened the survivors most. Not satisfied with money, mules, goods, and murder, the blacks carried off all the Nahua women in the party despite the entreaties of their husbands and their children. One mother who clung to her nursing infant paid an especially horrible price. As the terrified Spaniards and Nahuas watched, her black abductor tore the baby from her arms and dashed its brains on a nearby rock, saying he had no use for it. He then rode off with his screaming female prize.[2]

At times whites deliberately exploited blacks' reputation for cruelty to natives. Don Carlos Ribadenyra, a wealthy sugar planter and the *alcalde mayor* (chief magistrate) of the district of Teutila along Oaxaca's eastern border with Veracruz, counted on native fears of blacks to obtain land he had disputed with the village of Soyaltepec. In 1769, Ribadenyra paid residents of the newly created town of Amapa, populated by recently freed runaway slaves, to drive the indigenous locals from the lands he coveted. Ribadenyra had unsuccessfully tried to obtain them through the Spanish courts but had failed. Mexico City's *audiencia*, the highest tribunal in the viceroyalty, had just rendered a decision in favor of the natives after years of court battles. Frustrated, Ribadenyra decided that if he could not acquire the land legally, he would seize it illegally. The black mercenaries did their job. After less than a month of harassment and intimidation the Soyaltepec natives fled, Ribadenyra had control of the lands, and the historical record included another example of blacks' hostility toward Amerindians.[3]

These anecdotal incidents project a general impression of ongoing friction between blacks and natives throughout the viceroyalty over the entire colonial period. Indeed, few scholars challenge this perception in New Spain or in other parts of Latin America. Frederick Bowser, writing about sixteenth- and seventeenth-century Peru, stated that although African-native contact was often peaceful, it was more often violent.[4] James Lockhart, also commenting on Peru, concluded, "The relationship between Negroes and Indians was, in the main, one of strong mutual hostility."[5] In support of his contention, Lockhart points out that blacks acted as auxiliaries in the Spanish Conquest and occupied intermediary positions of de facto power between whites and natives. He asserts that from this middle power position, they quickly assimilated Hispanic culture in Peru and in other colonial New World settings, further alienating them from natives. Restall adds that "the dominant Maya tendency was to reject Africans, to imitate Spanish racial prejudices, to regard the African as one of the uglier faces of Spanish colonialism."[6] Magnus Mörner, one of the foremost authorities on race relations in colonial Latin America, observes that Spanish officials all over the Americas spoke out against blacks' abuse of natives. They complained of sixteenth-century Africans' sexual exploitation of indigenous women, seizure of indigenous lands and portable property, assaults on indigenous men, and transmission of corrupting influences, ranging from encouragement of vices to heretical religious ideas to revolutionary ideology.[7] All of these developments, by implication, caused natives to view blacks and whites alike as outsiders, conquerors, intruders, and exploiters, people to avoid as much as possible.[8] William Taylor's assessment of the colonial Mexican setting expressed this perception well when he stated that "contacts between villagers and non-Indians in central Mexico were frequent but not especially sociable."[9]

Despite widespread consensus on the predominantly hostile nature of black/native interaction, virtually every scholar who examines such interaction in colonial Latin America documents "exceptions" to this general rule. The pattern of "exceptions" invites consideration of an alternative reading of Afro-Mexican/Amerindian dealings, and many of the essays herein either implicitly or explicitly reinforce the need for such reinterpretation. Chapter 1 of this volume, by Ben Vinson and Matthew Restall, provides a case in point. The authors approach black/native relations from the perspective of *pardo* (persons of perceived black-Amerindian phenotype) and *moreno* (a euphemism for *negro*) militiamen's interaction with native Mexicans. They conclude that relations between Afro- and native Mexicans was generally antagonistic in nature. Restall and Vinson do, however, acknowledge that hostility was neither automatic nor universal. They observe that black militiamen "did not necessarily fight natives because they wanted or needed to, but because they were recruited [by Spaniards] for this duty." They point out that in northern areas of New Spain, on the margins of church and state influence, indigenous and Afro-Latin American peoples often voluntarily came together to create multiracial and multiethnic frontier communities.

As Castillo Palma and Kellogg state at the outset and conclusion of chapter 4, the inevitable interaction between black and indigenous inhabitants of Spanish America was both harmonious and hostile throughout the colonial period. They surmise that such ambiguity emanated from the nature of relations between the two groups. Intermingling by blacks, natives, and *castas* (mixed-race people) sprang from "interpersonal alliances" between members of these groups that naturally occurred in the workplace, on the street, and in the homes of plebeians. And the very nature of interpersonal relations runs the gamut from hostile to harmonious interaction.

Other scholars echo this more balanced assessment of Amerindian/ black relations in New Spain. Colin Palmer, a ground-breaking student of blacks' experience in Mexico, wrote that "Indians and Afro-Mexicans enjoyed an ambivalent relationship in early colonial New Spain. On the one hand, they established sexual unions; on the other hand, their relationship was often characterized by violent hostility."[10] Gonzalo Aguirre Beltrán, unquestionably the most renowned pioneer of early Afro-Mexican studies, provided an equally ambiguous interpretation of interaction between natives and blacks in Mexico. Beltrán recorded numerous instances of natives' mistreatment at the hands of Afro-Mexicans. He added, however, that the offspring of black-native unions were often raised in indigenous villages by their mothers and became fully integrated into those communities as equals and members of extended kin groups.[11] Woodrow Borah even suggests that the incidence of blacks tranquilly living side by side with native peoples might not have been as exceptional as many scholars thought. He asserts that Spanish officials unsuccessfully tried to prohibit blacks' presence in native Mexican villages because they saw such contact as "dangerous" to indigenous peoples.

Spaniards believed that blacks physically mistreated natives, stole and destroyed their property, and taught them bad habits. These misgivings, according to Borah, were exaggerated.[12]

This chapter goes even farther than the above revisionist constructions of a balanced, or even ambiguous, Afro-Mexican–Amerindian colonial relationship, and it turns the traditional hostile interpretation of interaction between the two groups on its head. I posit that in the colonial Mexican setting, blacks and natives engaged in more harmonious than antagonistic association with one another. To begin with, even those that accept the conflictive perspective of black-native relations acknowledge, along with Borah, that this perception may be overstated. As Lockhart has pointed out, colonial documents painted a "double image" of blacks in Spanish America. For example, notarial records often presented them as industrious and trustworthy; government documents, and to a lesser degree church records, usually portrayed them as undesirables—vile, unruly, dishonest, cruel, exploiters and corrupters of natives.[13] The probable explanation for this "double image" lies in the nature and function of each type of document. Local and viceregal officials often used public documents as tools for social engineering, as instruments to shape popular attitudes and beliefs. Colonial Mexico had a racially and ethnically pluralistic society within which white Spaniards and their creole descendants represented a small minority. The state's demeaning of blacks, natives, and castas, as well as discouraging harmony between these subordinate groups, enhanced and protected Spanish control over them. The Church too encouraged racist and ethnocentric mechanisms of control over persons of color and non-Hispanic ethnicity for the same reasons. Such strategies were reflected in the records public officials and clerics kept. As a result, state and church documents popularized negative perceptions of subaltern peoples and overemphasized instances of antagonistic interaction between them in order keep these groups divided and more easily controlled.

Notaries, on the other hand, proved less likely to portray blacks so negatively or to concern themselves with the nature of their relations with natives. Notaries commonly represented blacks as slave property or as free wage earners. As property, notaries tried to enhance bondpersons' value by providing generally complimentary descriptions of them; as contracted workers, notaries adopted a more neutral position on free blacks' person and character. Economically oriented notaries proved less likely than state and ecclesiastical officials to reflect the social prejudices and political biases toward blacks.

One probable reason for the lack of references to peaceful Afro-Mexicans in records describing native living spaces stemmed from post-1550 racially restrictive Spanish legislation aimed at protecting native peoples from abuse and consequent injury and death. Between 1540 and 1610, New Spain's indigenous population declined from an estimated 20 million plus to less than 1 million individuals. European conquerors incorrectly assumed that maltreatment at the hands of Spaniards and their black slave allies caused this demographic crisis.[14] Most scholars now blame the high morbidity on Old World diseases unintentionally introduced into a less complex New World disease environment by Europeans and Africans alike.[15] The steep native population decline did, however, offer Spaniards an unexpected advantage in securing control over the colony's material resources. Old World invaders assumed ownership of more and more land as huge tracts became depopulated due to widespread Amerindian deaths throughout the colony. This allowed the newcomers to redirect much of the production and to thereby shift primary market focus from Mexico to Europe.[16]

Fears of labor shortages created by the indigenous population decline, however, presented the conquerors with a dilemma. The same thing appeared to be happening in Mexico that had occurred on the Spanish Caribbean islands just decades earlier: the depopulation of the colony's indigenous residents. Who would work the new, post-1546 silver mines? Who would cultivate the large commercial agricultural estates in cochineal and sugar? Who would perform the myriad of menial tasks in the rapidly expanding Spanish urban centers springing up all over the viceroyalty? Spaniards did not risk their lives and surrender all their homeland social ties to do hard menial labor in the New World. Others would have to assume these roles on behalf of the new Ibero-American lords.

Such attitudes precipitated two strategies to avoid any labor crisis that would jeopardize Europeans' goal of liberation from menial labor as a reward for all the risks and sacrifices incurred while journeying to and conquering American lands like Mexico. Iberians would import an expensive but reliable supplemental labor force to relieve Amerindians of their most life-threatening tasks,[17] and they would limit physical contact between natives and non-natives by isolating indigenous peoples in their own communities through law and social practice. From about 1550 onward, the most probable reason why blacks and their Afro-casta offspring (or racially mixed persons of black African descent) appeared so infrequently in Spanish records of native communities was because under evolving colonial Spanish laws and social conventions, they were not supposed to be in native settlements. Thus, whether present or not, Hispanic record keepers seldom mentioned them unless they engaged in destabilizing behavior that required noting their presence. From the mid-sixteenth through the early nineteenth centuries, nearly the entire colonial period, Hispanic census takers infrequently acknowledged the presence of non-natives in native communities unless indigenous residents demanded such note by lodging complaints with royal authorities against Afro-Mexicans and other outsiders living among them.

The primary motivation for white Spaniards' separation of natives from black Africans did not initially stem from racist and ethnocentric attitudes; it arose from an attempt to protect indigenous peoples from perceived deadly physical abuse at the hands of European and African conquerors. In response the Spanish state and church, two of the most powerful corporate agents of colonial development, committed themselves to a two-tiered division of society. Both agencies encouraged a Hispanic and a native order, an arrangement they hoped would limit indigenous contact with non-natives to periodic workplace encounters and joint participation in religious ceremonies.

The crown principally relied on two additional strategies to accomplish this separation. First, Spaniards and other non-natives would occupy certain physical spaces—cities, towns, commercial agricultural and mining estates; natives would remain apart in their villages and townships—their indigenous "republics." Second, in areas where all the subpopulations necessarily resided in close proximity, namely the enclaves of Spanish residence, a set of colonial policies usually referred to as the *sociedad de castas* or *sistema de castas* discouraged native social contact with other groups. Based on racial and ethnic distinctions, this social order impeded cross-racial interaction and cultural diversity.[18]

By the time the demographic crisis began to abate, soon after the turn of the seventeenth century, whites' motive for isolating natives in their repúblicas and barrios had changed from safeguarding to controlling natives and other subject groups that had emerged, namely blacks and castas. Physical separation of blacks and natives represented both support for and a consequence of Ibero-Americans' middle- and late-colonial institutionalization of racism and ethnocentrism.[19] Amerindians welcomed and supported these apartheid laws and social restrictions as means to insulate themselves in their republics/villages or in their urban barrios. Their reward for embracing segregation was twofold. Indigenous isolation could diminish the likelihood of mistreatment at the hands of non-natives. Hispanic-imposed isolation and ethnocentrism also provided natives greater opportunity to preserve their cultural identity by limiting contact with other groups. Each of these considerations represented powerful incentives for indigenous ethnics to abide by segregationist Spanish laws, attitudes, and customs.[20]

Scholars do debate the effectiveness of colonial Mexico's apartheid legal and social conditions.[21] Yet whether effective or not, their very existence created a potential bias in record keeping. The fact that both blacks and natives occupied subordinate positions within the Spanish power structure discouraged specific references to peaceful interaction between members of both groups in public records. Documentation of harmonious interaction between blacks and natives might create positive popular attitudes toward black-native solidarity, which could pose a threat to minority white authority. Besides, the ordinary lives of blacks and natives did not interest royal officials unless the two groups flagrantly violated Spanish laws or behavioral norms. Peaceful black-native interaction within the confines of either group's ascribed physical spaces, rural native villages and urban barrios or in urban casta zones,[22] most likely was simply overlooked, misrecorded. Conversely, for both reasons of promoting black notoriety and white security, extraordinary instances of conflictive interaction involving crime and violence committed by blacks against natives received a good deal of documentary attention from Hispanic scribes. Thus, Spanish attitudes and social designs probably played a large role in dictating a historical record that perpetuated a myth of general hostility between blacks and indigenous peoples.

Natives may have also contributed to misconceptions concerning their relations with blacks. Social acceptance within indigenous communities rested primarily on ethnic identification.[23] As demonstrated below, outsiders who adopted local village or barrio ways were accepted regardless of their racial phenotype. Indeed, from at least 1550 onward, Spaniards tried to maintain divisions within the colonial society primarily based on racial otherness. Natives, on the other hand, distinguished subpopulations mainly on the basis of ethnic distinctiveness. Spanish/native commitment to these strategies of separateness probably led to an inevitable bias in reporting. Hispanic record keepers were predisposed to record data that validated and supported their apartheid policies. For their part, natives supplied Hispanic record keepers with misleading information, from the Spanish perspective of "otherness," about non-natives within Amerindian communities and barrios. To indigenous peoples, persons who lived like natives were natives even if Spaniards might define the same individuals as non-natives on the basis of their racial appearance. Given such different definitions of "*indio*," it was no wonder that colonial record keepers left us with a very imprecise record of African presence and behavior within native spaces.

Across the viceroyalty and throughout the colonial period in parish registries, in aggregate and in household census counts as well as in regional descriptions, Hispanic scribes more often than not failed to report the presence of non-natives in native communities. Spanish documents generally leave the impression that natives lived in indigenous pueblos; blacks, whites, and castas lived somewhere else. Eighteenth-century Jesuit Francisco Javier Clavijero, writing about the sixteenth-century conquest period, promoted such impressions in his *Historia antigua de México*.[24] The seventeenth-century bishop and later viceroy, don Juan de Palafox y Mendoza, made similar types of racial generalizations in his *visita* (inspection) report on his Puebla diocese.[25] Of the 144 settlements he toured between August and November 1643, Palafox noted the presence of Spaniards only in the zone's fifteen *cabeceras*, or head towns.[26] For example, he acknowledged black residents in the cabecera of Tepeaca and in the small town of San Lorenzo, a community of former runaway slaves near the sugar-growing town of Córdoba, Veracruz (much of Veracruz fell within the diocese of Puebla).[27] Of the 8 subject communities included in Manuel Valdes's census of the northern Veracruz district of Guayacoctla in 1781, 53 were recorded as all indigenous.[28] Don Agustín Ramirez's 1792 military census of the Valle San Francisco, within the Yxtahuac (San Luis Potosí) district, included 29 subject villages, of which only 6 had non-native residents.[29] A census compiled in 1777 for the district of Xicayan, Guanajuato, comprising the capital and 55 subject towns, listed the residents of 34 of these settlements as all indigenous.[30] Even along the Gulf coast, of the 6 communities that made up the jurisdiction of Mizantla, Veracruz, in 1746, only the district capital had non-native residents recorded.[31] A closer examination over time of local documents provides examples of Hispanic record keepers' underenumeration of non-natives in indigenous residential zones.

Constanino Bravo de Lagunas, the late-sixteenth-century magistrate for the district of Jalapa, Veracruz, in describing each of the capital's outlying subject villages, labeled them all simply as "*pueblos de indios*" and gave the number of inhabitants in each.[32] Two hundred years later the cleric assigned to compile the military census of 1791 in the district, Vicente Nieto, did nearly the same thing. Of the twenty-four villages he listed under the jurisdiction of the provincial capital of Jalapa, he acknowledged non-native dwellers in only four—Coatepec, Xicochimalco, Naulinco, and Xilotepec.[33] Residents of the other, more outlying settlements within the district were all listed as "indios." In fact, non-natives likely resided in most of the district's settlements.

San José Miahiutlan was one of Jalapa's subject villages. It sat just under thirty kilometers north of the district capital within the ecclesiastical and political jurisdiction of the cabecera of Naulinco at the outset of the struggle for independence.[34] San José was one of those "indio" villages Nieto had mentioned a generation earlier in his 1791 census. An entry in the ecclesiastical marriage registries for the town documents a non-native, a mestizo, resident within this all-"native" community. In 1811, this mestizo married an indigenous bride.[35] Two years later three Spanish couples living in the village exchanged nuptial vows.[36] Teocelo rested twenty kilometers south of the villa of Jalapa within the jurisdiction of neighboring Coatepec. Teocelo was another village Nieto had labeled a "pueblo de indios." In 1808 a mestizo inhabitant of the town took a free *parda* (an individual with a mixed native/black phenotype) bride.[37] Chiconquiaco was an even more outlying "native" village on the northern fringes of the district in Nieto's census. In 1813 a Spanish resident of Chiconquiaco married a parda, and a pardo wed a native woman.[38] Six years later a mestizo living in the same village took a free parda wife, and two other pardos married native women.[39] In 1821, the year of Mexican independence, a Spanish resident of Nieto's "indio" village of Tonayán married one of the community's native maidens.[40]

Amerindian pueblos represented the principal "regions of refuge," as Gonzalo Aguirre Beltrán called them, for natives trying to limit contact with non-natives.[41] Another, less racially restricted but nevertheless definably indigenous zone was the native barrio (a legally incorporated neighborhood) usually situated on the fringes of Hispanic urban centers. Although not as physically isolated from nonindigenous peoples as repúblicas de los indios, these corporate native urban sites allowed some insulation from potentially abusive whites, blacks, and castas. Fig. 9.1 shows a schematic representation of residential patterns for the eighteenth-century towns of Jalapa and Orizaba in central Veracruz. Based on a correlation of residency and race in the house-by-house Rivillagegido military censuses of the 1790s for each municipality, it shows a general pattern of concentric zones radiating outward from an urban core.[42] Although there was a good deal of racial overlap, white households dominated the central core zone. Black and casta households constituted a majority in the next zone, and native households outnumbered all others in the barrios resting within the outermost ring.

This overall pattern of residential distribution suggests two points. First, racial overlap, that is, the presence of a minority of persons from other racial groups in each of these zones, indicates—as Douglas Cope commented with respect to Mexico City—that there were limits to implementation of a

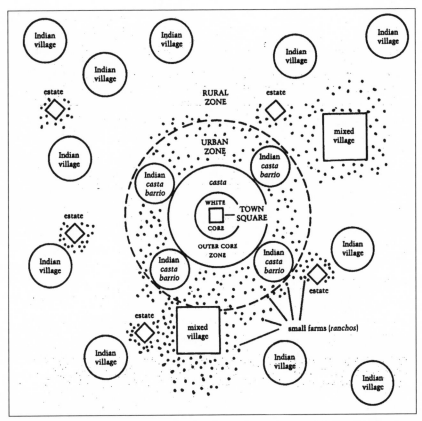

FIG. 9.1: *Schematic representation of eighteenth-century racial distribution in the villas of Jalapa and Orizaba, Veracruz. From Patrick J. Carroll,* Blacks in Colonial Veracruz: Race, Ethnicity and Regional Development, *2nd ed. (Austin: University of Texas Press, 2001), 116.*

strict separation of racial and ethnic groups in late-colonial Mexico.[43] Second, sandwiched between powerful whites in the urban core and natives on the urban periphery, castas and free blacks living in urban intermediate racial zones came into constant contact with both other racial groups. Greater proximity of blacks and Afro-castas than of whites to natives in terms of socioeconomic and political status further enhanced the likelihood of interaction between nonwhite groups. At the same time, relatively close proximity in terms of physical, social, economic, and political statuses among blacks, natives, and castas presumably impeded whites' ability to enforce their

legally institutionalized apartheid policies. Urban zones, where white segregationist laws and customs proved strongest, did not escape this pattern of
racially exogamous relationships among blacks, natives, and castas.[44] Despite
constant interracial contact in all three of these compressed urban zones,
documentation records no higher incidence of conflict between blacks or
their casta descendants and natives than for any other groups. This underscores the higher probability of generally peaceful relationships between persons of color in these spaces than is generally thought.

Some documents, most notably ones aimed at identifying those
required to pay tribute and serve in the militia, did take note of non-natives
in racially restricted indigenous zones. A 1653 tributary census of the native
barrio of Tequisquiapa within the provincial capital of San Luis Potosí provides a case in point. The second of the forty-one households enumerated
identifies Pedro Hernández, a free mulatto creole (a person of hybrid
black/white phenotype born in the New World) married to a Nahua woman
whose name did not appear in the record. Originally from Pachuca, Pedro
had resided in the barrio for two years by the time the count was taken.[45]
Data from his entry suggest a number of things about black-native relations
in this type of indigenous setting. First, blacks resided in urban native barrios despite the fact that their presence was not always recorded. Second,
blacks and Afro-castas did manage to establish harmonious social ties within the native community through marriage to native women. Third, the
inclusion of Pedro's name in the document and exclusion of his Nahua
wife's name illustrates the ongoing bias of Spanish record keepers. She was a
native, who was not supposed to marry a non-native; she would not appear
in the registry that recorded her husband because she occupied a racially
restricted social space reserved for natives. His registry separated non-
natives from natives even though in real life they lived side by side. Her
name would appear in native records only. And finally, Pedro's last name,
Hernández, indicates that he was Hispanicized. Natives seldom had surnames in Spanish documents. This enumerative pattern reflected the sense
of cultural distance from natives that Spanish record keepers felt. In
Spaniards' minds, natives could not culturally "fit" within Hispanic society
because they were "*gente sin razón*" (people who could not reason). The
inclusion of a last name for Pedro indicates that the Spanish scribe saw
Pedro as ethnically bridging both cultures.[46]

The third listing in the Tequisquiapa tributary count mentioned the
household of Antonio Hernández, also a free mulatto. Given that both
Pedro and Antonio shared the same surname and racial background and

the fact that they lived next door to each other leads one to assume that they might have been related. Antonio had migrated from the villa of León.[47] Unlike Pedro, Antonio was not married, perhaps because of the nature of his occupation. He was an *arriero*, or muleteer. The transient nature of Antonio's occupation, which probably took him away from his barrio residence frequently and for extended periods, made the establishment of strong social bonds with his native neighbors more difficult. This too might explain why he located next to Pedro and his native wife's home within this indigenous urban zone to reside near his kinsman in an alien setting. At the same time, Antonio's arriero occupation underscores a tentative conclusion drawn from Pedro's census profile. As a muleteer Antonio had regular contact with both the Spanish and the native populations of New Spain. This provided him the opportunity, as it did other Afro-Mexicans, to circumvent the post-1550 Spanish segregationist legal and social restrictions to racial and cultural integration within the colony. By physically traveling between spaces reserved for particular racial and ethnic groups, some non-natives inevitably found their way into Amerindian communities.

The entry for Juan Pasquel, head of the sixth household included in the Tequisquiapa census, provides yet further evidence of mundane Afro-Mexican social interaction in native pueblos. This charcoal maker and seller was listed as a "*lobo*," an individual who physically appeared to be the result of black-native miscegenation. Juan Pasquel had taken a native wife. The fact that he had no last name, had married a native, and lived in a native barrio suggests how deeply his Afro-Amerindian roots ran. The Spanish notary, by not reporting a surname for Juan Pasquel, implied his indigenous ethnicity. Through probable miscegenation the descendants of this "lobo" would inevitably acquire native racial as well as cultural identity even in Spanish records of the barrio's population.[48]

By the mid-seventeenth century Afro-Mexican women proved as likely to enter natives' segregated living spaces as Afro-Mexican men. María de los Reies and María de la Concepción were listed as free *negras* married to unnamed native men within the barrio of Tequisquiapa. And like the previously mentioned Juan Pasquel, they lacked surnames, indicating the record keeper's cultural classification of them as non-Hispanic, most probably native in this residential setting. María de Cuetto, a "mulata," did have a surname, but her entry included an even more obvious native cultural affiliation with her indigenous neighbors. The census taker enumerated her a "*natural*," a term almost always reserved for not fully Hispanicized Amerindians.[49]

All told, 108 individuals with racial identifications appeared in Tequisquiapa's 1653 household census. Of this total seventy-six were native, twenty mulatto, and twelve negro. Put another way, persons of Afro-Mexican identities represented nearly 30 percent of the racially identified population. Moreover, half the negros/as and a third of the mulattos/as listed as married within the census had native spouses.[50] These percentages illustrate the remarkable degree of black integration within native urban zones by the middle colonial period. They also indicate that blacks' presence did not represent a hostile intrusion into these residential zones. Afro-Mexicans occupied such spaces with native sanction and Spanish acquiescence so long as the contact remained peaceful or as long as the blacks lived like natives and became part of their indigenous communities.

Almost invariably, parish and royal tribute records for Amerindian villages identified most inhabitants as "*indios*." Whole registries titled "pueblos de indios" or "pueblos de naturales" listed individuals without reference to race or ethnicity because it was understood that all were supposed to be natives. In a number of instances, however, these same officials who ignored non-natives in a particular indigenous pueblo would in another context mention their presence. In 1570, don Hernán Gutíerrez Bustamonte, the royal tax collector for the archbishopric of Mexico, brought charges against two residents of one of the capital's native barrios for public fornication. He identified Xristobal, a mulatto, and María, a native, as the guilty couple. Catalina Pérez, a mestiza, testified against the pair, as did another neighbor, Pasqual Guzmán, a negro. The two were convicted and sentenced to eight months in jail.[51] This case illustrates not only the early presence of non-natives in native urban barrios, but also indicates the level of public openness displayed by these individuals in engaging in intimate forms of behavior.

Documents concerning the native pueblo of Tepecoacuilco, within the jurisdiction of Taxco, provide a second case in point. A 1759 tributary count for the town contained no references to Spaniards, blacks, or castas of any kind. In the same year, responding to petitions from the village's native residents, the viceroy, the marquis de Amarillas, reported an incident to the district magistrate, don Pedro de la Barrera. It involved a mulatto named Miguel de Chabarria, who resided in Tepecoacuilco. Indigenous villagers accused the mulatto of assault, extortion, and destruction of property.[52] De Chabarria's lawlessness was not the only thing that attracted notice. He had taken up residence within the village in compliance with the wishes of his employer. The Taxco magistrate, de la Barrera, had appointed de Chabarria

Minister of Weights and Measures within the community.[53] Miguel's ethnic rather than his racial "otherness" antagonized his neighbors. They petitioned a higher-ranking royal official, the viceroy, to enforce laws restricting non-native residence in pueblos de indios. Had de Chabarria not disrupted the peace, had he adopted native ways, his presence might have gone unrecorded. Underscoring this point, despite the mulatto's notoriety in the correspondence of the viceroy, he remained invisible on the tributary lists for the village.

A much more subtle indication of non-native presence in a native setting occurred in a document dated Mexico City, December 13, 1789. It recorded a betrothed couple from the nearby native town of Tenango del Valle. They applied to ecclesiastical authorities in Mexico City for dispensation from consanguinity restrictions to marry. Their petition not only documents Afro-Mexican presence in an Amerindian town, but also indicates just how deeply such individuals' roots sank in indigenous communities as well as the remarkable degree of upward mobility and acceptance blacks enjoyed if they adopted native ways.

Victoriano de la Cruz was the prospective groom; his intended bride's name was María Josefa. They were second cousins. Her grandmother and his grandfather were siblings, and this degree of consanguinity violated church law. In order to marry, they had to seek dispensation not from the itinerant priest that periodically visited the village, but from an ecclesiastical judge, one Bachiller José de Guzmán, of the archdiocesan capital, Mexico City. In the end what held up dispensation was not the question of consanguinity but the bride's racial identification. She and the rest of the community witnesses claimed she was native; the ecclesiastical judge said that she was "*al parece mulata*" (she appeared to be a mulatta). The ambiguity surrounding her identity may very well have reflected the differing emphasis Spaniards and natives placed on race and ethnicity in defining a person's identity. In the end, after over eight months of deliberation, the archbishop granted the dispensation and they finally married.[54]

An even more bizarre example of consanguinity and native/Afro-casta familial ties surfaced in the proceedings of a Mexico City ecclesiastical court. Again in 1789, third-degree cousins asked for permission to marry. Both parties were from the native village of Almolya, subject to the cabecera of Tleapetlahuaya. Antonio Esteban, the groom, was listed as a native. Simona Francisca, a mulata, was the bride. Simona was also the sister of Antonio Esteban's deceased first wife, Nicolasa. Antonio Esteban's maternal grandfather and Simona and Nicolasa's maternal grandmother were siblings. This relationship not only illustrated the contracting parties' family ties, but also demonstrated intergenerational continuity in native-black relations. Still other information included in the petition pointed to the fluidity of these ties. The bride was already carrying Antonio Esteban's child. Moreover, Antonio Esteban admitted to a concurrent illicit relationship with Simona and the dead Nicolasa's other sister, Rosa Efigenia, married to Julian Thomas, another native within the village. A simple petition for dispensation from consanguinity requirements turned into an attempt to arbitrate a potentially deadly conflict between village residents. Clerical judges agreed to grant the requested consanguinity exemption and allow the marriage provided that the groom promised to end his illicit relationship with the bride's sister. All parties involved accepted this condition, the court absolved the groom, the bride, and her sister from their sins, the marriage was performed, a yet unborn child was spared illegitimate status, and peace was preserved within the community.[55]

In a royal tributary count for 1720, don Raphael Hernández de Castilla was listed as the governor of the native village of San Luis de la Paz, a settlement in the mountains of western San Luis Potosí, bordering on the province of Puebla. The document identified Raphael and his wife, doña Andrea de la Cruz, as "indios." The fact that they both had the socially prestigious *don* and *doña* prefixes before their names indicates that because of his position as *gobernador* (native governor of the village), they enjoyed a measure of respect within the Hispanic world of the record keeper. The presence of a surname for him and the lack of one for his wife provide additional hints about life in native villages. Raphael's surname implies his acquisition of Hispanic culture. The fact that his wife did not have a surname suggests her native ethnic identification. More importantly from the perspective of black-native relations, Raphael was a widower with two daughters from a previous union. One of his daughters, Feliziana de la Cruz (no surname, with the prestigious *doña* prefix before her name), was married to Antonio Rodríguez, a mulatto.[56]

The Hernández family record is full of ethnic and racial implications. An Afro-casta had not only taken up residence within a native village in violation of Spanish law, but he had situated himself within a multicultural native family, the most politically and socially prominent family in the entire indigenous village. Spanish record keepers took note of this breach of the law and did nothing about it. Moreover, the governor's son-in-law was not the only Afro-casta listed in the village. Others had married into native families of lower socioeconomic and political status, indicating just how unexceptional such unions were. The twenty-six-year-old mulatto Nicolás Sánchez (with a last name) lived with his native wife, Lorena Quevedo (also with a last name), and their two children. The widow Juana de la Cruz (no last name and therefore a native both racially and ethnically) resided with her daughter Juana. Juana had no surname, which indicated native ethnic identification, but her race was apparently in question; the recorder simply noted that she was "*no al parece india*" (does not appear Indian). Only six Afro-castas and two negros were enumerated in this village of 311 inhabitants in 1720. The remaining 303 villagers were all designated as natives.[57] Afro-Mexicans made up only a small portion of the population, but every one of them had an indigenous spouse, indicating that they lived there not as outsiders but as integral members of village families.

CONCLUSIONS

Blacks and natives probably interacted more peacefully than not after the shock of the initial conquest period. From the second half of the sixteenth century onward, Afro-Mexicans and their casta descendants lived in rural and urban physical and social spaces restricted by Hispanic law, as well as by Spanish and native social customs, to natives alone. Amerindians did not object to the presence of these intruders in their zones as long as the newcomers did not act like outsiders. Social rank and acceptance within indigenous communities depended more on ethnic identification than on anything else. That was the case prior to the arrival of Spaniards and Africans and before Spaniards' mid-sixteenth-century legal validation of the integrity of native villages. Repúblicas de los indios made it possible for ethnic identification to remain the primary criteria for inclusion and social mobility within indigenous communities after 1550.

Spaniards showed concern over natives' failure to exclude blacks, black castas, and other racially designated non-natives from their villages. This deviation from the racist-based Hispanic social order, the *sistema de castas*, worried whites for several reasons. Initially (prior to about 1610) Spaniards feared that the presence of racially nonindigenous peoples in native settlements would lead to the extinction of the native population. After 1610, whites began to rely on racial distinctiveness to divide and control nonwhite subaltern groups. Natives' greater emphasis on ethnicity than race in conceding admission into their villages and barrios threatened the effectiveness of the white-engineered sistema de castas, and by extension whites' sociopolitical power. Yet whites had no choice but to accede to native practice in native-dominated physical spaces because of the limits of whites' power in colonial

Mexico. Ibero-Mexicans did dominate all aspects of life at the upper reaches of colonial society in their urban core areas and perhaps to a lesser degree on their commercial estates in the countryside. In urban casta zones and in native barrios, as well as in hinterland Amerindian pueblos, casta or native social orders dominated.[58] Spaniards did not have the power to enforce their designs in these social environments. Recognizing that such limitations threatened their overall power as a numerical minority in New Spain's socially complex racial and ethnic setting, they chose to underplay native, black, and casta nonascription to the Spanish emphasis on racial otherness in defining community membership and social rank. Spaniards downplayed native and other nonwhite noncompliance with the sistema de castas by understating the generally tranquil nature of native-black and native-casta relations and by overstating instances of conflict between these groups in the public records that whites kept. Such practices have led to a distorted historical view of Amerindians' interaction with blacks and castas. This chapter presents limited but suggestive evidence that Afro-native relations were indeed more harmonious than hostile in nature.

And why did Spanish and white creole record keepers distort the historical record, consciously or subconsciously? First and foremost, they did so to validate their own social values as reflected in their own self-interested social design, the racist and ethnocentric notions that justified whites' social elevation through the application of the sistema de castas. Even by the end of the colonial period, whites, whether *peninsulares* (Iberian-born Spaniards) or creoles (American-born Spaniards), represented just 12 to 13 percent of New Spain's population.[59] As a minority they relied, at least in part, on race and ethnicity as mechanisms of social control to maintain their power. Acknowledgment of limits to the effectiveness of this strategy in public records that dealt with indigenous villages and neighborhoods ran the risk of validating such subversive behavior, on one level. On another level it threatened to increase the likelihood of a challenge to white power by uniting persons of color. Such validation might encourage nonwhite subaltern solidarity against whites' power, the very thing Ibero-Mexicans feared most. By the end of the colonial period, these threats were real—as evidenced by the first stages of the Mexican struggle for independence under Miguel Hidalgo and to a lesser degree under his successor José María Morelos between 1810 and 1815.[60] For these reasons the colonial Mexican records Spaniards kept overstated the hostile and understated the harmonious nature of relations between natives and Afro-Mexicans in the colonial period—and in all likelihood did the same in other parts of Spanish America as well.

๑๑

NOTES

1. Mexico's Archivo General de la Nación (hereinafter AGN), *Mercedes*, vol. 5, f. 158.

2. Francisco González de Cossio, *Xalapa* (México City: Talleres Gráficos de la Nación, 1957), 56–57; Manuel B. Trens, *Historia de Veracruz*, 2 vols. (Jalapa: Gráficos del Gobierno de Veracruz, 1947), vol. II, 311–12.

3. AGN, *Tierras*, vol. 3543, expediente 3, fs. 13–14.

4. Frederick Bowser, *The African Slave in Colonial Peru, 1524–1650* (Stanford, Calif.: Stanford University Press, 1974), vii.

5. James Lockhart, *Spanish Peru*, 2nd ed. (Madison: University of Wisconsin Press, 1994), 172; see also Magnus Mörner, *Race Mixture in the History of Latin America* (Boston: Little, Brown, 1967), 46; Leslie Rout, Jr., *The African Experience in Spanish America* (London: Cambridge University Press, 1976), 117.

6. Matthew Restall, "Otredad y ambigüedad: Las percepciones que los españoles y los mayas tenían de los africanos en el Yucatán colonial," *Signos históricos* vol. II, núm. 4 (2000): 30–31.

7. Magnus Mörner, *La corona española y los foranos en los pueblos de indios de America* (Estocolmo, Suecia: Almqvist and Wisksell, 1970), 94–97.

8. Lockhart, *Spanish Peru*, 171–72.

9. William Taylor, *Drinking, Homicide and Rebellion in Colonial Mexican Villages* (Stanford, Calif.: Stanford University Press, 1979), 26.

10. Colin Palmer, *Slaves of the White God: Blacks in Mexico, 1570–1650* (Cambridge, Mass.: Harvard University Press, 1976), 64.

11. Gonzalo Aguirre Beltrán, *Regiones de refugio: El desarrollo de la comunidad y el proceso dominical en mestizoamérica* (México: Instituto Nacional Indigenista, 1987), 163–64.

12. Actually, Borah found that Spanish officials feared natives' contact with racially mixed persons (castas) and vagabonds of whatever phenotypical identification, including blacks. See Woodrow Borah, *El Juzgado general de indios en la Nueva España*, traducción por Juan José Utrilla (México: Fondo de Cultura Económica, 1987), 181.

13. Lockhart, *Spanish Peru*, 196.

14. Sherburne Cook and Woodrow Borah, *Essays in Population History: Mexico and the Caribbean*, 3 vols. (Berkeley: University of California Press, 1971, 1974, 1979), vol. II, 180–81; Charles Gibson, *The Aztecs Under Spanish Rule* (Stanford, Calif.: Stanford University Press, 1964), 136–41. For the best overall treatment of the introduction of Old World diseases to the New World see Alfred Crosby, *Columbian Exchange* (Westport, Conn.: Greenwood Publishing, 1972).

15. Cook and Borah, *Essays in Population History: Mexico and the Caribbean*, vol. II, 180–81; Gibson, *The Aztecs Under Spanish Rule*, 136–41.

16. Patrick J. Carroll, *Blacks in Colonial Veracruz: Race, Ethnicity and Regional Development*, 2d ed. (Austin: University of Texas Press, 2001), 7–14.

17. Ibid., 18–20.

18. Mörner, *Race Mixture*, 45–47; Carroll, *Blacks in Colonial Veracruz*, 7–11, 79–82.

19. Herein ethnocentrism involves discrimination on the basis of sets of acquired distinguishing traits such as language, religion, and dress. Racism involves bias on the basis of distinguishing inherited physical characteristics such as skin color, hair texture, facial features, and stature.

20. Patrick Carroll, "Los mexicanos negros, el mestizaje y los fundamentos olvidados de la 'Raza Cósmica': Una perspectiva regional," *Historia Mexicana* vol. XLIV, núm. 3 (enero–marzo, 1995): 432.

21. This debate is strongest about the effectiveness of the sistema de castas toward the end of the eighteenth century. Some scholars who emphasize the late-colonial strength of the sistema are Robert McCaa, Stuart Schwartz, Arturo Grubessich, Adriana Naveda, and Patrick Carroll. See Robert McCaa et al., "Race and Class in Colonial Latin America: A Critique," *Comparative Studies in Society and History* 21, no. 3 (July 1979): 433; Adriana Naveda, *Esclavos negros en las haciendas azucareras de Córdoba, Veracruz, 1690–1830* (Jalapa: Universidad Veracruzana, 1987), 142; Carroll, *Blacks in Colonial Veracruz*, 128–29, 213–14. Authors stressing the ineffectiveness of the sistema de castas by the eighteenth century include R. Douglas Cope, Norma Angélica Castillo Palma, Juan Pedro Viqueira Albán, Magnus Mörner, John Chance, William Taylor, Rodney Anderson, Patricia Seed, and Philip Rust. See R. Douglas Cope, *The Limits of Racial Domination: Plebeian Society in Colonial Mexico City, 1660–1720* (Madison: University of Wisconsin Press, 1994), xvi; Norma Angélica Castillo Palma, "Matrimonios mixtos y cruce de la barrera de color como vias del mestizaje de la población negra y mulata [1674–1796]" (paper presented at the X Reunion of North American Scholars of Mexico, Fort Worth, Tex., 1999), 22; Juan Pedro Viqueira Albán, *Propriety and Permissiveness in Bourbon Mexico*, trans. by Sonya Lipsett-Rivera and

Sergio Rivera Ayala (Wilmington, Del.: Scholarly Resources Inc., 1999), 7–8; Magnus Mörner, "Economic Factors and Stratification in Colonial Spanish America With Special Regard to Elites," *Hispanic American Historical Review* 63, no. 2 (May 1983): 367–68; John Chance and William Taylor, "Estate and Class in a Colonial City: Oaxaca in 1792," *Comparative Studies in Society and History* 19, no. 4 (October 1977): 485; Rodney Anderson, "Race and Social Stratification: A Comparison of Working-Class Spaniards, Indians, and Castas in Guadalajara, Mexico, in 1821," *Hispanic American Historical Review* 68, no. 2 (May 1988): 239–41; Patricia Seed and Philip Rust, "Estate and Class in Colonial Oaxaca Revisited," *Comparative Studies in Society and History* 25, no. 4 (October 1983): 707.

22. Carroll, *Blacks in Colonial Veracruz*, 115–16.

23. Ibid., 80.

24. Francisco Javier Clavijero, *Historia antigua de México* (México: Editorial Porrua, 1971).

25. Juan de Palafox y Mendoza, *Relación de la visita eclesiastica del obispo de Puebla, 1643–1646*, compiled by Bernardo García Martínez (Puebla: Editorial Nuestra República, 1997), 6–78.

26. Ibid., 6–7, 13–14, 15–19, 22, 24, 27–28, 34, 36, 37, 41, 50, 52.

27. Ibid., 12–13, 37.

28. AGN, *Historia*, vol. 72, f. 244; Peter Gerhard, *A Guide to the Historical Geography of New Spain* (Cambridge: Cambridge University Press, 1972), 132.

29. AGN, *Historia*, vol. 72, f. 65; Gerhard, *Historical Geography of New Spain*, 235.

30. AGN, *Historia*, f. 195.

31. Joseph Antonio Villa-Señor y Sánchez, *Theatro Americano*, 2 vols. (México: Impresa de la Viuda de Bernardo Hogal, 1746, 1748), vol. I, 279.

32. Constantino Bravo de Lagunas, *Relación de Xalapa, 1580* (México: Editorial Citlaltepetl, 1969), 23–77.

33. Vicente Nieto, *Padron de Xalapa* (México: Editorial Citlaltepetl, 1971), 18–22. For the listing of the four villages with acknowledged non-Indian residents, see pp. 18, 20, and 21.

34. Carroll, *Blacks in Colonial Veracruz*, map 4, p. 13.

35. Archivo Parochial de Naulinco (APN), libro 22, f. 3v.

36. Ibid., libro 19, f. 38.

37. Archivo Parochial de Coatepec (APC), *Matrimonios*, libro 5 [*sic*, 13], f. 19v.

38. Ibid., f. 6.

39. Ibid., libro 22, fs. 20v, 29.

40. Ibid., f. 31.

41. See Aguirre Beltrán, *Regiones de refugio.*

42. Ibid., 116.

43. Cope, *The Limits of Racial Domination,* 16–17.

44. Carroll, *Blacks in Colonial Veracruz,* 115–24.

45. Archivo General de Indias (hereafter AGI), *Audiencia de México,* Legajo 1043, unnumbered folios.

46. One final entry on Pedro worth noting is his designation as a creole. Many scholars ignore the fact that Afro-Mexicans and their descendants were at risk of being born outside Spanish America. Thus, the label *criollo/a* was not synonymous with a white born in the New World; it could also mean a black born in the Americas.

47. AGI, *México,* leg. 1043.

48. Ibid.

49. Ibid.

50. Ibid.

51. AGN, *Bienes Nacionales,* vol. 497, expediente 3, fs. 1–8.

52. AGN, *Alcaldes Mayores,* vol. 10, fs. 270–72.

53. Ibid., fs. 271–271v.

54. AGN, *Bienes Nacionales,* vol. 93, expediente 170, fs. 1–2.

55. Ibid., vol. 93, expediente 245, fs. 1–3.

56. AGI, *Audiencia de México,* Leg. 1043, unnumbered fs.

57. Ibid.

58. For brevity's sake, I have not addressed the casta social order in this chapter. For an explanation of its origin and operation, see Carroll, "Los mexicanos negros, el mestizaje y los fundamentos olvidados de la 'Raza Cósmica,'" 403–38.

59. Carroll, "Mexican Society in Transition: The Blacks in Veracruz, 1750–1830" (Ph.D. diss., University of Texas at Austin, 1976), 76.

60. Scholars debate whether the first popular stages of the Mexican struggle for independence under Miguel Hidalgo, José María Morelos, Vicente Guerrero, and others were racially or class based. I think these initial stages displayed both types of divisions, given the high correlation between race and class in late-colonial Mexico. Hugh Hamill's *The Hidalgo Revolt* (Gainesville: University of Florida Press, 1966) provides a representation of the early independence movement as a race war. John Tutino's *From Insurrection to Revolution in Mexico* (Princeton: Princeton University Press, 1986) is representative of works that interpret the early stages of the independence movement as a class-based conflict.

Bibliography of References

ARCHIVAL ABBREVIATIONS AND REFERENCES

AGAY   Archivo General del Arzobispado de Yucatán, Mérida, Yucatan, Mexico

AGEY   Archivo General del Estado de Yucatán, Mérida, Yucatan, Mexico

AGI   Archivo General de Indias, Seville, Spain

AGN   Archivo General de la Nación, Mexico City, Mexico

AGN-C   Archivo General de la Nación, Bogotá, Colombia

AGS   Archivo General de Simancas, Simancas, Spain

AHDC   Archivo Histórico de la Diócesis de Campeche, Campeche, Mexico

AHU   Arquivo Histórico Ultramarino, Lisbon, Portugal

AJP   Archivo Judicial de Puebla, Puebla, Mexico

ANC   Archivo Nacional de Cuba, Havana, Cuba

ANHQ   Archivo Nacional Histórico de Quito (recently renamed Archivo Nacional del Ecuador)

ANTT   Arquivo Nacional da Torre do Tombo, Lisbon, Portugal

APB   Arquivo Público do Estado da Bahia, Salvador, Brazil

APC   Archivo Parroquial de Coatepec, Veracruz, Mexico

APM   Arquivo Público Mineiro, Belo Horizonte, Brazil

APN   Archivo Parroquial de Naulinco, Veracruz, Mexico

BI   Biblioteca da Itamaraty, Rio de Janeiro, Brazil

BNM   Biblioteca Nacional de México, Mexico City, Mexico

BNRJ   Biblioteca Nacional do Rio de Janeiro, Brazil

DSACC   Diocese of S. Augustine Catholic Center, Jacksonville, Florida

GPA   Parochial Archives of Nuestra Señora de la Asunción, Guanabacoa, Cuba

IHGB   Instituto Histórico e Geográfico Brasileiro, Rio de Janeiro, Brazil

JCB   John Carter Brown Library, Providence, Rhode Island

PKY   P. K. Yonge Library Special Collections, University of Florida, Gainesville, Florida

Abbreviations of Published Works

ACMS   Salvador (Brazil). Diretoria do Arquivo e Divulgação. *Atas da Câmara Municipal do Salvador, Documentos históricos do Arquivo Municipal*. 10 vols. to date. Salvador, 1944–.

CHNPA   Salomon, Frank, and Stuart B. Schwartz, eds. *Cambridge History of the Native Peoples of the Americas*. Vol. 3, *South America*. Cambridge and New York: Cambridge University Press, 1999.

DH   Biblioteca Nacional (Brazil). *Documentos Históricos*. 110 vols. Rio de Janeiro, 1928–.

DHY   *Documentos para la Historia de Yucatan*. 3 vols. Mérida, Yucatan: Compañía Tipográfica Yucateca, 1936–1938.

Published References

Aguirre Beltrán, Gonzalo. *La Población Negra en Mexico: Estudio Etnohistórico*. Mexico City: Ediciones Fuente Cultural, 1946, and Fondo de Cultura Económica, 1989.

———. *Regiones de refugio: El desarrollo de la comunidad y el proceso Dominical en mestizoamérica*. México: Instituto Nacional Indigenista, 1987.

Alberro, Solange. "Juan de Morga and Gertrudis Escobar: Rebellious Slaves." In *Struggle and Survival in Colonial America*. Edited by David G. Sweet and Gary B. Nash. Berkeley: University of California Press, 1981, 165–88.

Alegría, Ricardo E. *Juan Garrido, el Conquistador Negro en las Antilles, Florida, México y California, C. 1503–1540*. San Juan de Puerto Rico: Centro de Estudios Avanzados de Puerto Rico y El Caribe, 1990.

Alencastro, Luiz Felipe de. *O trato dos viventes: Formação do Brasil no Atlântico sul*. São Paulo: Companhia das Letras, 2000.

Almeida, Maria Regina Celestino de. "Os índios aldeados no Rio de Janeiro colonial." Ph.D. thesis, Universidade de Campinas, 2000.

Almeida, Rita Heloísa de. *O Diretório dos índios: Um projeto de "civilização" no Brasil do século XVIII.* Brasília: Editora UnB, 1997.

Alvarado, Pedro de. *An Account of the Conquest of Guatemala in 1524* [1525]. New York: The Cortés Society, 1924.

Alves Filho, Ivan. *Memorial dos Palmares.* Rio de Janeiro: Xenon, 1988.

Anderson, Robert Nelson. "The Quilombo of Palmares: A New Overview of a Maroon State in Seventeenth-Century Brazil." *Journal of Latin American Studies* 28, no. 3 (October 1996): 545–66.

Anderson, Rodney. "Race and Social Stratification: A Comparison of Working-Class Spaniards, Indians and Castas in Guadalajara, Mexico in 1821." *Hispanic American Historical Review* 68, no. 2 (May 1988).

Arana, Luis, "Military Manpower in Florida, 1670–1703," "The Men of the Florida Garrison," and "Military Organization in Florida, 1671–1702." *The Military and Militia in Colonia Spanish America, St. Augustine, Florida.* St. Augustine: Department of Military Affairs, Florida National Guard, n.d.

Archer, Christon, "Pardos, Natives, and the Army of New Spain: Inter-Relationships and Conflicts, 1780–1810." *Journal of Latin American Studies* 6, no. 2 (November 1974).

———. *The Army in Bourbon Mexico, 1760–1810.* Albuquerque: University of New Mexico Press, 1977.

Arditi, Benjamín. *El Deseo de la Libertad y la Cuestión del Otro: Ensayos acerca de la Posmodernidad, el Poder y la Sociedad.* Asunción: Criterio Ediciones, 1989.

Arzans de Orsúa y Vela, Bartolomé. *Tales of Potosí.* Edited by R. C. Padden. Translated by Frances López-Morillas. Providence, R.I.: Brown University Press, 1975.

Ayala, Juan de. *A Letter to Ferdinand and Isabela, 1503.* Edited and translated by Charles E. Nowell. Minneapolis: University of Minnesota Press, 1965.

Bahamas in the Age of Revolution, 1775–1848. Nassau Department of Archives, Publication 16, 1989.

Bakewell, Peter. *Silver Mining and Society in Colonial Mexico: Zacatecas, 1546–1700.* Cambridge: Cambridge University Press, 1971.

———. *Miners of the Red Mountain: Indian Labor in Potosí, 1545–1650.* Albuquerque: University of New Mexico Press, 1984.

———. "Mining." In *Colonial Spanish America.* Edited by Leslie Bethell. Cambridge: Cambridge University Press, 1987, 203–49.

———. *Mines of Silver and Gold in the Americas.* New York: Variorum, 1997.

Bartra, R. *Wild Men in the Looking Glass: The Mythic Origin of European Otherness.* Michigan: University of Michigan Press, 1994.

Bastide, Roger. *African Civilizations in the New World*. Translated by Peter Green. New York: Harper, 1971.

Bateman, Rebecca B. "Africans and Indians: A Comparative Study of the Black Carib and Black Seminole." In *Slavery and Beyond: The African Impact on Latin America and the Caribbean*. Edited by Darién J. Davis. Wilmington, Del.: Jaguar Books on Latin America, Scholarly Resources, Inc., 1995.

Behar, Ruth. "Sexual Witchcraft, Colonialism, and Women's Powers: Views from the Mexican Inquisition." *Sexuality and Marriage in Colonial Latin America*. Edited by Asunción Lavrin. Lincoln: University of Nebraska Press, 1989, 178–209.

————. "Brujería sexual, colonialismo y poderes femeninos: Opiniones del Santo Oficio de la Inquisición en México." *Sexualidad y matrimonio en la América Hispanica*. Edited by Asunción Lavrin. Mexico City: Alianza-Conoculta, 1991, 197–229.

Bennett, Herman L. *Lovers, Family and Friends: The Formation of Afro-Mexico, 1580–1810*. Ph.D. diss., Duke University, Durham, N.C., 1993.

Bolland, O. Nigel. *Struggles for Freedom: Essays on Slavery, Colonialism and Culture in the Caribbean and Central America*. Belize City: Angelus Press, 1997.

Booker, Jackie. "Needed but Unwanted: Black Militiamen in Veracruz, Mexico, 1760–1810." *The Historian* 55 (winter 1993).

Borah, Woodrow. *El Juzgado general de indios en la Nueva España*. Traducción por Juan José Utrilla. México: Fondo de Cultura Económica, 1987.

Bourne, Edward Gaylord, ed. *Narratives of the Career of Hernando de Soto*. New York, 1904.

Bowser, Frederick P. *The African Slave in Colonial Peru, 1524–1650*. Stanford, Calif.: Stanford University Press, 1974.

Brading, David A. *Miners and Merchants in Bourbon Mexico, 1763–1810*. Cambridge: Cambridge University Press, 1971.

Braund, Kathryn E. Holland. *Deerskins and Duffels: The Creek Indian Trade with Anglo-Americans, 1683–1815*. Lincoln: University of Nebraska Press, 1993.

Bravo de Lagunas, Constantino. *Relación de Xalapa*. México: Editorial Citlaltepetl, 1969.

Brito, Domingos de Abreu e. *Um inquérito à vida administrativa e económica de Angola e do Brasil*. Edited by Alfredo de Albuquerque Felner. Coimbra: Imprensa da Universidade, 1931 [1591].

Brockington, Lolita Gutiérrez. *The Leverage of Labor: Managing the Cortés Haciendas in Tehuantepec, 1588–1688*. Durham, N.C.: Duke University Press, 1993.

Brooks, James F., ed. *Confounding the Color Line: The Indian-Black Experience in North America*. Lincoln: University of Nebraska Press, 2002.

Brown, Canter, Jr. *Florida's Peace River Frontier*. Orlando: University of Central Florida Press, 1991.

———. "The 'Sarrazota' or Runaway Negro Plantations: Tampa Bay's First Black Community, 1812–1821." *Tampa Bay History* 12 (fall/winter 1990).

———. "The Florida Crisis of 1826–1827 and the Second Seminole War." *Florida Historical Quarterly* 73 (1995): 419–42.

———. "Race Relations in Territorial Florida, 1821–1845." *Florida Historical Quarterly* 73 (1995): 287–307.

Brown, Kendall. "Workers' Health and Colonial Mercury Mining at Huancavelica, Peru." *The Americas* 57, no. 4 (April 2001): 467–96.

Buisseret, David, and Steven G. Reinhardt, eds. *Creolization in the Americas*. College Station: Texas A&M Press, 2000.

Bushnell, Amy. "The Menéndez Márquez Cattle Barony at La Chua and the Determinants of Economic Expansion in Seventeenth-Century Florida." *Florida Historical Quarterly* 56 (1978).

Buskirk, E. R. "Work Capacity of High-Altitude Natives." In *The Biology of High-Altitude Peoples*. Edited by P. T. Baker. Cambridge: Cambridge University Press, 1978, 173–87.

Cáceres, Rina. *Negros, mulatos, esclavos y libertos en la Costa Rica del siglo XVII*. Mexico City: Instituto Panamericano de Geografía e Historia, 2000.

Calado, Manuel. *O Valeroso Lucideno*. 2 vols. Belo Horizonte, 1987.

Campbell, Leon G. "Social Structure of the Túpac Amaru Army in Cuzco, 1780–81." *Hispanic American Historical Review* 61, no. 4 (1981): 675–93.

Cárdenas Santana, Luz Alejandra. "La transgresión erótica de Cathalina González, Isabel Uruego y Juana María." Paper presented at the VI Encuentro de Afroamericanistas Xalapa, Veracruz, 1996.

———. "El juego del intercambio en el siglo XVII. Inquisición, sexualidad y transgresión en Acapulco." In *Historia urbana: Segundo Congreso de Investigación urbana y regional*. Edited by Elsa Patiño and Jaime Castillo. México: Editorial de la Red de Investigación Urbana, 1999, 31–50.

Carmack, Robert M. "A Toltec Influence on the Postclassic Culture History of Highland Guatemala." New Orleans: Middle American Research Institute, Publication 26, 1968, 49–92.

Caro Baroja, Julio. *The World of the Witches*. Translated by O. N. V. Glendinning. Chicago: University of Chicago Press, 1964.

———. *Las brujas y su mundo*. Madrid: Alianza Editorial, 1996.

Carroll, Patrick. "Mexican Society in Transition: Blacks in Veracruz, 1750–1830." Ph.D. diss., University of Texas, Austin, 1976.

————. *Blacks in Colonial Veracruz: Race, Ethnicity, and Regional Development.* Austin: University of Texas Press, 1991 and (2nd ed.) 2001.

————. "Los mexicanos negros, el mestizaje y los fundamentos olvidados de la 'Raza Cósmica': Una perspectiva regional." *Historia Mexicana* XLIV, no. 3 (enero–marzo, 1995).

Castelnau-L'Estoile, Charlotte de. *Les ouvriers d'une vigne stérile. Les jésuites et la conversion des Indiens au Brésil, 1580–1620.* Paris, 2000.

Castillo Palma, Norma Angélica. "Matrimonios mixtos y cruce de la barrera de color como vias del mestizaje de la población negra y mulata, 1674–1796." Paper presented at the X Reunion of North American Scholars of Mexico, Fort Worth, Tex., 1999.

————. *Cholula: sociedad mestiza en ciudad India: Un estudio de las causas demográficas, económicas y sociales del mestizaje en Nueva España, 1649–1813.* México: Plaza y Valdéz and UAM, Iztapalapa, 2001.

Chance, John, and William Taylor. "Estate and Class in a Colonial City: Oaxaca in 1792." *Comparative Studies in Society and History* 19, no. 4 (October 1977).

Chatelain, Verne E. *The Defenses of Spanish Florida, 1565–1763.* Washington, D.C.: Carnegie Institute, 1941.

Clavijero, Francisco Javier. *Historia antigua de México.* México: Editorial Porrua, 1971.

Cline, Howard F. *Florida Indians II: Provisional Gazeteer with Locational Notes on Florida Colonial Communities.* New York: Garland Publishing, 1964.

Coker, William S., and Thomas D. Watson. *Indian Traders of the Southeastern Spanish Borderlands: Panton, Leslie & Company and John Forbes & Company, 1783–1847.* Gainesville and Pensacola: University Presses of Florida and University of West Florida Press, 1986.

Collections of the Georgia Historical Society. Savannah: Georgia Historical Society, 1909.

Conde Calderón, Jorge. *Espacio, Sociedad y Conflictos en la Provincia de Cartagena, 1740–1815.* Barranquilla: Artes Gráficas Industriales, 1999.

Contreras, Carlos. *Los mineros y el Rey, Los Andes del norte: Hualgayoc 1770–1825.* Lima: Instituto de Estudios Peruanos, 1995.

Cook, Noble David. "Sickness, Starvation, and Death in Early Hispaniola." *Journal of Interdisciplinary History* 32, no. 3 (winter 2002): 349–86.

Cook, Sherburne F., and Woodrow Borah. *Essays in Population History: Mexico and the Caribbean, Volume II.* Berkeley: University of California Press, 1974.

Cope, R. Douglas. *The Limits of Racial Domination: Plebian Society in Colonial Mexico City, 1660–1720.* Madison: University of Wisconsin Press, 1994.

Cornblit, Oscar. *Power and Violence in the Colonial City: Oruro from the Mining Renaissance to the Rebellion of Túpac Amaru (1740–1782)*. Cambridge: Cambridge University Press, 1995.

Corrêa Filho, Virgílio. *História de Mato Grosso*. Rio de Janeiro: Instituto Nacional do Livro, Ministério da Educação e Cultura, 1969.

Cortés y Larraz, Pedro. *Descripción geográfico-moral de la diócesis de Goathemala*. 2 vols. Biblioteca Goathemala, 20. Guatemala: Sociedad de Geografía e Historia de Guatemala, 1958.

Costa, F. A. Pereira da. *Anais pernambucanos*. 7 vols. Recife: Arquivo Público Estadual, 1951.

Covarrubias, Sebastián de. *Tesoro de la Lengua Castellana o Española*. Barcelona: S. A. Horta, 1943 (1674 ed., orig. 1611).

Craig, Alan K., and Robert C. West. *In Quest of Mineral Wealth: Aboriginal and Colonial Mining and Metallurgy in Spanish America*. Baton Rouge: Louisiana State University Press, 1994.

Crane, Verner W. *The Southern Frontier, 1670–1732*. New York: Norton, 1981.

Crosby, Alfred. *The Columbian Exchange*. Westport, Conn.: Greenwood Publishing, 1972.

Cutter, Charles. *The Legal Culture of Northern New Spain: 1700–1810*. Albuquerque: University of New Mexico Press, 1995.

Dakin, Karen, and Christopher H. Lutz. *Nuestro pesar, nuestra aflicción/Tunetuliniliz, tucucuca: Memorias en lengua náhuatl enviadas a Felipe II por indígenas del valle de Guatemala hacia 1572*. Mexico City: UNAM, 1996.

Davis, T. Frederick, ed. "United States Troops in Spanish East Florida, 1812–1813, III." *Florida Historical Quarterly* 9 (January 1931): 135–55.

——. "United States Troops in Spanish East Florida, 1812–1813, V." *Florida Historical Quarterly* 10 (July 1931): 24–34.

Deagan, Kathleen, ed. *Puerto Real: The Archeology of a Sixteenth-Century Spanish Town in Hispaniola*. Gainesville: University Press of Florida, 1995.

Deeds, Susan M. "First Generation Rebellions in Seventeenth-Century Nueva Vizcaya." In *Native Resistance and the Pax Colonial in New Spain*. Edited by Susan Schroeder. Lincoln: University of Nebraska Press, 1998.

Díaz, María Elena. *The Virgin, the King, and the Royal Slaves of El Cobre: Negotiating Freedom in Colonial Cuba, 1670–1780*. Stanford, Calif.: Stanford University Press, 2000.

Diouf, Sylviane A. *Servants of Allah: African Muslims Enslaved in the Americas*. New York: New York University Press, 1998.

Directório que se deve observar nas povoações dos índios do Pará e Maranhão. Lisbon, 1758.

Documentos Históricos. Biblioteca Nacional (Brazil). 110 vols. Rio de Janeiro, 1928–.

Douglas, M. *Purity and Danger: An Analysis of the Concepts of Pollution and Taboo.* London: Pelican, 1970.

Dowd, Gregory Evans. *A Spirited Resistance: The North American Indian Struggle for Unity, 1745–1815.* Baltimore: Johns Hopkins University Press, 1992.

Encinas, Diego de. *Cedulario Indiano.* Tomo 1. Madrid: Ediciones Cultura Hispánica, 1945–1946.

Ennes, Ernesto. *Os Palmares (Subsídios para a sua história).* Lisbon, 1938.

Enríquez Macías, Genoveva. "Nuevos documentos para la demografía histórica de la Audiencia de Guatemala a finales del siglo XVII." *Mesoamérica* 17 (1989): 121–83.

Farage, Nadia. *As muralhas dos sertões: Os povos indígenas no rio Branco e a colonização.* Rio de Janeiro: Paz e Terra, 1991.

Feldman, Lawrence H. "Vanishing Transhumant Cacao Planters: The Xinca of the Michatoya Drainage, Guatemala." *Actes du XLII Congrés International des Américanistes.* Paris: Société des Américanistes 8, 1976, 95–101.

———. *Indian Payments in Kind: The Sixteenth-Century Encomiendas of Guatemala.* Culver City, Calif.: Labyrinthos, 1992.

Fernández Molina, José Antonio. "Colouring the World in Blue: The Indigo Boom and the Central American Market, 1750–1810." Ph.D. diss., University of Texas, Austin, 1992.

Ferry, Robert J. "Encomienda, African Slavery, and Agriculture in 17th-century Caracas." *Hispanic American Historical Review* 61, no. 4 (November 1981): 609–35.

Few, Martha. *Women Who Live Evil Lives: Gender, Religion, and the Politics of Power in Colonial Guatemala, 1650–1750.* Austin: University of Texas Press, 2002.

Foster, George. *Culture and Conquest: America's Spanish Heritage.* Chicago: Quadrangle Books, 1960.

Fowler, William R., Jr. *The Cultural Evolution of Ancient Nahua Civilizations: The Pipil-Nicarao of Central America.* Norman: University of Oklahoma Press, 1989.

Friedmann, Nina S. de. *La Saga del Negro: Presencia Africana en Colombia.* Bogotá: Instituto de Genetica Humana, Facultad de Medecina, Pontificia Universidad Javeriana, 1993.

Funari, Pedro Paulo A. "A arqueologia de Palmares: Sua contribuição para o conhecimento da história da cultura afro-americana." *Liberdade por um fio: História dos quilombos no Brasil.* Edited by João José Reis and Flávio dos Santos Gomes, 26–51. São Paulo: Companhia das Letras, 1996.

Gabbert, Wolfgang. *Becoming Maya or Mestizo: Ethnicity and Social Inequality in Yucatan since 1500.* Tucson: University of Arizona Press, 2004.

Gadsden, James. "Defences of the Floridas: A Report of Captain James Gadsden, Aide-de-Camp to General Andrew Jackson." *Florida Historical Quarterly* 15 (April 1937).

Gage, Thomas. *Travels in the New World* [*The English-American,* 1648]. Edited by J. Eric S. Thompson. Norman: University of Oklahoma Press, 1958.

Gallay, Alan. *The Indian Slave Trade: The Rise of the English Empire in the American South, 1670–1717.* New Haven, Conn.: Yale University Press, 2002.

Gandon, Tania Almeida. "O índio e o negro: Uma relação legendária." *Afro-Asia* 19–20 (1997): 135–64.

Garcés G., Jorge, ed. *Las minas de Zamora: Cuentas de la Real Hacienda, 1561–1565.* Quito: Archivo Municipal, 1957.

García Añoveros, Jesús María. *Población y estado sociorreligioso de la diócesis de Guatemala en el último tercio del siglo XVIII.* Guatemala: Editorial Universitaria, 1987.

García Bernal, Manuela Cristina. *La Sociedad de Yucatan, 1700–1750.* Seville: Escuela de Estudio Hispano-Americanos, 1972.

———. *Población y Encomienda en Yucatan bajo los Austrias.* Seville: Escuela de Estudio Hispano-Americanos, 1978.

García Pelaez, Francisco de Paula. *Memorias para la historia del antiguo reino de Guatemala.* Notas e índice anomástico y toponímico de Francis Gall, Biblioteca Goathemala. Vols. XXI–XXIII., 3rd ed. Guatemala, C.A.: Sociedad de Geografía e Historia de Guatemala, 1968–1973.

Garrido, Margarita. *Reclamos y representaciones: Variaciones sobre la política en el Nuevo Reino de Granada, 1770–1815.* Bogotá: Banco de la Republica, 1995.

Gellert, Gisela. "Ciudad de Guatemala: Factores determinantes en su desarrollo urbano (1775 hasta la actualidad)." *Mesoamérica* 27 (1994): 1–68.

Gerardo-Suarez, Santiago. *Marina, Milicias, y Ejército en la Colonia.* Caracas: Casa de Reeducación y Trabajo Artesanal de El Paraíso, 1971.

Gerhard, Peter. *A Guide to the Historical Geography of New Spain.* Norman: University of Oklahoma Press, 1993.

———. *The North Frontier of New Spain.* Norman: University of Oklahoma Press, 1993.

Gibson, Charles. *The Aztecs Under Spanish Rule.* Stanford, Calif.: Stanford University Press, 1964.

Giddings, Joshua R. *The Exiles of Florida.* Columbus, Ohio, 1858.

Gómara, Francisco López de. *Cortés: The Life of the Conqueror by His Secretary* [1552]. Berkeley: University of California Press, 1964.

Gomes, Flávio dos Santos. "Fronteiras e mocambos: Protesto negro na Guiana brasileira." *Nas terras do Cabo Norte: Fronteiras, colonização e escravidão na Guiana brasileira, séculos XVIII–XIX.* Edited by Flávio dos Santos Gomes, 225–318. Belem, Pará: Gráfica e Editora Universitária, 1999.

———. "'Amostras Humanas': Índios, negros e relações interétnicas no Brasil Colonial." *Raça como retórica: A construção da diferença.* Edited by Yvonne Maggie and Cláudia Barcellos Rezende, 27–82. Rio de Janeiro, 2002.

Gomez, Thomas. *L'envers de l'Eldorado: Economie coloniale et travail indigene dans la Colombie du XVIème Siecle.* Toulouse: Assosiation des Publications UTM, 1984.

González, Nancie. "The Neoteric Society." *Comparative Studies in Society and History* 12 (1970): 1–13.

———. "New Evidence on the Origin of the Black Carib." *Nieuwe West-Indische Gids* 57, nos. 3–4 (1983): 143–72.

González de Cossio, Francisco. *Xalapa.* México City: Talleres de la Nación, 1957.

Grahn, Lance. *The Political Economy of Smuggling: Regional Informal Economies in Early Bourbon New Granada.* Boulder, Colo.: Westview Press, Dellplain Latin American Studies, No. 34, 1997.

Greenblatt, Stephen. *Marvelous Possessions: The Wonder of the New World.* Oxford: Clarendon Press, 1991.

Gutiérrez Pineda, Virginia, and Pineda Giraldo, Roberto. *Miscegenación y cultura: La Colombia Colonial, 1750–1810.* Tomo 2. Santafé de Bogotá: Ediciones Uniandes, 1999.

Guzmán, Angela Inés. *Poblamiento e Historias Urbanas del Alto Magdalena: Tolima, Siglos XVI, XVII y XVIII.* Santafé de Bogotá: Eco Ediciones, 1996.

Hamill, Hugh. *The Hidalgo Revolt.* Gainesville: University of Florida Press, 1966.

Hann, John H., ed. *Apalachee: The Land between the Rivers.* Gainesville: University Presses of Florida, 1988.

———. "St. Augustine's Fallout from the Yamassee War." *Florida Historical Quarterly* 68 (1989): 180–200.

———. *Mission to the Calusa.* Gainesville: University of Florida Press, 1991.

———. *A History of the Timucua Indians and Missions.* Gainesville: University Press of Florida, 1996.

———. "Documentation Pertaining to the Asile Farm." San Luis Archaeological and Historical Site, Tallahassee, n.d.

Hannertz, Ulf. "The World in Creolization." *Africa* 57 (1987).

Haslip-Viera, Gabriel. "The Underclass." In *Cities and Society in Colonial Latin America.* Edited by Louisa Schell Hoberman and Susan Migden Socolow. Albuquerque: University of New Mexico Press, 1986.

Hassig, Ross. *Mexico and the Spanish Conquest*. London and New York: Longman Group, 1994.

Helms, Mary W. "The Cultural Ecology of a Colonial Tribe." *Ethnology* 8, no. 1 (1969): 76–84.

Herrera, Robinson Antonio. "The People of Santiago: Early Colonial Guatemala, 1538–1587." Ph.D. diss., University of California, Los Angeles, 1997.

Himmerich y Valencia, Robert. "The 1536 Siege of Cuzco: An Analysis of Inca and Spanish Warfare." *Colonial Latin American Historical Review* 7, no. 4 (fall 1998): 387–418.

Hoffman, Paul. *The Spanish Crown and the Defense of the Caribbean, 1535–1585*. Baton Rouge: Louisiana State University Press, 1980.

———. *A New Andalucía and a Way to the Orient: The American Southeast During the Sixteenth Century*. Baton Rouge: Louisiana State University Press, 1990.

———. *Florida's Frontiers*. Bloomington: Indiana University Press, 2002.

Hoover, Robert. "Spanish-Native Interaction and Acculturation in the Alta California Missions." In *Columbian Consequences*. Edited by David Hurst Thomas. Vol. 1. Washington, D.C.: Smithsonian Institution Press, 1989, 395–406.

Hudson, Charles. *Knights of Spain, Warriors of the Sun, Hernando de Soto and the South's Ancient Chiefdoms*. Athens: University of Georgia Press, 1997.

Hulme, Peter. *Remnants of Conquest: The Island Caribs and Their Visitors, 1877–1998*. Oxford: Oxford University Press, 2000.

———. "Yellow and Black in the Caribbean: Racial and Ethnic Classification on St. Vincent during the Revolutionary Wars of the 1790's." Paper given to the Department of Anthropology, University of Wisconsin—Madison, March 2000.

Hulme, Peter, and Neil L. Whitehead, eds. *Wild Majesty: Encounters with Caribs from Columbus to the Present Day, an Anthology*. Oxford: Oxford University Press, 1992.

Hunt, Marta Espejo-Ponce. "The Process of the Development of Yucatan, 1600–1700." In *Provinces of Early Mexico*. Edited by Ida Altman and James Lockhart. Los Angeles: UCLA Latin American Center, 1976.

Instituto do Açúcar e do Álcool. *Documentos para a história do açúcar*. 3 vols. Rio de Janeiro, 1954–1963.

Israel, J. I. *Race, Class and Politics in Colonial Mexico, 1610–1670*. London: Oxford University Press, 1975.

Jefferson, Ann F. "The Rebellion of Mita: Eastern Guatemala in 1837." Ph.D. diss., University of Massachusetts, Amherst, 2000.

Jones, Grant D. "The Ethnohistory of the Guale Coast through 1684." In *The Anthropology of St. Catherine's Island: 1. Natural and Cultural History.* Edited by David Hurst Thomas et al. New York: Anthropological Papers of the American Museum of Natural History, vol. 55, pt. 2, 1978.

———. *The Conquest of the Last Maya Kingdom.* Stanford, Calif.: Stanford University Press, 1999.

Jopling, Carol F., ed. *Indios y Negros en Panamá en los Siglos XVI y XVII: Selecciones de los documentos del Archivo General de Indias.* Antigua, Guat., and South Woodstock, Vt.: CIRMA and Plumsock Mesoamerican Studies, 1994.

Juarros, Domingo. *Compendio de la historia de la Ciudad de Guatemala.* 3rd ed. 2 vols. Guatemala: Tipografía Nacional, 1936.

Karasch, Mary. "Os quilombos do ouro na capitania de Goiás." *Liberdade por um fio: História dos quilombos no Brasil.* Edited by João José Reis and Flávio dos Santos Gomes, 240–62. São Paulo: Companhia das Letras, 1996.

Kepecs, Susan. "The Political Economy of Chikinchel, Yucatan, Mexico: A Diachronic Analysis from the Prehispanic Era Through the Age of Spanish Administration." Ph.D. diss., University of Wisconsin—Madison, 1999.

———. "Mayas, Spaniards, and Salt: World Systems Shifts in 16th-Century Yucatan." In *The Postclassic to Spanish-Era Transition in Mesoamerica: Archaeological Perspectives.* Edited by Susan Kepecs and Rani Alexander. Albuquerque: University of New Mexico Press, forthcoming.

King, Stewart R. *Blue Coat or Powdered Wig: Free People of Color in Pre-Revolutionary Saint Domingue.* Athens: University of Georgia Press, 2001.

Klein, Herbert. "The Colored Militia of Cuba: 1568–1868." *Caribbean Studies* 6, no. 2 (1966): 17–27.

Klos, George. "Gracia Real de Santa Teresa de Mose: A Free Black Town in Spanish Colonial Florida." *American Historical Review* 95 (1990): 9–30.

———. "Blacks and the Seminole Indian Removal Debate, 1821–1835." In *The African American Heritage of Florida.* Edited by David R. Colburn and Jane L. Landers. Gainesville: University Press of Florida, 1995.

———. "*Cimarrón* Ethnicity and Cultural Adaptation in the Spanish Domains of the Circum-Caribbean, 1503–1763." In *Identity in the Shadow of Slavery.* Edited by Paul E. Lovejoy. London: Continuum, 2000, 30–54.

———. "The Central African Presence in Spanish Maroon Societies." In *Central African and Cultural Transformations in the American Diaspora.* Edited by Linda M. Heywood. Cambridge: Cambridge University Press, 2002, 227–41.

———. "Conspiradores esclavizados en Cartagena en el siglo XVII." In *Afrodescendientes en las américas: Trayectorias sociales e identitarias: 150 años de la abolición de la esclavitud en Colombia*. Edited by Claudia Mosquera, Mauricio Pardo, and Odile Hoffman. Bogotá: Universidad Nacional de Colombia, 2002, 181–93.

Korth, Eugene V. *Spanish Policy in Colonial Chile: The Struggle for Justice, 1535–1700*. Stanford, Calif.: Stanford University Press, 1968.

Kraay, Hendrik. "Entre o Brasil e Bahia: as comemorações do Dois de Julho em Salvador no século XIX." *Afro-Asia* 23 (2000): 49–88.

Kramer, Wendy. *Encomienda Politics in Early Colonial Guatemala, 1524–1544: Dividing the Spoils*. Boulder, Colo.: Westview Press, 1994.

Kuethe, Allan J. "The Status of the Free-Pardo in the Disciplined Militia of New Granada." *The Journal of Negro History* 56, no. 2 (1971): 105–17.

———. *Military Reform and Society in New Granada, 1773–1808*. Gainesville: University of Florida Press, 1978.

———. *Cuba, 1753–1815: Crown, Military, and Society*. Knoxville: University of Tennessee Press, 1986.

Langfur, Hal. "Uncertain Refuge: Frontier Formation and the Origins of the Botocudo War in Late Colonial Brazil." *Hispanic American Historical Review* 82, no. 2 (2002): 215–56.

Landers, Jane. "African-American Women and Their Pursuit of Rights through Eighteenth-Century Spanish Texts." In *Haunted Bodies: Gender and Southern Texts*. Edited by Anne Goodwyn Jones and Susan V. Donaldson. Charlottesville and London: University Press of Virginia, 1997.

———. *Black Society in Spanish Florida*. Urbana: University of Illinois Press, 1999.

Lane, Kris. *Pillaging the Empire: Piracy in the Americas 1500–1750*. Armonk, N.Y.: M. E. Sharpe, 1998.

———. "Taming the Master: Brujería, Slavery, and the Encomienda in Barbacoas at the Turn of the Eighteenth Century." *Ethnohistory* 45, no. 3 (summer 1998): 477–507.

———. "The Transition from Encomienda to Slavery in Seventeenth-Century Barbacoas (Colombia)." *Slavery & Abolition* 21, no. 1 (April 2000): 73–95.

Las Casas, Bartolomé de. *A Short Account of the Destruction of the Indies*. Translated by Nigel Griffin. New York: Penguin, 1992.

Leite, Serafim, ed. *História da Companhia de Jesús no Brasil*. 10 vols. Lisbon: Livraria Portugalia, 1938–1950.

———. *Cartas do Brasil e mais escritos de P. Manuel da Nóbrega (opera omnia)*. Coimbra, 1955.

Le Page, R. B., and A. Tabouret-Keller. *Acts of Identity: Creole-Based Approaches to Ethnicity and Language*. Cambridge: Cambridge University Press, 1985.

Lestringant, F. *Cannibals*. Berkeley: University of California Press, 1997.

"Letters of Montiano, Siege of St. Augustine." *Collections of the Georgia Historical Society*. Savannah, 1909, 20–43.

Lewis, Laura A. "Colonialism and Its Contradictions: Indians, Blacks and Social Power in Sixteenth and Seventeenth Century Mexico." *Journal of Historical Sociology* 9, no. 4 (December 1996).

Linebaugh, Peter, and Marcus Rediker, *The Many-Headed Hydra: Sailors, Slaves, Commoners, and the Hidden History of the Revolutionary Atlantic*. Boston: Beacon Press, 2000.

Littlefield, Daniel F., Jr. *Africans and Seminoles: From Removal to Emancipation*. Westport, Conn.: Greenwood Press, 1977.

Livi Bacci, Massimo. "Return to Hispaniola: Reassessing a Demographic Catastrophe." *Hispanic American Historical Review* 83, no. 1 (February 2003): 3–51.

Lockey, Joseph Byrne. *East Florida, 1783–1785: A File of Documents Assembled and Many of Them Translated*. Berkeley: University of California Press, 1959.

Lockhart, James. *Spanish Peru, 1532–1560: A Social History* [1968]. 2nd ed. Madison: University of Wisconsin Press, 1994.

———. *The Men of Cajamarca*. Austin: University of Texas Press, 1972.

———. *The Nahuas after the Conquest: A Social and Cultural History of the Indians of Central Mexico, Sixteenth through Eighteenth Centuries*. Stanford, Calif.: Stanford University Press, 1992.

Lockhart, James, and Stuart B. Schwartz. *Early Latin America: A History of Colonial Spanish America and Brazil*. Cambridge: Cambridge University Press, 1983.

Lokken, Paul. "Undoing Racial Hierarchy: Mulatos and Militia Service in Colonial Guatemala." *SECOLAS Annals* 31 (November 1999).

———. "From Black to *Ladino*: People of African Descent, *Mestizaje*, and Racial Hierarchy in Rural Colonial Guatemala, 1600–1730." Ph.D. diss., University of Florida, Gainesville, 2000.

———. "Transforming Mulatto Identity in Colonial Guatemala, 1670–1720." Paper presented at the American Historical Association Annual Meeting, San Francisco, January 2002.

Lovejoy, Paul. *Transformations in Slavery: A History of Slavery in Africa*, 2nd ed. Cambridge: Cambridge University Press, 2000.

Lovell, W. George. *Conquest and Survival in Colonial Guatemala: A Historical Geography of the Cuchumatán Highlands, 1500–1821.* Rev. ed. Montreal & Kingston: McGill-Queen's University Press, 1992.

Lovell, W. George, and Christopher H. Lutz. *Demography and Empire: A Guide to the Population History of Spanish Central America, 1500–1821.* Dellplain Latin American Studies, No. 33, Boulder, Colo.: Westview Press, 1995.

———. "A Dark Obverse: Maya Survival in Guatemala, 1520–1994." *Geographical Review* 86, no. 3 (1996): 398–407.

———. *Demografía e imperio: Guía para la historia de la población de la América Central Española, 1500–1821.* Guatemala City and South Woodstock, Vt.: Editorial Universitaria and Plumsock Mesoamerican Studies, 2000.

Lovell, W. George, and William R. Swezey. "The Population of Southern Guatemala at Spanish Contact." *Canadian Journal of Anthropology* 3, no. 1 (1982): 71–84.

Lovell, W. George, Christopher H. Lutz, and William R. Swezey. "The Indian Population of Southern Guatemala, 1549–1551: An Analysis of López de Cerrato's *Tasaciones de Tributos.*" *The Americas* 40, no. 4 (1984): 459–77.

Lucena Salmoral, Manuel. *Piratas, Bucaneros, Filibusteros y Corsarios en América.* Madrid: Editorial Mapfre, 1992.

Luján Muñoz, Jorge. "Fundación de villas de ladinos en Guatemala en el último tercio del siglo XVIII." *Revista de Indias* 36, nos. 145/146 (1976): 51–81.

Lutz, Christopher H. *Historia sociodemográfica de Santiago de Guatemala, 1541–1773.* Serie Monográfica: 2. CIRMA: La Antigua Guatemala, 1982–1984.

———. "Evolución demográfica de la población no indígena." In *Dominación española: Desde la conquista hasta 1700.* Vol. ed. Ernesto Chinchilla Aguilar. *Historia General de Guatemala,* vol. II. Gen. ed. Jorge Luján Muñoz. Guatemala: Asociación de Amigos del País, Fundación para la Cultura y el Desarrollo, 1993, 249–58.

———. "Evolución demográfica de la población ladina." In *Siglo XVIII hasta la Independencia.* Vol. ed. Cristina Zilbermann de Luján. *Historia General de Guatemala,* vol. III. Gen. ed. Jorge Luján Muñoz. Guatemala: Asociación de Amigos del País, Fundación para la Cultura y el Desarrollo, 1994, 119–34.

———. *Santiago de Guatemala, 1541–1773: City, Caste, and the Colonial Experience.* Norman: University of Oklahoma Press, 1994.

———. "Santiago de Guatemala (1700–1773)." In *Siglo XVIII hasta la Independencia.* Vol. ed. Cristina Zilbermann de Luján. *Historia General de Guatemala,* vol. III. Ed. gen. Jorge Luján Muñoz. Guatemala: Asociación de Amigos del País, Fundación para la Cultura y el Desarrollo, 1994, 185–98.

Lutz, Christopher H., and W. George Lovell. "Core and Periphery in Colonial Guatemala." *Guatemalan Indians and the State: 1540–1988*. Edited by Carol A. Smith. Austin: University of Texas Press, 1990, 35–51.

———. "Survivors on the Move: Maya Migration in Time and Space." In *The Maya Diaspora: Guatemalan Roots, New American Lives*. Edited by James Loucky and Marilyn M. Moors. Philadelphia: Temple University Press, 2000, 11–34.

Lyon, Eugene. *The Enterprise of Florida: Pedro Menéndez de Avilés and the Spanish Conquest of Florida, 1565–1568*. Gainesville: University Press of Florida, 1974.

Macías Domínguez, Isabelo. *Cuba en la primera mitad del siglo XVII*. Sevilla: Escuela de Estudios Hispano-Americanos, 1978.

MacLeod, Murdo J. *Spanish Central America: A Socioeconomic History, 1520–1720*. Berkeley and Los Angeles: University of California Press, 1973.

Madigan, Douglas Glenn. "Santiago Atitlán, Guatemala: A Socioeconomic and Demographic History." Ph.D. diss., University of Pittsburgh, 1976.

Mahon, John K. *History of the Second Seminole War*. Gainesville: University of Florida Press, 1967.

Marchena Fernández, Juan. *Oficiales y soldados en el ejército de America*. Seville: Escuela de Estudios Hispanoamericanos, 1983.

———. "The Social World of the Military in Peru and New Granada." In *Reform and Insurrection in Bourbon New Granada and Peru*. Edited by John R. Fisher, Allan J. Kuethe, and Anthony McFarlane. Baton Rouge: Louisiana State University Press, 1990.

———. *Ejercito y milicias en el mundo colonial Americano*. Madrid: Editorial Mapfre, 1992.

Marin, Rosa Elizabeth Acevedo. "Prosperidade e estagnação de Macapá colonial: As experiências dos colonos." In *Nas terras do Cabo Norte: Fronteiras, colonização e escravidão na Guiana brasileira, séculos XVIII–XIX*. Edited by Flávio dos Santos Gomes. Belem, Pará: Gráfica e Editora Universitária 1999, 33–62.

Martin, Cheryl English. *Rural Society in Colonial Morelos*. Albuquerque: University of New Mexico Press, 1985.

Martin, Joel, *Sacred Revolt: The Muskogees' Struggle for a New World*. Boston: Beacon Press, 1991.

Maximilian, Prinz von Wied. *Travels in Brazil in the Years 1815, 1816, 1817*. London, 1820.

McAlister, Lyle N. *The "Fuero Militar" in New Spain, 1764–1800*. Gainesville: University of Florida Press, 1957.

McBride, Dwight A. *Impossible Witnesses: Truth, Abolitionism, and Slave Testimony*. New York: New York University Press, 2001.

McCaa, Robert, et al. "Race and Class in Colonial Latin America: A Critique." *Comparative Studies in Society and History* 12, no. 3 (July 1979).

McEwan, Bonnie, ed. *The Spanish Missions of La Florida.* Gainesville: University Press of Florida, 1993.

McFarlane, Anthony. *Colombia Before Independence: Economy, Society, and Politics under Bourbon Rule.* Cambridge: Cambridge University Press, 1993.

Meireles, Denise Maldi. *Guardiães da fronteira: Rio Guaporé, século XVIII.* Petrópolis: Vozes, 1989.

Meisel Roca, Adolfo. "Esclavitud, mestizaje y haciendas en la Provincia de Cartagena 1533–1851." In *El Caribe Colombiano: Selección de textos históricos.* Edited by Gustavo Bell Lemus. Barranquilla: Ediciones Uninorte, 1988.

Mello, José Antônio Gonsalves de. *Tempo dos Flamengos: Influência da ocupação holandesa na vida e na cultura do Norte do Brasil.* 2nd ed. Recife: Governo de Pernambuco, Secretaria de Educação e Cultura, Departamento de Cultura, 1978.

———. *Henrique Dias, Governador dos crioulos, negros e mulatos do Brasil.* Recife: Fundação Joaquim Nabuco, Editora Massangana, 1988.

Metcalf, Alida C. "Millenarian Slaves? The Santidade de Jaguaripe and Slave Resistance in the Americas." *American Historical Review* 104, no. 5 (1999): 1531–59.

Miles, Suzanne W. "The Sixteenth-Century Pocom-Maya: A Documentary Analysis of Social Structure and Archaeological Setting." *Transactions of the American Philosophical Society* 47. Philadelphia: American Philosophical Society, 1957, 733–81.

Mina, Mateo. *Esclavitud y Libertad en el Valle del Río Cauca.* Bogotá: Fundición Rosca de Investigación y Acción Social, 1975.

Mintz, Sidney, and Richard Price. *An Anthropological Approach to the Afro-American Past: A Caribbean Perspective.* Philadelphia: Institute for the Study of Human Issues, 1976.

Moreau, Pierre. *História das ultimas lutas no Brasil entre holandeses e portugueses.* Translated by Leda Boechat Rodrigues. Belo Horizonte: Livraria Itatiaia Editora, 1979.

Moreau de Jonnès, Alexandre. *Aventures de guerre au temps de la République et du Consulat.* Paris: Pagnerre, 1858.

Mörner, Magnus. "La política de segregación y el mestizaje en la Audiencia de Guatemala." *Revista de Indias* XXIV: 95–96 (1964): 137–51.

———. *Race Mixture in the History of Latin America.* Boston: Little, Brown, 1967.

———. *La corona española y los foranos en los pueblos de indios de América.* Stockholm: Almqvist and Wiksell, 1970.

————. "Economic Factors and Stratification in Colonial Spanish America with Special Regard to Elites." *Hispanic American Historical Review* 63, no. 2 (May 1983).

Morse, Richard M. "Latin American Cities: Aspects of Function and Structure." *Comparative Studies in Society and History* IV (1961): 473–93.

Mott, Luiz. "Brancos, pardos, pretos e índios em Sergipe, 1825–1830." *Anaís da História* 6 (1974): 139–84.

Moya Pons, Frank. *Despues de Colón: trabajo, sociedad, y política en la economía del oro.* Madrid: Alianza Editorial, 1987.

Mulroy, Kevin. *Freedom on the Border: The Seminole Maroons in Florida, the Indian Territory, Coahuila, and Texas.* Lubbock: Texas Tech University Press, 1993.

Narrative of a Voyage to the Spanish Main in the Ship "Two Friends." Facsimile of 1819 ed. Gainesville: University Presses of Florida, 1978.

Naveda, Adriana. *Esclavos negros en las haciendas azuareras de Córdoba, Veracruz, 1690–1830.* Jalapa: Universidad Veracruzana, 1987.

Nazzari, Muriel. "Vanishing Natives: The Social Construction of Race in Colonial São Paulo." *The Americas* 57, no. 4 (April 2001): 497–524.

Newson, Linda A. "Indian Population Patterns in Colonial Spanish America." *Latin American Research Review* 20, no. 3 (1985): 41–74.

Ngou-Mve, Nicolas. *La traite et l'esclavage de Noirs au Mexique de 1580–1640.* Ph.D. diss., L'Université de Toulouse-le Mirail, 1987.

Nieto, Vicente. *Padron de Xalapa.* México: Editorial Citlaltepetl, 1971.

Nieuhof, John. *Memorável viagem marítima e terrestre ao Brasil.* São Paulo: Editora da Universidade de São Paulo, 1981 [1682].

O'Brien, Greg. *Choctaws in a Revolutionary Age, 1750–1830.* University of Nebraska Press, 2002.

O'Gorman, Frances. *Aluanda: A Look at Afro-Brazilian Cults.* Rio de Janeiro: Livraria F. Alves Editora, 1977.

Olsen, Margaret M. "*Negros horros* and *Cimarrones* on the Legal Frontiers of the Caribbean: Accessing the African Voice in Colonial Spanish American Texts." *Research in African Literatures: The African Diaspora and Its Origins* 29, no. 4 (winter 1998): 52–71.

Orser, C. E., Jr. *In Search of Zumbi: The 1993 Season.* Normal: Illinois State University Press, 1993.

Ortiz, Fernando. *Cuban Counterpoint: Tobacco and Sugar.* New York: Knopf, 1947.

Oviedo, Gonzalo Fernández de. *Historia General y Natural de las Indias.* Books I–VIII, Biblioteca de Autores Españoles, v. 117. Madrid: Atlas, 1959.

Palafox y Mendoza, Juan de. *Relación de la visita eclesiastica del obispo de Puebla, 1643–1646.* Compiled by Bernardo García Martínez. Puebla: Editorial Nuestra República, 1997.

Palmer, Colin. *Slaves of the White God: Blacks in Mexico 1570–1650.* Cambridge: Cambridge University Press, 1976.

Palomo de Lewin, Beatriz. "Esclavos negros." In *Siglo XVIII hasta la Independencia.* Vol. ed. Cristina Zilbermann de Luján. *Historia General de Guatemala,* vol. III. Gen. ed. Jorge Luján Muñoz. Guatemala: Asociación de Amigos del País, Fundación para la Cultura y el Desarrollo, 1994, 135–48.

Pardo, J. Joaquín. *Efemérides para escribir la historia de la muy noble y muy leal ciudad de Santiago de los Caballeros del Reino de Guatemala.* Guatemala: Tipografía Nacional, 1944.

Parker, Susan R. "Men Without God or King: Rural Settlers of East Florida, 1784–1790." *Florida Historical Quarterly* 64 (October 1990): 135–55.

Patch, Robert W. *Maya and Spaniard in Yucatan, 1648–1812.* Stanford, Calif.: Stanford University Press, 1993.

Peñas Galindo, David Ernesto. *Los Bogas de Mompox: Historia del Zambaje.* Bogotá: Tercer Mundo Editores, 1988.

Perdue, Theda. *"Mixed Blood" Indians: Racial Construction in the Early South.* Athens: University of Georgia Press, 2003.

Pinto Soria, Julio César. *Estructura agraria y asentamiento en la Capitanía General de Guatemala: Algunos apuntes históricos.* Guatemala: Universidad de San Carlos, Centro de Estudios Urbanos y Rurales, 1980.

———. "Apuntes históricos sobre la estructura agraria y asentamiento en la Capitanía General de Guatemala." In *Estudios sobre la Guatemala colonial.* Edited by Stephen A. Webre. Serie Monográfica 5. South Woodstock, Vt., and La Antigua, Guatemala: Plumsock Mesoamerican Studies, and Centro de Investigaciones Regionales de Mesoamérica, 1989, 109–40.

Poma de Ayala, Felipe Guaman. *El primer nueva corónica y buen gobierno,* 3rd ed. Edited by John V. Murra and Rolena Adorno. Mexico: Siglo XXI, 1992.

Porter, Kenneth Wiggins. *The Negro on the American Frontier.* New York: Arno Press, 1971.

———. *The Black Seminoles.* Edited and revised by Alcione M. Amos and Thomas P. Senter. Gainesville: University Press of Florida, 1996.

Price, Richard. *Maroon Societies: Rebel Slave Communities in the Americas.* Baltimore: Johns Hopkins University Press, 1973.

———. "The Miracle of Creolization: A Retrospective." *New West India Guide* 75, nos. 1, 2 (2001): 35–64.

Priestly, Herbert. *José de Gálvez, Visitor-General of New Spain (1765–1771).* Berkeley: University of California Press, 1916.

Puntoni, Pedro. "A guerra dos bárbaros: Povos indigenas e a colonização do sertão do nordeste do Brasil, 1650–1720." Ph.D. thesis, Universidade de São Paulo, 1988.

———. *A mísera sorte: A escravidão africana no Brasil holandês e as guerras do tráfico no Atlântico Sul, 1621–1648.* São Paulo: Editora Hucitec, 1992.

Pupo-Walker, Enrique, ed. *Castaways: The Narrative of Alvar Núñez Cabeza de Vaca.* Berkeley: University of California Press, 1993.

Recinos, Adrián. *Pedro de Alvarado, conquistador de México y Guatemala.* Mexico City: Fondo de Cultura Económica, 1952.

Records of the British Public Record Office Relating to South Carolina, 1663–1782. Edited by A. S. Salley. Atlanta and Columbia, S.C., 1928–1947, 88–95.

Reis, João José. "Escravos e coiteiros no quilombo de Oitizeiro, Bahia, 1806." In *Liberdade por um fio: História dos quilombos no Brasil.* Edited by João José Reis and Flávio dos Santos Gomes. São Paulo: Companhia das Letras, 1996, 332–72.

Reitz, Elizabeth J. "Zooarchaeological Analysis of a Free African American Community: Gracia Real de Santa Teresa de Mose." *Historical Archaeology* 28 (1994): 23–40.

Restall, Matthew. *The Maya World: Yucatec Culture and Society, 1550–1850.* Stanford, Calif.: Stanford University Press, 1997.

———. "Heirs to the Hieroglyphs: Indigenous Writing in Colonial Mesoamerica." *The Americas* 54, no. 2 (October 1997): 239–67.

———. *Maya Conquistador.* Boston: Beacon Press, 1998.

———. "Interculturation and the Indigenous Testament in Colonial Yucatan." In *Dead Giveaways: Indigenous Testaments of Colonial Mesoamerica and the Andes.* Edited by Susan Kellogg and Matthew Restall. Salt Lake City: University of Utah Press, 1998, 141–62.

———. "Otredad y ambigüedad: Las percepciones que los españoles y los mayas tenían de los africanos en el Yucatán colonial." *Signos históricos* II, no. 4 (2000).

———. "Black Conquistadors: Armed Africans in Early Spanish America." *The Americas* 57, no. 2 (October 2000): 171–205.

———. "La falacia de la libertad: La experiencia Afro-Yucateca en la edad de la esclavitud." In *Rutas de la Esclavitud en Africa y América Latina.* Edited by Rina Cáceres. San José: Editorial de la Universidad de Costa Rica, 2001, 289–304.

———. *Seven Myths of the Spanish Conquest.* New York: Oxford University Press, 2003.

———. *The Black Middle: Slavery, Society, and African-Maya Relations in Colonial Yucatan.* Stanford, Calif.: Stanford University Press, forthcoming.

————. "Manuel's Worlds, Richard's Worlds: Black Yucatan and the Colonial Caribbean." In *Slaves, Subjects, and Subversives: Blacks in Colonial Latin America*. Edited by Jane Landers. Albuquerque: University of New Mexico Press, forthcoming.

Restall, Matthew, Lisa Sousa, and Kevin Terraciano. *Mesoamerican Voices*. Cambridge: Cambridge University Press, forthcoming.

Richter, Daniel K. *Facing East from Indian Country: A Native History of Early America*. Cambridge, Mass.: Harvard University Press, 2001.

Rodríguez, Pablo. *Sentimientos y vida familiar en el Nuevo Reino de Granada*. Santa Fé de Bogotá: Editorial Ariel, 1997.

Rodríguez Baquero, Luis Enrique. *Encomienda y vida diaria entre los Indios de Muzo (1550–1620)*. Bogotá: Instituto Colombiano de Cultura Hispanica, 1995.

Romero, Mario Diego, and Kris Lane. "Miners and Maroons: Freedom on the Pacific Coast of Colombia and Ecuador." *Cultural Survival Quarterly* 25, no. 4 (winter 2002): 32–37.

Rout, Leslie, Jr. *The African Experience in Spanish America*. London: Cambridge University Press, 1976.

Rubio Mañé, J. Ignacio. *Archivo de la Historia de Yucatán, Campeche, y Tabasco*. 2 vols. Mexico City: Imp. Aldina, Robredo y Rosell, 1942.

Russell-Wood, A. J. R. "'Acts of Grace': Portuguese Monarchs and Their Subjects of African Descent in Eighteenth-Century Brazil." *Journal of Latin American Studies* 32 (May 2000).

Salomon, Frank, and Stuart B. Schwartz, eds. *Cambridge History of the Native Peoples of the Americas*. Vol. 3, *South America*. Cambridge: Cambridge University Press, 1999.

Salvador (Brazil). Diretoria do Arquivo e Divulgação. *Atas da Câmara Municipal do Salvador, Documentos históricos do Arquivo Municipal*. 10 vols. to date. Salvador, 1944–.

Salvador, Frei Vicente do. *História do Brasil, 1500-1627*. 5th ed. Notes by Capistrano de Abreu, Rodolfo Garcia, Frei Vinâncio Willeke. São Paulo: Edições Melhoramentos, 1965.

Santos, Jocélio Teles dos. *O dono da terra: O caboclo nos candomblés da Bahia*. Salvador: Sarah Letras, 1995.

Sauer, Carl O. *The Early Spanish Main*. Berkeley: University of California Press, 1966.

Saunt, Claudio. *A New Order of Things: Property, Power, and the Transformation of the Creek Indians, 1733–1816*. Cambridge: Cambridge University Press, 1999.

Schafer, Daniel L. "'A Class of People Neither Freemen nor Slaves': From Spanish to American Race Relations in Florida, 1821–1861." *Journal of Social History* 26 (1993): 587–609.

Schwartz, Stuart B. *Sugar Plantations in the Formation of Brazilian Society, Bahia, 1550–1835.* Cambridge: Cambridge University Press, 1985.

———. "The Formation of a Colonial Identity in Brazil." In *Colonial Identity in the Atlantic World, 1500–1800.* Edited by N. Canny and A. Pagden. Princeton: Princeton University Press, 1987.

———. *Slaves, Peasants, and Rebels: Reconsidering Brazilian Slavery.* Urbana and Chicago: University of Illinois Press, 1992.

———. "Brazilian Ethnogenesis: Mestiços, mamelucos, and pardos." In *Le Nouveau Monde, Mondes Nouveaux: L'Expérience Américaine.* Edited by S. Gruzinski and N. Wachtel. Paris: Editions Recherche sur les civilisations: Editions de l'Ecole des hautes études en sciences sociales, 1996, 7–28.

———. "Cantos e quilombos numa conspiração de escravos haussás, Bahia, 1814." In *Liberdade por um fio: História dos quilombos no Brasil.* Edited by João José Reis and Flávio dos Santos Gomes. São Paulo: Companhia das Letras, 1996, 373–406.

Schwartz, Stuart B., and Frank Salomon. "New Peoples and New Kinds of Peoples: Adaptation, Readjustment, and Ethnogenesis in South American Indigenous Societies (Colonial Era)." In *Cambridge History of the Native Peoples of the Americas.* Vol. 3, pt. 2. Cambridge: Cambridge University Press, 1999.

Seed, Patricia, and Philip Rust. "Estate and Class in Colonial Oaxaca Revisited." *Comparative Studies in Society and History* 25, no. 4 (October 1983).

Sharp, William F. *Slavery on the Spanish Frontier: The Colombian Chocó, 1680–1810.* Norman: University of Oklahoma Press, 1976.

Sherman, William L. *Forced Native Labor in Sixteenth-Century Central America.* Lincoln: University of Nebraska Press, 1979.

Shoemaker, Nancy. "How Indians Got to Be Red." *American Historical Review* 102, no. 3 (June 1997): 625–44.

Silva, Ignácio Accioli de Cerqueira e. *Memorias históricas e políticas da provincia da Bahia.* 6 vols. Salvador, 1925.

Sluiter, Engel. "Livro que dá razão ao Estado do Brasil." *Hispanic American Historical Review* 29, no. 4 (November 1949): 518–62.

Solórzano Fonseca, Juan Carlos. "Las comunidades indígenas en Guatemala, El Salvador y Chiapas durante el siglo XVIII: Los mecanismos de la explotación económica." *Anuario de Estudios Centroamericanos* 11, no. 2 (1985): 93–130.

Soulodre-La France, Renée. "Socially Not So Dead! Slave Identities in Bourbon Nueva Granada." *Colonial Latin American Review* 10, no 1 (2001): 87–103.

———. "'Los Esclavos de su Magestad!' Slave Protest and Politics on Jesuit Haciendas in Late Colonial New Granada." In *Slaves, Subjects, and*

Subversives: Blacks in Colonial Latin America. Edited by Jane Landers. Albuquerque: University of New Mexico Press, forthcoming.

Spalding, Phinizy. *Oglethorpe in America.* Athens: University of Georgia Press, 1984.

Spanish Land Grants in Florida. 5 vols. Tallahassee, Fla.: Historical Records Survey, 1940–1941.

Spaulding, Karen. *Huarochirí: An Andean Society under Inca and Spanish Rule.* Stanford, Calif.: Stanford University Press, 1984.

Stern, Peter. "Marginals and Acculturation in Frontier Society." In *New Views of Borderlands History.* Edited by Robert Jackson. Albuquerque: University of New Mexico Press, 1998.

Stern, Steve J. *Peru's Indian Peoples and the Challenge of Spanish Conquest: Huamanga to 1640.* Madison: University of Wisconsin Press, 1982.

Strathern, M. "Cutting the Network." *JRAI* 2, no. 3 (1996): 517–35.

Tandeter, Enrique. *Coercion and Market: Silver Mining in Colonial Potosí, 1692–1826.* Albuquerque: University of New Mexico Press, 1993.

Taracena Arriola, Arturo. *Invención criolla, sueño ladino, pesadilla indígena: Los Altos de Guatemala: De región a Estado, 1740–1850.* San José, Costa Rica: Editorial Porvenir, 1997.

Taylor, William. *Drinking, Homicide, and Rebellion in Colonial Mexican Villages.* Stanford, Calif.: Stanford University Press, 1979.

Techo, Nicholas del. *Historia de la Provincia del Paraguay de la Compañia de Jesús.* 5 vols. Madrid: A. de Uribe, 1897.

Thomas, David Hurst, ed. *Columbian Consequences, Vol. 2: Archaeological and Historical Perspectives on the Spanish Borderlands East.* Washington, D.C.: Smithsonian Institution Press, 1990.

Thompson, E. P. "Moral Economy of the English Crowd in the Eighteenth Century." *Past and Present* 50 (February 1971).

Thompson, J. Eric S. "The Maya Central Area at the Spanish Conquest and Later: A Problem in Demography." In *Maya History and Religion.* Edited by J. Eric S. Thompson. Norman: University of Oklahoma Press, 1970.

Thompson, Robert Farris. *Flash of the Spirit: African and Afro-American Art and Philosophy.* New York: Vintage, 1984.

Topping, Aileen Moore, ed. "United States Troops in Spanish East Florida, 1812–1813." *Florida Historical Quarterly* 9 (January 1931): 135–55.

———. *An Impartial Account of the Late Expedition Against St. Augustine Under General Oglethorpe.* Gainesville: University Press of Florida, 1978.

Toral, André A. de. "Os índios negros ou os Carijó de Goiás: A história das Avá-Canoeiro." *Revista de Antropologia* (São Paulo) 27/28 (1984–1985): 287–325.

Toribio, Almeida Jacqueline. "Race, Language, and Ethnic Identity among Dominicans." Paper presented at Pennsylvania State University, 2002.

Tovar Pinzon, Hermes. "De una chispa se forma una hoguera: Esclavitud, insubordinación y liberación (1780–1821)." *Nuevas Lecturas de Historia*, no. 17, 1992.

Trens, Manuel B. *Historia de Veracruz*. 2 vols. Jalapa: Gráficos del Gobierno de Veracruz, 1947.

Triana Antorveza, Adolfo. "Estado-Nación y Minorias Etnicas." In *Grupos Etnicos, Derecho y Cultura*. Bogotá: Funcol-Quadernos del Jaguar, 1987.

Tutino, John. *From Insurrection to Revolution in Mexico*. Princeton: Princeton University Press, 1986.

Twinam, Ann. *Miners, Merchants and Farmers in Colonial Colombia*. Austin: University of Texas Press, 1982.

Vainfas, Ronaldo. *A heresia dos índios: Catolicismo e rebeldia no Brasil colonial*. São Paulo: Companhia das Letras, 1995.

Veblen, Thomas T. "Native Population Decline in Totonicapán, Guatemala." *Annals of the Association of American Geographers* 67, no. 4 (1977): 484–99.

Victoria Ojeda, Jorge. *Mérida de Yucatán de la Indias: Piratería y estrategia defensiva*. Mérida, Yuc.: Ayuntamiento de Mérida, 1995.

Victoria Ojeda, Jorge, and Jorge Canto Alcocer. "San Fernando Ake: La Comunidad Negra del Nororiente Yucateco (1796–1848)." Unpublished manuscript, 1997.

Villagutierre Soto-Major, Juan de. *Historia de la Conquista de la Provincia de el Itza* [etc.]. Madrid, 1701.

Villa-Señor y Sánchez, Joseph Antonio. *Theatro americano*. Vol. I of 2 vols. México: Impresa de la Viuda de Bernardo Hogal, 1746, 1748.

Vinson III, Ben. *Bearing Arms for His Majesty: The Free-Colored Militia in Colonial Mexico*. Stanford, Calif.: Stanford University Press, 2001.

Viqueira Albán, Juan Pedro. *Propriety and Permissiveness in Bourbon Mexico*. Translated by Sonya Lipsett-Rivera and Sergio Rivera Ayala. Wilmington, Del.: Scholarly Resources Inc., 1999.

Voelz, Peter M. *Slave and Soldier: The Military Impact of Blacks in the Colonial Americas*. New York and London: Garland Publishing, 1993.

Volpato, Luiza Rios Ricci. *A conquista da terra no universo da pobreza: Formação da fronteira oeste do Brasil, 1719–1819*. São Paulo: Editora HUCITEC, 1987.

———. "Quilombos em Mato Grosso." In *Liberdade por um fio: História dos quilombos no Brasil*. Edited by João José Reis and Flávio dos Santos Gomes. São Paulo: Companhia das Letras, 1996, 213–39.

Von Mentz, Brígida. *Pueblos de indios, mulatos y mestizos, 1770–1870: Los campesinos y las transformaciones protoindustriales en el poniente de Morelos*. México: CIESAS, 1988.

————. *Trabajo, sujeción y libertad en el centro de la Nueva España: Esclavos, aprendices, campesinos y operarios manufactureros, siglos XVI a XVIII.* México: CIESAS and Porrúa, 1999.

Wade, Peter. *Gente negra, nación mestiza: Dinámicas de las identidades raciales en Colombia.* Translated by Ana Cristina Mejia. Bogotá: Ediciones Uniandes, 1997. First published as *Blackness and Race Mixture: The Dynamics of Racial Identity in Colombia.* Baltimore: Johns Hopkins University Press, 1993.

Wagner, Roy. *The Invention of Culture.* Chicago: University of Chicago Press, 1975.

Warner, Rick. "Indios Amigos in the 'Conquest' of Nayarit." Paper presented at the American Society for Ethnohistory, Quebec City, October 2002.

Warren, Jonathan W. *Racial Revolutions: Antiracism and Native Resurgence in Brazil.* Durham, N.C.: Duke University Press, 2001.

Webre, Stephen, A. "Water and Society in a Spanish American City: Santiago de Guatemala, 1555–1773." *Hispanic American Historical Review* 57, no. 1 (1990): 57–84.

Weisman, Brent R. "The Plantation System of the Florida Seminole Indians and Black Seminoles During the Colonial Era." In *Colonial Plantations and Economy in Florida.* Edited by Jane Landers. Gainesville: University Press of Florida, 2001, 136–49.

Werner Cantor, Erik. *Ni Aniquilados, Ni Vencidos: Los Emberá y la gente negra del Atrato bajo el dominio español, Siglo XVIII.* Bogotá: Instituto Colombiano de Antropología e Historia, 2000.

West, Robert C. *Colonial Placer Mining in Colombia.* Baton Rouge: Louisiana State University Press, 1952.

Whitehead, Neil L. "Carib Ethnic Soldiering in Venezuela, the Guianas and Antilles: 1492–1820." *Ethnohistory* 37, no. 4 (1990): 357–85.

————. "Ethnic Plurality and Cultural Continuity in the Native Caribbean. Remarks and Uncertainties as to Data and Theory." In *Wolves from the Sea: Readings in the Archaeology and Anthropology of the Island Carib.* Edited by Neil L. Whitehead. Leiden: KITLV Press, 1995.

————. "Ethnogenesis and Ethnocide in the Settlement of Surinam." In *History, Power and Identity, Ethnogenesis in the Americas, 1492–1992.* Edited by J. Hill. Iowa City: University of Iowa Press, 1996, 20–35.

————. "The Crises and Transformations of Invaded Societies: The Caribbean (1492–1580)." In *Cambridge History of the Native Peoples of the Americas.* Edited by Frank Salomon and Stuart Schwartz. Vol. 3. Cambridge: Cambridge University Press, 1999, chap. 10.

————. "Lowland Peoples Confront Colonial Regimes in Northern South America, 1550–1900." In *Cambridge History of the Native Peoples of the Americas.* Edited by Frank Salomon and Stuart Schwartz. Vol. 3. Cambridge: Cambridge University Press, 1999, chap. 14.

———. "Tribes Makes States and States Make Tribes. Warfare and the Creation of Colonial Tribe and State in Northeastern South America, 1498–1820." In *War in the Tribal Zone*. Edited by R. B. Ferguson and Neil L. Whitehead. 2nd ed. Santa Fe and Oxford: School of American Research Press and James Currey, 1999, 127–50.

———. "Native Society and the European Occupation of the Caribbean Islands and Coastal Tierra Firme, 1492–1650." In *A General History of the Caribbean*. Vol. III. Edited by C. Damas and P. Emmer. London: UNESCO Publications, 1999, chap. 7.

———. "Hans Staden & the Cultural Politics of Cannibalism." *Hispanic American Historical Review* 80, no. 4 (2000): 721–51.

Whitten, Norman. *Black Frontiersmen: Afro-Hispanic Culture of Ecuador and Colombia*. Prospect Heights, Ill.: Waveland Press, 1986.

"William Dunlop's Mission to St. Augustine in 1688." *South Carolina Historical and Genealogical Magazine* 34 (1933): 1–30.

Williams, Caroline A. "Resistance and Rebellion on the Spanish Frontier: Native Responses to Colonization in the Colombian Chocó, 1670–1690." *Hispanic American Historical Review* 79, no. 3 (August 1999): 397–424.

Wood, Peter H. *Negroes in Colonial Carolina, from 1670 through the Stono Rebellion*. New York: Norton, 1974.

Woodward, Ralph Lee., Jr. "Crecimiento de población en Centroamérica durante la primera mitad del siglo de la independencia nacional." *Mesoamérica* 1 (1980): 219–31.

———. "Population and Development in Guatemala, 1840–1879." *SECOLAS Annals: Journal of the Southeastern Council on Latin American Studies* 14 (1983): 5–18.

Worth, John H. *Struggle for the Georgia Coast: An Eighteenth-Century Spanish Retrospective on Guale and Mocama*. Athens: University of Georgia Press, 1995.

Wright, Irene. "Our Lady of Charity." *Hispanic American Historical Review* 5 (November 1922): 709–17.

———. "Dispatches of Spanish Officials Bearing on the Free Negro Settlement of Gracia Real de Santa Teresa de Mose." *Journal of Negro History* 9 (1924).

Wright, J. Leitch, Jr. "A Note on the First Seminole War as Seen by the Indians, Negroes, and Their British Advisors." *Journal of Southern History* 34 (November 1968): 565–75.

Zulawski, Ann. *They Eat from Their Labor: Work and Social Change in Colonial Bolivia*. Pittsburgh: University of Pittsburgh Press, 1995.

Index